Joseph and Emma:

A Love Story

Volume II

Joseph

and

Emma:

Volume II

by Marsha Newman and Buddy Youngreen

Salt Lake City, Utah

Acknowledgments

No one person, or even two, is ever entirely responsible for a work such as this with its extraordinarily wide scope. We consider it an honor and a calling to treat the significant material pertaining to the personal relationship between the Prophet Joseph Smith and his Elect Lady, Emma Hale Smith. Therefore, first among our sincere acknowledgments must, respectfully, be Joseph and Emma Smith for the exemplary lives they led and the incredible legacy they left to us, the generations who look back with awe upon their accomplishments.

In our own lives there have been many who have provided information, consultation, encouragement, and inspiration. We would like to thank Gene Newman, our publisher and consultant for his faith in the project and the investment of time and heart, as well as finances.

We extend special thanks to Scott Fullmer, our editor and consultant, for his many hours of dedication and work, as well as the sacrifices of his family, and especially for his love for Joseph and Emma. His assistance has been invaluable.

Thanks also go to Lorena Normandeau, Joseph's and Emma's great-granddaughter for consulting on the manuscript and proofreading, to Gracia N. Jones and Michael Kennedy, also descendants of Joseph and Emma, for technical assistance and support, to Larry Porter and Lyndon Cook for background information on early church history, and to Barbara Miller, Marilyn Mann, Elizabeth R. Crofts, and Russell K. Jorgensen for consultation and proofreading.

Finally, we appreciate all the wonderful authors who have researched and written excellent historical books on the Smith family, the events, and the times. Many fine literary works have contributed essential material for the writing of this historical novel, Joseph and Emma: A Love Story, and are listed in the bibliography.

Sincerely,

Marsha Newman and
BuddyYoungreen

Chapter One

"The Spirit of God Like a Fire Is Burning"

The woman stood like a statue in the frosty, bleak hours of early dawn. She had already been up for hours, tending sick children, collecting eggs from the biddies, and had just finished skimming cream off the milk. Bread was rising on the sideboard in neat little rows of doughy lumps, which would bake into tasty doughnuts for breakfast. She left behind a snug home, with delicious smells and a warm fire. Wrapped like a mummy with long, woolen scarf about her head and neck, a heavy, gray dress over ankle-length petticoats, and a full length, black cloak enveloping all, she stood facing the structure slowing taking shape on the crest of the hill. It was soon to be known as the Kirtland Temple, and was fast becoming the wonder of the state.

In just three years, the Latter-day Saint settlement at Kirtland, Ohio had transformed a sleepy village into a busy, bustling town of several thousand. Newly converted Mormon immigrants left family farms and businesses to gather with others of their faith to Kirtland, where Joseph Smith, the young prophet from New York,

1

had settled. The first three years had marked the growth of an industrious community of millers, wheelwrights, tailors, printers, teachers, farmers, and craftsmen of all kinds. A spirit of sacrifice and unity characterized the expanding town. Most homes housed more than one family, as established citizens made room for newcomers. Hastily constructed cabins and farms were quickly filling in like quilt-work patches over the rolling hills. However, even more important than building homes for the new converts was building the House of the Lord in a manner acceptable to deity.

Emma Smith drew a deep breath of frigid air and started her walk up to the temple site. It was February 1834. When the winds from Lake Erie screamed across the countryside, a woman could scarcely stand against it. Boats and barges caught on the water in a squall could capsize, with all the crew lost to a turbulent grave. This morning only a slight breeze wafted away her cloudy puffs of breath. She carried a basket filled with fresh, hot biscuits and jars of warm apple cider to men she knew were already at work on the temple. In her basket was bounty of another kind: warm socks knitted during late night hours beside her hearth, socks for feet that often were shod only in scraps of leather — loosely termed boots. She knew the socks would be as highly prized as her biscuits and cider.

Emma was a familiar figure to the temple workers of Kirtland. As long as she had flour, eggs, and butter she brought them bread. Sometimes her treasure basket contained bits of salt pork, fried crispy on the outside while succulently salty and tender inside. Then they truly had a treat, and blessed her name in their prayers. When she did not come, as sometimes happened, they knew there was no food in Emma's larder. Word would quickly fly around Kirtland, and supplies would turn up on the Smith doorstep. A miller would scrape his barrels and fill a flour sack for her, or a farmer would slaughter a pig and haul a side of pork to the Smith home.

Her words of gratitude were warmly given — not effusively, for that would embarrass her benefactors, but genuinely, with a gentle press of the hand and look of delighted surprise. Emma Smith had large, dark eyes, deep-set with long, black eyelashes. Those brown eyes could express more than her lips would ever speak, for she was an intensely private woman, not given to sharing her heart or her opinions with anyone but her husband, Joseph. Even he wondered if he truly knew the depths of her soul. She was perhaps just as intense about her deepest religious feelings as he. Where expressions of love and praise for God bubbled up from Joseph like a fountain, in Emma the waters were still and very deep, her love for deity being the guiding force of her life from childhood. As a girl, having been so devout in her Methodist faith, the folks of Harmony, Pennsylvania had commonly speculated that she would be a minister's wife. How a good, young Methodist woman fell in love with the unique and notorious "boy prophet" was a marvel to those friends who knew them both. Other young women, less serious and sober than Emma Hale, might have been swept off their feet by the handsome young prophet from Palmyra, but Emma never made rash decisions. Her choice to elope with Joseph and brave the anger of her father was agonizing, but not impulsively made. She loved her father and family. However, she admired and passionately adored the uneducated, unpolished, highly visionary young man from Palmyra.

They made a remarkable couple, both tall and with regal bearing. Joseph Smith stood six feet two inches. He was broad-shouldered, with powerful arms and hands. While Emma was dark-haired with warm, olive skin, Joseph was fair-haired, especially in the summer months, and fair-skinned, possessed of startling, blue eyes that could hold an audience entranced for hours. Joseph was loved by his people with fervent adoration, and he loved them in return, as a shepherd does his flock. Emma was universally regarded as an angel of mercy and admired for her stamina and stoicism in the face of hardship. She was a friend to those hungry and cold. She would give her own warm bed to strangers and sleep on the floor by the hearth, wrapped in her cloak. However, no one but Joseph knew the secrets of her heart.

Joseph and Emma Smith had been married seven years, buried four of their first six children, lived in seven locations in three different states, never had a home they could call their own, and were entirely dependent on the charity of family and friends for food, clothing, and shelter. It was as if the parting words from her father, Isaac Hale, would haunt Emma throughout her married years to Joseph: "If you go off with that plowboy from Palmyra, you'll never know joy, you'll never know happiness, but you'll be no stranger to sorrow. That husband of yours will be more married to the cause of his golden Bible and that new church than he ever will be to you or your children."

Still, here in the Western Reserve of Ohio, Emma was to find her solace. She now had two beautiful, healthy children, and the time she and Joseph spent in this new gathering place for their growing church was generally happy, though it would be short-lived.

This morning, Emma hurried through the cold to distribute the bounties to men who were chipping, polishing, and fitting rocks into place to form the walls of the holy structure. A cry of welcome greeted her, rippling down the foundation line and ringing from the heights of the unfinished walls. "Sister Emma, " they called, "Bless you!" One by one they climbed down from their perches and respectfully came around for their warm biscuits and pork. Emma accepted

4

a simple "thank you" but brushed aside any profuse expressions. She was simply doing her duty to God and her fellow man. It was the least a good Christian woman could do, especially since the men worked with cold-blue fingers to chip away at rock. Just a shy smile and quiet appreciation gratified her most, as well as the realization that the wife of the prophet must always set the example. Her untiring efforts rallied the other women of Kirtland who also dealt with hunger, cold, death, and grinding poverty. How could they complain while the prophet's wife managed a smile and a kind word for all? Angel or queen: she was often likened to one or the other, and both connoted the unreachable, unattainable image which Emma unconsciously inspired.

Indeed, all the women of the Smith family behaved themselves like royalty. Lucy Mack Smith and her daughters, Sophronia, Katherine, and Lucy, as well as Jerusha Barden Smith, Hyrum's tender young wife, all bore the mantle of "first family of the restoration" with determination to be worthy of their callings. They gave untiring service to those around them, while often called on to bear testimony of the divine origin of the Book of Mormon. There was no pettiness in their natures, no tendency to complain or feel sorry for themselves no matter what their temporal condition. Having traded comfortable homes and a peaceful life for the cause of the gospel of Jesus Christ, they held their standard high and went about the work with a song on their lips. Women of their time had no illusions about the nature of life on this earth. They never supposed that *it should* be easy, or ever *would* be. Hunger was ever a wolf at the door, and they knew they were entirely dependent on God for their daily bread. They lived with death at their elbows, and each time a woman faced childbirth, she faced that possibility, either for herself or her children. Emma Smith had already lost four children to harsh frontier life in early America, and Mother Smith had lost three.

Emma seldom spoke of these wrenching experiences or the feeling of loss embedded in her heart. Only Joseph knew how she yearned, pleaded, even begged for more children, healthy children. Little Julia and Joseph were a comfort and a beginning, but she longed for a full nest. The namesake, Joseph, was just over a year old now, walking like a miniature sailor on a rolling deck, and running from Emma to hug his father's legs whenever Joseph was around. Longing for a new baby had begun to possess her again as she saw her little one developing. Sometimes in their most tender, intimate moments Joseph heard her whispered plea, "Give me a baby to keep." This he hoped for as well, sharing Emma's yearning for more children.

After seven years of marriage he still found her beautiful, womanly, and a prized counselor, for her wisdom was practical, sensible, and far-sighted. He often marveled at having found a wife who would accept his doctrinal teachings then lead the way in living them. His calling was receiving truth and teaching it, hers was serving humanity and living revealed doctrine, for Emma followed St. Paul's counsel to "be ye doers of the Word, not hearers only." She didn't see angels as Joseph did, but she saw Christ in the lean, hungry, cold-reddened faces of every person she served.

Once the biscuits had been given to the workers and eaten, and the socks received with praise, Emma inquired after her husband. "Is Joseph around?"

"He was here before I was," Levi Hancock reported, "But I expect he is meeting with the brethren over in the printing office."

Emma glanced at the small building just behind the temple. Yes, there was a light flickering from inside. No doubt they were meeting to discuss the problem of the mortgage on the temple. Payment was due and there was no money. She said a silent prayer that he would have good news when he came home for midday meal. With a friendly wave in response to the chorus of thank you's, she started back down the hill to her home over the Whitney store. Her doughnuts would have risen by now. Time to put them in the oven for breakfast. The glimmer of sun was feeble, but welcome. Perhaps they were in for a winter thaw.

Joseph Smith had sent his loyal disciple, Brigham Young, to Canada in the summer of 1832 to invite well-known construction contractor, Artemus Millet, to join them in Kirtland and oversee the construction of the temple. Millet convinced Joseph and the others that brick should not be their main building material. They explored a local quarry and found beautiful limestone. This became the principal element for the thick walls of the temple. Brother Millet had brought his expertise and considerable fortune with him. Joseph asked him for a thousand dollars, but Millet gave much more than that. He gave as long as he had means, and he gave his time in supervising the building design. Levi Hancock and Truman Angell worked alongside him as supervisors. Joseph and his brothers headed up efforts in the rock quarry, working long hours, chiseling and hauling stone. Every able-bodied Latter-day Saint sacrificed in order to erect the House of the Lord, as they loved to call it, for they believed that God would pour down upon them great spiritual blessings in that temple.

Now, in February of 1834, the industrious Mormons were so impoverished that the mortgage on the temple lot was in foreclosure.

The thousands of dollars it would take to pay the mortgage were impossible to raise. Numerous appeals to the members of the church had raised only a small portion, and that had comprised the "widow's mite." Joseph felt the oppression of poverty, combined with the necessity of obeying the Lord's command to build His temple. Prayers were long and fervent. Still, no help came.

Then the week of foreclosure was upon them. A desperate meeting in the printing office seemed to produce no great solutions. Still, Joseph ended it with a promise that God would provide for them. He went to work in the quarry until midday when Heber C. Kimball came riding hurriedly in to fetch him back to town. A company of new converts from Bolton, New York had come to Kirtland, led by a wealthy landowner and farmer, John Tanner. He and his family had converted to the church after reading the Book of Mormon, inspired by the preaching of Simeon Carter, and a miraculous healing.

John Tanner had been a man of no small means in New York, running a successful farm, harvesting acres and acres of timber, and running a prosperous hotel on the shores of Lake St. George. He had been incapacitated for six months with vicious boils and fever blisters on his left leg. No amount of treatment had been successful. The doctors had told him the leg must be amputated. Tanner had not walked for six months, but kept his leg elevated and resting on pillows. When he heard the Mormon missionaries preach a funeral service in Bolton, he invited them to come to his home to preach to him. With many of his neighbors gathered one evening, the missionaries preached on the restoration of the gospel of Jesus Christ and asked Tanner if he believed his leg could be healed.

Tanner was a man of faith. "If God wills it," was his reply.

Simeon Carter took him by the hand and commanded him to arise and walk in the name of Jesus Christ. Tanner walked three quarters of a mile to the lake to be baptized. Subsequently, most of his family joined with him in conversion to the peculiar sect known as Mormons.

John Tanner liquidated his financial holdings and began the journey to Kirtland, Ohio so he could be of assistance in building God's kingdom. The day after he arrived in the burgeoning Ohio town Tanner met with Joseph Smith and the temple committee. When told of the imminent foreclosure, he freely gave thirteen thousand dollars to save the temple, and gave the rest of his considerable fortune to aid the destitute church. Joseph was overcome with gratitude, and marveled once more at the working of the Lord in providing means when every earthly alternative failed.

The public came from all over the area to see the Kirtland temple. Newspapermen and politicians came to scorn but left marveling. It outshone every other place of worship in the countryside, even though the Mormons had not a penny to their names. How could such an impoverished people erect this building? How did they? They sacrificed every other thing in their daily lives to do it. They considered it a privilege to work on the house of the Lord. Indeed, everyone, women and children included, counted it not labor, but an act of devotion to contribute. They gave all they had to the cause — time, effort, and even precious heirloom china to be crushed and added to mortar so the walls of the temple would glisten. They also sewed altar cloths and wove rugs.

Women took over the chore of providing for their families, while their men built the temple with rifles in one hand, under guard against attack from their enemies. With united effort and the resources of a few wealthy men like Artemus Millet, John Johnson, and John Tanner, the structure steadily climbed skyward.

Hyrum started the foundation trench when ground was broken on June 5, 1833, and less than two months later, twenty-four church leaders met to lay cornerstones. From that time on, through March 1836, the primary focus of the church in Kirtland was building the House of the Lord. They accomplished in three years what their enemies swore could not be effected in three decades. It was a great unifying effort. Men with wagons and teams hauled the limestone. Others, like Joseph, who had no wagon to contribute, worked the quarry. Timber for the temple was cut from nearby woods and dried. The kiln, heated to extreme temperatures, caught fire several times.

Often, men labored all day in the quarry or on the walls, returning home weary and worn, with nothing more to eat than a bit of cornmeal and milk. For those who lacked cows, supper was cornmeal and water. It was a treat to get a bit of molasses or meat. Women toiled almost around the clock in some seasons, spinning and knitting hundreds of pounds of wool to become clothing for the laborers, or temple carpets and curtains. Clothing was a constant problem. The physical efforts of the men in quarrying, climbing scaffolding, and working with stone, bricks and mortar wore out pants and shoes faster than normal activity would have. Some men, including Brigham Young, went without shoes in the summer. Most of them wore ragged pants to work and had one good pair reserved for Sunday meeting. Brigham Young, Heber C. Kimball, and Parley P. Pratt were among the destitute. At one point they had nothing at all to eat and borrowed money from a friend to keep their families from starving.

The burden endured by the saints wore heavily on the young prophet and his counselor, Sidney Rigdon. They felt accountable to the saints as their leaders, though their personal circumstances were no better than the others. Provisions from the church's general store were soon exhausted, being traded on credit, and there was no cash to re-supply them. Citizens of Ohio, who opposed the flood of newcomers, found a way to harass the Mormons. They passed a law against being poor!

If a person was suspected of being destitute and possibly becoming a ward of the community, he was escorted out of town, directed to return from whence he had come. It was self-defense on the part of non-Mormons in the area. Old-timers had seen their city triple in size. They felt it had been wrested from them by extremists who believed in a strange God and a strange theology. Life had been simpler and more prosperous before the Mormons. They believed their only hope to regain control of their town was to get rid of Joseph Smith.

Subsequently, Joseph's life was constantly in danger. When lit-igation didn't stop him and trumped up charges failed, he was the object of continual threats. The church assigned men to act as his bodyguards day and night, even sleeping in his home to protect him. Through all of this, Joseph continued to function as prophet, receiv-ing continual revelation for and in behalf of specific individuals, as well as for the entire church. Many such revelations had already been published as the "Book of Commandments," and were accepted as scripture by the saints.

Joseph had assigned that publishing task to Oliver Cowdery and William W. Phelps in Independence, Missouri. These men compiled early revelations and started printing them in the Phelps home, but persecution started in Independence as well. The Phelps home was razed, the family turned out, and the press destroyed. The Gilberts, Morleys, and Partridges were all turned out of their homes, the men tarred, feathered, and threatened with death if they didn't move on.

Soon, much of Joseph's time was taken in corresponding with church leaders in Missouri. He drew up and sent petitions and letters outlining abuses perpetrated on the Mormon settlers to Governor Dunklin of Missouri. With the church press destroyed in Missouri, Joseph directed the establishing of a new press in Kirtland to publish church documents. He sent word to Oliver to return to Ohio and head up that effort.

One cold night in late February, Parley Pratt and Lyman Wight arrived in Kirtland with information for Joseph concerning the plight of the saints in Missouri. They sat by the Smiths' hearth, warmed their chapped hands and faces, and poured out the agonizing story of their Missouri Zion.

"Colonel Pitcher of the Missouri militia has disarmed the saints, and now they are defenseless. They have been burned out and chased off. The children are terrified and have nightmares. Bishop Partridge's land was set on fire, while hysterical women and children huddled together in his home. He was snatched from his home by a mob and his clothes torn off. After a severe beating they tarred and feathered him."

At this Joseph shuddered, remembering his own ordeal. Emma listened anxiously, thinking of her own two precious children asleep upstairs. It all seemed too close, too possible, even right here in Kirtland.

"There's more, Joseph. Mob leaders came back the next day and threatened death to all, as well as the destruction of the entire settlement. Bishop Partridge, Phelps, Morley, Gilbert, Whitmer, and John Carlin offered themselves as ransom, even unto death, if the mob would only let the saints stay in peace. . ." Parley's voice broke.

On that sobering note, they all fell silent. Lyman Wight, tough as a frontiersman could be, finished the narrative, for Parley could no longer speak. "The upshot of it all is, our folks promised to leave. Now they're living on the banks of the Missouri, or along the river bottoms. Some are starving and freezing, but what choice do they have?"

Emma asked anxiously, "And what of the Colesville saints? Are they still. . . alive?"

Lyman gave her fragmented news of her old friends as Joseph broke down and sobbed. These were his friends too, close to his heart. They had shared much with him, and now they were all suffering for the sake of the gospel he had shared with them. He had sent them to "Zion" in Missouri. He felt responsible.

"I should have stood with them."

"You would have been killed by now," Wight tersely assessed.

Emma asked, "Why do they hate us so?"

Parley answered. "Sister Emma, we upset their community. They mistreat their slaves. We don't; we baptize them. They fear the Indians; we teach them and help them. Some of us have preached that the city of Independence has been consecrated for the Lord's kingdom. A few have said the righteous remnant of the Indians will one day possess the land. You can imagine how that upset the locals. What's more, we built good solid log houses while most of them live in sod huts. We have a large enough population to control the political vote. Most of all they think we're crazy to believe in angels and miracles, healing, and the imminent coming of Christ. I guess, all in all, they're jealous and afraid of us, and that spells violence."

"Here is a letter from Brother Phelps for you, Joseph." The young prophet read it aloud, stumbling over parts his tears blurred.

"The condition of the scattered saints is lamentable and affords a gloomy prospect. No regular order can be enforced... We are in Clay, Ray, Lafayette, Jackson, Van Buren, and other counties, and cannot hear from one another oftener than we do from you... brethren, if the Lord will, I should like to know what the honest in heart shall do? Our clothes are worn out; we want the necessaries of life, and shall we lease, buy, or otherwise obtain land where we are, to till, that we may raise enough to eat? Such is the common language of the honest. . . to do the will of God. I am sensible that we shall not be able to live again in Zion, till God or the President rules out the mob. . . The mob swears if we return we shall die! If, from what has been done in Zion, we, or the most of us, have got to be persecuted from city to city. . . we want to know it; for there are those among us that would rather earn eternal life on such conditions than lose it; but we hope for better things and shall wait patiently for the word of the Lord."

Parley turned to Joseph. "We need help. We need revelation."

In a broken voice Joseph answered, "And you shall have it. Will you stay the night, brethren?"

"That's a kind offer, Brother Joseph. We gladly accept."

Emma took the men upstairs to a small alcove with two cots. It was the best they had to offer, for Emma and Joseph were already giving shelter to another family who were crowded into a small bedroom downstairs. Joseph could not sleep that night, dispirited by reports of his Missouri friends in such dire circumstances. He pleaded with the Lord for direction. Before the night was over he had his instructions. The next day he wrote a letter directing the saints to petition President Andrew Jackson regarding their situation. They were to request federal troops for protection. They were also to press their grievances before Missouri Governor Jonathan Dunklin at the same time. Joseph then recorded a new revelation requiring him to raise an army for the aid of the saints in Zion.

Emma was amazed. "An army! You don't mean you'd go to battle?"

"I do mean it!"

"But Joseph, our men aren't soldiers, they are farmers, husbands, and fathers."

"God will make of them what they must be."

"And who will lead them?"

"I will, and Lyman will." Joseph stood at the foot of their bed. He was undressing for bed, stripped down to his long johns and bare feet. Emma scrutinized her husband. He was hard-muscled from years of physical work, but he scarcely looked like a soldier.

"You haven't any military experience! You're their spiritual head. How does it look for a prophet to be training with a musket and bayonet?"

"How does it look for a prophet to sit by his warm fire while his friends are being driven and killed? Even Nephi had to take up arms to fulfill the Lord's plan. You can be a man of God and a military leader too; Moroni was."

Emma drew a deep breath. She knew it was no use debating against her husband. When he felt directed by the Spirit, no argument held sway with him. Still, the thought of him leading a bloody battle was so repugnant to her, she could scarcely endure it.

"How can a fight help our cause? Surely you don't imagine the people of Missouri will look more favorably on us if you lead an army there. It will only make them fear us more."

Joseph pulled his nightshirt over his head. His face appeared from the folds of the shirt. He was grinning. "I *hope* to throw the fear of God into the whole state of Missouri! We're peaceable folks, but we aren't cowards!"

He sat down on the foot of the bed and took her hand in his. "Now, Emma, you don't think I intend to ride into Missouri to burn farms, and murder men, women and children, do you? I simply intend to train our men in self-defense and offer a show of strength to the Missourians. After all, you never know when our people in Kirtland may need the protection of a trained militia. You and our children could be next to be thrown out of our house into the freezing cold."

Emma was incredulous. "Ohio is far too civilized for that. No matter how our enemies detest us, there are laws to protect innocent people here."

He smiled ruefully and shook his head. His wife was sitting straight up in bed, her dark hair protected by a fluffy white cotton cap, and her nightgown laced up to her neck. He seemed to catch a mental glimpse of her, cloaked and trudging through snowy woods, her nose reddened by the wind and her face pinched with hunger and fear.

"I pray that you are right, Emma! I am learning not to trust lawyers and judges, or to rely on constitutional protection. We live in a time when we must protect our own, for no one else will do it for us."

The campaign started the next day. Parley and Lyman went to all the nearby Mormon settlements to raise volunteers for the military expedition that would become "Zion's Camp." They solicited funds and goods as well. From the depths of their own impoverishment the Ohio Saints could contribute but little -- two hundred and fifty-one dollars, ten wagonloads of goods and about two hundred volunteers. During this time, Emma had a constant parade of volunteers through her home, coming for supplies and consultation with Joseph, sleeping before the kitchen hearth. Joseph traveled to New York and the eastern Ohio church settlements and collected another two hundred dollars. It would take about two months to complete the preparations.

Wilford Woodruff, a recent convert, was one of the volunteers. He stayed at the Smith home several days. One afternoon, Emma returned from visiting the sick to find Joseph and Wilford indoors tanning a wolf hide, which they had stretched over her two good kitchen chairs. They were somewhat chagrined to be discovered using her home for such a messy project, but Emma's good humor over the matter won her Wilford's admiration.

Zion's Camp mustered on May 5, 1834 with Joseph as commander. The men had a sense of mission; they were going to rescue their brethren. Emma went to the schoolhouse, still under construction, and sat in the shade of a maple tree, listening to her husband's farewell address before his departure to Missouri. He spoke with zeal and determination to rally the saints to the cause and his faithful friends to his side. And they stood with him: Sidney and Brigham, Parley, Orson Hyde, the Johnson boys, the Tanners, Wilford Woodruff, and Joseph's own kith and kin, Hyrum, Samuel, William, Don Carlos, and cousins George A. Smith and young Jesse Smith.

Emma heard her husband vow he was ready for martyrdom if it were God's will. She held little Joseph on her lap. Fanny Alger, Emma's young helper and nursemaid, sat beside them on the grass with three-year-old Julia. Even as she warded off waves of anxiety, Emma felt the enthusiasm of the ragged army of men and boys gathered to reclaim Zion and establish it for the Lord. It was almost a crusade, and everyone was in high spirits. Emma gazed off at the newly begun "House of the Lord," so recently their focus.

The day was warm, but she was out of sorts. It was all well and good for Joseph to go off on his high adventure. She would be left to provide for the needs of their family. With him gone, she would have to take over his chores, and she would manage because it was her duty. She wouldn't complain, not to him or to anyone else. But Joseph was the reason she had endured privation for the last seven years, and would yet endure more. He had just better not get himself killed!

That was precisely the startling news she read the following July in an Ohio newspaper:

"A letter has been received by a gentleman in this neighborhood, direct from Missouri, stating that a body of well-armed Mormons, led by their great prophet, Joe Smith, lately attempted to cross the river into Jackson County; a party of Jackson County citizens opposed their crossing, and a battle ensued, in which Joe Smith was wounded in the leg, and the Mormons obliged to retreat; finally, Smith's leg was amputated, and he died three days after the operation."

"Fanny!" Emma called to her youthful boarder and helper. "Just look at this story! It can't be true! I would know if Joseph died. I don't believe this! I *won't!* Read it, Fanny, dear. Tell me what you think."

Fanny took the newspaper article and her face went white. She sat down and looked up at Emma. "I don't believe it, either. Still. . . what if it's true? Why would they print such gross falsehood?"

"They would print anything to hurt our cause. They probably think such news will weaken our faith and throw us into panic. Well, when my husband lies dead at my feet, I'll believe it!" She stomped over to the hearth, crumpled the paper, and hurled it violently into the fire.

Her hunch proved true. The false news report stirred up a furor. The saints began coming to the Smith house in a stream, some of them weeping. They were mostly older folks or wives who had been left behind when Zion's Camp departed. They wanted reassurance that Joseph was still alive. Emma calmly offered her belief that the newspaper article was false. She had no evidence her husband had been either wounded or killed. Later she had a visit from Mother Smith and Jerusha.

"Poppycock!" Lucy proclaimed. "That newspaper report is a pack of lies! Joseph and Hyrum are alive; I know it! I saw them in a dream. They were sick, but not dead! I jumped from my bed and knelt in prayer for my boys. Nobody can tell me my sons are dead. I know better. They'll come home fit as fiddles, mark my word!"

Because of Emma's faith and Lucy's spirited assurances, the worries of the saints abated. A calm spirit carried the day, and the saints went confidently about their daily work, inspired by Sister Emma. Meanwhile, Emma steeled herself to await the truth -- whatever it might be.

No better news was immediately forthcoming. Other newspaper accounts described the Mormon army as being wiped out by cholera. Kirtland was plunged into depression. Worry over the fate of husbands and sons was overwhelming the women in the settlement.

Emma went about urging optimism and soothing fears. She was a well-known figure, with her basket over her arm, carrying bread, fruits and vegetables to neighbors, walking to the doors of many homes from which loved ones had gone to serve. The Kirtland saints clung to her faith, and the solace they found in repetition of Mother Smith's dream. Emma, herself, did not know how she maintained faith in the face of the newspaper allegations, but these days away from Joseph actually strengthened her reliance on the Lord. God was her solace and comfort. She found herself murmuring simple prayers as she stirred the stew pot or kneaded bread. She called her household together for prayer and instructed her little girl to say, "Thank you that Father is still alive and coming home." Her lifelong faith in God gave her courage while awaiting her husband's return.

Zion's Camp, as the Mormons called their militia, was an exercise in obedience. Two hundred men formed an unlikely army, unregimented, un-trained, mostly on foot, walking nine hundred miles to western Missouri. Joseph, not to set himself apart from his men, walked his share and nursed blisters, just as his men did. They tried to maintain a low profile and would separate when coming to a town, walking around if they could, or sending men a few at a time through it to purchase food and other necessities. Knowing his enemies would seek his life, Joseph assumed different names, while his identity as their leader was closely guarded. His young cousin, George A. Smith, a boy of seventeen, was so guileless in his appearance that they usually let him answer the oft-asked questions, "Who are you? Where are you going? Who is your leader?"

George A.'s round eyes would blink behind his glasses. He would hitch up his striped pants, made from bed ticking, shift his massive two-hundred-plus pounds to the other foot, squint nearsightedly into the face of his inquirer, and answer. "Oh, we're from the East. Where are we going? Why, to the West. Our leader is first one, then another." Such illuminating answers usually discouraged the curious population of the countryside.

Joseph had his hands full keeping discipline and good spirits among the company. He reminded them every morning at prayer that they were the "Camp of the Lord," but such sentiments didn't prevent murmurs as the men grew weary of walking. They found many occasions to complain over the simple, hastily-prepared food. Arguments broke out. Joseph constantly pleaded and begged the men to conduct themselves as emissaries of the Lord. It turned out to be a time of winnowing. The good wheat separated from the chaff, and men who proved themselves faithful during the tedious march of Zion's Camp would prove faithful in future trials as well.

The little band of would-be rescuers reached western Missouri after two months and was disappointed to find that Governor Dunklin refused to keep his word to help the displaced saints recover their lands. He had earlier sympathized with the plight of the persecuted Mormons and said he was duty-bound to help them recover their stolen properties, but when faced with demands to do so, he withdrew his support. After all, it would take extensive military commitment in and about the countryside to reinstate the Mormons and preserve long-term peace. It would also cost his state plenty; with no guarantee the angry Missourians would allow the hated Mormons to live peacefully with them when the military eventually retired from the field.

Joseph faced a painful decision: If he took his militia into Jackson County, there would surely be bloodshed. Public opinion would not be with the Mormons. Without the support of Governor Dunklin and protection of the state, could his people successfully retake their lands? As disappointed and dispirited as his men, Joseph came to the realization they must abandon the mission and relocate the saints. The people of Clay County, just north of Jackson County, seemed willing to offer a sympathetic hand, and the Mormons had already begun tentatively to settle there.

Frustration at not being able to fight or avenge their fellow saints threw some in the camp into angry rebellion. Joseph repeatedly warned the men that the spirit of contention would bring down Heaven's judgments on them. It finally happened. Most of them contracted cholera; fourteen died, including Joseph's young cousin, Jesse Smith. There was no medicine to help them. Whiskey and a dip in cold water was the only treatment they knew. There weren't even coffins. Men were rolled up in their blankets and buried on the bank of the Missouri River. Joseph and Hyrum also came down with the disease and were so sick they thought they would not survive. Hyrum had a vision of their mother, Lucy, praying for them, and he knew they would recover because of her righteous prayer. A few brave men, not yet taken by the sickness, cared for the many, exposing themselves continually to the dreaded disease in aiding their comrades.

As the members of Zion's Camp slowly recovered from the effects of cholera, they began to make their way home. Over land, across rivers, by barge, or on foot, they straggled back to Kirtland.

It was early August before Joseph finally walked into Emma's kitchen. It was hot and he was tired, but he was home! He looked like a woodsman, his hair longer than usual, his skin deeply tanned, his chin uncharacteristically covered by a scruffy beard. His pants were dirty, and his shirt had lost one sleeve. He carried a rifle across his shoulders.

From just outside the back door, Emma heard a noise from somewhere in the store, and before she could leave the churning, a large figure filled the doorway. She stifled a scream. Then, as she recognized her husband, she jumped to her feet and gave a cry of relief.

"Joseph! I knew you were not dead. You're home! You're alive! But just look at you! You look like a savage."

He grasped her hand and pulled her inside through the open doorway. When he pressed her into his arms and kissed her, she finally sighed, ". . . like a *wonderful* savage."

"And you are as beautiful as ever. Where are the children? I have thought of my family every day. Call them in. Tell them their *father* is home!"

"Fanny," Emma called. "Oh Fanny, bring the children! Their father wants them!"

Immediately, Fanny Alger appeared at the top of the stairs with the little ones. "Brother Joseph!" she exclaimed, her face shining. She had baby Joseph in her arms, and helped Julia down the stairs, urging the little girl on. At the bottom, she presented the children to their smiling father, the frontiersman. He opened his arms for both of them, and held and kissed them many times, though the baby wailed at the strange man with a beard. Emma hooked her husband's arm, as they walked back into her kitchen. There, in privacy, Joseph held his wife and two children in the circle of his arms, savoring their fragrance and soft skin. "It's good to be home," he murmured against Emma's ringlets. "I *love* home. . . *my* home, and *my* family."

"I'm *so* glad — so very glad — you're home. It's been too long! All the newspapers reported you dead. We heard about the cholera. What happened?"

He sat down, still holding his children. "Shall we call Fanny in so she can hear too?"

They all sat down while Joseph rehearsed the successes and tragedies of Zion's Camp, from the miracle flash flood at Fishing River, which saved them from their enemies, to the scourge of cholera, which infested the camp.

"I'm afraid we were not much help to the Missouri saints. We did contribute what goods and money we had, and made temporary peace with our enemies. Now we must either sell our land to them, or buy theirs. We have negotiations going on now to purchase the lands we need. Emma, I had to choose: compromise or see my men die in battle with Missouri mobocrats. Sylvester Smith wanted to fight, and denounced me, accusing me of all sorts of evil. I'm sure he thinks me a coward, but I could not order my men to die."

"You did the right thing," Emma consoled him. "But surely some good came from all this!"

"Well, I learned who my real friends are — who will bear tribulation and who won't; who's a complainer, and who's not; who believes in a prophet, and who doesn't. Hyrum, Brigham, Heber, Lyman, and Wilford — they're all like Peter of old, rock solid. I think we also gained a great deal of valuable experience on how to move a body of people. We traveled nearly two thousand miles going and returning. Still, I would do it all again for the knowledge we gained and the proving of my men."

He turned to include Fanny. "What has happened here in my absence?"

She quickly directed his attention back to Emma. "Sister Emma has been an angel to the saints, comforting them when they thought you were dead. Without her influence, they might have lost faith."

"And what of my children?"

"Their mother told them every day their father loved them and would soon be home."

He smiled with pleasure at the report. Emma was embarrassed by the lavish praise, yet Joseph knew it was all true.

The next week, Sylvester Smith — unrelated to Joseph and always an agitator — voiced grievances against Joseph before the Kirtland saints, calling him a would-be king, a despot, and a fallen prophet. He also accused Joseph of taking consecrated money. Joseph spent the week calling on witnesses to vindicate himself before his church peers. When no one else would substantiate Sylvester's claims, he finally acknowledged the error of his ways and asked for forgiveness. Joseph forgave him, but Emma never could. She was outraged that he could spread such lies and merely be forgiven upon request. Joseph went beyond forgiveness and later called him to be his scribe.

It took a family wedding to finally banish the troubled feelings of the past few months. Samuel Smith, Joseph's younger brother, had fallen captive to the gentle, sweet ways of Mary Bailey. She was so shy and tender of feelings that Emma had wondered if she would survive the embarrassment of being courted. Mary managed, though barely. Samuel was the bachelor catch of Kirtland. He was tall — as all the Smith men were — broad-shouldered, handsome, and quiet. Everywhere he went the young women whispered and giggled. In short, Samuel had his pick of the eligible young ladies. He was only impressed by one — the sweet, pure, meek Mary Bailey, dearest and best friend to Agnes Coolbrith, the young lady whom Don Carlos was courting.

By August, with Joseph and Hyrum home at last, Samuel's wedding became the celebration of Kirtland. The saints wanted a reason to rejoice. Zion's Camp had been an exercise in sheer obedience, hardly a victory to rejoice. Now, the Smith wedding provided welcome diversion and lifted the spirits of the whole town.

"Samuel has certainly chosen a fine wife," Joseph commented to Emma while she plumped a goose down pillow she and Joseph were giving the newlyweds.

"And what exactly does that mean?" Emma teased. "Do you say that because she is pretty, or sweet, or blessed with a comfortable dowry?"

"My assessment goes even further. She loves him!"

"And why not? All the Smith men are extremely good catches — all handsome, strong, and appropriately pious. All except my husband, that is. No one could call you pious tonight. You're enjoying yourself more than anyone else here, I believe."

"And you are far too serious. You can't be proper every moment. Come here, my saintly wife. Your husband bids you to dance with him."

He led her outside where a small brass band was playing, bowed to her, and began gracefully weaving in and out. Emma immediately joined the high spirit of celebration, and the small yard around Father Smith's home was awhirl. Samuel and Mary, at first the center of attention, found it convenient to slip quietly away from the festivities, and before anyone missed them, were gone in a borrowed carriage to a tiny cabin Samuel and his brothers had built on the outskirts of town. But the band played on into late afternoon, and Joseph and Emma enjoyed this wedding almost more than they had their own.

The School of the Prophets resumed upstairs in the Whitney store above Emma's kitchen. Building started up again on the House of the Lord, as well as work on other buildings. Additional land was set aside for building more schools for the priesthood brethren. That was all right with Emma, since she had accommodated the School of the Prophets in her home. Meanwhile she had been selecting songs for a hymnbook, as the Lord had commanded her to do.

"When shall we have our hymnal?" Joseph asked one evening, looking over his wife's shoulder as she sat at the desk.

Emma sighed and paused in her work. "Perhaps I am too careful. It's taking longer than I thought. I'm including songs the saints already know and love. Some of the words have to be changed to be in harmony with our doctrine; Brother Phelps is helping me with that. I feel a great responsibility. We all know how important music is in any worship service."

"When will you be ready to give it to Brother Williams for printing? Frederick asks me almost every time he sees me."

"I'm really not sure. If done in haste, it would be unsatisfactory, and I don't want that. There are so many favorite songs our people love to sing, and I must make sure the words are appropriate to the doctrine the Lord has revealed." She paused thoughtfully, rubbing the back of her neck.

"It's been helpful to have Fanny do the household chores," Emma said. "I wonder though. . . she is old enough to court and marry. Many young men drop by to visit now that she's about."

Joseph pondered, "Has she said anything about marriage?"

"No. She seems content. But it is only natural for a girl her age to want children of her own."

"Yes," he agreed. "I must ask her."

Emma looked up. Just for a moment her heart skipped a beat. What did he mean exactly? That night by the fireside, when Joseph first told her of the restoration of the ancient order of plural marriage, came back to her like a shaft through her heart. She understood it — or at least she thought she did — after reading and rereading every scripture connected with the principle. But understanding was not the only thing. Accepting it was well nigh impossible. She glanced at her husband with their son on his knee and the old feeling of rebellion returned to her heart. To share him! To *lose* him! To think that she was not all to him as he was to her! She might scream her protest if she didn't regain control. And what good would that do? It would just alarm Joseph and provoke another scene. So, with supreme effort, Emma put such thoughts aside. She would not allow herself to be tormented. Nor would she give in to hysteria.

"Our Brother Phelps has submitted a new restoration song," with a strained voice, she changed the subject. "It is called, *The Spirit of God Like a Fire Is Burning.*"

Her husband put his hands on her shoulders and bent to murmur in her ear. "Sing it for me, Emma-rose. I haven't heard you sing in a long time."

Emma's voice caught in her throat at that old, sweet endearment. Then she coughed and cleared her throat, hiding from him the emotions that welled up inside. He must not know how desperately she longed to possess him body and soul for herself alone. After a moment, Emma's clear soprano voice rang out. The song was both stirring and melodic. It was truly an anthem to the God and the Lamb.

> *"The spirit of God like a fire is burning!*
> *The latter-day glory begins to come forth,*
> *The visions and blessings of old are returning,*
> *And angels are coming to visit the earth.*
>
> *We'll sing and we'll shout with the armies of heaven,*
> *Hosanna, hosanna, to God and the Lamb!*
> *Let glory to them in the highest be given,*
> *Henceforth and forever! Amen and Amen!"*

Listening to his accomplished wife, Joseph was moved. His smile of admiration was the balm of Gilead to Emma's heart. "It's beautiful, Emma. It must be sung for the dedication of the Lord's house."

The warmth of summer quickly gave way to the snows of December. The next time the Smiths all met together was December 9, 1834. Fall harvest was long since over. Snow had come early to Kirtland that year, and work on the temple had slowed. Emma's work was at the spinning wheel, and making quilts and cloaks, and sewing clothes for Joseph and her children. Her hands were never idle, for if her own family was provided for, there were many others in need, and Emma considered it her duty to care for them as well. Joseph's work was cut out for him, caring for the needs of his own family while holding together the church. Everyone who had a problem, no matter how petty, wanted the prophet's guidance on it. If a man cut his arm or broke his leg, he wanted Joseph's blessing. If neighbors quarreled, they must have it settled by the prophet. Joseph was up early, long before daylight, chopping wood, carrying water from the spring, clearing snow, ordering supplies for the store, and responding to legal threats. Sometimes it seemed impossible to progress the work of the church for all the minutiae that stole his time.

It was a snowy night when the Smiths gathered for a "blessing party." Joseph Sr., as First Patriarch of the Church, had determined to bless each one of his children and their spouses.

"Father, Mother! Come in here by the fire! Welcome! You're almost the last to arrive. Our newlyweds are yet to come." Joseph took his mother by the arm and guided her right to the hearthside. After the brisk night air, the home was cozy and welcoming. The fragrant smell of the feast rushed upon them. Emma had been baking all day, and the sideboard was lined with her famous pastry. They were to be the treat of the evening, after a banquet prepared by many family members. Lucy and Joseph Sr. made the rounds embracing their family.

The home was abuzz with family greetings. Even Calvin Stoddard, Sophronia's husband, seemed unusually cordial and friendly tonight. Stoddard was often a reluctant participant in family gatherings, having relinquished a mission call, declining to leave his family and farm. Sophronia quietly insisted on staying close to her family, though her husband rebelled in his own way against the religious zeal of the Smiths. Katherine stood by her sister's side, sharing with her the burden of a rebellious husband. Jenkins Salisbury, for all he loved his dark-haired wife, had one great weakness — the potent, alluring fruit of the vine. More often than Katherine would admit to her family, her husband imbibed until drunk. Her father and mother agonized over their two daughters whose husbands could not live the gospel of Jesus Christ, which held the rest of the family together.

Tonight, however, nothing could dampen the good feelings all around. Christmas was close at hand. Thoughts of the Savior's birth permeated the occasion. Father Smith beamed on his family, a patriarch with a faithful posterity upon whom he was about to bestow the only gift he had to give — his blessing, as a father and patriarch in Israel.

"Oliver!" Lucy greeted their dear friend with genuine warmth. He had stayed often and long at her home, and seemed more like a son than a friend. "I'm glad you're to be the scribe for these blessings. Father Smith would be happy to include you as well."

True to his genteel upbringing, Oliver bowed to the matriarch, then tucked her hand under his arm and escorted her to a chair. "I would, indeed, cherish such a blessing. Perhaps another time. I wouldn't want to intrude upon this family occasion. I am here to record, not to participate."

The door opened with a gust of winter air, and Samuel came in with Mary. Joseph Sr. crossed the room to heartily embrace the young couple.

"Now we can begin! You are here and that makes our family complete. Mary, you're looking healthy and happy. My boy must be taking good care of you, eh Samuel?"

"I'm trying to, Father." Samuel beamed, and Mary clung closely to his arm. Sweet Mary blushed profusely, her musical voice so soft as to be a whisper as she responded, "Samuel is a perfect husband, Father Smith."

"Good! Glad to hear it! This is a great night!" Joseph Sr. exclaimed. "We'll have a word of prayer, then a song, and the blessings, then the food which has been prepared for us." He turned about, signaling William and Don Carlos. "Boys, set these

31

chairs in a circle, just here. I want spouses next to each other. Leave the circle open nearest the hearth. Mother is going to offer prayer, then she'll sit in her chair by the fire."

The Smith men began pushing and arranging the chairs and stools as their father had directed. Soon everyone took a seat and the hubbub quieted down. Upon their father's request, his children sat in order of birth around the circle with their spouses at their sides. Emma on her husband's left, then Joseph with Sophronia and Calvin on his right. Mary sat close to Samuel, frequently glancing at his strong profile, trying hard to be discreet, though obviously much in love.

Mother Smith stood in the center of the circle and prayed with all the rejoicing of a strong, loving mother for her posterity. Her zealous spirit endeared her to her children. They each knew Lucy was their staunchest defender and supporter. She had no sooner finished than Father Smith stood up, drew his spectacles out of his pocket, and took Lucy's place in the center to address his children and their spouses.

"My children, I am now old, and my head is white: I have seen many years compared to those enjoyed by many. I am now in my sixty-third year, and my frame is feeble because of the many trials and fatigues which I have endured in this life. I have not attained to the age of my fathers, neither do I know that I shall, but I desire, and for a long time have desired, to bless my children before I go home."

Father Smith paused, looking around fondly on his sons and daughters. Then a shadow stole across his face. His eyes became watery, and he looked upon his wife with sadness.

"*. . . I look upon you before me, and I behold a lack; three seats are, as it were, empty. The Lord in His just providence has taken from us at an untimely birth, a son. My next son, Alvin, as you are all aware, was taken from us in the vigor of life in the bloom of youth: my heart often mourns his loss, but I have no disposition to complain against the Lord. Another has been taken also, in his infancy. I pray that my loss may be abundantly supplied, and made up in additional blessings, and that His grace may attend me and His Holy Spirit be shed abroad in my heart, that I may pronounce such blessings upon your heads as will be fulfilled.*"

A profound spirit had settled over the little group. With snow gleaming white and still outside the opaque windows, and the glowing fire casting warm shadows across the room, a hush wrapped them each in tender thoughts of eternal family ties. Husbands and wives glanced affectionately at one another, then around the circle of brothers and sisters. Salisbury gazed steadfastly at his shoes, and Calvin Stoddard looked sheepishly at his wife. Their father's voice had grown a little raspy, and welled-up tears caused him to pause in his remarks until he regained his composure.

"Oh, my children, my dear children, it is my privilege as your father to bestow upon you the blessings you are entitled to from God, the very Eternal Father of us all. If you will be patient, I desire to bless each of you, along with your spouses. I shall begin with Hyrum, our eldest, at this time and place."

He walked around the outside of the circle and placed his hands on his son's head. All the love of a father filled his bosom and he could scarcely begin, so strong was the emotion that surged through him.

"Hyrum. . . Thou hast borne the burden and heat of the day; thou hast toiled hard and labored much for the good of thy father's family. Thou hast been a stay many times to them, and by thy diligence they have often been sustained. . . I now ask my Heavenly Father, in the name of Jesus Christ, to bless thee with the same blessing with which Jacob blessed his son, Joseph; for thou art his true descendant and thy posterity shall be numbered with the house of Ephraim. . . Thou shalt be blessed with the good things of this earth in rich abundance. The Lord will multiply his choice blessings upon thee and thy seed after thee, and thou, with them, shalt have an inheritance in Zion. . . Thy name is written in heaven and thy salvation sealed on high."

He then blessed Jerusha, a beloved daughter-in-law.

He turned next to Joseph, and stood for a long moment with his hands on his son's shoulders, the memories of him as a young lad with shining countenance, fresh from the presence of angels, coursed through the older man's mind. The words of a blessing began to crowd out all other thoughts, and he rested gnarled hands on his son's fair hair.

"Joseph, my son, I lay my hands upon thy head in the name of the Lord Jesus Christ, to confirm upon thee a father's blessing.

"The Lord thy God hast called thee by name out of the heavens: Thou hast heard His voice from on high from time to time, even in thy youth. The hand of the angel of His presence hast been extended toward thee, by which thou hast been lifted up and sustained; yea, the Lord hast delivered thee from the hands of thine enemies; and thou hast been made to rejoice in His salvation; thou hast sought to know His ways, and from thy childhood thou hast meditated much upon the great things of His law. . . For all these things the Lord, my God will bless thee.

"Thou hast been called, even in thy youth to the great work of the Lord, to do a work in this generation which no other man would do as thyself, in all things according to the will of the Lord. A marvelous work and a wonder hast the Lord wrought by thy hand, even that which shall prepare the way for the remnants of His people to come in among the gentiles, with their fulness, as the tribes of Israel are restored.

"I bless thee with the blessings of thy forefathers, Abraham, Isaac, and Jacob; and even the blessing of thy father Joseph, the son of Jacob. . . Thousands and tens of thousands shall come to a knowledge of the truth, through thy ministry; and thou shalt rejoice with them in the Celestial Kingdom. . . Thou shalt see thy Redeemer come in the clouds of heaven, and with the just receive the hallowed throng, with shouts of hallelujahs, praise the Lord, Amen."

The son sat reverently beneath the hands of his patriarch, while Father Smith trembled with the energy of the Holy Spirit coursing through him. Emma waited with a prayer in her heart to be worthy of a blessing from the Lord and to understand His words to her. With the fire of prophecy still burning within, Joseph Sr. turned to Emma, placed his hands upon her dark curls and blessed her abundantly.

"Emma, my daughter-in-law, thou art blessed of the Lord for thy faithfulness and truth, and thou shalt be blessed with thy husband, and rejoice in the glory which shall come upon him. Thy soul hast been afflicted because of the wickedness of men in seeking the destruction of thy companion, and thy whole soul hast been drawn out in prayer for his deliverance; rejoice, for the Lord thy God hast heard thy supplication.

". . . Thou shalt ever remember the great condescension of thy God in permitting thee to accompany my son when the angel delivered the record of the Nephites to his care. Thou hast seen much sorrow because the Lord hast taken from thee three of thy children. In this thou art not to be blamed, for He knows thy pure desires to raise up a family, that the name of my son might be blessed.

"And now, behold, I say unto thee. . . thou shalt bring forth other children, to the joy and satisfaction of thy soul, and to the rejoicing of thy friends. Thou shalt be blessed with understanding, and thy little ones the way of life, and the holy angels shall watch over thee and thou shalt be saved in the kingdom of God, even so, Amen."

The Lord had heard her prayer and would bless her with more children! It was the desire of Emma's soul. Julia and little Joseph were her heart's delight, but she sorely missed the babes she had laid in the dark earth. Emma prayed constantly to be strong enough and worthy enough to receive more children for her husband — healthy children who could climb upon his knee, and wrestle with him, work with him, and learn the ways of God from their father's lips. Emma put her face in her hands, so overcome with joy that she was afraid her emotion would embarrass her. Joseph reached over and took her hands in his, kissed them, and held them securely through the other blessings. Emma bowed her head and let the renegade teardrops fall unimpeded.

Joseph Sr. blessed each of his children in order of their ages. Calvin Stoddard and Jenkins Salisbury were admonished to repent of their rebellious ways, and God would yet bless them. William Smith was also cautioned to control his passions. The hand of the Lord had chastened him, for he had not practiced "meekness." But tonight, the spirit of meekness was prevalent in the whole group, and when the blessings were done and duly recorded by Oliver, they enjoyed the feast prepared for them with rejoicing and hope for the future.

Emma's blessing of more children filled her heart with satisfaction and anticipation. As she said goodnight to each of her guests, she seemed to glow with an inner light. Her sister-in-law, Katherine, hugged Emma as they slipped past her out into the cold December air, and whispered, "You look like the mother of our Lord tonight. Mary, herself, could not have glowed more beautifully than you, Emma. You will be a mother again soon, I just know it."

Emma kissed her sister's cheek with gratitude and went to bed that night, hugging the comfort of the blessing to her heart. She would look back on it with hope over the next troubled years.

In February 1835, Joseph was inspired to organize a Quorum of Twelve Apostles. Men were selected who had proven themselves in the furnace of Zion's Camp. They were Heber C. Kimball, Orson Hyde, David Patten, Parley and Orson Pratt, Brigham Young, Luke and Lyman Johnson, William McLellin, John Boynton, Thomas Marsh and William Smith. They were called to be special witnesses of Christ in all the world, traveling and bearing testimony as the Savior's apostles had done in New Testament times.

He also organized a Quorum of Seventy, which included his cousin, George A. Smith, Joseph Young, and even Sylvester Smith, once Joseph's accuser. Emma thought her husband too generous, but Joseph was not one to hold a grudge. Sidney Rigdon and Frederick G. Williams served as Joseph's counselors. Oliver Cowdery had become Associate President of the church, and Hyrum Smith and Joseph Smith Sr., who had already been sustained Patriarch of the church, were appointed Assistant Presidents.

Joseph was becoming more satisfied. The organization and governing bodies of the church were growing. It had not all come to him in one sweeping inspiration. He was learning line upon line, precept upon precept, the fuller organization and higher doctrines of the kingdom. With trusted men assuming more and more responsibility, Joseph had time to turn his thoughts back to study and inspired writing. In March, with winter passing, he sent the Twelve east on missions, while work progressed on the beloved House of the Lord.

"Joseph, a Mr. Chandler would like to speak with you. He says he has brought something that will be of interest to you."

"I'm really quite busy now, Emma. Can he come back?"

"I think you'll want to see what he has."

Joseph looked up from his conversation with Oliver. He was clearly impatient with being interrupted. "Who is he?"

"Mr. Michael Chandler is an Irishman." She paused, then added with a trace of a smile, "He has a friend with him, a Mr. Benjamin Bulloch, and. . . Egyptian artifacts."

Both men gave her their full attention. She went on serenely, her hands neatly clasped over her apron front. "He has them with him."

Her husband pushed back his chair. "Really?"

Emma nodded. Pleased that she now had his attention, her brown eyes twinkled. "Yes, really!"

Emma's face was a study of amusement; Joseph's was a study of expectation and decorous reserve. He stepped out of his little office to meet Mr. Chandler, and Oliver followed close behind.

Chandler was somewhat older than Joseph, considerably short-er, and packed into a brown, cotton suit almost two sizes too small. His narrow mustache looked like a slit in his face, for his lips were so thin they disappeared under it. He wore a monocle — strictly for effect, Joseph thought — and had the habit of rocking back and forth on his toes. He waited expectantly beside the larger and bulkier Benjamin Bulloch.

"Mr. Smith, is it?" Chandler's squeaky voice assailed him the moment Joseph entered the room. "I have with me wonders of the ancient world! I am the possessor of Egyptian mummies straight from the tombs of Egypt! I also have papyri on which wonderful characters are written — hieroglyphics, as the inscriptions are called! I have been told you are a translator of ancient languages."

"I am familiar with *some* ancient writing."

"Ah, so you are a student of antiquity," Chandler beamed.

"Do you wish to show me the artifacts or merely talk about them?"

"You're a man of action! Excellent! I am too. But first, let me present my companion, Mr. Bulloch. He has shared my adventure almost from the first. We have been to New York and placed several mummies in museums. We even met with other scholars who referred me to you."

"And I'm pleased to introduce you both to my associate and scribe, Mr. Oliver Cowdery. Now, what is the history of these papyri?"

Noting Joseph's impatience, Chandler plunged in. "Right to it — we'll get right to it! I have the papyri here in my bag." He looked up from unbuckling his satchel of treasures. "The mummies — a gift from my uncle, Mr. Antonio Lebolo, formerly a celebrated trader and world traveler, now deceased, rest his soul — are still at the waterfront landing in Fairport. I didn't want to transport all my treasures until I knew you were interested." He reached into a dilapidated valise and drew out a papyrus, rolled and secured with twine.

"Here! You may unroll it and peruse it if you desire."

If? Joseph looked at the little man with amazement. *If* he desired? He took the ancient writing from Chandler, and unrolled it with care. Excitement built as strange, but not unfamiliar, characters lay before him. Oliver watched over Joseph's shoulder. From the doorway, Emma could feel the surge of exhilaration in her husband. Joseph looked over the scroll intently and took care to conceal the thrill that leapt within him.

"What will you do with these artifacts, sir?"

"Sell them, that's what! I'm in need of money. I know nothing of Egyptian antiquities. If you're a man who understands them, so much the better. I'll sell you my mummies and include the papyri. Here, what about these hieroglyphics? What do they mean?"

Joseph accepted the challenge to decipher the meaning of the Egyptian symbols Chandler was pointing out. He politely exited the room with the papyrus he had been studying, but returned quickly with a written translation, which he handed to the surprised Chandler.

"Aha!" Chandler exclaimed, turning to his friend Bulloch. "Exactly as the learned scholars have told me."

"Whom did you consult?" Joseph was curious.

"Oh, various professors, of course — the very best scholars." Curiously he asked, "Whom did you consult?"

Joseph responded simply, "The Holy Spirit."

Chandler and Bulloch glanced at each other, eyebrows raised in skepticism. Chandler went on. "None of the scholars of antiquity want the task of the full translation. And," he dropped his voice, rocking backward on his heels, ". . . none would meet my price."

"I see. Well, my friend, Mr. Cowdery, and I would like to examine your mummies to see if they are truly as you report. I have other associates, as well, with whom I'd like to consult."

Joseph let the men out the front door, looking back at Emma as he went and grinning like a boy. They hurried up the hill to the printing office where William W. Phelps and Sidney Rigdon were in deep conversation about the printing of a book to be called "Doctrine and Covenants."

Introductions were made and Rigdon immediately asserted his authority.

"We'd like to see a certificate of authenticity."

"Certificate? My artifacts need no certificate," Chandler protested. "They speak for themselves and are obviously centuries old — but still in perfect condition," he concluded hastily.

"If you have mummies, why did you not bring them?" Sidney asked, his bushy eyebrows raised in challenge.

"It's a long way here from Fairport Harbor. Suppose I ha not found Mr. Smith at home? But they are safe at the ship under lock and key."

"Shall we take a trip to Fairport?" Joseph asked his friends.

"I would like to see them," Phelps began to strip off his apron. "It's a fine day, and I've been at work too long. Let me change my trousers before we go."

So they took Sidney's carriage to Fairport Harbor and saw for themselves the actual Egyptian mummies, which Chandler was hawking. They appeared authentic and were perfectly preserved, almost beautiful to Joseph's appreciative eyes.

The church leaders returned home making plans to buy the artifacts. The church was not financially able to pay Chandler his price, and Joseph was deeply in debt personally, since his name appeared on most church financial transactions. However, the news of the curiosities from Egypt spread like wildfire through the little Latter-day Saint community, and several men of means raised the funds to pay for them. Mother Smith even gave her life savings to help pay the fee. Mr. Chandler was completely satisfied, for by his private assessment, twenty four hundred dollars was far more than the prize was worth. But Joseph knew better.

Oliver and William Phelps then turned their attention to helping Joseph translate this new acquisition. To Oliver, it seemed like old times. Only this time, nothing was hidden; he was as able as Joseph to look upon the papyri. He rejoiced that Joseph had the gift to translate, for he knew his friend had no formal training in the Egyptian language, only what God revealed.

"In the land of the Chaldeans, at the residence of my fathers, I, Abraham, saw that it was needful for me to obtain another place of residence." (Excerpt Book of Abraham, Chapter 1)

Joseph stopped, astounded. He and Oliver looked at each other in awe, overcome with an astonishing realization. "Oliver, can it be? Can it truly be that we have a record of Abraham? If so, it is a miracle! I can hardly believe it."

Oliver was no less exhilarated. "And the Lord has delivered them, like an excess of grain, shaken down and flowing over, into our hands!" He grasped Joseph's arm. "Could it be a recompense for all our tribulation?"

"It is like manna from heaven to feed our souls."

The mummies and papyri were eventually placed on display in an upper room in the Kirtland Temple after it was dedicated. They were the subject of much interest and a means of revenue, since a continual stream of visitors wanted to view them.

While the School of the Prophets continued in Joseph's home, his brother, William, decided to organize a school of debate in his house. William was a natural leader himself and sometimes chafed under his secondary role to his older brother. A week before Christmas, William invited Joseph to a "friendly discussion." Joseph went in the sleigh, with the frosty winter breeze ruffling his hair, remembering his youth in Palmyra and Manchester, where he had often participated in a debate group. On this occasion, however, he had some misgivings about the appropriateness of debating principles of the Lord's gospel. Those misgivings were confirmed as the evening wore on and the discussion eventually took a contentious tone. After quietly listening through many speakers and heated words, Joseph finally spoke.

"Brethren, I fear this debate school will not result in good, if it is continued." His blue eyes showed concern. "Just witness the heated arguments raised on both sides of this issue. If we continue in this same manner, every matter, large and small, will come under adversarial discussion, and we will quickly be divided instead of united."

William frowned. He dearly loved a good debate, and being very quick-witted, often prevailed. William's fair cheeks began to flush with emotion. Joseph had no right to spoil a perfectly respectable diversion.

"Brother Joseph, debate schools have been deemed good and profitable for society for many years. The best minds have participated and encouraged them."

"Perfectly understandable, since many points of religious doctrine and procedure have been invented by men. In the restored gospel of Jesus Christ, that is not the case."

William was not satisfied. "Sound doctrine will stand discussion."

"With whom?" Joseph challenged him. "Will you debate Christ's doctrine with Him?"

William flushed a deep red now, and stood up. "You have no right to speak so. Do you intend to insult me? And in my own home?"

Joseph answered quietly, "If my memory serves me, I built this home for you."

A profound and embarrassed silence had fallen over the men seated about the room. They had all seen Joseph invoke the rights of his prophetic position before, but none of them wanted to be in the middle of a family feud. Hyrum rose and attempted to soften the feelings.

"Brother William, let us keep our tempers. I have something to say."

William turned on him angrily. "You may speak if you will not abuse the school in my house. I have organized a respectable debate school, and will not allow any man to cast aspersion on it in my presence." This he said as he turned back to Joseph.

Before Hyrum could soothe the argument between his brothers, Joseph took exception with William's implication and also stood. Now the three brothers faced each other, and tension mounted.

44

"When has Hyrum ever abused you or proceedings in your home? You have no reason to accuse him. In fact, you mean those remarks for me because I have reproved the contentious spirit here tonight. It is as ugly a spirit as I have ever seen, and I will not tolerate it just because you are my brother."

Joseph Sr. had entered the room quietly, hearing loud voices. He was embarrassed to have his grown sons arguing before their priesthood brethren. "Silence!" he commanded in no uncertain terms, his eyes flashing. All three brothers stood reproved by their patriarch. Joseph and Hyrum had the grace to defer to him and started to sit down. But William was like a stallion with the bit in his mouth. He drew himself up to his full stature and retorted, "I will not be silenced in my own home! I shall say whatever I please, and who will say me nay?"

Joseph Sr. and Lucy were living in the home with William's family. Father Smith saw the necessity of halting this confrontation before it erupted any further. He counted on Joseph's usual even temper to counteract William's rash words.

"All right then. William, it is your home. Say what you will, but let the others hold their tongues."

Joseph saw in his mind's eye the months of work he had personally done on William's home — the food and other necessities he had provided his brother's family when they were in need. Anger flashed hot within him.

"I will speak," he asserted, "For I built this house, and therefore have as much right as you do. Everyone here has had opportunity to voice his feelings tonight, and I shall do the same. William, I tell you the spirit of the devil is here, and this is proof of it!"

Before anyone could restrain him, the hotheaded William rushed his older brother, pushing him backward into the doorframe.

Joseph jerked at his loose fitting frockcoat to free himself for the tussle, but William was too swift for him. Shoving his shoulder solidly in Joseph's ribs, William almost knocked him off his feet. Every man in the room jumped up to stop an all-out fight. William's fists were cocked when Jared Carter pulled him back, only to catch the brunt of his host's fury in a blow to his cheekbone. Hyrum and William McLellin grappled with William, while Joseph clutched his ribs. He had had a weakness on that side ever since the beating and tarring at Hiram, Ohio. Now he felt a crack that doubled him over.

"Let go!" William bawled. "I won't be reproved just because he fancies himself a prophet."

Brigham pushed himself between the brothers and faced William like a lion. "I fancy him my prophet, and ask by what authority you silence his counsel."

Hyrum had his arm under Joseph's, holding him erect. Joseph's face was drawn and pale. Mother Smith came rushing into the room, though her husband tried to hold her back.

"Boys!" she reprimanded, "Shame on you! In front of company no less! Joseph, you had best leave. William! What has gotten into you? Father, can you not stop this dispute? All this debate nonsense — I'm ashamed of you all. This is my house too, and I want peace restored."

The tiny woman was ablaze with righteous indignation. Brigham helped Joseph on with his coat, and together with Hyrum walked him out to his carriage. The snow had stopped, and the night was bitter cold. As Joseph drew the cold air into his lungs, he felt another stab of pain in his ribs.

"I'll be all right," he asserted through clenched teeth.

"I'll see you home," Hyrum said, climbing up in the carriage, while Brigham helped Joseph hoist himself into the rig.

The few minutes it took to get home were agony for Joseph. When Emma opened the front door she was amazed to see her husband doubled over in pain. Her face reflected surprise that an evening at his brother's home should result in a broken rib for her husband.

"Well," she said, "I should have thought my husband safe in the bosom of his *family*. So, this is the way debate school ends!"

She helped him upstairs to bed, bound his rib cage snugly with strips of cloth. He winced, and once he cried out, as she wrapped and pulled the cloth tight.

"Which is hurt more, your ribs or your pride?" she asked wryly.

"Neither! My friendship with my brother."

"William was always hotheaded. If you're to be his friend, you must be more of a peacemaker like Hyrum, than a debater like he is. How did Mother take it?"

"She threw us out."

"I'm not surprised. I'd have done the same."

Joseph turned over as his wife directed, groaning miserably. "I think the debate club died tonight."

Even if the men had wished to continue, their women put a stop to it. Mother Smith didn't stop chewing on it until early hours of the morning, when her husband had long since fallen into exhausted sleep. Emma knew better than to chide her husband more. It was clear that his feelings were more pained than his ribs. He and William had always walked a delicate line with each other. That line had now been crossed. When brothers fall out, the devil walks in, she thought. We have enemies enough to contend with. We don't need arguing and fighting right in our midst. If it has come to this, how long can our dream of Zion stand?

Days later, William wrote a letter of abject contrition to his brother and begged forgiveness for his "passions." True to his nature, Joseph wrote back, forgiving, counseling, and pleading that the enmity between them cease. Soon thereafter, a family gathering was held. Both men covenanted with each other that they would not allow such a spirit to come between them again. Emma and Lucy were called in to witness the covenant. The rift was healed, but it was symptomatic of the depths of the violent emotions beginning to surface in Kirtland.

By February 1836, Emma's collection of Sacred Hymns for the church was published, bearing the date of 1835. The objective of the book was spelled out in the preface: "As the song of the righteous is a prayer unto God, it is sincerely hoped that the following collection has been selected with an eye single to His glory . . . " Emma had finally completed the task given her of the Lord. The book contained words to ninety favorite hymns, edited in some cases to be in harmony with the doctrines of the church.

In early March of 1836, the Kirtland temple was nearly completed. Joseph's growing family moved into larger and more comfortable quarters, and on March twenty-seventh, the House of the Lord was dedicated. During the last few months of construction, the saints had worked at a feverish pitch. Brigham often stayed late into the night working on the mortar, pressing the crushed glass and china into it, his hands bleeding from the sharp edges. His devotion became legendary. When the outside walls were finished in January, the lower room was readied for painting. The ladies made white curtains of canvas to be raised and lowered, dividing the large, lower assembly room into sections. Brigham sacrificed attending Hebrew class to do woodwork painting and window glazing.

Paralleling the physical preparations throughout 1835 and early 1836, Joseph tried to prepare the people spiritually as well. He preached that they were to prepare for a "solemn assembly," that the Lord would appear and endow His people with great gifts of the Spirit. He met with all his trusted brethren who had been summoned to Kirtland for the festivities, and he admonished them, "Great blessings await us at this time, and they will soon be poured out upon us, if we are faithful in all things. Therefore, be prepared in your hearts. Be faithful. We must all be perfectly obedient."

Knowing that for him perfect obedience meant compliance with the difficult and dreaded commandment of plural marriage, Joseph prayerfully determined to go to Levi Hancock, his old friend, and instruct him in the principle. Then he would have to tell Levi that the Lord had instructed him to take Fanny Alger, Levi's niece, as a plural wife. So Joseph determined he would go and do the things which the Lord had commanded.

Two men sat on a bench in the nearly completed temple. Levi waited patiently and expressionless while Joseph explained the understanding he had gained of the practice in the Old Testament of plural marriage. "Brother Levi," Joseph began with all the fortitude he could muster:

"The Lord has revealed to me that it is His will that righteous men shall take righteous women, even a plurality of wives, that a righteous race may be sent forth upon the earth, preparatory to the ushering in of the Millennial Reign of our Redeemer — for the Lord has such a

high respect for the nobles of his kingdom that He is not willing for them to come through the loins of a careless people - therefore; it behooves those who embrace that principle to pay strict attention to even the least requirement of our Heavenly Father."

Despite Joseph's trepidation, Levi had a spiritual witness of the principle and had already anticipated Joseph's request for Fanny's hand. He agreed to perform the ceremony in the spirit of humble obedience to commandment.

With even greater apprehension, Joseph next went to Emma to ask for her consent. He knew it would be painful for them both, but he also knew that they must pass every test God used to try their souls. Emma wept. Joseph wept. Only her conviction of Joseph's divine calling as the Lord's prophet enabled her to eventually give her consent. Still, it tore her heart, and she never acknowledged the marriage afterward.

Fanny was at first taken aback by the proposal, frightened at what it would mean, and was most reluctant to offend Emma, the woman who had taken her in and taught her so much. After much fasting and prayer, Fanny obtained an undeniable spiritual witness that Joseph's teaching on plural marriage was correct. They were married simply, in private, and Fanny went to live elsewhere afterward. Their marriage was the first step in the restoration of the ancient principle of plural marriage for the latter-day dispensation of the Fullness of Times.

The dedication of the Kirtland temple proved the most exciting day of the saints' sojourn in Kirtland. They were seemingly triumphant over their enemies. Their efforts at building had often been blocked by businessmen who wouldn't sell lumber to them, or loan money, or even sell food to them for daily sustenance. They posted a guard around the temple to protect it, and established a bodyguard contingent for Joseph as well.

Finally, the grand day arrived! Lots had been drawn, for there were not seats enough to accommodate everyone. Someone had a brilliant idea: little children could sit on their mothers' laps and thereby free up more space for others. The idea spread rapidly. Soon the great hall was filled with people, and not only were children sitting on laps, but many grownups were as well. Everyone wanted to be a part of the dedication.

The congregation of about a thousand began to assemble by seven o'clock in the morning. The services began at nine. All were dressed in their finest attire. Children's faces had been scrubbed pink. Feet were encased in newly knitted socks, with shoes if they had them. Hair was curled; noses were powdered. Cravats were carefully tied, and boots were polished. The saints presented themselves in proper decorum before their Lord. And they sang! Oh, how they sang!

Emma's hymnal was in abundant circulation. The temple assembly made a most joyful noise, singing, sometimes almost shouting their praises to God. The sacrifices they had made were but dim memories now as their objective was finally being realized. Joseph sat with Sidney Rigdon and Oliver Cowdery behind elevated pulpits at the west end of the main floor sanctuary. Sidney read Psalms Ninety-six and Twenty-four. After the choir sang a beautiful response, he proceeded to speak for two-and-one-half hours. His address caused every eye to fill with tears. He told them there were many large houses of worship in the world, but this one, built with their own sweat and sacrifice, was erected by divine decree so that the Lord could reveal Himself to his people.

Emma sat with the choir and had the great satisfaction of watching her husband. Joseph sat facing the congregation; a breeze blew gently through open windows into the crowded room while sunlight illuminated his face. She rejoiced that she had chosen him over typical comforts of home and hearth. Joseph stood at Sidney's signal to be sustained as prophet, seer and revelator of the Lord's church. He stood tall and straight. The pure white shirt he wore was the work of her tireless hands. The white cravat about his neck, marking him a minister of the gospel, she had stitched. He had never been more handsome.

All at once, the people on either side of her were standing in unanimous affirmation that they accepted Joseph as their president and would uphold him as such by their prayers of faith. Joseph beamed with love and gratitude, showering back on his people the adoration they imparted to him. Emma stood quietly, with dignity, and many eyes were also turned on her, the prophet's Elect Lady. It was, for her, a supreme moment.

Singing began again:

"Now let us rejoice in the day of salvation.
No longer as strangers on earth need we roam.
Good tidings are sounding to us and each nation,
And shortly the hour of redemption will come."

Emma didn't need a book, for she knew this hymn, and the others she had compiled, by heart. She looked around. The singing was lifting, lifting, and then she looked up. Somehow, she sensed angels there in God's house. She had heard other voices but had not known what they were until now. She seemed to hear silken robes rustling and heavenly voices praising the Father and the Son, just as hers did. Could her own sweet, angel children be among them? The thought caught at her heart. She was in her sixth month of pregnancy and felt the child within her respond to her thought. She gently caressed her sweet babe, and sensed others with her as well, raising angelic voices to God in praise. She was not usually a person of visions. Her husband had that gift. But she was a woman of courage, faith, and commitment in the face of terrible personal trials, and now she had her heart's desire — to sing with the angels, *her* angels!

Later in the proceedings Joseph gave the dedicatory prayer. It was a long prayer of rejoicing and praise. Joseph's voice carried to the four corners of the building. In its power, it thrilled his wife; in its humility, it brought her to tears. This house of God was being consecrated for the spiritual endowments and ordinances of God. Here the blessings of heaven would be poured out upon the people who had built it in their poverty against all odds. When he finished, the choir burst into rejoicing as they raised their voices in thanksgiving. When their final notes faded away, Don Carlos Smith blessed the sacrament and supervised the elders in passing the bread and wine.

Emma sat through seven hours and counted them as one. When they finally dismissed, the people left reluctantly. Everywhere about her, she heard people testifying of personal visions and angels. Joseph came down from the pulpit and headed toward Emma. This was a time they should share. She had played almost as large a role in the proceedings of this day as he had, for her unwavering support made his role possible. But a throng of enthusiastic, well-wishing saints pushed them further and further apart. His name resounded through the assembly hall, "Brother Joseph! Brother Joseph!" Everyone wished to speak to him; everyone wanted his blessing.

Emma watched her husband over the heads of the crowd. He looked for her, even while he greeted people. Sometimes their eyes would meet, but they were prevented by the pressing crowd from even touching hands. Finally, she gave up and went home to wait for him.

It was nearly dark, and Emma was still waiting for her husband, when she heard a peculiar noise outside. Then she heard shouting. Was it a mob? Were they so incensed by the success of the saints that they would fall upon the people now, on the evening of their greatest accomplishment? Something told her no; this was a special moment. Emma grabbed little Julia's hand and hurried outside. She was not alone. The rutted, dirt road was thronged with people all looking toward the temple. Some she recognized as friends. Some were not members, and some of them had harassed the temple builders, stealing supplies, tearing down fortifications, and doing all they could to stop the work. Now, all the citizens of Kirtland looked with amazement, as a pillar of fire seemed to rest on the top of the newly dedicated House of the Lord.

The temple stood aglow as if in the midst of a fiery furnace, and a loud, rushing of mighty wind was heard. The building seemed ablaze, but not consumed, as the power of God baptized it with fire and the Holy Ghost. Many saints stood in the streets, with uplifted hands, rejoicing and bearing testimony to this spiritual manifestation from heaven. Emma raised her clear soprano voice and, for one more refrain, began to sing with all her heart:

> *"The spirit of God like a fire is burning,*
> *The latter-day glory begins to come forth!*
> *The visions and blessings of old are returning,*
> *And angels are coming to visit the earth!"*

Chapter Two

"... Best of Times... Worst of Times"

Is this Don Carlos? — *my* little grandson? Land sakes, he's as tall as a tree!"

Mary Duty Smith — Joseph's paternal grandmother — sat in a high-backed chair with a lap quilt about her legs, greeting her burgeoning family. She was tiny and delicate, chilly even in this soft May climate, white-haired and regal, though her shoulders were now bent with age. Still, she held court as a queen might, greeting each grandchild and great-grandchild with expressions of amazement and joy.

"Joseph," she said, tugging on her son's shirtsleeve, "I believe all your sons are taller than you are." She patted Don Carlos' hand. "And I think this one is the handsomest of all!"

The youngest son grinned broadly and knelt down beside his grandmother's chair. Her eyes brightened and she put her hand on his head as if to bless him.

"You're a good boy," she spoke with satisfaction. "Favored of the Lord, I can tell. Be true to the Lord and your family. That's all God requires of us."

Don Carlos kissed her wrinkled, papery hand, and moved aside for others to greet their matriarch. Joseph and Emma moved forward to take his place. Joseph went down on one knee before his grandmother. Emma stood beside the chair with two children clutching her skirts and hiding from this strange, elderly lady. Emma was expecting her baby in another month. She and the children had waited while Joseph and Hyrum had gone to Fairport to escort their grandmother home in a carriage. Julia and little Joseph had talked of nothing else all day except their great-grandmother. Would she like children? Could they sit on her lap? Did she know their father when he was little? Now, great Grandmother was here, and they were too shy to greet her. Emma took Grandmother Smith's hand in hers, noting the coolness of her thin, dry skin. A sudden premonition of growing old herself, surrounded by grandchildren, flooded her mind, and she shivered momentarily even while smiling warmly at the older woman.

"Ah, Joseph," Grandmother Smith murmured in satisfaction. "I see you brought your family tonight. Such fine children, and. . . "she looked up at Emma, "and a well-favored wife, about to bear you more posterity, it seems."

"Yes. This is my wife, Emma. She's been eager to meet you since she learned you might pay us a visit."

Emma felt an instant kinship with the bright-eyed, elderly woman. She pressed her fragile hand and explained. "I wanted to visit you upon your arrival, but Joseph said you were fatigued from your trip. I don't doubt it. We were all so surprised to hear that you would undertake such a journey at your stage in life. But, oh, how happy we are to have you here! Grandmother Smith, this is a great day for us."

The old matriarch's face glowed with the many expressions of love she had enjoyed that night.

"This is a great day for me! To see my children's children — and their children! — happy and living righteously in the Lord! A

Christian mother could ask no more." She shook her grandson's shoulder affectionately. "And this one — this boy has made us all proud. Why just look at the city he has built, and a large, beautiful house of the Lord. It's a wonder, an absolute wonder! I have walked completely around that building and looked inside. It must be the Lord's dwelling place, for His Spirit whispered to me in there. Who would have thought a mere boy could start a church that is the wonder of the whole countryside? Your ancestors have been men of valor and honor, Joseph, so I'm not surprised. . . but I am pleased, very pleased."

Her approbation meant a good deal to Joseph, for not all his father's family had accepted him or his calling. The Smith family members were independent thinkers, and none more so than Joseph. Only one of his uncles refused to even discuss the new religion or Joseph's spiritual gifts. Tonight however, other uncles, Silas and John, who had joined the church and gathered to Kirtland, were bringing their families to see Grandmother Smith.

Joseph, looking into her eyes, became for a moment the little tow-headed boy of Palmyra. Fleetingly he longed for simpler times, running through the fields, playing in the forest, jumping off the hay wagon and stumbling into the old pond to wash off the dust. His heart ached within him for the childhood left behind, but still mirrored in his grandmother's eyes. To her he would always be "little Joseph," and that suddenly seemed so comforting. Joseph's eyes were wet as he leaned forward to kiss her soft, creased cheeks.

With a breaking voice, the matriarch whispered in his ear. "I have had a blessing! To be kissed by the prophet of the Lord!"

At that, Joseph's heart expanded until he thought his chest would burst. He controlled an emotional sob as he stood again and beamed down on his grandmother. Then Samuel and Mary crowded up from behind, and he stepped aside to give them place.

It was a rich evening, full of reminiscence and family anecdotes. Cousins played in the corners of the room, and then as evening approached, they started the age-old, favorite game of hide-and-seek. Uncles, aunts, brothers and sisters sat long into the night sharing stories and jokes, while Grandmother Smith gazed with deep satisfaction on her expanding family.

Finally, the evening grew late. The children were called inside. All gathered before the fireplace where a few embers glowed, and Joseph Sr. offered a family prayer in thanksgiving for his mother. She was a woman who would rather spend her last few days with her family than remain in her own comfortable home. The journey had taken the last reserves of her strength, and they knew she was weakening rapidly. Emma and Lucy helped Grandmother Mary to bed, slipping the voluminous nightgown over thin, frail shoulders, and tucking her in bed with warm bricks at the bottom of the blankets to warm her chilly feet.

She patted each woman's hand and whispered a final word of thanks and blessing. Then she closed her eyes. Tiny blue veins crisscrossed her paper-thin eyelids as she sighed and allowed herself to settle into a deep, comforting sleep. Emma looked back on the tiny figure barely a bump in the covers. Then she quietly slipped out and closed the door behind her. No one knew exactly when the deep slumber became the sleep of the ages, but Mary Duty Smith passed out of this world that night with a smile on her lips. The family gathered once more the next day to bury their mother and grandmother in view of the new temple, which she had so heartily admired.

A little over a month later, Emma gave birth to their second healthy, baby boy. It was a fairly easy birth, but all the women attending her, especially her mother-in-law Lucy, watched the child anxiously for any signs of distress. There were none. The baby wailed lustily, even before the birthing was complete. His skin turned a rich pink, and he grabbed at the sheets covering his mother.

"He's a strong one, this boy!" Mother Smith spoke with satisfaction, as she sponged the child with warm water.

Rebecca Williams attended Emma. "Here, I'll help you sit up a little. You can hold him in just a moment." To the anxious look in Emma's eyes, she answered the silent question, reassuring her friend, "Yes, he is healthy and strong. Are you?" Emma looked white as a ghost.

"I'm tired, but all right. I just want to hold my baby."

"His father says the same."

"You can bring Joseph in now."

A few minutes later, Joseph came to the bedroom, peered around the doorway, then grinned like a schoolboy. His mother had the baby wrapped in a light cotton blanket and handed the tightly swaddled figure to him. Dark, bright eyes looked up into his father's blue ones, and a little rosebud mouth pouted with the outrage of birth. Joseph was delighted with his son and walked about the room, holding the child in the crook of his arm and talking to him.

Lucy asked, "What will you call this little fellow?"

Emma and Joseph looked at each other, then at Rebecca. Joseph answered, "Frederick! Emma and I want to name him after our dear friend, Frederick Granger Williams. What do you think, Rebecca? Is it a good name?"

Naturally robust with a rosy complexion, Rebecca now blushed with the compliment to her husband. Her voice choked with emotion, she simply replied, "The best!"

Joseph smiled at Emma, the two of them enjoying the happiness of a strong healthy son and the pleasure of honoring a dear friend. So, Freddy was the boy's name, and he thrived right from the start.

It was the best of times for Joseph and Emma. Though material goods were still scarce, spiritual blessings abounded. The School of the Prophets moved into the newly dedicated temple, and almost every day Joseph brought home another story of prayers answered there. In some ways she missed hosting the men, serving them hot bread, and hearing her husband give instruction to their friends. In January, they had begun studying Hebrew with a Jewish teacher, Joshua Seixas, for Joseph wanted all priesthood leaders to be educated in languages. He intended that they go on to learn many languages, thereby becoming better able to spread the Lord's word. He led the class in scholarship and was soon reading the scriptures in Hebrew. Emma had the benefit of each new insight Joseph gained, for he shared it with her.

One night, soon after Freddy's birth, Joseph sat beside the bed as she lay curled up with the baby in the circle of her arms. Her husband confided in her a spiritual witness that she would cling to until her dying day.

"When we picked up Grandmother Smith at Fairport, the barge captain had heard of the temple as well as the persecution of the church. He asked if it had all been worth our sacrifice. I imagine sometimes you must think back on your father's warning and wonder the same thing."

A smile crept over his wife's lips and she shook her head no, but he went on.

"Well, in case you wonder, I want to tell you of the Lord's blessing on us in the temple last April. It happened just a few days after the dedication. It was the first Sunday in April. We had held services there. You recall, don't you?"

"Yes."

"Did you see Oliver and me retire behind the veils after the sacrament was served?"

"Yes."

"I. . . I never told you what happened to us then. I wanted to get it down in writing first, as a testimony to the world."

His eyes left Emma and little Freddy, for he looked beyond them, and his face took on a familiar white light. Even his hair seemed almost translucent, and his voice trembled with deep humility.

"We saw the Lord standing upon the breastwork of the pulpit, before us; and under His feet was a paved work of pure gold, in color like amber. His eyes were as a flame of fire; the hair of His head was white like the pure snow; His countenance shone above the brightness of the sun; and His voice was as the sound of the rushing of great waters, even the voice of Jehovah, saying: I am the first and the last; I am He who liveth, I am He who was slain; I am your advocate with the Father. Behold, your sins are forgiven you; you are clean before me; therefore, lift up your heads and rejoice. . . For behold, I have accepted this house, and my name shall be here; and I will manifest myself to my people in mercy in this house. . . "

Emma lay perfectly still watching her prophet-husband. He fairly quaked with the power of the words he spoke. Light seemed to spill from him and flow over her bed, her baby, and herself. A renewed energy of body and soul surged through her. She was weary with the daily grind of work, children, and frugal living, but at this moment she seemed far richer than a queen.

He went on to say that the Prophet Elijah had given him the keys of sealing power, giving eternal validity to the performance of all gospel ordinances for both the living and the dead, and told him that the great and dreadful day of the Lord was near. He added that this was the fulfillment of Malachi's prophecy that Elijah would be sent to turn the hearts of the fathers to the children and the children to the fathers. When Joseph had finished, the trembling and the light disappeared, his gaze turned back to his wife and son watching him. He drew a deep breath and shook his head slightly as if in an effort to come back to the present world.

Suddenly Emma was frightened. She cried out, "Oh Joseph, will I lose you to that other world? It is far more glorious than this one we share. How can I hope to hold you here by me, when the angels of heaven and the very Son of God call you away to a place I cannot go?"

A sob welled up from her breast. Joseph quickly went to her and took her in his arms. "Emma! My Emma-rose. Are you afraid? Is that what I hear? I thought you would welcome this glorious witness."

She pressed her face against his shoulder. "I do," she choked out. "Oh, I do! It is so very beautiful. But I can't join you in that kind of communion. It's not my calling. It's yours, and I fear you prefer that world to this. One day, I'll lose you to it, and I can't stand that thought."

She wept in earnest, and the baby soon began to wail as well. Joseph scooped them both into his arms, holding and rocking mother and son to calm them. Soon his warmth and soothing took its effect. Emma regained her composure, her sobs diminished, and her arms around his neck loosened. She lay back against the pillow, drained from the experience, and reached up to touch her husband's face.

"Joseph, my Joseph, I have a jealous heart when it comes to you. I cannot share you. Maybe God will curse me for wanting you all to myself. I can't help it. Without you and your light, my world would be dark as night. Promise me you won't choose that world of angels and leave me here on earth alone. I. . . I. . . couldn't bear it."

Joseph regarded his wife with deep affection. Emma held such a tight rein over her heart. It was rare for her to reveal her anxieties or the depth of her love. He kissed her forehead, her eyelids, the tip of her nose, and the curve of her soft lips. The baby whimpered and Joseph kissed him too. His emotions as a father and husband were almost harder to speak than his witness of the Lord. They were all interwoven with the pattern of his life and his divine calling.

"I'll never leave you. . . not until my work here on earth is finished. Even then, God will have to pry me away from you. Don't cry, Emma, my love, my heart."

And Emma's soul was comforted.

"Do the saints think of material blessings when God promises He will pour out His blessings upon them?" Oliver, Joseph, and Sidney were deep in serious discussion over the financial state of the church.

"Apparently they do," Joseph sighed. "They have sacrificed so much that when the Lord speaks of blessings, their minds naturally rush to relieving their poverty."

"Material blessings are easier to count than spiritual blessings. Those aren't necessarily obvious for years, even generations." Sidney had a firm grasp on human nature.

Joseph reassured them. "The Lord will free us of our debts in His own time."

"I hope He hurries," Oliver shook his head. "The temple is mortgaged to the hilt. The supplies we signed for — the mortar, the benches, the furnace, the belfry — those debts will all come due next spring."

Sidney had pushed back from their meager dinner, balled up his fist, and pounded the tabletop. "I feel utterly defenseless in the grip of the gentile banks. I wish the saints could deal only with other faithful members. I don't trust the economic stability of the country. President Jackson is going to ruin our national economy by giving his favored, private banks huge deposits and having no national standard for banking. Speculation and panic are bound to run wild."

"At least, it is in our favor right now," Joseph observed. "With the government accepting bank notes for land, it enables us to sell property and enjoy more economic prosperity than ever before."

"It's false prosperity, though," Sidney counseled. "The value of land is entirely subjective. What a man will pay today has nothing much to do with what he will pay tomorrow. You can't build an economic base on speculation."

"I agree, and for that reason, I feel impressed to start a bank of our own to keep our people out of the clutches of callous bankers."

"Start a bank?" Oliver broke in.

"Yes! One that we can control. Our people are used to trading services for goods. If we started a bank. . . "

"I don't know, Joseph." Sidney was hesitant.

"Many communities have chartered banks of their own. Ashtabula, Ravenna, Warren — they all operate on a smaller scale than a state bank, but at least they can fund their own projects, keep that money in their own community, and thereby control their own destiny."

Oliver had been sitting back, listening, calculating. His face showed the signs of maturity. The fine features of youth had thickened a little, and his hair was thinning. Marriage and Missouri had mellowed him. He had married Nancy Whitmer and enjoyed immensely his brotherly status with David and John Whitmer. He often contemplated the boyish enthusiasm that had linked his life forever with Joseph Smith.

His personal relationship with Joseph had been revitalized with the recent work on the Egyptian papyri. It had seemed almost like old times, only better. This time he could see the ancient writing and examine the papyri to his satisfaction, and Joseph's ability for transliteration was not dimmed. To the contrary, it seemed heightened. Oliver's respect for his friend burned even brighter than before.

Now, Oliver looked at Joseph pensively. Did his prophetic abilities extend to financial spheres as well? Debt hung so heavily over the church that Joseph could hardly speak of anything else. Thirteen thousand dollars was still owed on the Kirtland Temple.

"God always expects us to help ourselves," Joseph warmed to his subject. "We will sell bonds and subscriptions and start our bank with twenty thousand gold and silver dollars in reserves. We won't limit investment to only those of substantial means. We'll sell inexpensive bonds to all who wish to participate. Everyone can have a share."

There was silence. Oliver and Sidney pondered the proposition.

The door to Sidney's room opened, and Hyrum showed George Robinson, Rigdon's son-in-law, in before him. "What are we hatching?" Hyrum asked.

"A bank of Kirtland," Oliver looked up at Hyrum. "What would you say to such a proposal?"

"Well, I don't think the government gives bank charters to churches." Hyrum ventured.

"I don't propose a bank charter for the church," Joseph grew impatient. "It would be strictly a civil matter. It would have duly appointed president, cashier, manager, and clerks. I'm thinking of Frederick Williams, Warren Parrish, Oliver, Sidney, you, myself, David Whitmer and Newel Whitney as officers. The people would respond to the idea of our own bank if we were all behind it."

"We haven't any banking experience," Hyrum protested.

"But we have an interest in protecting our people from the greedy bankers of Painesville and Amherst. They charge exorbitant interest. They keep a stranglehold on our expansion by refusing to loan us money for new equipment or building. If we had a cooperative effort, just imagine what we could accomplish!"

Joseph was obviously committed to his proposition. "We can obtain a state charter, abide by rules of banking, sell bonds and subscriptions, and fund our own growth by the inspiration and direction of the Lord."

Oliver finally caught fire from Joseph's enthusiasm. He leaned forward, his chair legs coming down with a thud. "I'm with you, Joseph. It is better that interest be collected by a bank founded by our own people than to leave that money in the hands of our enemies. Our community is growing fast now that the temple is done. People are gathering here from all the eastern states and Canada. We should be able to succeed just on the basis of our growth. Sidney, do you have any doubt of our ability to run a bank?"

Rigdon scratched his neck and conceded the argument. "No, not of our ability. We do lack some in experience, but common sense tells me that banking can't be that difficult. However, great care should be taken to see that our money is sufficiently backed with gold and silver. Do you agree, Joseph?"

"Certainly! Everyone knows paper money is only paper without gold reserves to back it." He was so excited now, having won over his friends, that he paced the room, stopping occasionally to clap one or another on the shoulder to emphasize a point.

"I already have a name for the bank — *the Kirtland Safety Society Bank!* This will not be just another bank. I want people to know their money is safe with us. I will personally guarantee all the transactions."

"Joseph!" Hyrum warned. "Do you think that is prudent?"

Joseph was adamant. "The people must know their money is safe. Oliver, I want you to print up stock certificates when we get everything in order, and we'll begin selling shares immediately. Now we need to procure a bank charter from the state capital."

Sidney stood and offered his hand to Joseph. "To demonstrate my good faith, I'll buy the first two thousand shares."

Joseph grasped his shoulder with a vise-like grip. "I appreciate that kind of support, Brother Sidney!"

Later, Emma considered her husband's newly proposed venture with grave concern. She was the one who had to turn people away when the goods of the church store had been given out on credit and not paid for. Joseph's heart was too big to be a financier. He trusted too much and forgave too easily.

"Well, I'm certainly not alone in this," Joseph reasoned. "Brother Sidney has pledged himself to the first two thousand shares of stock. Oliver, David, Frederick — they all see the potential. Emma, we are being strangled by hostile bankers. They control our purse strings and our lives. I can't stand that anymore. If I must owe money, let me owe it to a man of integrity."

She was rocking their little Freddy. He was just five months old, a dark-haired child with serious brown eyes. Emma listened to her husband's plans with sober misgivings. She felt as though she were throwing water on his great idea, but she had a suspicion that others were so in awe of his position they agreed with everything he said. It was tempting to think that the Lord's prophet could do no wrong. It simply wasn't true. Though well-intentioned, Joseph was fallible.

"So many people personally owe you money now, we could fund the bank ourselves if they all paid," she observed dourly.

Joseph was dismayed at Emma's tone. It was unlike her to be cynical. The burdens were pressing on her too heavily. Years of going without, of putting off creditors and scrimping to put food on the table were taking their toll on his wife. He must find a way to provide financially for her and his family. The bank was the answer. Of that he was quite sure.

"Oliver is the logical choice to go to Philadelphia for engraving plates." Joseph presented the entire concept to a choice group of trusted friends. "He has experience in printing and will know the best price for the dies and plates, as well as good quality. While he is gone we must obtain the formal banking charter. Sidney, Frederick, Warren, David, and I have been working on drawing up a petition to the legislature in Columbus. It is nearly complete, but we are undecided on a courier. He will have to represent us all, and it may take several weeks. Brother Hyde, Sidney has suggested you. Is this an assignment you would be inclined to take?"

Orson Hyde was a quiet man, but known to be a shrewd bargainer, and had proven his loyalty to Joseph and the church many times. His dignified deportment served him well in any company, and he was tireless in doing his duty.

"I consider it a privilege. When do you want me to go?"

"Right away. Oliver is leaving tomorrow for Philadelphia. Our petition will be ready within the week, and you should go *posthaste*. Private bank notes have more than doubled in the last few years, and I see no reason why Kirtland should not have its own bank as soon as possible."

Unfortunately, the legislature in Columbus didn't share Joseph's view. While Oliver ordered the plates they needed and had them inscribed with "The Kirtland Safety Society Bank," Orson sat for days in the hallowed halls of government only to have the Kirtland bank petition rejected. There had been too many inflammatory reports of the Mormons over the last few years, and the state legislators were not interested in encouraging greater expansion in Kirtland. Orson returned dejected and empty-handed.

Joseph responded by calling a meeting on January 2, 1837 of the proposed bank officers.

"Certainly it is a blow," he said, "But we shouldn't be surprised nor daunted. We have experienced opposition every step of the way. Our enemies do not want us to succeed. They didn't want us to build a temple, but we built it! They are afraid of us, brethren — afraid of our growing numbers and afraid of the society we want to create."

"There is another option," David Whitmer ventured. "It is to open without a charter. Many private banks have no charter from the state."

"But is it legal?" Hyde asked.

David answered Orson, but looked straight at Joseph. "In 1816, the Ohio legislature passed a law prohibiting bank operations without official incorporations, and they imposed a hefty fine on all officers associated with such a venture. *However*, that law has been ignored as obsolete and impractical. It has been declared invalid by attorneys, and even the current legislature."

Joseph weighed the alternatives. "There is risk in anything we do. If we do nothing, we are subject to the whims of our enemies. If we strike out on our own, they might use an antiquated law against us. But success is its own spokesman. I would rather take a risk than be strangled as we have been."

"We'll need to reorganize somewhat," Frederick Williams got immediately to the point.

"And, we'll need a new name," Oliver pointed out, "one compatible with the dies already cast. To re-do them would be far too expensive. Any suggestions?" He threw it open to the group.

"If it isn't a 'bank,' it is an 'anti-bank,' a financial institution owned by its members." Warren Parrish observed. "Could we simply add that to the notes?"

Oliver considered the proposal. "The Kirtland Safety Society Anti-Banking Company — that's quite a mouthful, and will have to be stamped on the notes *after* they are printed."

"Can you do it?" Joseph asked.

"Yes," Oliver hesitated. "I see no alternative."

"Good," Joseph was anxious to get on with the plans. "We will accept land for stock shares — shares of $50 minimum. Since the value of land is going up every day, I anticipate our assets will increase quickly. That should bring in much needed capital."

Notes were issued on January 6, 1837 for the new Kirtland Safety Society Anti-Banking Company. Many mortgaged their lots and homes for quick and ready cash — Kirtland Bank notes.

Eventually the Smiths came to own one-sixth of all the stock in the Kirtland Safety Society Anti-Banking Company. Some thought that owning shares in the company would be the making of their fortunes, since they could buy shares worth fifty dollars face value for twenty-six cents per share. For a fifty-two dollar investment they would have stock worth ten thousand dollars — on paper. Speculation joined up with Farmer Brown's cow and jumped over the moon. Prices shot up. Goods and services doubled within a few months. An acre lot which could be purchased for six dollars in January sold for forty-four dollars by June. Tailors, carpenters, milliners, coopers, and glaziers all tripled their prices, and people paid them — at least they promised to pay them. They ran up exorbitant charges for merchandise, expecting inflation would enable them to make more money to pay their debts. After all, they had built the Lord's temple and been promised blessings. There was an air of excitement in Kirtland. Were they not a chosen people, and would God not reward them with riches? Why, eventually, the very streets could be paved with gold!

The bubble began to burst when local businessmen, not of the faith, refused to take the Kirtland Anti-Banking notes. Others collected them and took them to the bank demanding to redeem them for gold coinage. Against Joseph's cautions, Warren Parrish honored every request. Within a few weeks, their reserves had dwindled considerably. Paper money became worthless to everyone but the most faithful of saints.

At the same time, the banks in all parts of the United States were plunging toward failure. Joseph was notified that his Kirtland Anti-Banking notes were not acceptable for the debts the church owed in the east. Creditors refused them, since the bank had no charter from the state.

The bubble of prosperity did burst after just a month. In February, Joseph and Sidney as chief officers were served with a charge of illegal banking. Grandison Newell, a wealthy businessman in Kirtland with a particular hatred for Joseph, brought the lawsuit.

Emma had rarely seen Joseph so discouraged. His enthusiasm and sense of destiny usually carried him on a high tide through all opposition. Now he simply sat by the fireplace, his elbows resting on his knees, his head bowed.

"There is nothing to do but shut down the bank," he said woodenly.

"But Joseph, so many of our people have invested in it. *We've* invested in it. The whole Smith family has put almost all their assets into the bank. So have the other leaders of the church. They'll have worthless stock if you close the bank."

"I know! But what else can we do? All the other bank officers will be charged with illegal banking activities, as I have been, unless we close. The fine is one thousand dollars. I have no doubt my enemies will convict me, despite the fact that we did nothing other private banks haven't done. Besides, we are at the point of collapse anyway. There is no reserve backing for the money. All the gold and silver we had has been dispersed. I issued warnings, but was ignored. Warren Parrish felt that in order to establish confidence in the paper money, we had to redeem every note with gold. It didn't even go back into the hands of the saints; it was withdrawn by our enemies."

They were both silent for several minutes, contemplating financial ruin.

"I need to issue a word of warning to the saints about the spirit of speculation and greed that has taken over. I'm concerned about the morale of our people as well. Oliver has lost confidence and wants to get out of the printing office as well as the bank. He has asked Sidney and me to buy him out. I feel as though I'm trying to stop a run-away locomotive."

Emma couldn't stand seeing him so dejected. She went to him and knelt beside him, taking his face in her hands.

"Joseph, your enemies have not the power to harm you as long as God is with you. Wait on the Lord. He knows all, and He has reasons for allowing this persecution. Our vision is not always *His* vision. Be patient and it will all work out."

Joseph sighed. "You are the most forbearing wife I know of. Most women would be borne down to the dust with the problems you have overcome. In fact, is there even any food in your larder right now?"

She smiled tenderly. "Let me worry about that."

"No, I must know. How are you feeding our family and all the friends who stop by?"

"I am frugal. You know that. I set some food on the table, and some I hold back in the cellar. We still have ham, bacon, flour, honey, even some apple butter I made last fall. Our larder is first cousin to that of the widow who fed Elijah — our cruse of oil never runs out."

He put his head on her shoulder. "What would I do without you?"

"You know I'll never forsake you, not as long as I know you love me."

"And do you know that?"

Emma took her husband in her arms. "Yes, I do. After all, you kidnapped me and married me."

"You were willing enough." He relaxed and leaned against her.

"Well, I didn't have much choice. It was almost indecent, allowing you to kiss me as you did. Marriage seemed preferable to disgrace."

"Disgrace? You are older. I knew little of love and courting. You were obviously the initiator."

"Hah!" she feigned offense. "You wooed me in Josiah Stowell's parlor."

"Yes, but you followed me there. And you kissed me first."

"That had nothing to do with it. Before I knew what was happening. . . "

72

"I kissed you like this." Her husband silenced her with a tender, longing kiss.

Finally she murmured, "Yes, something like that. How could I refuse to marry you after that? It was shameless."

"Completely shameless." He persisted in nuzzling her. "You might have resisted my improprieties."

"Perhaps," she whispered. "But how could I? You won my heart."

Emma smiled, pleased with her little success in making her husband forget the storm clouds gathering over his head.

The bank continued to do business, issuing notes only the faithful accepted. Among many who had invested in the bank, feelings grew bitter. A schism soon developed between Joseph and his friends, Oliver, David, and Martin, who criticized the whole banking effort. When the second petition for a charter failed to win approval, other officers began to grumble. The paper money was almost worthless, and the gold and silver reserves were gone. Some threatened to sue.

Joseph and Emma were at Frederick G. Williams' home one day in spring when a mob of angry men gathered outside, shouting threats and demanding Joseph be given up. It terrified the children, and Joseph was about to surrender, when Rebecca Williams pulled a dress and bonnet out of her trunk. A tall, robust woman with a good sense of humor and a cool head, she threw the dress over Joseph's head, put a shawl around his shoulders, and tied the bonnet under his chin.

"There!" Rebecca exclaimed, "They'll never know you, 'Aunt Trudy!' Pull that bonnet down a little further and stuff your cheeks with cotton wool. Emma, you keep the children calm. I'm going to walk 'Aunt Trudy' out to our carriage. She is lame and has to be driven home, you know."

"Will it work?" Joseph was dubious.

"Better than surrendering, isn't it?"

"I suppose. . . Let's go!"

Rebecca tucked her arm through "Aunt Trudy's," gave her a cane, and led her, limping, from the parlor, out the side door, and to the buggy hitched beneath the hickory tree. "I'm so glad we had this visit, Auntie. Now, you stay off that leg until Dr. Williams says your knee is all better. Pardon me, sir. My Aunt Trudy is on her way home. Excuse me, excuse me!"

The angry mob fell back from her path as she escorted her old, bent "auntie" to the carriage under the trees. Her twelve-year-old son, John, helped "Aunt Trudy" into the rig. Men in the mob were still yelling for Joe Smith to show himself. Some at Rebecca's elbow were complaining that Smith was hiding on the premises, and they would search the place to find him.

"Well, Mr. Perkins," Rebecca confronted the loudest of the men, " you're welcome to search my house. Try not to frighten my children any more than you already have. You'll find Dr. Williams in the parlor attending to his correspondence. Sister Emma and her daughter are upstairs. We've had a delightful day visiting. I'm sure she'll be glad to see you, but I can promise you, Joseph Smith is not in our house."

The men looked at each other. They were confused. Reports had it that Smith was at the Williams' home, and they were determined to haul him before a judge, for one of their own had sworn out a warrant against him.

"I'll go in and search," a particularly loud man volunteered. "The rest of you stay out here. If he is there, I'll bring him out. No sense scaring the young'uns." Eyes ablaze, he entered Rebecca's house.

"Goodbye Auntie. Take care of that leg now, or Dr. Williams will be upset with you."

"Aunt Trudy" settled back into the carriage and waved her handkerchief as John clucked to the horse. The mob of about two-dozen men still milled around in the Williams' yard, trampling the flowers and complaining about the "Safety Society Bank."

Their leader finally satisfied himself that Joseph was not in the house and came stomping out, thoroughly perturbed. Rebecca and Emma laughed about the incident later on, but Joseph knew persecution was just beginning. There would be the devil to pay before this was over.

One year after the April 3, 1836 vision of the Savior to Joseph and Oliver, another conference was held. The membership of the church commemorated their formal organization of 1830. Wilford Woodruff, though a recent convert, was already a trusted friend of Joseph and Emma. He compared the outpouring of the Spirit as "something similar to the Pentecost that St. Paul spoke of at Jerusalem."

Before the conference was over, Joseph announced that the Lord had directed missionary work to begin in the British Isles. A murmur rippled through the congregation. Who would be the first to go? The names fell from Joseph's lips, and the men stood up.

"Brothers Heber C. Kimball and Orson Hyde are called to open the missionary work in the British Isles. Brethren, get your affairs in order and prepare to go by June."

Two months later, the First Presidency set Heber and Orson apart to head a church mission to England. Also set apart were Willard Richards and Joseph Fielding, a new English convert, who had come to America with his sister, Mary Fielding. This first mission to England had been urged by Canadian brethren who wanted to spread the gospel to family and friends abroad. It was to prove a huge success and started an influx of European converts, which would soon double the size of the Kirtland church.

After the missionaries departed, Joseph and Sidney spent two days in deep discussion.

Rigdon was adamant. "I tell you, it is time to get out of the banking venture, Joseph! We've been in court six times, and charged with illegal banking. Our fines are overwhelming. We must let Warren Parrish and Frederick Williams succeed us, if that's what they desire."

Joseph already knew he must acquiesce, but was racked with guilt. Sidney took a more objective view of the dilemma, but Joseph felt responsible to everyone who had lost money. Nor was money the only thing on his mind.

"Sidney," he said solemnly, "we are losing the battle. There is a great schism growing in the unity of the brethren. Perhaps I deserve the criticism from Oliver, David, and Martin. I was too overbearing in urging their participation."

"It's no one's fault. It's the times. . . bad times for the whole country."

"Yes, but I promised those notes would be good. I guaranteed them personally."

" So you're guilty of a little optimism!"

Joseph shook his head. "How does it look now to resign from the bank? If we withdraw our support, chaos will reign. Eventually, the people will turn on us. Apostasy is at our doorstep."

Sidney observed the sallow complexion of his friend and prophet. Joseph didn't look well. Normally he was robust and hearty. Now he looked as though he hadn't slept in months. Sidney shoved a calloused hand through his hair. He knew Joseph was right. The United Order had gradually been phased out when it failed to establish prosperity. Now, every effort to make the bank work had failed, and they were more deeply in debt than ever.

Sidney stood up and began to pace. "We have done everything we can. There is no cooperation among the brethren. Jared Carter and Oliver Granger want to take over my stock, and I intend to transfer ownership to them. You should consider doing the same."

Joseph's face was haggard. There were threats on his life necessitating a constant bodyguard. On his way to and from Painesville, he had been waylaid more than once. Emma and the children were anxious, and each strange noise frightened them. Joseph had commissioned a larger home to be built earlier in the spring, but only one man still worked on it. Jonathan Crosby was so devoted to Joseph and Emma that he went on with the work, even when he had no pay and no food for his own family. Now, with three children and a constant stream of visitors, Joseph desperately needed more space for his family. He was growing weary with the burden of admonishing, encouraging, and giving counsel that was rejected. He spent his days preaching, organizing quorums and defining their responsibilities, in addition to defending himself from continual criticism from close friends. Only a select few remained steadfast. Sidney was his most loyal supporter. Brigham also remained faithful. Oliver, on the other hand, would hardly speak to him. David Whitmer, whom Joseph had once designated as his successor to guide the church in his absence, had become sullen and hostile. Joseph began to search each face for signs of loyalty or disaffection.

A few days after his conversation with Sidney, Joseph spoke with his close friend and counselor, bank cashier, and local constable, Frederick G. Williams. Williams had opened up the Safety Society building for him. The prophet had been there since early morning, reviewing the records and trying to reconcile assets with debts. He had been examining the ledger.

Joseph pushed back his chair. "Frederick, I am concerned. There appear to be some irregularities in the ledger. Not only has Warren been issuing worthless bank notes, but it's possible he has lined his own pockets as well."

"That's a serious charge." Williams frowned, looking over Joseph's shoulder at the ledger.

"I hardly know what else to think in light of what I have read. If it isn't true, I'd like an explanation."

"Joseph, Warren is your scribe, and he's been with us in the banking venture from the beginning."

Joseph was impatient. "I know, but there is something amiss, and I mean to get to the bottom of it."

Williams folded his arms over his chest, rocked back on his heels, and asked Joseph, "How will you do that?"

"I want you to issue a warrant to search his trunk."

"There isn't sufficient evidence. I won't issue a warrant on suspicions."

"It's more than suspicions. I believe there is evidence he has personally profited from the bank when everyone else is suffering."

Williams shook his head. "I've never seen it, and I work closely with him. I think if he were misusing money, I would know."

Joseph paused and looked hard at the man whose friendship was so dear to him that he and Emma had named their son after him. He had been the most generous of men with time and resources when he first came into the church. Now he seemed less willing to sacrifice. He was a learned man and one of the best pupils at the School of the Prophets. Joseph had always admired Frederick's fine mind and knowledge, coupled with a great spirituality, but perhaps there was a shadow of pride threatening to spoil the mix.

"Where is your loyalty, Frederick?" Joseph asked in humble, measured tones, dreading the answer.

"My loyalty is with truth and fairness." Frederick's haughty answer sounded more like a politician's than a friend's.

"Then, in the pursuit of truth, I would like a warrant to search Parrish's trunk."

Williams was obstinate. "I flatly refuse to issue a warrant. I know him to be honest."

Joseph's gaze never wavered. "I insist," he pressed quietly, "for if you will give me a warrant, I can get to the bottom of this. If you do not. . . " He paused a moment, regretting the force he must exercise. "If you do not, I will release you from your office in the church."

Frederick G. Williams returned the gaze of his prophet without flinching. Where a mere difference of opinion should have been resolved peacefully between friends, Frederick had now hardened his resolve. He had given his life and his fortune to the church, but he would not forfeit his sacred honor.

Frederick's eyes narrowed, his face flushed, and he spat back, "Then release me, and we will strike hands upon it."

It hit Joseph like a physical blow. Next to Sidney, Frederick G. Williams was the most trusted friend he had. But Joseph would not be thwarted in this important matter. He drew a deep breath, shook his head, and resolutely replied, "Very well then, from henceforth I drop you from my quorum, in the name of the Lord!"

"So be it," Williams responded, shook hands, and backed away. When he neared the doorway, he abruptly turned and went out.

It was raining outside. Joseph heard the drumming on the tin roofs. As he followed Williams outside, a low rumble of thunder rolled across the night sky. He watched Frederick jump into his carriage and drive smartly away, with huge drops of rain splattering on the top of his buggy. Sorrowfully, Joseph started his walk home. This was a friendship he did not want to lose. Nor could he actually drop Williams from the quorum without a consenting vote by the priesthood. Joseph pondered the encounter. Couldn't Frederick see how important this was? Why had he refused? Had he lost confidence in him as a leader and a prophet? It was clear he could no longer count on Frederick's allegiance.

Joseph walked home, heedless of the rain, and entered his house thoroughly soaked. That night he rehearsed the whole event to his wife. He was so despondent that Emma insisted on some herb tea to settle his stomach.

"I don't want anything for my stomach! It isn't my stomach that hurts; it's my heart. I love Frederick like a brother. Emma, I couldn't be more upset if it had been Hyrum! I feel like storm clouds have gathered over the whole city and are about to break with vengeance upon us."

"Perhaps you pressed Frederick too far. He has his pride, you know."

"Do you think I am wrong then?"

"I wasn't there, but I do know that Frederick has been a loyal friend, and you might have been more patient with him."

Now Joseph was thoroughly downcast. "Maybe you're right. . . I am sorry we ever started the bank. It seemed so right, and it went so wrong. Satan is using all his means to destroy this church. I'm afraid I have not only failed with the bank, I have failed with the church. The Saints trusted me, and I made promises I can't keep. We are as destitute as anyone. There are debts I have signed for, church debts that I personally guaranteed! I may never be able to pay them off. Oh, Emma! What am I to do?"

She had no answer for him. She had been turning away creditors for months. They had been living on gifts from friends and borrowed goods. She could scarcely feed her own family on the supplies they had, and every day there were visitors to provide for as well. People constantly came to see Joseph for counsel or help. She could not simply ignore them. Even the ham hocks and johnnycake had to be rationed. She was grateful she always had enough flour to make bread. With a slice of warm bread, men always thought they were well fed. But freshly baked bread would not satisfy the demands of the courts.

"I think Sidney was right. You have to withdraw. Your continued allegiance to the bank only confuses the people, and they think all will be well as long as you are the president. They don't understand the complexities, and you will shoulder the blame. Sylvester Smith is openly condemning you as a fallen prophet."

"Sylvester has dallied on the edge of apostasy since Zion's Camp. Nothing I could do ever satisfied him. When the food was bad, I was to blame. When he pulled his hamstring, I was to blame. He thinks a prophet should be able to *command* the Lord in all things, not *reveal* the Lord in all things. I have never pretended to have influence with God. If I had, I would surely have saved my own children. All I can do is reveal the will of the Lord. When the people won't listen, I can't prevent the consequences.

"I feel as though the hounds of hell are after me! Every way I turn, I encounter hatred and accusation. I can endure the persecution of non-members. I can face their lies and threats on my life and not be daunted. But, oh the agony of looking a friend like Frederick G. Williams in the eye and seeing disillusionment. . . even hatred! It is more than I can bear!"

His voice broke, and his chest expanded with a deep effort to stay in control. Emma went to him, and he wrapped his arms about her waist, burying his face in her hair. She knew his emotions, always sensitive, were even more so lately. He made no effort to hide his faults from the people, or to pretend to be better than they. In his own revelations, he humbly suffered the reprimands of the Lord and thought all men should do the same, and then take counsel of God to correct their ways.

Emma put her husband to bed that night with a cold cloth across his head and eyes. Even discounting the effects of distraught emotions, he didn't seem well. She woke many times to his tossing and turning. Several times he cried out in his sleep, and once he sat straight up in bed with such a wail that young Jared Carter jumped up from his guard post and pounded on the door, asking if all was well. Emma soothed Joseph back to sleep, noting that he seemed warmer than usual and that his eyes were bloodshot. She put her hand on his cheek. He held it there, murmuring about her cool touch.

Morning came and Joseph tried to get dressed, but fell back into bed with the effort. Now Emma was truly concerned. Joseph was seldom sick. He was so hale and hardy that she had almost thought him impervious to normal illnesses. Not now. She brought him chicken broth and bread, but he wouldn't eat. His temperature was high, so she sponged him down every hour, but he seemed to sink deeper and deeper into lethargy. Had it been winter, she would have suspected pneumonia. But it was June and the sun was shining; the days were beautiful. There was very little sickness going around the community.

Emma turned away every visitor except their closest friends. When her brothers-in-law, Hyrum and Samuel, came to see Joseph, she hoped they might comfort him.

"Hyrum, will you pray for me?" Joseph asked his older brother.

Hyrum glanced at Emma on the other side of the bed. The brothers were as alarmed as she was. Joseph's complexion was sallow, and dark circles ringed his eyes. His lips were pale, and his breath sour. Hyrum had seen their older brother Alvin die with similar symptoms.

"Where does it hurt, Joseph?"

"Mostly my head. . . and my heart. The light hurts my eyes. Every noise jolts me. I have no appetite. My stomach won't hold food. I can't think. My only peace comes when someone prays for me. Please, Hyrum, Samuel, won't you pray for me?"

Samuel knelt beside Hyrum, and the two men pleaded with the Lord for a blessing on their brother. They took turns praying for the better part of an hour. When they finished, Joseph was finally sleeping peacefully. Emma took her brothers-in-law to the kitchen and served them milk and cornbread. She sat with them and rehearsed her conversation with her husband the night he fell ill.

Hyrum agreed with her point of view. "Joseph has to withdraw from the bank as well. It will be hard. We've all lost money. Our family invested as much as anyone. I personally don't want the members thinking the Smiths are behind this venture any longer. To prolong it will simply result in greater losses."

Emma nodded. "I think Joseph is suffering more over his estrangement from Frederick and other friends than problems with the bank. Send Father over, Hyrum. Perhaps he can help ease Joseph's mind."

That evening Lucy and Joseph Sr. came to see their son. Emma had scarcely shown them into the bedroom when William and Don Carlos knocked on the door as well. She was especially glad to see William. The friendship was not always as strong as it should be between brothers. Emma welcomed them warmly and took comfort from Don Carlos's embrace. This youthful brother-in-law was growing at a remarkable rate. He was taller now than any of his brothers. Peach fuzz still on his young face, he was quickly becoming a fine figure of a man as his shoulders filled out his shirt, and long legs raised him above a crowd.

The small bedroom was crowded. Lucy looked like a little doll tucked in between her men-folk. She sat beside her son's bed and held his hand. Though the effort to speak was tiring for Joseph, he told his family of the concerns weighing on his mind.

Then he asked, "Do the people blame me?"

"Shh. No, Joseph," Mother Smith quickly tried to assuage Joseph's fear. "The people love you. Oh, a few have turned away, but the people as a whole love you. They understand the entire country is having financial problems."

Joseph appealed to his father, the Patriarch. "What shall I do? Oh, Father, my heart is sick within me! And this very day another summons came from Painesville. Grandison Newell is accusing me of trying to have him murdered."

Lucy cried out. "That man is a curse! He will not rest until he gets you convicted on some account. Murder, indeed! I'll oblige him, if he is so determined that someone threaten his life!"

Don Carlos smiled at Emma across the room and patted his mother's shoulder.

William spoke up, "I'll stand trial in your place, Joseph!" He reached for his brother's hand.

"William!" Joseph's voice broke. After a moment he continued. "God bless you for that, William. I know you would, too. Still, it is me they want. It's my blood they're after. Just ride with me when it is time to go."

"I will!" his brother affirmed ardently.

Joseph Sr. drew a deep breath and counseled his son. "It is time to turn your back completely on the bank. Too much damage has been done in your name. The abuses will not stop until the people understand that their prophet is no longer connected with this establishment. Right now, they still think you are. You must make it perfectly clear you have severed all ties."

Joseph looked from one family member to another. All of them nodded. His mother pressed his hand, understanding the burden that had brought him down into the depths of personal hell.

"I have weighed alternatives and tried to make reasonable decisions. But everything has gone awry," Joseph admitted humbly. "Father, you are my patriarch; please bless me!"

His father stepped to his bedside and laid calloused hands on Joseph's head. He pleaded for the Lord of Heaven to bless the church and lead the people back from the brink of disaster. Those in the room were silent for a time after the blessing was finished. They were well aware that the fragile thread holding the church together was confidence in Joseph. They also knew that thread was in danger of breaking.

Finally, Joseph broke the silence. "Father, I will abide by your counsel. I will instruct Sidney to transfer my stock in the bank and resign my position."

His father nodded approval. "One day we will see the purpose in all this. It may serve only to pare away the rotten portion of the church and leave the sweet fruit. You will soon discover who your true friends are. If a man prizes money above the teachings of the Lord, he has no place in heaven beside Abraham, Isaac, and Jacob. If he will leave the church over this, he would not have endured to the end, for no doubt there are more rough waters ahead."

Joseph Sr. looked down on the wretched face of his son. He patted Joseph's hair, awkwardly, roughly, and with a choked voice counseled, "Sleep now, my son. Place this in the Lord's care and rest. God's church needs you well. Your family needs you well!"

A week later the newly called missionaries left for England. They came to see Joseph before departing, and their unwavering testimonies served to strengthen him. Orson Hyde, Heber C. Kimball, Willard Richards, Joseph Fielding and others went without purse or scrip to journey to the British Isles. They would carry the restored gospel to the land of their ancestors. It was with deep affection that Joseph bade them a fond farewell and blessed them that their efforts would bear fruit. It was hard to say goodbye to faithful friends when others were turning against him. As Joseph's health started to improve, Sidney proposed a mission to Canada for them. Emma felt Joseph was still far too weak, however, he was determined to go. He needed some relief from his troubles and the incessant charges filed against him.

He and Sidney started for Fairport, but were detained at Painesville when a warrant was served on them. They appeared before a local judge. He ruled the warrant had no legitimate grounds. They started out the door of the court and were met by the constable with another warrant. This was also dismissed. Wearily, Joseph started to leave the courtroom again, only to be served yet a third time. The judge dismissed the third warrant also. After a fourth was served and ruled unsubstantial, Joseph and Sidney entered the carriage, turned it around, and started back to Kirtland. Joseph fell into bed that night, totally worn out and disconsolate.

The next morning Emma was hopeful. "Surely you'll not try to go again."

"I must. I cannot stay here another day. I feel the demons of hell hovering over me. Emma, please understand. I hate to leave you to face my creditors and my enemies, but a woman cannot be held responsible for her husband's debts. It is only me they want. I think I can regain some of my strength, if I just get away for a while. I need to preach again, to commune with the Lord. A crisis is coming, and I fear the consequences. For my family and friends I must find strength."

So Emma packed a knapsack full of food to sustain her husband. He went to his children, held each one on his lap, kissed them, and said goodbye. Last of all, he kissed Emma and waved apologetically. He and Sidney spent five weeks in Canada where the thirty-year-old prophet — now president of one of the fastest growing religions in America — slowly regained his good spirits. Joseph's severe trials of the tempestuous year had served to solemnize his once effusive preaching.

Emma continued in Kirtland as always, greeting church members with constant reaffirmation of the prophet's love for them, and helping out when possible with food and supplies. She eased the ache of missing her husband with work. Emma tended her family garden, cared for their children and home, showed the Egyptian mummies and papyri to curiosity seekers, and attended public meetings as her husband's representative. She heard the rumors spread by Oliver Cowdery, David Whitmer, and Frederick Williams but continued to greet them as friends. She had known and loved these men for years and continued now to reach out to them, her brown eyes silently pleading that they stay true to her husband and his work.

Joseph and Sidney returned from Canada, stronger than when they had left. Joseph's recovered stamina was tested on the return trip. They were set upon soon after they docked at Fairport by a mob bent on taking them back to Painesville for yet another trial. By the good graces of a sympathetic innkeeper, they escaped.

That night was black and starless. With the drunken mob still whooping and laughing in the inn, Joseph and Sidney ran out the kitchen door and guessed at the way home. Their best cover was in the trees. The ground was swampy, but the woods offered protection. They had no sooner slipped into the shadows when their absence was discovered, and shouts of outrage came from the tavern. Joseph and Sidney stumbled through the underbrush, sometimes tripping over logs, wading knee deep in filthy, stagnant water. Smoky torches sent flickering light through trees and brush while angry voices drew closer. Finally, Joseph pulled Sidney behind a fallen tree, hiding under its prickly branches.

"Don't breathe so loudly."

"Can't help it. . . " the older man panted. "Can't. . . catch. . . my breath."

"Shh! They're getting closer."

Sidney held his breath as long as he could, then exhaled carefully. His lungs felt as though they would burst. Joseph's back muscles were burning from constantly crouching as he ran. They tucked their heads in like a couple of tortoises and tried to melt into the shadows of the night. After a time the angry hunting party passed them by. When the cursing of the mob had completely faded away, the two men started off again, eventually abandoning the dark wooded shelter to find the familiar road home to Kirtland.

Joseph fell against the door of his house. It was bolted shut, so he pounded. Emma opened it within seconds. He stumbled past her into the house, Sidney hard on his heels. Emma gasped. She had been waiting for her husband since the previous morning when a traveler from Fairport reported Joseph and Sidney had disembarked and were heading home. Now here was her husband, filthy, wet, smelly, with his hair matted and his clothes torn. An equally battered Sidney all but collapsed in front of her fireplace. She brought them each a clean nightshirt and took the dirty clothes they shed to the washtub outside.

Once Sidney was settled in bed, she and Joseph looked at each other by glowing candlelight. He was exhausted, but not despondent as she had seen him last.

He drew her close with a deep sigh. "I guess you wonder what happened."

"No," she replied. "I can tell what happened. Oh, Joseph, I thought being chased by mobs was behind us when we moved to Kirtland. I believed you'd be safe here, surrounded by friends." Her voice softened as her heart ached for him. "Come to bed, husband, you need sleep. There is time to hear the whole story after you've had some rest."

"How are the children? How are you, Emma? Has it been difficult since I left?"

Nestled together, they pulled up the covers, and Emma fit right into the curve of his body, his arm draped around her slender waist. "The children are fine though they have missed you terribly. So have I. But there has been so much to do, I've had little time to be lonely. I have managed to store potatoes, carrots, onions, and apples in the food cellar. I knew my husband would eventually return," — she sounded a little wry, — "and I wanted to have a good food supply for us."

"Any news?"

"You have a letter from your attorney in Missouri, Alexander Doniphan."

Joseph was already drifting off. "You can tell me all about it tomorrow."

"*Dear Mr. Smith,*" Joseph read Doniphan's letter the next morning. "*I have recommended to the legislature of Missouri that the Mormons be allowed to permanently settle in Daviess and Caldwell Counties. Seeing that these two areas are sparsely settled and want the improvement of good, industrious people, I consider that Mormons could be a valuable asset to the state of Missouri if the fear and prejudice. . . could abate. I urge your immediate attention to the desperate plight of your people in Missouri and advise a personal visit by yourself to settle their difficulties. I am certain that with your influence, many of the misunderstandings may be laid to rest. Without such personal intervention, I fear the worst. Sincerely yours, Alexander Doniphan*"

"I must go back to Missouri," Joseph concluded reluctantly as he met with Brigham, Sidney and Thomas Marsh.

"Well, you have trouble here as well," Brigham confided. "While you and Brother Rigdon have been away, I have delayed my mission to the east in order to oppose apostates who are attempting to split the church. Joseph, I'm sorry to tell you Martin Harris has thrown in with the troublemakers."

His hazel eyes turned hard as he reported the schism of the last few months. "Parrish has gathered support from such hardheaded dissenters as Sylvester, John Boynton, Luke Johnson, Cyrus Smalling, and Joseph Coe."

Joseph shook his head. "I'm not surprised about Sylvester and Warren, but Luke and Martin, as respected priesthood leaders, lend credibility to all this."

"You've yet to hear the worst. The temple has been profaned."

Joseph and Sidney reacted in alarm.

"There was violence in the House of the Lord! Sunday morning, the first part of August — right after you left — Parrish and his friends occupied the Aaronic pulpits while Father Smith, Brothers

Taylor, Whitney, and others took their places in the Melchizedek pulpits. Parrish and Boynton began interrupting the proceedings, shouting down the speakers and creating such a clamor the ushers came to take them out of the building. Boynton and the others pulled out their weapons and rushed into the congregation, threatening to blow the brains out of anyone who opposed them. It was an awful scene.

"The apostates made charges against you, accusing you of departing from the faith, and leading the people to financial ruin. They are calling for a vote to remove you from office."

Joseph looked so dejected that Brigham wondered if his friend would reply at all. Sidney paced the floor and denounced the apostates with all the energy of wounded dignity. But Joseph sat in deep sorrow, without speaking. When he finally raised his head, he noted, "And you came back to defend me." A bleak smile crossed his lips.

Brigham simply said, "Always!"

"When will the vote be taken?"

"This Sunday."

Joseph turned to Sidney. "Brother Rigdon, you conduct the meeting, and give the apostates their voice, their chance to condemn themselves. I pray that Martin will come to his senses. He has been my friend and benefactor a long time."

He turned back to Brigham. "This is disappointing news, how disappointing I cannot tell you. And the worst may not be over. How many of my brethren will I lose to this spirit of greed?"

Sunday morning, September 3, 1837, dawned warm and clear. The sky was as blue as Joseph had ever seen it, and the late summer sun was bright with the promise of autumn. He awoke early and spent hours in prayer, searching the will of God and examining his own shortcomings. No reassuring thought crossed his mind. No angel appeared to comfort and instruct him. It seemed that he must weather this crisis on his own.

He walked into the temple, burdened with grief -- not with fear that the people might cast him off as their prophet, but grieving over the spirit of opposition infecting his friends. Across the room, he spotted Martin Harris looking haggard. Martin did not meet his eye. Soon Sidney began the meeting. A song was sung. A prayer was raised to the Lord, and speakers were given the chance to voice their feelings. John Taylor asked permission to speak. Eloquent, educated, and a recent Canadian convert to the church, Taylor reasoned persuasively with the wavering saints.

"From whence do we get our intelligence and knowledge of the laws, ordinances, and doctrines of the kingdom of God? Who understood even the first principles of the doctrines of Christ? Who in the Christian world taught them?" He threw out the challenge to the congregation.

"If we, with our learning and intelligence, could not find out the first principles, which was the case with myself and millions of others, how can we find out the mysteries of the kingdom?" His voice began to rise now with authority and conviction. He turned and pointed. *"It was Joseph Smith, under the Almighty, who developed the first principles, and to him we must look for further instruction."*

All eyes were turned upon their leader. Sidney stood, and after reproving the spirit of apostasy among them, called for a vote. "Will you retain Joseph Smith as your prophet, seer and revelator?" When the vote carried unanimously, he proceeded to call for a vote on the rest of the priesthood leadership. Frederick G. Williams was dropped from the presidency. Luke Johnson was removed from the Quorum of the Twelve Apostles. Warren Parrish was relieved of his priesthood responsibilities. A great winnowing was refining the membership of the church.

Then Sidney turned the meeting over to Joseph for instruction of the saints. Ignoring for the moment their economic problems, Joseph sought to raise the level of understanding in the principles of faith and obedience. All decisions, temporal and spiritual, must be based on those principles. He spoke with such authority that the saints left with renewed confidence in their prophet.

Joseph and Emma, with their growing family, took dinner that day at William Smith's home. After a long rehearsal of his missionary efforts in Canada and the near disaster at Painesville, Joseph read to William from Doniphan's letter then said, "I have known for some time I must return to Missouri. The brethren there need direction and cheering. Will you go too?"

It was mid-September. Crops were in. William had just finished a home he had been building for Brother Bollinger. He had been paid mostly in goods, but there was some cash that had come from it as well. The proposed journey seemed suddenly appealing.

"I believe I would like that. Whom else have you asked?"

"Brother Sidney and Vinson Knight. Hyrum is leaving next Monday. The rest of us will leave the end of the month. We should be back in time for Christmas."

Emma sat knitting and talking to her sister-in-law, Caroline, while the children played nearby. Emma heard her husband's proposal to his brother and knew she would soon face more months without him. Her only consolation was that when Joseph was gone, so were his bodyguards. Life was quieter without a living prophet of God in her daily routine — but empty.

On September 27, 1837, Joseph left once more for Missouri. His brothers, Hyrum and William, went with him. He had settled a few debts and met with the quorums, counseling caution, fiscal responsibility, sacrifice, unity, and attention to the poor. He tried to offset a general atmosphere of rebellion and hardheaded opinions.

A river of apostasy was running, and he could not control the flow. The Kirtland saints grew more impoverished. The bank had dissolved in July, and people papered their walls with useless Safety Society notes. Even those who had been wealthy, such as John Tanner and Artemus Millet, were brought down to poverty, without means to even feed their families. Tanner had neither horse nor ox to pull a wagon. But where would he go? Most of them still considered Kirtland their gathering place. They had cast their lot with the church, and were determined to ride out the tide.

In October, Emma was called one dark night to go to Hyrum's home. Jerusha, her sweet sister-in-law, had fallen gravely ill after the birth of her daughter, Sarah. Lucy was watching over the baby and the other four children, while Jerusha was failing fast. Emma was one of the most knowledgeable in the city on the healing power of herbs. She took with her a small supply of lavender oil and other ointments. She had been saving them for a time when a loved one was truly ill. Money was so scarce she didn't know when she would be able to purchase more. This, however, was a crisis. Jerusha had never been strong. Her constitution was generally delicate, and she had borne six children in ten years. Five years earlier they had each lost a child. Now Jerusha had wasted away, and Emma instantly feared for her sister-in-law when Mother Smith showed her into the sick room.

"Jerusha, dear, it's Emma. I've come with some ointments I want to try on you."

Jerusha whispered, "It's no use. Save your medicines for one it can help."

Emma spoke a little more forcefully. "Jerusha, open your eyes. I cannot help you if you won't try. I'm going to rub your back, temples, and throat with healing oils. Here, I'll help you turn over. See, that wasn't so hard. A deep breath now — take a deep breath. How does that feel? Does it ease the pain a little?"

"Um hmm, a little. Thank you, Emma," Jerusha coughed as she tried to respond. "Mother said you would come, but I fear you are too late. I saw angels last night. They came to tell me the other side is beautiful, with rare and lovely flowers." She opened glazed eyes and tried to smile. "They will take me to that land of flowers."

Mother Smith and Emma listened to her carefully. Their eyes met as both women recalled hearing others recite visitations from across the veil just before dying. Emma scrutinized her sister-in-law. Jerusha was wan, her skin almost transparent, and the whites of her eyes were yellow. Emma glanced around the room in despair. Her heart sank within her. Jerusha could not last another twenty-four hours. And what of the children, with their mother dead, their father gone? Hyrum was away in Missouri. He wouldn't even know for weeks. Tears filled her eyes. Fury rose up in her, fury at the harshness of life. Why should a delicate young mother like Jerusha have to live in such impoverished circumstances? She should have had a warm, lovely home, not this drafty cabin. She should have had dresses to grace her beauty, not these shapeless, quickly-woven garments. More than that, she should have a husband by her side to clasp her to his breast and bid a loving farewell to the mother of his children. Instead, she would die without seeing her beloved a last time; die after the effort of giving him a beautiful baby girl. It was unfair; tragically unfair!

"Oh, Jerusha! Don't go! Smell this lavender oil! Let me massage it into your temples and throat. Take a deep breath. It's good for your system. Jerusha, dear Jerusha, think of your baby, your children. Live for them, for Hyrum. He loves you. If he were here, he would take you in his arms and carry you to the temple and bless you there."

Jerusha opened her eyes and smiled weakly at Emma. "Would he? Do you think so?"

"Yes! He would, and he would kiss you and bless you and love all the sickness away."

A tear rolled down Jerusha's cheek. "Yes. I know he would. Hyrum loves me, doesn't he Emma?"

"Yes, dear. He loves you, and even now he is thinking of you, praying for you. Can you hear him, Jerusha?"

"I believe I can. Where are my children?"

Lucy stroked her daughter-in-law's damp hair. "In the next room, dear. Mary Fielding is caring for them."

"Call them in."

Emma started to protest, but her sister-in-law feebly raised her hand against the objection. "I must see them."

Mother Smith nodded her concordance, so Emma stepped to the doorway and motioned for Mary to bring in the children. The little ones gathered around their mother's bedside. They were all solemn, especially John, the eldest. Jerusha touched each one briefly then fell back exhausted against her pillow. She spoke in a small voice, as though it already came from beyond the grave.

"Tell your father when he comes that the Lord has taken your mother home and left you for him to take care of. I love you, my darlings. Be good. . . for me."

The effort was exhausting. Her eyes fluttered and closed. Emma and Mary quickly herded the children back to the other room. Mother Smith stayed back and held her daughter-in-law's hand. Within the hour, Jerusha Smith took a shuddering last breath and died with a peaceful smile upon her lips. Emma sat beside her bed, weeping. As she pulled the sheet over her beloved sister-in-law, a sweet, delicate fragrance of roses seemed to float in the air. Emma looked quickly about the room, almost expecting to see Jerusha's angels. But the room was dim, the candles burned low. She could detect nothing unusual, except a lovely scent of flowers lingering over the dead woman's bed.

Weeks later, Emma sat in a sewing circle with friends and Lucy. She looked around the circle. Mary Fielding was there, along with Hepzibah Richards. Both had brothers on the English mission. Strikingly attractive, with dark eyes and hair, young Zina Huntington sat beside Caroline Crosby, whose husband was still working on a new home for Emma and Joseph. Another young woman — Eliza R. Snow — sat with the ladies, next to Lucy. She and her brother Lorenzo had recently converted to the church. Both were well educated, and Eliza had already established a reputation as a poet and a teacher. Emma smiled at her. They were quite naturally good friends. Both women were refined, polished, and commanded respect. By any observer's standard, Emma was the more beautiful of the two. Even after bearing five children, her figure was slim, and her complexion smooth and clear. Curls hung in clusters against the nape of her neck. Only her deep-set, brown eyes showed the cares that had overtaken her in recent years. They were sadder, less inclined to sparkle, and more quick to flash when confronted with injustice.

Zina's high voice was heard reporting events that had transpired at the temple the previous evening. "My brother, Oliver, said it was a terrible scene. Men who have turned away from the faith — I think William McLellin was among them — have become the most bitter of enemies. Every time our brethren try to meet, they use every means to make a disturbance. Why, last Sunday, *in the sacred temple itself,* mind you, apostates broke into the meeting *with daggers.* I don't know what the world is coming to! Daggers in the temple of the Lord!"

Hepzibah scarcely looked up from her embroidery. "I have given refuge twice now to Brother Brigham. He said Warren Parrish is trying to garner enough support to depose the prophet. Brother Brigham stood up and rebuked them and declared that they were going to sink themselves to hell with such actions. They were so angry at his condemnation they chased him clear out of town. He sneaked back to our house, and we hid him in an upstairs closet."

Zina's eyebrows were raised in wonder. "Hepzibah, I would have been frightened to death. Weren't you scared?"

The plump cheeks flushed, but the ample Hepzibah Richards simply settled into her chair more firmly and answered shortly. "No! And Brother Brigham is right. They cannot hurt a prophet of God; they can only hurt themselves by this villainy. If they ever try to search my house. . . well, I have my brother Willard's rascal-beater in the corner, and I know how to use it."

Mother Smith spoke up. "You're a good woman, Hepzibah Richards. I know a little about persecution, I can tell you. You just have to stand your ground."

Eliza spoke in smooth, cultured tones. "We must all remember that we are in Sister Emma's home. This particular subject must be quite distressing to her."

Emma's glance was appreciative. She had been unusually tired and nauseated of late, and suspected she was with child. Her emotions had been on edge, and now she responded quietly, with great control. "Thank you, Eliza. It *is* upsetting. I have heard more and more about it lately. Evidently certain brethren are trying to wrest control of the church from Joseph. I have written to him several times, so rest assured, he is not unaware."

Lucy's voice was bitter. "'Certain brethren' indeed. To think that Oliver Cowdery, David Whitmer, and Martin Harris would turn on Joseph when they have practically been members of the family. What can they be thinking? If they try to bring him down, they are working against the Lord's anointed, and the judgment of the Almighty will be on them. Mark my words, the three witnesses of the Book of Mormon are in danger of hellfire — knowing the divine calling of Joseph and then trying to depose him!"

Emma spoke gently, "Mother, please. . . "

Lucy sputtered, then clamped her lips shut.

Caroline Crosby had sat silently through the preceding discussion, her attention on her embroidery. When silence prevailed for a few moments, she timidly told her own story. "Did you all see the blaze last night? I awoke at midnight to voices shouting 'Fire!' The ground looked as light as day. A very strange sensation ran through me. I threw open my front door and saw the printing office in flames. Men were running with buckets of water to control the blaze, but it was useless."

Every woman had put down her sewing, and all eyes were glued to Caroline's face. The recent fire was uppermost on everyone's mind. She went on hesitantly. "We walked up to the site this morning. The printing office, lock, stock, and barrel, with many copies of the Book of Mormon are all destroyed. I'm so thankful the temple and other buildings didn't burn. I'm not as brave as Hepzibah. I'm frightened! I saw some of the apostates. I know the men who did it."

She burst into tears. Emma spoke as soothingly as possible. "Caroline, the Lord has His eye upon us. The powers of adversity cannot prevail as long as we trust in God."

Mother Smith spoke up. "Well, I suppose you all know that my husband, the Patriarch of the Church, and well into his years, was *attacked* — physically attacked — in the temple! Warren Parrish tried to drag him from the stand when he was testifying of Joseph. Oliver Cowdery, our justice of the *peace*, would do nothing to help him; nothing whatsoever! There, Emma," she stated triumphantly, "You may shush me all you will, but Oliver Cowdery and others are turncoats and intend to bring my husband up before a court on charges of riot in the temple! Can you imagine?"

Eliza gave a half laugh. "Mother Smith, no one would possibly convict your good husband of riotous behavior. Everyone can attest to his dignity, his patriarchal demeanor. He has more distinction than all his accusers put together. But Emma is quite right. We must guard our tongues. Our role is to maintain some aspect of civility throughout all this. Our calmness and reason could inspire better judgment and rationality from the men."

Emma smiled with gratitude at her new friend. "Ladies, I am pleased to relate that my husband will soon return to our midst. He is on his way home from Missouri, and we may expect him before Christmas. I have hope he can restore order here."

Lucy's bright eyes narrowed, but in deference to her daughter-in-law, she looked down at her needlework and refrained from comment.

A couple of days later, Emma was hurrying home before an impending storm. Her children ran ahead of her, while she held her eighteen-month-old, Freddy, in her arms. Unexpectedly, she stumbled right into the arms of Oliver Cowdery, their old friend.

"Oh, my gracious! Freddy, shh, you're all right! Oliver, I'm so sorry. I didn't see you. I was watching those clouds gather. It looks like a storm is brewing."

"Yes, it does. . . Are you quite well, Emma?"

By now she had calmed little Freddy, and fixed her direct gaze upon Oliver. He began to fidget. Emma's deep brown eyes could be arresting.

"I'm as well as can be expected with my husband away. I do what I can to help build up the church, while others do what they can to tear it down."

Oliver's response was solemn and deliberate, "No one wants to *tear down* the church, Emma. Some of us just feel that certain changes have to be made."

Her voice now became low and insistent. "*What* changes exactly has the Lord revealed to you?"

"Well, obviously, Joseph's proposal for financial self reliance hasn't worked. . . "

"You could have helped Joseph with that, Oliver — you *and* David. He needed your help."

". . . and his revelation for the building of Zion in Missouri hasn't proven out."

"Joseph can't be everywhere, do *everything*! He has to rely on *faithful* friends to help with God's work. Oliver, where is your faith? Are you for Joseph or against him?"

Cowdery clenched his teeth and a muscle in his cheek twitched. His voice was flinty when he replied. "I have *faith* in my own convictions. Joseph has failed us as a prophet, here and in Missouri. I can't stand with him any longer or I'll be a ruined man."

"You've lost confidence in Joseph, then?" Emma persisted, even as her child squirmed and whimpered in her arms.

"I'm afraid so."

"Oh, Oliver!" she exclaimed. "What about the Book of Mormon? What about the revelations and visions you have shared with him? Can you so easily forget your testimony of Christ, of angels, and eternal glory?"

He put out his hand in front of his face as if to brush her words aside. "I forget nothing, but I'm afraid my path lies in a different direction now."

"Don't, Oliver," she pleaded. "You will live to regret such a course. You cannot separate Joseph from the church. It is his calling. You can only separate yourself from it. Why risk your eternal welfare over temporal matters? Do you think God cares about our *money*? What really matters is our faithfulness, our obedience, our sacrifice. Take care, Oliver. You may lose the best friend you ever had. . . and perhaps your very soul."

"Mother," little Julia called. "It's waining on me!"

Five-year-old Joseph tugged at Cowdery's coattail. "Uncle Oliver, come to my house! I miss you!"

The two adults stood, their eyes locked in mute debate as the rain shower began in earnest. Emma could see prideful resolve had hardened this dear friend. Oliver tipped his hat to Emma and walked past her, silently. Large, splashy raindrops fell on Emma's cheeks. . . or was it just the rain?

Joseph returned home on December 10, 1837. The happiness of his homecoming was marred by accounts of the rough handling of his father in the temple, the death of his sister-in-law, Jerusha, and reports of the burning and looting now occurring regularly throughout the city. Hyrum came home to four sorrowing children and their baby sister who dearly needed a mother. He didn't want any other wife. He had plainly told Joseph so when earlier discussions of plural marriage had taken place. Now he had no one in mind that might be willing to take over the considerable duties of mother to five children.

Joseph counseled him, "This is not the time for the niceties of courtship, Hyrum. You need a helpmeet and your children can't wait. Mary Fielding has been helping out in your home ever since her brother left on an English mission. Emma has informed me this woman gave tender and loving care to Jerusha and your children, right up to the last. Pray for confirmation, for it is God's will that you marry Mary Fielding immediately!"

Hyrum shook his head doubtfully. Hyrum knew Mary Fielding, an English woman and recent convert who had come down with her brother, Joseph, and sister, Mercy, from Canada. She was intelligent, faithful, independent, and with some means of her own, but he doubted she would accept him.

"I foolishly made some rather uncomplimentary remarks about her before we left for Missouri, not knowing her well, nor understanding her kindness. I've come to feel she is a remarkable woman, but I'm certain she must hold my words against me."

101

Joseph smiled and simply shook his head no.

Mary had known Hyrum primarily as the prophet's brother. She never considered him a potential husband, or herself a stepmother. However, a few weeks after his return, Hyrum put on his best suit of clothes, dampened and combed his hair, straightened his cravat — mourning over that simple exercise, for Jerusha had always done it for him — and went to knock on Mary's door. She showed him in. Mary Fielding looked down at her folded hands while he recited the reason for his visit. His face was gaunt and hollow. He was a man in mourning, driven by the need for a wife.

Could she forgive him a prior thoughtless remark and come to love him? Could she marry him and become a mother to his children? Hyrum Smith's gentle soul was evident in his face. By the flickering firelight, with the first snow of winter falling thick and fast outside her door, she felt the warming grace of love stirring within. Mary reached out and touched his bowed head. Hyrum's shoulders heaved as he heard the clipped, precise British tones affirm that she would, indeed, accept him as a husband. So, Hyrum Smith gratefully married thirty-six-year-old spinster, Mary Fielding on Christmas Eve, December 24, 1837.

The ever-faithful Brigham Young was driven from Kirtland by a mob in late December. Joseph admonished Brigham to remember the words of the Savior, "When they persecute you in one city, flee to another." Joseph and Sidney conferred before a special meeting in the temple on December 30 to discuss the question of how best to deal with Oliver, David, and Martin, all of whom now declared Joseph a fallen prophet. They had an impressive array of support. Luke and Lyman Johnson, John F. Boynton, and William McLellin — all former apostles — and many others were calling for Joseph to step down. They accused him of failing to obtain the true word of God pertaining to the church in Kirtland. In their opinion, they constituted enough authority to govern the church without Joseph. He was wounded to the heart. These men had been with him since the beginning of the church. They were pillars in that early organization. Now when they looked at him, it was as though they had never rejoiced together, prayed together, or served the Lord together. Joseph had to find a way to shore up the rickety timbers of his organization. Days earlier he had called for a meeting of the high council and all the quorums. When they met, he and Sidney spoke at length, condemning the usurpation of authority and calling for the excommunication of the opposition faction. Sidney made accusations against them, only to have them hurled back in his face by the embittered apostates.

On that frigid December day, Joseph and Sidney faced the bleak prospect of a divided church and a city in complete chaos. In addition to problems with apostasy, Grandison Newell had again brought legal charges against Joseph. Another court appearance would, no doubt, result in mob action if not imprisonment. Joseph had no other option but to authorize an exodus from Kirtland.

Along with Sidney, he met with close friends in Father Smith's home a fortnight later to discuss the unpleasant task before them. The curtains were drawn, the doors bolted, and trusted bodyguards were stationed in the shadows of the trees.

The anxiety-ridden prophet gave directions for them to follow, after he departed Kirtland. Then he added, "One thing, brethren, is certain, I shall see you again, let what will happen, for I have a promise of life five years, and they cannot kill me until that time is expired."

The small circle of men noted the firelight illuminating Joseph's face, casting shadows over his determined features. His certainty lent courage to them. One by one, they stood and embraced him, often too choked up to utter more than a gruff farewell, then cautiously left the home, dispersing quickly into the dark chill of the night.

No sooner had they gone than Joseph's four brothers entered; the door was locked and bolted shut once more. Joseph paced before the hearth, addressing his father and brothers.

"If I leave the city and direct the faithful saints to follow, the violence will burn out. I know there is a place for us in Missouri. The saints there are overcoming the prejudice the Missourians first had against us. The Missouri legislature has given us two counties of our own to settle. It is the only place to go from here."

His father, the patriarch, spoke up in support. "I agree, and the sooner the better. I have heard threats on your life that anger me. In fact, I think you should leave tonight! Mobs are already searching for you, mobs led by so-called friends."

"I'm not concerned about myself, but I fear for Emma and the children."

Hyrum offered his plan. "Joseph, I have felt for a long time that it might come to this. The question is not *if* you should leave, but *how* exactly you can accomplish it without being waylaid and murdered on the road. I have a plan. Before he moved his family to Far West, Levi Hancock left me a pine box prepared for whatever unlucky soul might be in need. I think you are that soul!"

Joseph stopped and stared at his brother. "A pine box?"

"Yes. Your enemies won't think to look for you in a coffin."

Joseph shuddered. "I don't know. I've never imagined a coffin for a bed," he said wryly.

Stalwart and normally silent, Samuel spoke up. "I agree with Hyrum. Do you think you can simply mount a horse and calmly ride out of the city? You would be shot before you could get out of sight."

"I must see to Emma and the children. Emma has already begun packing a few things, since I warned her it might come to this, but she is in a delicate condition again and needs my help. I didn't think we'd have to leave quite so soon."

His father warned him, "Tonight is hardly soon enough. Don Carlos says there are roving bands of men looking for you down by the river even now. You'll put your family at risk if you go back."

The youngest brother, Don Carlos, volunteered, "I'll pack up everything, Joseph, and drive Emma and the children to Norton. We'll meet you there."

Joseph twisted his hands behind his back. He stopped in his restless pacing in front of Hyrum. Of a sudden his complexion paled, and his brothers heard him whisper, "The Spirit warns me even now to make my escape as soon as possible. . . ."

As he was hesitating, a rock shattered the window, and angry voices from the dark woods shouted for him to come out. William stepped to the door and commanded the mob to go back to their homes. Hyrum pulled Joseph to the pantry and hid him inside.

"We want Joseph Smith!" the mob leader called out.

"I'm here! Take me," Joseph Sr. shouted bravely.

"Not you, grandpa! Where's yer boy, the fallen prophet?"

"That's no concern of yours! This is my home and property! What mischief are you men up to? You're all trespassers and I order you off my grounds."

Both William and Father Smith ducked as a rock came hurtling from the darkness. It bounced off the doorframe and glanced off William's shoulder. Cheers and shouts exploded from the mob.

Joseph Sr. started to get his musket from behind the door, but Hyrum stopped him. "We can't give them any excuse for violence!"

Father Smith bellowed out, "We have laws in this town, and I mean to have you all thrown in jail. Go on back home now!"

Nervous laughter mocked his threat. "Turn Joe over right now or we'll fire the house."

Tall, powerful, Stephen Markham, along with other guards who patrolled the thicket of trees outside, now joined the Smith men surging from the doorway and shouting defiance. The sight of five strong, bold Smith men backed up by determined bodyguards, caused a few of the attackers second thoughts, and the mob began to melt back into the shadows. Someone flung a torch to the ground, but it was dampened immediately in the dirty snow. Markham and the bodyguards rushed into the thicket, and the pursuit soon became a rout.

When certain the danger was past, the Smith men turned back inside to conclude the plans they had been discussing. Joseph emerged from the pantry, his face white. He admitted to Hyrum, "I'm ready. I can't have my entire family endangered." He went to his father and embraced him.

"Steady, Father! Those men are half your age!"

"Those men don't have half my heart! They can't threaten my home and family like that!"

Joseph sent Samuel outside with directions to Markham to contact Sidney with a message to meet Joseph, for both men needed to leave Kirtland immediately. The Smith men waited another hour, until absolutely confident the mob had dispersed then quickly rode to a barn where Levi Hancock had stored his ox cart before leaving for Missouri. As town mortician, Levi's makeshift hearse was a familiar sight, not liable to arouse any suspicion, even with mobs searching for Joseph. Samuel opened the barn door. By lantern light, Joseph embraced his father and brothers and bade them an emotional farewell, then he started to climb onto the cart, but paused on seeing the new pine coffin.

"If anyone stops the wagon they won't have the nerve to look in the coffin. It's the safest place for you," Samuel urged.

Joseph was still hesitant. Trying to lighten the moment he joked, "I'm not really looking for another home, with our new one barely finished. I don't think Emma will like this one nearly so well."

"Emma will never have to see this one. It's only temporary — hopefully. Now, quickly, Joseph! Time's a-wasting!"

Joseph jumped onto the cart. "Brothers, God willing, we will meet again in a few days. If He is not willing, I'll see you in the sweet bye-and-bye. God bless you all."

Then, quelling an eerie feeling, Joseph climbed into the freshly made pine box, wrapped his cloak around himself, and his brothers covered him with straw. Hyrum saw Joseph's face drawn with anxiety as they secured the lid on the pine coffin. Don Carlos sat in the back beside the coffin, huddled beneath a black cloak and wearing a widow's veil over his face.

William, after hitching up a horse, climbed onto the driver's box, put on a mortician's stovepipe hat, wrapped himself in the folds of a heavy deerskin robe, and gathered up the reins. He clucked to the horse, and the rough hearse rolled out of the barn into the dark, frigid night. William carefully drove the cart and contents southward, past darkened houses securely bolted. Most of the citizens of Kirtland were uneasy and some were already making preparations to leave, to face the uncertain prospects of journeying in the dead of winter all the way to Missouri.

In their bedroom, Emma was awaiting any news of her husband, after turning away two groups of torch-bearing thugs earlier that night. Emma heard the rumbling sounds of carts rolling past her house. She peered out into the unfriendly night. All she saw was Levi's old wagon carrying some poor soul to his final resting place. Emma shivered. It could be Joseph, she thought. Lately, such thoughts had haunted her more and more. The newspapers, which circulated in the city, cursed and vilified her husband. Men appeared at her door almost every day demanding to see Joseph, shoving past her to peer into her home. I have less right to our few scanty belongings than the most obscure passing stranger, she thought, and less time with my husband than his lawyers. Tonight she had waited later than usual, praying for Joseph to come home.

In the darkness, snow clouds swirled round and round, obscuring the disappearing hearse. William spoke soothingly to the laboring horse, while Carlos looked about on all sides, watching for mobs that might still be beating the bushes for Joseph.

The creaking cart moved along its way, as it bore a shivering Joseph confined inside a cold, pinewood coffin. Outside the town limits, far away from roving mobs, William reined in the mare, climbed into the wagon box, and with Don Carlos yanked the top from the pine box. Joseph's white face appeared, and he sat up quickly, grateful for a breath of fresh air.

William whistled a prearranged signal, and shortly Sidney Rigdon emerged from the cover of trees. He was clad in heavy, winter clothes. He held his own bay by the reins and led Joseph's prancing, snorting black mount, Ol' Charley.

Joseph greeted his friend and counselor, "I'm glad *that's* over! You all right, Sidney?"

Rigdon blew on stiff his hands and nodded yes.

Joseph and Sidney leaped to their horses and rewrapped their cloaks. Then, waving a hasty farewell to Joseph's brothers, the two men rode out at full, thundering gallop down the dark road that led to far away Missouri and the new promised land.

Chapter Three

Trial By Ice

The old sleigh creaked and rocked as it mastered the frozen ruts of the Ohio back. It hadn't been the best the wainwright had ever constructed, but it was ready, and Emma could not wait for a new sleigh to be built. Don Carlos had helped her hitch the horses to it and had driven it back home through the dark shadows of night. They packed the sleigh with as many essentials as they could fit in, then nestled the children, still sleeping, in between the trunk, the mummy crates, and the rocking chair. The feather tick had gone in first, so the children cuddled together in a warm bed and slept while their uncle clucked to the horses and the sleigh eased along the icy road that led them away from Kirtland.

They planned to reunite with Joseph in Norton, Ohio the next evening. The children were so excited by a long sleigh ride that their high spirits made the arduous trip almost tolerable. Emma thought back to another journey by sleigh she had made seven years earlier with Joseph, Sidney and Edward Partridge. She had been pregnant then too. Now, she was expecting for the fifth time, and the rocking of the sleigh upset her already queasy stomach.

"Mama, when will we see Papa?" little Julia asked sleepily when she awoke.

"Soon, darling."

"How soon?"

"By nightfall, I should think. Is that about right, Carlos?" Emma knew the distance to Norton, but wondered if her brother-in-law was aware of any possible pitfalls she wasn't.

"Yes. I believe if you're a very good girl. . . " Don Carlos glanced back at the nearly seven year old child, "and don't tip the sleigh off the road. . . "

"I couldn't tip the sleigh off the road," the indignant girl interrupted.

". . . and don't spook the horses so they run away. . . "

"I *would never* spook the horses. That's silly, Uncle Carlos."

". . . and don't lose your doll so we have to stop and search for it. . . "

"*Mama,*" Julia protested, altogether too serious for her years, "you know I would *never* do such things."

". . . If — and I emphasize *if* — you can manage to patiently ride and enjoy the clear weather and fresh air," Don Carlos dragged out the much sought for resolution, "*then* we should see your Papa by nightfall."

He was almost right. It was well past dark when they stopped the sleigh in front of the only mercantile store in Norton, Ohio where Joseph had instructed his family to meet him. Emma was exhausted with the effort of caring for three active children, keeping them warm on a frosty day, and trying to appear cheerful while subduing her anxiety during the lengthy trip. Don Carlos went into the store and greeted his brother. After a thankful embrace, Joseph hurried outside. He reached up to help Emma, and his apprehensive wife fell into his arms, giving way to her relief at seeing him well and safe.

Safety was an illusion. He and Sidney had dodged two groups of angry Kirtland citizens who were still hunting them. With Joseph's family safely here, they now waited for Phoebe Rigdon and the children. Just before midnight, as Sidney paced the floor and imagined terrible things, a lumber wagon creaked to a stop just outside. The little village of Norton consisted of only a dozen houses and this mercantile store. There were two lights still burning in town, and Phoebe was standing in the wagon trying to determine if her husband waited at either of those two flickering lights. Her son and three daughters were huddled in the bed of the wagon. Sidney rushed from the store to his family and wept with relief that they had arrived safely.

Joseph procured a wagon with a canvas covering for his family. It afforded only a little more shelter than they had in the sleigh. Brother Brooks, owner of the store, provided him with food, boots, gunpowder, grease for the wheels, and other supplies. So by January 18, 1838, Joseph and Emma's eleventh anniversary, the Smiths and the Rigdons again set out on the nine-hundred-mile journey to Far West, Missouri. Don Carlos returned to Kirtland to help the rest of the Smith family prepare for their move west.

The first leg of the long journey would take them to Columbus, then on to Eaton, Ohio. The wagons served well enough on sunny days, but they were of little comfort in a snowstorm. Twice riders came upon the group, searching for Joseph and Sidney, having vowed to kill them if the two church leaders were discovered. Joseph occasionally lay beneath the covers in the back of the wagon, while his children perched on his back and solemnly eyed the frustrated pursuers.

Just forty miles west of Norton, the Ohio sky turned dark gray and a wind picked up until soon the travelers were all chilled.

"Joseph," Emma urged, "Isn't there a farmhouse or a barn where we can take shelter? That storm will close in on us within the hour."

"I've been looking over the fields. The last few acres are well-cultivated. There must be a home nearby."

"Can we chance telling them who we are?"

"Probably not. I know George Lyons has not given up his search yet. He swore by an oath on his mother's life to find me and kill me. If we locate a farmhouse, we'll use your maiden name for safety's sake."

Just as the wind became intolerable and the children were fussing in the drafty wagon, Joseph saw on the right side of the road, a long lane going toward a substantial farmhouse; smoke blustered from the chimney, lights glowed from the windows. Perhaps there would be good folks who would clear a bit of floor for them to sleep on. Joseph tugged the horses' reins and pulled his wagon off the road onto the lane. Sidney and family, close behind them, followed suit. When the wagon stopped, Emma climbed into the back where little Julia was diligently keeping her two brothers beneath thick quilts. All too often, a small head would pop out from under the quilts and bright eyes would peer around. Julia tugged them back down and scolded them roundly.

"Mother, are we staying at this house?" she asked.

"We'll see. Your father is talking to the owners now."

"Will we have something hot to eat? I'm tired of cold bread and cold pork."

"Perhaps we'll cook tonight. It all depends on if they have room for us."

The little girl surveyed the rambling farmhouse. "It *looks* like they have lots of room."

"Maybe so, but with the Rigdon family, we are quite a few."

Julia nestled back beneath her blankets confidently. "They have room. I want hot soup with onions and beef and carrots in it. I want hot biscuits. I want to warm my hands in front of a hot fire. And, Freddy, I want you to stop pushing me with your feet! Right now!"

"Children! Be patient just a while longer. Look, Papa's going in. It must be all right."

Joseph had knocked on the door. Before Sidney could even get to the doorstep, the heavy, wooden door opened and a short, burly man with a shock of dark brown hair greeted them.

"You folks are in a desperate straits to be traveling in this storm. Where are you headed?"

"To the western border of Missouri," Joseph answered.

"That's a piece."

"Yes, I guess it is. We have families in our wagons, and we are hoping you might have room to put us up until the storm is over. We'll sleep on the floor. We're not choosey."

"Mother," the farmer called to his wife, "got some folks here need a shelter from the storm."

"Well, what are you doing holding open the door? Git them inside before we all freeze."

Life was hard in 1838, and it was the unspoken rule of the day that you shared home and hearth with travelers. People never knew when they would be the travelers needing a Good Samaritan. Joseph and Sidney stepped inside gratefully, exchanging greetings with Abigail and Thomas Babcock.

"Thank you kindly, Mrs. Babcock. We have our families in the wagons," Sidney took his hat off in the presence of the lady and continued to plead their cause. "His wife," and he indicated the prophet, "is in a delicate condition, and we are hoping to find some warmth and comfort more especially for her."

"Well, you're welcome here. We don't have a lot, but we are warm and well-fed, maybe too well-fed," the ample Mrs. Babcock joked. "Let's bring those children and their mothers in by the fireplace. I have two bedrooms in the back of the house. We used to use them for our own children, but they're all grown up now with families of their own. Your families can each use one, Mr.. . . . ?"

"Hale," Joseph finished her sentence.

". . . and Brooks," Sidney contributed.

"Thank you kindly." Joseph was truly grateful. He thought of the countless families he and Emma had given their beds to and noted how true the scripture is; the good which people do comes back to them. He and Sidney went out to help their wives and children in from the storm.

Joseph took little Freddy from Emma's arms and helped her out of the wagon. Then, scooping young Joseph up into the crook of his other arm, with Emma holding Julia's hand, they hurriedly entered the warm farmhouse. The smell of food cooking almost made Julia drool, and Emma squeezed her hand tightly to prevent her from begging for dinner immediately.

"You're very kind," Emma gratefully greeted Abigail Babcock.

"I've been in the cold before, too. Come on in here and warm yourselves by the fire. Are you children hungry?" Abigail's knowing eyes caught the pained look on Julia's face.

"Yes, ma'am," Julia responded politely, as her mother had taught her.

"Then, sit right down here, and have some of my hot soup and bread."

Julia looked up at her mother with eyes dancing. "See," she whispered in Emma's ear, "God does hear our prayers."

Emma sat down at the long wooden table. All at once, the energy seemed to drain from her, and she put her head down on her arm, too exhausted to move. Joseph knelt beside the fireplace with his sons at his knee, warming their chapped hands and faces. Sidney's family of three daughters, and a young son named after Joseph, followed Thomas Babcock down into the larger bedroom. It had a tiny coal stove and a bed, with room on the floor for the children. After riding and sleeping on the jolting bed of a wagon, the steady floor of the farmhouse actually seemed inviting. Best of all, it was warm.

The Babcocks were hospitable folks. They were happy to have company, and often used their house as an inn. On a howling winter's night it was good to have pleasant conversation and trade news with people from the east. Thomas Babcock had built his home himself on land he had homesteaded. He shook his head over the state of the country, now in deep financial trouble. He didn't trust banks and would rather *forgive* a man a debt, than accept a promissory note and never get payment. Joseph and Sidney did not argue with him.

With full bellies and warm toes, the children finally bedded down on the floor in their separate rooms, with parents in bed beside them. Joseph was just drifting off to sleep when he heard banging on the front door. It sounded rather insistent. *Hopefully, more travelers needing shelter,* he thought. Then the banging stopped and he heard voices. Shortly, he heard his own name, then Sidney's, spoken with vehemence and rancor. He glanced at Emma. She was sound asleep, snuggled down into the warm covers.

More voices interrupted and rose in volume until he heard them declare distinctly, "He can't be far. I've tracked Joe Smith from Kirtland. How he manages to escape me, I can't tell. Must be the devil protects his own."

"Well, no such scoundrel has stopped here, I can tell you. Now, do you want to stay, or are you moving on?"

"In this storm? We'll stay, if you can find a warm corner for us."

"Don't have much room. We put two families in the spare bedrooms already, but it's warm by the kitchen hearth, if you want to put down your bedroll there."

"Two families, huh? One wouldn't be ol' Joe Smith's, would it? I wanna have a look-see. If I find that cheatin' fraud, we'll be diggin' his grave by morning."

"These families are the finest of folk. I won't have you bothering them. They just got their children to sleep."

The other voice became louder, moving toward the bedroom. "If they're really decent people, we don't mean them no harm. But if it's Joe Smith, you don't want the likes of him here. Better have a quick look."

With that, the nearest bedroom door swung open and three bearded faces peered into the dark room just by Joseph's head. He sat up as Emma awoke. If there were to be a scuffle, he didn't want her and the children involved.

One of the intruders growled, "You be from Kirtland, Mister?"

"I'm from New York," Joseph replied honestly.

"Ever heard of Joe Smith?"

"I've heard of him."

"We're looking for him. They say he's a big man. How big are you?"

"Not as big as my father, but too big for a lickin', my mother says."

The ringleader laughed hoarsely then asked suspiciously, "Where are you headed?"

"West. I hear there's land to be homesteaded."

The three men looked at each other, shrugged and stepped back. Closing the door, they muttered, "Sorry to bother you."

Joseph lay back down. He could hear them talking around the fireplace late into the night, bravely vowing to kill ol' Joe if they ever got their hands on him. Emma finally fell into a fitful sleep once Joseph assured her everything was fine. He got little rest that night, listening to threats on his life. Joseph's family slept a little late the next morning, and when they rose to see if they could be on their way, the three pursuers had already ridden on.

The morning was frosty and cold, and the snow was about four inches deep. The Smiths and Rigdons thanked their hosts and departed with the best of feelings between them. Their wagons rolled on toward Missouri, following the tracks of their relentless, would-be slayers.

The two families made their way slowly toward Columbus, Ohio, approximately 120 miles from Norton. There they would lay in more supplies, perhaps find a place to stay for a few days, then forge on to Eaton, another ninety miles or so. Emma anticipated the worst, and while it was true that the wagon slipped and bumped along the way and the weather vacillated between cold and frigid, she found an unexpected consolation. For the first time in years, she had her husband to herself. There were no crowds pressing in to hear his every word. There were no streams of hungry strangers eating her food and wanting her husband's attention. There were no church demands, no meetings, no translating — only hour after hour in the wagon beside Joseph, talking and planning and tending to their children together. When Emma reflected on this, she realized blessings often come in strange disguises, and reminded herself not to anticipate how God answers prayers. Having her husband almost exclusively to herself, except when they stopped for the night and ate their meager supper with the Rigdons, was an unanticipated treasure. Though her hands and feet were often cold, Emma's heart warmed under the steady sunlight of Joseph's undivided attention.

Joseph had an amazing gift of focusing on the person to whom he was speaking. He never seemed distracted during conversation. Instead, he plumbed the inner thoughts of his companion. When he talked with Sidney, he drew out the deepest thoughts of his friend. When he talked with his children, he soon knew all their little grievances and their jokes. But only with Emma did he find the personal depths of his own heart being probed. Much like their early days of marriage, he talked for hours about revelations that came to him from heaven, of the visions and dreams he had. He spoke so easily about ancient days that he seemed to live outside the boundaries of time.

"Joseph, what do you see for the church?"

"I have two visions of the church. One is a time of trouble, with great persecution, greater than we have yet known, and one is a time of plenty and of rejoicing, when the church of God will shine forth in glory. The saints have so much to learn and yet remain proud in their ignorance. That pride will reap the whirlwind. People must all learn humility before they can be the tools God means for them to be."

"I thought we learned a good deal of humility in Kirtland."

"Some did. I know I had much to learn," Joseph thoughtfully shook his head as he pondered his own actions. "Some I fear for. Take Oliver for instance. Oliver has changed in the last year. We used to be as close as brothers. Working on the papyri together was an oasis of the spirit. But money has laid its hand on Oliver, and now he is in its grasp. From the time he went to Philadelphia and bought the engraving plates to print bank notes, he has not been the same."

"Perhaps it was wrong to assign him to monetary matters," Emma mused.

"No, we all must have a chance to prove ourselves and be tested in all things. For some, money is the temptation, for others, it may be pride, position and influence. If we cannot stand in the furnace of temptation, we will never become refined like pure gold and worthy to stand before our Lord."

Watching the horses' twitching tails as they plodded along, Emma asked thoughtfully, "And in which furnace do you stand?"

Joseph was silent, reflecting on her question. Finally he sighed and said, "Perhaps overreaching, believing my visions for the church must happen just as I see them. I suppose my own lack of humility and patience. I see so much more for our people than they dream of for themselves. Perhaps I prescribe their failure by demanding too much?"

"Maybe so, at least with Frederick Williams. I don't know about Oliver or David Whitmer."

"I'm afraid those two have infected each other with a spirit of rebellion. It is natural for brothers-in-law to confide in each other, but I'm afraid they fuel the fires of apostasy in each other."

"Oliver claims you owe him money for the press."

"I do. It seems I owe everyone. I signed all bank documents and guaranteed all bank debts personally. I never dreamed the venture would fail. I was so sure it was the right thing to do, and I still think it could have worked if we had not given out our gold and silver backing. In any case, I have given all my earthly assets to try to repay those notes. I simply haven't any more to give. Oliver knows that. He knows I've never gotten rich from the church. He, however, has reached a point where money is more important than the law of consecration, or sacrifice. We must be willing to give all we possess for the common good. And to tell the truth, I am not envious of prosperity. Comfort makes cowards of us all, and we prefer to take our ease by the fireside instead of sacrificing and working for the Lord."

Emma knew her husband spoke with the conviction of a full participant. Joseph had always given everything they owned to further the cause. Consequently, they owned little. She had her feather tick, her rocking chair, and her Bible. Back in Harmony, she owned six acres of land as part of her Hale inheritance, but doubted she would ever see that land again. They still had the Book of Mormon transcription and the Egyptian mummies and papyri. They were priceless, but not in a worldly way. She had concealed the mummies in the wagon and the manuscript in the false bottom of her trunk, carefully hidden in case they were stopped and searched.

"Is there no sacrifice too great?" she queried.

"Emma, if you knew what I know of the celestial kingdom, you could answer that question yourself. Did Christ set a limit on

His sacrifice? Did He say, 'This is too much?' And if He had, would any of us have assurance of forgiveness for our sins? Our crowns of glory are burnished by the same principle of sacrifice the Savior mastered. We may not give to that same degree, but we can give what we have, until we are one day called upon to give our very lives as the final sacrifice."

"I hope that's a long time off."

He glanced sideways at her profile. Her brow was still clear and unlined, her nose straight and fine, though her cheeks were more sunken than usual. When she was tired, as she so often was now, her right eyelid drooped slightly. To others, it might have spoiled her otherwise perfect features, but for Joseph, it was a tender reminder of that difficult first birth that almost cost her life. He loved that little imperfection. Now he put his arm around her shoulders and pulled her to him.

"You will live a good, long life, Emma-rose. Even after I am gone, you will enjoy our children and grandchildren."

"Hush!" she reprimanded him. "Don't talk so. We'll enjoy those grandchildren together."

He shook his head slightly. "God has a different work for me. Yet He will see that all things happen for the best in our lives."

After another two weeks of travel, they arrived in the small town of Dublin, Indiana, west of Eaton, Ohio, and asked a resident to direct them to the house of Phineas Young. When the two wagons lurched down the lane to the Young home, a welcome figure hurried out to meet them. Brigham knew they were coming and had been watching for them. In December, he had barely escaped Kirtland with his life, and fled with his new wife and children to his brother's home in Dublin for safety. He and Mary Ann Angell Young were waiting to continue the journey to Missouri with Joseph and Sidney.

"We are prepared to travel on with you, Brother Joseph. How long will you need and ready yourselves for the rest of your trip?" Brigham was eager to travel with Joseph, whom he loved above all other men.

Joseph was weary and a little doubtful. "I can't say. I'll need provisions, and I have wagon wheels needing repair. But. . . I have no money. I have given it all away trying to settle debts and provide the necessities for my family. I thought I might earn some small means by chopping wood for the good folks around here."

He held up a hand to silence Brigham's protests. "I'm not bad at splitting rails, chopping and stacking wood. I'm certainly good for something useful besides preaching."

"I know. I worked beside you in the stone quarry. You can out-work most men, but I don't believe that is what the Lord wants now. The saints in Zion need their prophet. In fact, I think the Lord knew the Missouri saints would not survive without you. You've got to go on to Far West, but. . . " he paused in deep thought for a moment. "Right now you need to rest. Be assured you shall have the means to continue your journey. The Lord will provide."

Actually, it was Brother Tomlinson who provided the means by which Joseph could continue the journey. He was trying to sell his farm. He had offered it to several prospective buyers. They had been interested but unwilling to meet his price.

One afternoon, Brigham knocked on the door of the Tomlinson farmhouse.

"Afternoon," he tipped his hat politely. "Could I have a word with your husband?"

Suspiciously the prune-faced, reluctant woman asked, "What for?"

"Business, madam."

"Don't do business with strangers." With that she slammed the door in his face. Her husband was a new member of the church and knew Brigham and Phineas well, but she had rejected all opportunities to listen to their radical new doctrines.

Still determined, Brigham knocked energetically until the door opened a crack and the same wizened, wrinkled face peered up at him.

"I am here to see Mr. Tomlinson about the sale of his farm."

Her eyes squinted, and she made a raspberry sound through pursed lips. The door slammed irrevocably, and Brigham realized he would have to locate the man himself. So, he tramped through the snow, down the beaten path to a two-story barn. Pushing back the bolt, he stepped in and hollered, "Brother Tomlinson? Are you in here?"

From the loft a voice replied, "Up here. Who's asking?"

"Brother Brigham."

Immediately, a round, red-cheeked face appeared. Tom Tomlinson was a good-natured fellow with broad cheekbones and full lips.

"Ladder's over yonder. Come on up. It's warmer up here."

In the dim light, Brigham found the ladder and climbed it. Tomlinson sat on a pile of hay, his hands cradling a cup of steaming liquid.

"Taking your afternoon tea?" Brigham asked.

"Yep."

"Isn't it warmer in by the fire?"

"Yep. But it's quieter out here."

Brigham nodded, remembering the shrill voice of Mrs. Tomlinson. "Have you had any luck in selling your place?"

"Not yet. Haven't met too many wanting to buy a farm in winter. These Indiana storms send 'em scurrying for cover, like bears hibernating. Maybe in the spring I can sell out and head for Missouri to join the saints."

"What does your missus think of that?"

Sheepishly, Tomlinson admitted, "She don't know about it yet."

"Um-hmm. I see. Will she go?"

All bravado, the man threw out his chest and declared, "I'm the one who says we stay or we go. If I go, she goes." Then he laughed and relaxed, confessing, "'Less, of course, she digs in her heels."

Brigham nodded. He knew the Lord would just have to convince his feisty little wife to move to Missouri.

"Brother Tom, I have it from the Lord. If you will share your good fortune with His chosen prophet, Joseph Smith, you will soon sell your property."

Tomlinson meditated on that for a moment. After a couple of minutes, he simply asked, "If I git my askin' price, I'll give the Lord's prophet three hundred dollars."

Brigham was touched by the man's faith. "You're a good man, Brother Tom. The prophet lost everything to the mobs of Kirtland. He is penniless, his wife is expecting, and he hasn't enough money for provisions to get him to Missouri. Whatever you share with him goes to the cause of building the kingdom."

"I'd be honored to give it all to him."

And he did. When Mr. James Porter arrived from Chicago three days later and bought the Tomlinson two-hundred-acre farm, Tom and Cecilia packed two wagons with provisions, seeds, herbs, furs, furniture and a nanny goat with her kid — and readied themselves to move out west. Tom got his price for the farm, and Joseph got three hundred dollars.

The Smith family was ready to leave Dublin and travel on. Sidney, however, was in no condition to go anywhere. He had all but succumbed to violent headaches and chronic depression. Phoebe had hidden his malady from friends as long as she could. She was a loyal woman and loved her husband deeply. She knew most of the saints revered him second only to Joseph as their leader. She did not want gossip about her husband. Phoebe traced his headaches and chronic, erratic behavior directly back to the tarring incident at Hiram. He had never quite been the same since. Sidney had become more frail, and his strength to work or preach was somewhat diminished. However his commitment to the restoration was as strong as ever, even though he was at the point of exhaustion. The last few weeks, riding in the open January air, had brought on chills, fever, headaches, and labored breathing. It was foolhardy for him to travel.

"You shall stay here," Phineas Young settled the matter with aplomb. "My family and I will go on with Brother Brigham and Joseph. But you are welcome to use my home as long as you like. When you are ready to follow us to Zion, close it up, or find a family to buy it and bring me the money. It may help us acquire a farm in Missouri."

Phoebe's eyes filled with tears. She was not usually an emotional woman. She was educated and cultured, now living on the edge of poverty and enduring indignities for the sake of religion and the man she loved. She could sacrifice all else, but she could not bear to lose her husband, and that had seemed like a distinct possibility as she had driven their wagon over icy roads.

The little party of friends stayed a few more days, long enough to acquire more provisions and to enjoy nights of preaching to each other by firelight in the small parlor. Their testimonies of Christ and His latter-day work rang with the fervor of visionaries and dedicated servants. Before parting, Joseph, Brigham, and Phineas pronounced a blessing of health and recovery on Sidney, admonishing him to follow them as soon as he recovered. Phoebe waved farewell, then gratefully prepared soup for her shivering husband and their children, whom she kept busy reading and doing schoolwork. It was the best way to keep their energetic minds occupied with things other than quarreling.

The departing families turned their wagons west once more. Their horses struggled through the deep snow. Children whimpered or quarreled. Beneath heavy robes, Emma rubbed her expanding stomach to soothe her baby when bumps and jolts shocked her system. She was bigger with this baby than she had been with the others. Cooking at night by campfire was a bitterly cold affair. Her hands and face would glow from the warmth of the fire, while an icy chill penetrated her feet and back.

Emma grew quieter as they neared their next resting place; so did her husband. Emma had heard rumors that Levi Hancock had left Kirtland months ago with orders to take Fanny Alger to Missouri. She had also heard they were delayed somewhere in Indiana. She wanted to ask her husband about it, but couldn't bring herself to disturb the precious bond of the last few weeks. She knew he had discussed the principle of plural marriage with a few close confidants, but as yet, the church was not required to practice it. The firestorm of public fury was so hot over the Kirtland Safety Society Anti-Banking notes that more fuel could create an inferno the church might not survive.

Emma knew Joseph had the capacity to love abundantly. Once, in the early days of Kirtland, Joseph had been preaching to a small congregation, and was so inspired by his vision of heaven that he sealed up the entire group of men and women to himself for eternity. His view of eternity was greater than he could describe, and his love for all the members of the church was deeply felt. Emma did not doubt that he was perfectly convinced God had commanded him in regard to plural marriage. They had never spoken of his marriage to Fanny. Emma had given her consent when it happened, but had since refused to acknowledge it. God might command, and she might obey, but she didn't have to like it. Silence was her characteristic defense against pain, both physical and emotional.

Traveling through eastern Indiana, Emma began to dread separation from Joseph, if only for an hour. She imagined them meeting Levi Hancock and Fanny at every stop.

Finally, the wagon caravan pulled up in front of a rural mercantile shop on the outskirts of a small town. It was an impressive red brick building. Emma entered, filled with anxiety. Signs were hung advertising tempting goods inside. Most desirable of all for the children was the horehound candy they found in a barrel. While they pestered their mother for the sweets, the proprietor handed Joseph a note. Emma saw him from the corner of her eye as he stood before the window and read the message. Then he went back to the pot-bellied stove to talk quietly with the storeowner. Within a half hour the door opened, letting in a blast of frigid air. Emma looked over little Joseph's head, and her heart dropped. There was Levi. He strode over to Joseph and embraced him in a bear hug. There was much slapping on the back and beaming. Stories were swapped, news exchanged. Emma and Mary Ann Young carefully planned the purchase of further provisions, answering a hundred questions from their children, and all the while Emma silently pleaded with God that Levi would leave, alone. After an hour of visiting, he did leave, and she sighed with relief. Sitting heavily in the chair at the end of the counter, Emma found herself trembling.

"Emma, are you all right?" Joseph had seen her groping her way to the chair.

Her voice was tight with the effort to retain self-control. "I'll be fine. I'm just glad you're here with me. I half expected you to go with Levi."

Joseph reassured her. "I would never leave you, Emma. Don't worry; I am here."

She smiled weakly, and he knew she needed rest. "Brother Brigham, Brother Phineas, I need to get my wife a place to lie down. This has been a long trip for her."

Brigham nodded in agreement, "Brother Hancock and his family have invited us to stay with them. Shall we stop for the night there?"

Emma rose from the chair, "No. . . I don't want to overburden the Hancocks. After all, don't they have their niece with them as well?"

Mr. Stuart, the proprietor, answered, "Why yes. A young lady by the name of Fanny is with them, but I'm sure if they invited you, they have enough room."

"Isn't there any other place we can go? I just hate to be a burden, and three more families would be quite a handful." Her eyes turned to Joseph now, pleading for him to understand.

He turned to Stuart. "What other Mormon families are in the area?"

"The George Anderson place is another two miles down the road. Their place is small, but I'm sure they would be happy to put you up."

"If you would please send someone ahead of us, to let them know we need a place." He looked at Emma sympathetically. She breathed deeply and held back tears. He understood.

Brigham and Phineas Young, with their families, went to temporary residence with Levi Hancock. The Smith family went the extra two miles down the road. The Andersons moved their children out to sleep by the hearth and gave the Smiths a room of their own. It was small, but adequate, and it had a comfortable bed, which was not jolting, rocking, or bouncing in a wagon. Emma lay down while Mrs. Anderson fed the children cabbage soup.

Emma fell fast asleep in minutes. By the time she awoke, hours later, Joseph had the children gathered for family scripture reading and prayer. She awoke to the sound of his voice reading holy writ as only he could. She was grateful beyond words for this warm house, warm bed, and understanding husband.

Joseph spent three days there and it was enough. Unhappy with the delay, Emma demanded all his time during the daylight, holding his arm when they walked about, pleading to go with him everywhere he went. With difficulty he made the two-mile trip to Levi's one evening to see Fanny and to discuss future arrangements. He gave Levi money for her keep, and counseled him not to bring her to Far West until things were more settled.

The Smiths had come through Dayton and Eaton, Ohio, and had stopped in Dublin, Indiana. Now with the Youngs, they would cross the rest of Indiana, all of Illinois, and enter Missouri from Quincy. Emma stopped counting the days and the miles. It became a matter of simple endurance. After Indiana they didn't stop again for any significant length of time. Their goal was to make twenty miles a day. So the wagons ground on, through snow and freezing rain, across frozen ruts and frozen streams. Stopping at night, sleeping in covered wagons, letting down the end flaps and securing them against the wind, they bundled up together in narrow wagon beds. Rising came early as they pressed on, crossing from Indiana into Illinois over the Wabash River. It was frozen solid. They crossed the Illinois River, a little over forty-five miles west of Springfield, on a barge ferry still operating on the South Bend.

February was bitter cold. The children even stopped complaining. They found it did no good and it used up energy. They learned to simply endure. Some time, some day, some year, this would all be over, if they could just get through each day. Little Freddy would often climb under his mother's robe, onto her lap, and rest his cold cheek against her bosom. She cuddled him there, protecting her youngest from the biting wind, even while her back and hips ached with the jouncing of the wagon wheels.

Other groups of saints joined them along the way, moving steadily toward the heart of their precious Zion, believing a new promised land was theirs in Missouri. At night, they built campfires for cooking, and melted snow for drinking and watering the animals. They crowded around the fire and shared stories of faith to bolster their courage. The little caravan had by now grown to ten families, and finding a farmhouse or barn to shelter them all became impossible. Joseph and Brigham made rounds at night, checking on each family, examining wagon wheels and axles, inspecting animals' hooves and general health.

When the time came for sleep, Emma cherished the moment she would curl up against the warm curve of her husband's body and feel his breath against her cheek. She was always cold except when nestled against Joseph. He was always warm. She listened to the sounds of the camp die down, heard her children breathing softly, sometimes sighing in their sleep, and she prayed they would all live through this trip and that she would remember these precious nights with Joseph when she grew old.

They reached the mighty Mississippi by the end of February. They camped on the bank of the river at Quincy, Illinois. Joseph, Emma, and family were invited to stay with Judge John Cleveland and his family, new converts to the faith. They allowed themselves only two days, for there was a pressing need to go on.

The frigid weather, which had made their journey so miserable, now proved to be their friend, for the Mississippi River was caught in its icy grip and frozen so fast they could take their horses and wagons across. Joseph and Brigham left early in the morning to walk the river's edge and examine the ice's thickness and determine the best place to attempt the crossing.

"I'm not sure we can chance it," Brigham shook his head. "Look here, the ice is solid only about five feet out, then it's broken up in chunks."

"Yes, but look farther out," Joseph pointed to the middle of the frozen river. "Over there the larger chunks have lodged against each other. It's thick and, while it is rough, it looks passable."

Brigham was dubious. The creaking and groaning of ice moving with the undercurrent was nerve wracking. Occasionally, they heard a loud crack, almost like a gunshot, and a large ice floe would break and move.

"If it thaws, even a little, while we are trying to get everyone across, our families' lives will be in danger. I don't like it, Joseph. It is too risky."

Joseph stood with his hand on his horse's neck, soothing the animal, as he continued to consider. Brigham was right. It was risky. His grandfather would have said it was cold enough to freeze a witch in her pot. Then, as he sought to divine Heaven's will, he seemed to see their little party of wagons, horses, and people crossing over safely, almost as the children of Israel did the Red Sea.

"Look, Brigham, there's a flatboat, icebound, but close enough to the shore we might use it to reach the heavier ice in the middle. Let's try it."

They tested the barge and found it quite stable. On its decks lay long planks, which they soon found helpful to stretch out as a path to reach across the ice. After using these planks to reach the middle of the river, they decided the sooner they could get their people started, the better chance they would have of a successful crossing. So, with the rushing sound of water flowing only a few feet beneath their boots, they hurried back to camp and announced the crossing would take place early the next morning.

That night the temperature sank to zero. Emma sat for a long time before the fireplace in the Cleveland home, dreading the dawn and the last freezing leg of their journey. Joseph sat beside her, more silent than usual, pondering the sacrifices he had asked of his family and followers. Emma was busy with the mending in her lap.

"Do you wish we could simply settle down in a comfortable little home like this one and never set foot out in the cold again?" Joseph searched her secret soul.

"You have read my very thoughts." She smiled at him, "You must truly be a seer."

"It doesn't take a heavenly vision to reveal such a natural wish to a husband's mind." He tried to discern her telltale signs of fatigue — her eyelid drooping, her hands trembling — for he knew she would not tell him.

"Perhaps the time is not far away when you can rear your children in peace and sit before your own fire. I'm hopeful our presence in Far West will help stem the fears of the Missourians. They'll see we are peaceable, reasonable folks. I have to stop the tactless boasting of the saints. They aggravate the population when they claim the land belongs rightfully to them as heirs of Zion. True or not, you don't make friends with such talk!"

Emma glanced at him while her needle went on flying in and out. "Do you really think you can reverse the tide?"

"I'll do all I can. I never really envisioned the church's permanent headquarters at Kirtland. It was surrounded too much by worldly influences. The church needs space. It needs isolation to grow the way it should. It must be taken out of the world, as we know it, and given a chance to incubate, mature, and break forth from its chrysalis like a great, beautiful butterfly. When that happens it will spread across the whole earth, calling God's chosen from every country."

Emma smiled. Her husband's vision of the church far exceeded the creaking, weather-beaten wagons rolling torturously across the frozen, rutted roads of Illinois. "And how long will all this take? Twenty years? Fifty? Will we see it?"

Joseph was silent, staring into the fire. After a few minutes he spoke, "I have seen it already, but time has no meaning in heaven, and I can't put a timetable on it. I just know the day will come when the gospel will be the only hope in a very dark world."

Emma put down her sewing, tucked her needles in her little bag. "Then I guess we had better be getting on to Far West to build your Zion."

Joseph protested, "*Your* Zion too."

She put her hand on his cheek. "You are my Zion, my refuge. Come, it's time to sleep. Four o'clock comes early."

Joseph lay awake beside his wife, long after weariness nudged her into deep slumber. He was concerned for Emma. He knew she meant what she had said. Her testimony was in him, their love, her witness of him as a prophet. That personal attestation was great encouragement to him, but he wondered if she would stand true if he were not there. How many of his followers would? How many were truly converted to the restored gospel, not just converted to him as their leader? And how many had come looking for power? There weren't many Newel K. Whitneys or Joseph Knights.

He lay in the darkness thinking of the friends who formed the backbone of the church. Gratitude filled his heart. How very far they had all come since Cumorah. He could not let them down. Kirtland had blossomed with great expectations and had died with great disappointment. Now Kirtland's faithful were uprooting their families in the hope of finding a new haven in Missouri. His own parents and family were following somewhere close behind. He had to get to Far West quickly in order to solve the problems among neighbors and quell the spirit of rebellion, which Oliver and David were spreading.

Joseph's longtime friends felt they were on equal footing with him, and refused to sacrifice any more for the good of the kingdom. He was heartsick, for sacrifice was truly their test; God *requires* sacrifice. Most men, when blessed by heaven, bear fervent testimony of the goodness of God. But when stripped of earthly possessions, hated, hunted, beaten, spit upon, sick, and penniless, they blame an unjust heaven.

As he continued to ponder, Joseph seemed to see a great field, while a fierce wind separated the wheat from the chaff. The wheat would fall back to earth to blossom green again in fruitful soil. The chaff was gathered up in a whirlwind, whipped around in a frenzy, then scattered across the land to fall on barren ground as dust. The church would yet suffer the whirlwind, for the Lord needed fruitful Saints to blossom. Joseph knew that in the process his heart would be broken by the separated chaff that once were his friends.

Emma awakened when Joseph did, fixed a small breakfast of biscuits and milk for her family, then bundled the children up with warm clothes and blankets. Joseph had prepared the wagon the night before and now took each sleepy child, carried him out, and tucked them all together into the wagon quilts. In the early morning dark, he and Emma said an emotional farewell to the Clevelands, thanking them for two wonderful days of comfort and warmth. Joseph took up the reins, and the wagon once again began its groaning course toward the river camp.

The camp was already broken, though the sky was still pitch black. Brigham was riding back and forth down the line of weary travelers, helping where he was needed and encouraging each family with the promise that this was the last leg of their journey. Two families decided to stay in Quincy until spring, and they pulled out of the group, and headed to town to seek lodging for the rest of the winter. Ropes securing the loads on the remaining wagons were checked and tightened. Axles and wheels were tested once more. The men driving the teams were burly figures padded by layers of clothing, thick coats and cloaks, with rags wrapping their faces until only their eyes showed. The women and children were packed into the depths of the wagons like rabbits in their burrows.

The first families in line didn't see the course Brigham and Joseph had laid out for them until their rigs were actually on the frozen river. The men formed their caravan into a long dark line which rolled along the bank for miles until they came to the ice-bound flatboat. Joseph led the way. Brigham brought up the rear. The men sat in their wagons and watched by dawn's thin light as Joseph got down, tugged on the bridles, and urged the nervous horses onto the flatboat, then onto the river of ice. Immediately there was a loud crack from the ice, and the horses tried to rear, but Joseph kept a firm grip and calmed them down. Emma's head appeared from under a canvas flap.

"I'll get out and help."

"No! Stay where you are."

"But I just add weight to the wagon. It'll be lighter without me. I'm coming out."

"I don't want you to fall on this ice. It's rough. I'll send Jacob here to help you. I've got to put down more planks for the wagons. It'll be smoother that way, and their wheels won't break through the ice."

"I'll be fine. Go put those planks down and let's get across."

Brigham and two other men came cautiously across the flatboat and were already lifting planks to position them on the ice. Joseph worked with them, laying the boards end-to-end in a long line toward the other bank. Once the planks were in place, Joseph came back to the skittish horses, grasped the reins and began urging them farther and farther out onto the frozen river. The wagon rolled onto the planks with a jolt and slowly made its way toward the middle of the river, where the planks ran out. The sharp creaking and groaning of the ice spooked the horses, and they began to fidget in their traces. The sudden noise also frightened the children, now thoroughly awake. Their cries, combined with the wagon and ice sounds, only added to the cacophony during this laborious crossing.

Emma lost sight of Joseph. He went back to the beginning of the plank trail, leaving Jacob, the fifteen-year old son of Abner Jacobs, to help her with the horses. The boy held them firmly while men began laying out more planks. Other men had come from Quincy to help, and they worked the entire day getting the wagon train across the Mississippi.

By the time the Smith wagon made it to solid ground, it was daylight. The men threw a rope around two large tree trunks and made a pulley to help the other wagons across. Joseph, seeing his family secure, kissed Emma's brow, and started back across the ice with Brigham and the others.

Through the open flap of her wagon, Emma could see the caravan on the same agonizing path she had just completed. Once tested, it was determined the ice would sustain several wagons if spaced out enough. They divided up the planks and used them for three different paths, inching them forward, little by little across the shifting, crackling ice floes. The last few wagons moved their trail a little upstream from the path of first crossing. The ice was more solid where horses and wagons had not been. The river was a little wider there, but the surface less damaged. By the time Brigham's wagon ventured out onto the ice, it was three o'clock in the afternoon. Joseph had retrieved his champion black gelding, Charley, and rode him across the frozen river, the horse's hooves cracking the weakened ice with every step.

Finally, the last wagon was safely across, with Mary Ann Young walking behind it, carrying her youngest daughter. On the Missouri side, the women had already built a large bonfire and the company gathered around it. Dusk was upon them. The temperature was dropping, and supper was a poor affair of cold biscuits, fried salt pork, and a few carrots bought in Quincy. Before the weary pilgrims could finish their meal, the lowering clouds ushered in a snowstorm. They pulled the wagons into a circle, covered their teams with heavy quilts, and huddled down in wagon beds, each family struggling with its own particular problems. Snow mounted up on the top and sides of their canvas coverings and eventually provided insulation for them, as they snuggled in their wagon beds. Children fell into exhausted sleep; horses stopped fidgeting, and the world settled into a deep quiet.

The next day dawned cloudy but not as cold as the last two months had been. Emma breathed a sigh of relief, for she sensed a corner had been turned and warm weather was coming. Joseph frowned. Warm weather meant melting snow and mud for wagons to navigate. That would be even more difficult than ice. Then too, three more rivers — the Salt, the Chariton and the Grand — had to be crossed before they arrived at Far West, still over two hundred miles away.

Within the hour, wagons moved out across the rolling plains of northern Missouri. This was the western frontier. The clapboard or log homes of Indiana and Illinois were gone. The well-worn roads from one town to the next had disappeared. They followed a trail mapped out by cavalry scouts and other travelers, but it was just a rutted, bumpy path. They saw an occasional wooden cross reaching up out of a snowy field. What mother had left her husband or child there in a shallow grave, Emma wondered? She watched them until they were lost behind a bend in the trail.

The third day, they came to a log cabin tucked between the trees on the side of a knoll. No welcoming smoke wafted from the chimney. No animals wandered in the yard. Joseph drove up the incline to the home and started to get down from the wagon to knock at the door. A small board moved at the window and the barrel of a rifle was thrust out. From inside the cabin a man's hoarse voice called, "Who be ye?"

"Friends," Joseph replied. "Just wondering if there are Christian folks in these parts."

"Wouldn't know about that. Where ya headed?"

"Ray County."

"Huh! You're a fer piece. Better be gittin' on."

"Guess we will." Joseph turned to go, when the board moved again revealing bright eyes overshadowed by bushy, white eyebrows.

"How many are ye?" their inquisitor asked.

"About ten families?"

"Ain't Mormons are ye?"

"Why do you ask?"

"Too many Mormons already been through here. They want our land. Reckon they'll be a fight, cause we aim to keep it for ourselves. Now, one more time, are ye Mormons?"

"We come from Ohio and we're headed west to settle."

"Keep on headin' then! This here land's already been settled."

The musket barrel held steady, sighted right on Joseph, until he turned his wagon back down the road. That was their first welcome to Missouri, and Joseph learned two valuable things: one, they were on the right trail and two, they were not welcome.

The weather turned milder, warmer in the day, though below freezing at night. The snow soon disappeared from the ground, and children began to beg to walk. Emma's spirits began to rise, though her back ached with every bump. The sun was shining. They passed several lakes still frozen over and sparkling in the winter sunlight. Emma rubbed a sore spot at the base of her spine. Soon she would trade this bumping, jolting wagon for a new home in Far West.

At last, the company came to the north fork of the Salt River after stopping twice to re-nail iron bands on wagon wheels. It was a long, meandering river, moving slowly through a wide meadow. In the summer it might even be a beautiful spot. Across the river, the bank rose steeply onto a plateau. Bare-limbed trees fringed the river's far side, while spindly skeletons of bushes were on the near side. They followed the river half a mile upstream looking for a barge to ferry them, for the river had thawed. Abner's son reported the ferry sunk downstream from their original stopping place.

"What do you think?" Joseph asked when Brigham returned from reconnoitering.

"There's a pond a little way from here where the river pools and the current is slow. Ice chunks seem solid, though they're a few inches below the surface."

"Let's go take a look."

Joseph rode with him back to the pond, and they urged their horses out into the freezing water and onto the submerged ice. The horses were skittish. The ice tilted dangerously, but it held. Joseph and Brigham looked at each other with dread. It was the only way across.

They rode back and led the wagons to the pond. Emma watched with growing alarm as she saw water flowing freely over the surface of the ice. When they were lined up on the bank, Joseph gathered all the families together and outlined the procedure.

"The men will take their teams and wagons into the water — it's not deep here, only a few inches. There are solid ice chunks just a few feet out, beneath the water's surface. You'll have to walk your horses onto them to get to the other side. Women and children, there is a canoe here at the edge. You'll use the canoe, to reach the ice, and walk from there about a hundred yards to the other side. We'll take the canoe with us to get from the ice to the far bank. Any questions?"

A little ten-year-old girl called out. "Brother Joseph, can't you just pray for a miracle and get us across?"

He swung her up into his arms and turned to Brigham. "Well, Brother Brigham, can't we do that? Shall we pray for a miracle?"

Brigham bit down on his lip as though in thought and nodded slowly. "You know, Abigail, I've been praying for miracles the whole way. Haven't you?"

"Yes, sir," the child nodded affirmatively, her pig-tails bobbing vigorously.

"And, do you think we've had any?"

"Yes, sir. We made it across the mighty Mississippi River okay."

"Well, there you have it," Joseph assured her. "Lots and lots of miracles! And I think this little pond is another miracle. It's still partially frozen, otherwise we'd have to wait for warm weather to cross."

Then Joseph led the way. He and Abner took the Jacobs' team, one man on each side of the horses, grasped the bridles and reins and plunged the animals into the icy river. The animals tried to rear, but the men persisted and urged them on. By the time they reached solid ice the freezing water was two-and-a-half feet deep. They ran the horses up onto the ice chunks, and the big beasts lunged forward, glad to get out of deep water. The wagons lumbered up onto the shifting, tipping sheet of ice. The anxious group at the water's edge was silent, fearfully watching the desperate operation before them. Once on the ice, with just a few inches of water to walk through, Joseph and Abner could easily lead the horses across. Then, at the farthest edge of the submerged ice, they plunged once more into thigh-deep, icy water, and thrashed through onto solid frozen ground beyond.

The women and children broke into wild cheering. The first wagon had made it! Abner's wife and four children stepped into the little canoe, and with Brigham walking beside them in the freezing water to steady the vessel, they moved out to the submerged ice. They clamored out of the canoe, and moving as fast as they could without slipping, made their way across the ice sheet, until they reached its edge. Brigham held the canoe while the Jacobs family once again stepped into it, and the men on the far side pulled them to safety.

So it went, one family after another. Emma and the children were the fourth family to go. Joseph had taken a family across and was returning from the far bank when Emma started out. Brigham steadied the canoe for them. When she stepped from the canoe into the ankle-deep, icy water, her breath caught in her chest. She stopped for a moment, her eyes wide open.

"Sister Emma, are you all right?" Brigham asked.

"I . . . I . . . I can't breathe."

"I know," he said tersely.

Then she realized he was standing in the icy water up to his thighs, and she didn't say another word about the cold. She held little Freddy, and helped her other children out of the vessel. Brigham picked up the canoe.

Julia screamed out, "Mama, I can't feel my feet!"

"It's all right, darling. Just keep moving."

"No!" the little girl cried. "I want to go back!"

"We can't go back, Julia. Keep moving!"

Joseph, seeing his family on the ice, immediately plunged toward them.

Little Joseph, only five years old, looked up at his mother, tears streaming down his face. Emma's heart almost broke when she looked down and saw his pleading look.

"I'm c-c-c. . . cold!" he whispered, his teeth chattering.

"We're almost there, children, almost there! Hurry, hurry!"

Julia slogged through the icy water, pulling on her mother's long skirt. They were within a few feet of the far side when the girl slipped. The drag on Emma's skirt threw her off balance. She went down on one knee, still holding Freddy. Brigham let go of the canoe to grasp Emma and the children just as Joseph reached the traumatized group. He climbed onto the ice, causing it to tilt precariously. All Emma could say was, "Oh, oh. . . Oh!" The water had soaked her long heavy skirts, and shocked her system.

Joseph raised her up as Brigham took young Joseph and Julia in his arms. "Emma! Emma! Are you all right?"

She shook her head.

"Hold on to me. We're going to the canoe."

But the canoe had drifted away. All he could do was clutch her tightly in his arms and plunge into the deeper water on the edge of the pond. Involuntarily a muffled cry broke from Emma as Joseph staggered up the bank and finally onto dry ground. Julia was still crying lustily in Brigham's arms while the year-and-a-half-old Freddy wailed in sympathy. Other men brought the Smith wagon out of the water just minutes later. The wheels were dripping, but bed and belongings were dry.

Joseph carried Emma to the wagon, helped her off with her wet clothes, and wrapped her in a quilt. Mary Ann Young, already safely across, took Julia and stripped her down, wrapped her in a quilt, and quieted her cries with warm stones for her feet. Once he had Emma safely settled, Joseph started back for another trip across the pond, as she tried to stop him.

"Joseph, how can you go again? You've been in that freezing water too long."

"I have to. Keep the quilts warm for me." And he went back into the pond once more.

Finally, the last family had crossed, all without serious mishap, and night closed in around them. The men stood around the fire steaming; their wet pants sizzled as they dried and warmed themselves. The women cooked a huge pot of boiling soup and took it around to families still in their wagons. Emma tried to get out and help, but she was simply too exhausted. So for once she lay back in her wagon bed, her little ones clustered close around her, and let others cook and serve. She could hear her husband encouraging the others with stories of Far West and the beauty of the prairie just to the north. She drew back the canvas curtain and peered out at him. There he stood, warming himself by the fire, loving his life, loving his friends, even loving the challenges that daunted other men. A rush of emotion ran through her. Love for him rose up within her as she closed the curtain and curled up, struggling to gather a little warmth into her bones. She also tucked the quilt more tightly around her three children. Throughout her life Emma would remember the Salt Creek crossing, and all other hardships were measured against it.

Chapter Four

"Never, No Never!"

mma permitted herself the pleasure of watching the sunrise from the warm comfort of a clean, soft bed in George and Lucinda Harris's home. The sun rose in delicate shades across the clear, eastern sky. She lay quietly, reflecting on their arrival the day before in this frontier town called Far West, Missouri. Bishop Marsh had notified the people that the prophet was coming, and their wagon train entered town to the strains of a brass band with a large crowd gathered to welcome them. Emma had traveled nine hundred miles, swaying, jolting, freezing, but conquering the trial by ice. Since crossing Salt Creek, she had felt perpetually numb through and through. She automatically responded to the needs of the children, but more than that she could not manage.

Three days out from Far West, supply wagons met them on the trail. Thomas Marsh had sent food, bedding, firewood, and even a brand new coat for the prophet. That last night in the wagon under the stars, she and Joseph had lain awake talking.

"I almost dread what's coming," he mused. "I'll have to confront Oliver and David, and I fear they are beyond reason. Church leaders in Far West have already called them to account, but they refuse to respond."

"We'll see them soon, Joseph. Surely you can rekindle friendship and the testimony of the work."

"I hope I can, but complaints are mounting. They are staying with William McLellin in Daviess County and stirring up trouble from there. McLellin has become a dyed-in-the-wool apostate. He'll certainly be no good for their testimonies."

Emma sighed, thinking of the many close friends who had turned on them in the past year. Oliver and David were terrible losses. They were forever woven into the tapestry of the genesis and organization of the church. She could close her eyes and picture their faces as they had been at Fayette, aglow with the fire of heavenly revelation. She remembered the excitement in their voices as they recounted experiences with angels and the golden plates. She had seen Oliver's head bowed with Joseph's many nights over the translation of the *Book of Mormon*, and more recently, the Egyptian papyri.

"Oh, Joseph. My heart hurts for them; especially for Oliver! How can he turn on us, knowing all he does about the restoration of the gospel?"

"Sometimes concerns for things of this world overcome even the elect. Perhaps that is why God never blessed us with lands and money."

Incredulously, she turned to look into his face. "Joseph, we've had lands and money, but you've turned everything over to the church. We don't have anything because you gave it all away!"

He was surprised. It had not occurred to him that way. "Emma, are you angry?"

Her indignation gave way and she settled back down into his arms. "No. Just amazed that you don't recognize the extent of our sacrifices."

He continued to meditate on the problems awaiting him. "We're going to lose William Phelps and probably John Whitmer as well. They've been selling church land — selling off lots without consulting anyone, and worse yet, they keep the money for themselves."

"How can they?"

"The spirit of rebellion has overcome them. They have transferred title to the land in Far West in such a way as to encumber Edward Partridge and make him liable for over three thousand dollars. They've been demanding immediate payment."

"That's outrageous!"

"Of course, it is. And they know Edward hasn't any money to pay those debts. The whole church together can't raise three thousand dollars right now. The government isn't demanding payment. The dissenters are. They bring lawsuits against the brethren just to annoy them."

"You'll set things right," she assured him confidently. "That's why we're here. Your influence will make the difference. Call the dissenters in. Go to each of them and let your friendship win them back."

"I'll certainly try. These are my best friends. I can't just give up on them." Then he reflected a moment and said, "Well, almost 'best' friends. You, Emma, have stayed by me through everything. I've never had a better friend than you, and I pray to be all that and more to you."

Now, musing over these memories, Emma rested in a soft bed, gathering strength to start the day without him. Joseph was already up and gone, and she knew he was exclusively hers no more. Reclining against pillows, Emma could see the new frock so thoughtfully provided for her by the ladies of Far West. It was hanging on a peg in their room. It was her favorite color, a dark plum skirt, with a lighter shade for the bodice. It looked more than ample for her gaunt figure, though she was now six months into her pregnancy. Traveling these past two months, she had been thoroughly wrapped and concealed beneath her voluminous cloak, but the dress beneath was a disgrace. It was stained and soiled beyond reclaiming. When she first saw the new dress hanging in the room, she had clasped it to her heart, overcome with gratitude.

Emma soon roused and quickly dressed in the cool morning air, taking extra time with her hair, smoothing the graceful skirt, and straightening her collar. Last of all, she pinched a little color into her cheeks. She would not be dowdy in the company of Lucinda Harris. George Harris had offered the Smiths space in his house until a proper home could be erected for them. This was a large home with a great fireplace and oversized kitchen. It boasted three bedrooms, one of which was temporarily given over to Joseph, Emma, and little Freddy. The other children slept in the third room with two older Harris children. Lucinda Harris ruled over this commodious estate like a queen at court. She had black hair, fine and curling against her neck, and eyes as blue as the spring sky. They turned at a moment's notice from twinkling and laughing to flashing with command. Her figure was undamaged by giving birth to four children, and she had the habit of using her second best Sunday dress for every day wear. Emma, while grateful for the generous accommodations and kind attention, was not unconscious of Mrs. Harris' open admiration of Joseph.

"Sister Smith, I'm so glad you had a chance to rest this morning. Your husband has already taken breakfast and told me he will likely be away all day. He has left you in my hands, so I have planned a wonderful day for us. First, we'll see to the children, then if you don't mind walking a bit, we'll go to the bishop's storehouse and choose his best wool. Then I thought you might want to work on clothing for your new little one. Of course, it's just a suggestion. If that's too taxing after your long trip, you can simply sit and relax and tell me about your adventures."

Emma stifled a sense of annoyance. The woman was just being kind. "Indeed, I'm not sure I would know how to simply sit and relax. Already I'm feeling like a caged bird, after being outdoors so long. But I don't wish to disturb your daily activities or be a bother."

146

Lucinda waved the suggestion away. "Oh, it is no bother to have the prophet and his wife in my home. You're a woman I admire. It must be a difficult life, married to a man whom everyone else under the sun claims as their own."

Emma was taken aback to hear her own thoughts voiced by a stranger. Perhaps the wishes of her heart were not so unusual. Emma listened as Lucinda chattered on about things of a personal nature. She wondered if Mrs. Harris had heard the rumors of plural marriage that had so inflamed Kirtland. She kept her thoughts to herself. She would be the last to speak of *that* principle.

"I want to see Oliver," Joseph told Thomas B. Marsh.

Marsh looked around the room. The leaders of the church in Missouri were gathered with Joseph for consultation: David Patten, George Hinkle, Brigham Young, John Corrill, George Robinson, and Joseph's recently arrived brother, Samuel H. Smith.

Thomas shook his head. "Cowdery won't meet with us. He says we have no authority over him."

"He'll recognize mine," Joseph said quietly.

David Patten spoke up. "He's infatuated with the law, and fancies himself a potential law partner of Alexander Doniphan. He has declared 'the law is my theme,' and threatens all the leaders with lawsuits. I doubt he'll meet with you either. He prefers to sue us. He has caused so much trouble, I think he's beyond reason."

"I'd like to think our friendship could overcome these problems. Old Lucifer has hold of his coattails now, whispering in his ear. I can't believe he'll actually give up the cause of Zion for a mess of pottage. He must come around."

Patten held up two fingers. "Cowdery already knows you're here. I told him just last evening. I passed him in the street and pointed out brother Harris' home where you are staying. Well sir, he turned on his heel and headed in the other direction."

Joseph stared soberly at David. Oliver was far-gone then.

Thomas Marsh took up the order of the day. "We have held several councils which Oliver rejects as unlawful, stating we have not the authority to try him or the other dissenters. Now it is time to officially, once and for all, call Oliver Cowdery to account for misdeeds. George, read the counts against him."

George W. Robinson took up the paper, which cited nine offenses, and assuming a dignified stance, cleared his throat and read them aloud in his deep, raspy voice.

"Number one is persecuting the brethren with vexatious lawsuits."

Thomas turned to Joseph. "Oliver, David, and John know our debts are not due to be paid for many months, but are attempting to embarrass and impoverish us by demanding immediate payment."

George continued, "Seeking to destroy the character of Joseph Smith, Jr. by falsely accusing him of adultery." He paused, cleared his throat, and glanced about the room.

Joseph sat calmly, quite unperturbed. "This is a charge Oliver has made before. He knows it is not true. Go on, George."

Robinson rushed on to the next charge. "He is charged with not attending meetings and treating the church with contempt; fourth, denying he will submit to any ecclesiastical authority or revelations whatever as regarding his property or temporal affairs; fifth, selling his land in Jackson County contrary to holy revelation.

"Sixth, he is accused of sending an insulting letter to the High Council and to the president of the council while they were attending to the duties of their offices; seventh, he has left his church calling for the sake of filthy lucre, and has turned to the practice of law."

Patten spoke pointedly, "Which he practices against *us*."

George went doggedly on. "Eighth, he has disgraced the church by being connected with bogus money-making; and ninth, dishonestly retaining notes after they have been paid. He has forsaken the cause of God and returned to the beggarly elements of the world."

Robinson's voice gradually rose in indignation as he finished with emphasis and slammed the paper down on the desk. He looked triumphantly at his prophet as he finished the accusations against Oliver.

Joseph, however, did not return the glance. Instead, he sat gazing steadfastly out the window. How could the sun be shining so brightly? For a moment he thought he heard a whistle, one like Oliver used to make while walking along the Susquehanna River. That day in April when they had first met in Harmony, Oliver had been the answer to Joseph's prayers for a scribe! Joseph almost smiled, remembering the hot sun, the cool water, and the angel commanding them to baptize each other. Was he the only one to remember that it was Oliver's hand which had written down the entire translation of the *Book of Mormon?* Joseph's breath caught in his chest as a pain seared him. Oh, my friend, he silently lamented. How have you come to this? Put the mantle of godliness back on! Oliver, come back! Come back to the Lord! Where are you, my friend?

Joseph turned to Thomas Marsh. "And are the charges similar for David and John Whitmer, Luke and Lyman Johnson?"

Marsh nodded an affirmation. Joseph questioned further, "And there are witnesses to support these allegations?"

"Yes, as many as you need."

"Well, then, send them letters to the effect that if they refuse to recognize the jurisdiction of this council, the charges against them will be sustained, and they will be considered no longer members of the church. Perhaps they will yet humble themselves and repent."

George quickly entered that directive in the minutes of the meeting. Then the council took up other matters of concern, including the deeding of certain property to Joseph for the building of a home.

Brigham had sat quietly through the entire discussion. He could see the pain it was causing his friend. He knew how Joseph agonized over the disaffection of close his friends. As for himself, Brigham had never really warmed to Oliver. Brigham, at this juncture, had only two desires: to build a comfortable home for his family and to be the truest friend Joseph Smith ever had.

"Brother Brigham," Thomas turned to him. "Have you considered which town lot you might want to build on? There are still a few available."

Brigham shook his head thoughtfully. "No. I believe I'll leave the town lots to other folks. I prefer farmland outside of town a few miles, close enough to pester my friends at will, and far enough to stay out of politics."

That won him a smile from Joseph. When the meeting was dismissed, Brigham bade his friend a fond farewell for the time being and rode eastward toward a little valley he had already selected as a worthy place for Mary Ann and the children. Joseph looked after him with a twinge of regret. They had traveled countless miles together, and Brother Brigham had become a strong right arm. Joseph sensed he would need that strength before long.

Joseph spent the next few weeks traveling the length and breadth of adjoining Carroll County, surveying and laying out land southeast of the Caldwell County seat, planning for the arrival of the Kirtland saints, whom he knew were making their way to Missouri. Looking over the fertile, rolling fields which were just beginning to show prairie grass and a few yellow and purple flowers,

Joseph envisioned the saints joined in cooperative farming, putting those fields under cultivation and all families benefiting from the proceeds. An inspired plan had already formed in his mind on organizing agricultural companies, a plan he called "Big Field United Firms." It would enable them to feed thousands of immigrants flooding into northwestern Missouri and would turn the state into the most efficient farmland in the United States.

Another project needed Joseph's immediate attention. John Whitmer had been commissioned to keep a history of the church. Not much of a writer, he nevertheless had accumulated copious notes, notes he now refused to turn over to the church. Joseph had personally asked for the notes so the history could be compiled. John still refused. Joseph then decided that before more time elapsed, he would personally write the history, since he alone knew it most thoroughly. This he now commenced during early morning and late evening hours in the Harris home. Joseph had more time than anticipated to work privately. The church was so well organized in Far West, with Marsh, Patten, and Young bearing most of the burden, his time was free more often than expected to preach and to write. He was also anxious to resume the printing of church publications. Oliver had brought the church printing press with him from Kirtland but held it against the debts he said Joseph owed him. It was Oliver's "pound of flesh," and he was relentless in his demands.

Oliver refused to come to a council meeting or answer charges, refused to cooperate in any way with the new Missouri church authorities, or consider the impoverished nature of the church members. Instead, he pressed lawsuits to extract every possible penny from those he had so recently considered brothers. He boasted that Joseph would vindicate him. For all Joseph's heart yearned after his friend, vindication could come only from God.

A bright spot of April 1838 was the arrival of Sidney Rigdon with his family and a group of saints. When a rider from Haun's Mill, on Caldwell County's eastern border, brought word that Rigdon was nearing the city, Joseph, along with Thomas Marsh, arranged a town celebration. Wagons were assembled with food, clothing, and bedding for the newcomers. Arrangements were made for living accommodations until individual houses could be erected. The company of one hundred twenty people reached town on April fourth. Joseph and Emma with their children stood at the head of the band, which played a welcome tribute to the weary travelers.

A wagon ground to a stop in front of the Smiths, and Sidney climbed down. He looked around with surprise at the elaborate welcome, choked up with emotion, then turned to Joseph and embraced him without a word. After several thumps on the back and much clearing of the throat, he offered his gratitude.

"Joseph, it's a grand welcome!"

"The long journey from Kirtland is over. Are you well, Sidney?"

"Yes, well enough."

Sidney looked around at the growing settlement. The houses were just rough-hewn log homes, but well built and sturdy. The town seemed promising enough.

"The church seems to be prospering, Joseph." Sidney observed.

"It is. We have six stores doing a thriving business, and we raise a house every day. Lots have been laid out in a precise manner. We've saved a choice city lot for you. It's just off the town square, near my own."

"Have you received a revelation regarding another temple?"

"Not yet. Right now we must find additional land and housing for the immigrants flooding in. Older settlers feel Mormons should be confined to Caldwell County, but there's no practicality in that. We are only just starting to grow. As more and more saints arrive, we'll burst the seams of Caldwell. Already a few have ventured into the upper counties of Missouri."

Sidney was quickly caught up in the excitement of expansion and settlement. "Joseph, you must show me the other counties. I have hope we may finally be permitted to worship God in our own way."

Thomas Marsh stood up on a log bench, motioned for the band to be still, and taking off his hat, proceeded to issue a welcome to the exhausted travelers on behalf of the town of Far West. After his short speech, the newcomers gave a hearty shout of hurrah, and accepted the feast provided for their families. The day was cool, but almost perfect for a picnic and a party. Night had fallen by the time they were all settled into host homes for the time being.

The church convened conference during a blustery April. Joseph and Sidney each spoke in their spellbinding way. Oliver and the other dissenters steadfastly refused to attend. Before the three-day sessions began, Joseph learned that Oliver and David were back from their trip to Richmond, and he wanted to ride out and pay them a visit.

Joseph talked it over with Emma in the parlor of the Harris home. "Letters pleading for reconciliation were sent to the dissenters. They have not answered. I have gone as far as it is appropriate to go. They must repent, and if their pride will not allow them to, it is time they are cut off. To keep them in their positions with such hypocrisy and rebellion as they show, flies in the face of every spiritual witness God has given them."

Emma sat back in a rocking chair, hands clasped in her lap. She watched her husband, and thought back to the first time she had seen him, young, innocent, and new in his calling. Now Joseph's face showed maturity. The years had bestowed determination. Joseph knew he was the Lord's spokesman. Love caused him to be reticent, but respect for his office filled him with resolve. Who knew better than Emma how he agonized over the loss of dearly loved comrades? When his friends were cut off, Joseph's heart would bleed.

Inevitably, excommunication claimed Oliver Cowdery, Martin Harris, David and John Whitmer, Luke and Lyman Johnson, W.W. Phelps, William McLellin and John Boynton. When the ordeal was over and the church divested of many original leaders, Joseph and Emma sat up many a night sadly burying the memories of good friends and good times past. The church would never be the same without them, for they had contributed much, talked with angels, and given years to further the Kingdom of God.

Emma was nearing her confinement. The saints raised a log home for the Smiths, and Emma went to work braiding rugs to cover the rough floors, and making mattress covers. If they could only live in peace for a few years, the saints would turn this rough frontier into a civilized township. Already they had a schoolhouse, where the children met during the week and the saints met on Sunday for Sabbath worship. Julia very proudly skipped her way to school, while Emma stood with young Joseph and Freddy, watching her until she disappeared from sight around the curved path to school.

As humble as her home was, Emma was happy to again have a house of her own. Mrs. Harris and her constant chatter wore on Emma. Still, Lucinda had thoughtfully given her a beautiful tablecloth when they had left for their new home. Emma was grateful, but she was more grateful not to lie in bed waiting for Joseph to finish conversations with George and Lucinda. He was often up late there, either in consultation with the brethren or writing his history of the church. She would rather have him at her kitchen table than at Lucinda's. Petty perhaps, but, she reasoned, her role as his wife should not be undermined by anyone.

While Julia went to school to learn her letters, Emma taught little Joseph, by repetition, short verses of scripture and various homilies such as "A stitch in time saves nine," which he sang out every time she took out her needlework. He always begged to go with his sister to school, but Emma couldn't bear to be separated from him yet, so she placated him with promises of next year and filled his time with planting a small garden and caring for their cow and sheep. Freddy tagged along after his brother with the lurching, rolling steps of a toddler.

Before long, the Smiths' cabin was filled with visitors seeking audience with Joseph. Unlike her days in Kirtland, Emma decided she was not personally responsible for feeding everyone who came to her home. She politely referred them to the bishop, if they needed temporal help. There were a few guests, however, in whom she took particular delight.

Prominent Clay County attorney, Alexander Doniphan, came looking for Joseph one day. Emma had heard Joseph speak highly of Doniphan's role as a member of the Missouri legislature. This man was instrumental in the creation of Caldwell, their "Mormon" county. Letters had passed between her husband and Doniphan. Now, hearing Joseph was living there, Alexander came on horseback, seeking the Mormon prophet.

"My husband is at work inside. He gave me strict instructions that he not be disturbed for a few hours." Emma looked full into the face of the "Friend of the Mormons." Doniphan was a strong, handsome man, tall and broad-shouldered. His dark hair hung in locks out from beneath his palm leaf hat. He had a wide brow, square jaw, and commanding eyes. One look at his face revealed the character of the man: honest, straightforward, and indomitable.

Emma paused only momentarily, then continued. "However, Mr. Doniphan, my husband considers you a true friend and values the services you have performed for our people. I am sure he will be happy to see you. Please, tie up your horse beneath the shade tree, and I'll tell him of your arrival."

Emma didn't know if she was out of breath from hurrying, or if the lawyer's presence had flustered her. In any case, she was flushed with excitement when she entered Joseph's workroom.

"You'll never guess who is here to see you."

Joseph frowned at the interruption and continued his writing. "Emma, how do you spell *partishunned?*"

"P-a-r-t-i-t-i-o-n-e-d," she quickly spelled out. "Joseph, we have a special guest!"

Now he looked up, surprised. Emma was rarely so enthusiastic about visitors. "Who is it?" he asked, somewhat expectantly.

"Alexander Doniphan!" his wife announced triumphantly.

He stood up. "Really?"

"Yes, and he is just tying up his horse. He'll soon be at the door. Quite an impressive man, I must say."

A smile played on her husband's lips. His raised his eyebrows. "Must you now? Well, let us greet this impressive man."

He preceded her out the door, giving Emma time to smooth her hair and change her work apron for a nicer one. Doniphan was, indeed, already at the door. Joseph welcomed him with a hearty handshake.

"Alexander Doniphan, it is so very good to see you again. My wife said our visitor was a 'very impressive man,' and she is not given to undue praise."

Emma pressed her lips together to keep from showing any hint of embarrassment.

"Mr. and Mrs. Smith," Doniphan executed a swift, shallow bow. "I come unannounced and therefore hesitate to interrupt."

"Not at all. You are a most welcome interruption, and, "turning to Emma, "my wife thinks so too."

A spot of color appeared instantly in Emma's cheeks, but she would not let herself be flustered. She stepped forward, hand extended as though holding court. "Mr. Doniphan, it is a pleasure to have you in our home. Do come in. It is our privilege to wait upon you."

Doniphan noted that Mrs. Smith was obviously a woman of propriety. He would have anticipated nothing less in Joseph Smith's wife. He had met Joseph in 1835 when Zion's Camp came to rescue the Missouri saints. Joseph had exercised true discipline by not wading into a difficult circumstance and making local matters worse. One night, on the north bank of the Missouri River, Doniphan had advised him against violent reaction to the persecution of his people. Any violence, no matter how deserved, against the civilians of Jackson and Clay Counties would immediately result in a full-scale battle with the Missouri regulars. The two men had talked for hours. It was clear the Mormon leader had come with every intention of demonstrating military strength as a backing for his destitute people. His militia expected a fight, but they did not expect to be slaughtered, and that would have been the result had the state militia been called up. Joseph had listened to Doniphan and concluded he was right. Doniphan was glad to find Smith a cool, clear-minded man, who simply wanted to relieve the suffering of his people instead of exacting vengeance.

Doniphan had introduced a bill into the Missouri legislature designating Caldwell and Daviess Counties as acceptable settlement lands for the Mormons. The bill passed, but it was a disappointment to Joseph, since revelation had stipulated Jackson County as the place to be dedicated for the Second Coming of Jesus Christ. However, Joseph was willing to settle north, and wait upon the Lord for fulfillment of prophecy. Doniphan knew Smith was looked upon as an infallible leader by his people, but he was humble enough to be teachable when the need arose. Alexander was his match both in stature and in leadership, and in questions of law, he was the undisputed superior. Joseph took his advice and disbanded Zion's Camp. That was the beginning of great mutual admiration, and this reunion was truly enjoyable for both men.

Emma brought out a loaf of bread, hot from the oven, and served it with honey she had bought from the church store.

"Your husband is a courageous man, Mrs. Smith."

That pleased her. Any sincere compliment to Joseph brought a warm response. "I believe he is, General."

"Most spiritual and military leaders promote their own positions of power. Your husband shows extraordinary good sense and humility, despite being "the Mormon Prophet." Doniphan's stern visage had now dissolved into a smile.

Emma looked at her husband.

"I'm sure you have met a few of our prominent dissenters who consider him much less than a prophet."

"If you refer to Mr. Cowdery and Mr. Whitmer, yes, I've had conversations with them. David Whitmer was the first to retain my services as a lawyer. Cowdery must file half a dozen lawsuits a month against your husband and other Mormon leaders. If I believed those indictments, I would consider Joseph Smith a real villain. Luckily, I have met your husband under truly difficult circumstances, and I know him to be a person of integrity and reason. Mr. Cowdery and Mr. Whitmer seem to have devolved into common pettifoggers."

Doniphan turned to Joseph now. "They are stirring up more trouble for you here. I'm afraid it could turn nasty, as it did in Jackson and Clay Counties. The locals are already suspicious of the masses of Mormons moving in, and land speculators see a threat to their control. Now, with the Whitmers, the Johnsons, and Cowdery all spreading rumors, claiming Missouri will be run by your revelations, the old-timers here are almost ready to fight. The governor feels the pressure to appease his constituency. At the first sign of violence, he will presume your people are the troublemakers. He'll remember earlier confrontations, and I'm afraid there will be no more mercy."

Joseph was not surprised. "We will not invite a fight, but I can tell you now, the saints are sick of persecution. We are the most peaceable of people, but we will not suffer again in silence. Where was mercy in Jackson and Clay Counties? You saw our people. They were starved, destitute, freezing, homeless. Sometimes a man has to stand up for his God-given rights. Some things are worth dying for. We will not be forced from our homes again."

Doniphan observed Joseph's wife, apparently expecting a child. Three small children had entered the front room during their father's impassioned remarks. Now they stood beside their mother, staring solemnly at Joseph and at him.

"I am trying to help you, Mr. Smith. . . help you to counteract the damage your erstwhile friends are doing to your reputation. But the old-timers are saying they won't allow Mormons to vote themselves into office. They also say the Mormons are not confining themselves as was stipulated, but are over-running the surrounding counties as well. You can't let that happen."

"I can't control it! Wagon trains come here every day, but I don't know everyone who leaves the company and settles outside our area. Our people are mostly farmers. They want enough land to cultivate and to make a good living, the same as others do. So they creep farther and farther out."

"How many more people are we to expect will move here?"

"I honestly don't know. Converts across the nation and from Europe and Canada want to gather here with us."

Doniphan shook his head. "I'm not sure we can accommodate all your growth. The legislature will not appoint more land for Mormons."

"The Lord has designated Missouri as the gathering place for the church, so I will leave it in His hands."

Doniphan looked quizzically at his host. The man did not equivocate. He had grown in determination since their first meeting. He was only Smith's friend, not a follower, so he did not call him a prophet, but he admired the man too much to see him fail.

Emma enjoyed Mr. Doniphan's company. He was a gentleman in every way: kind, intelligent, and refined. She listened to his counsel and feared he was right. Though virtually isolated in Far West, she occasionally read a newssheet from other parts of the state. The news usually included something about the growing "Mormon menace."

"Are we, indeed, a menace?" she wondered aloud.

Doniphan's eyebrow lifted as he considered her question. "You, Madam, in particular, I deem to be a formidable menace to the state of Missouri. . . for you are a lady! You will civilize us, I'm afraid. You and your sister saints will tame us with your delicious cooking, and hobble us with manners. You will grow flowers, build churches and schools, replace the buckboards with surreys, and beckon our men to your firesides by nine o'clock at night. You'll tame us with families and responsibilities. There'll be no one left for the constables to lock up, and the undertakers to bury after a gunfight."

Emma knew he was flattering her, but she smiled at his eloquence in doing so. He went on, "Mrs. Smith, if all our legislators could sit at this table and enjoy such a visit as I have had, they would turn all our crude state into Mormon land. But," he shook his head sadly, "not having had that opportunity, they will continue to fear you. They fear the Mormon power. They fear your husband's influence. Mark my words, a storm is brewing."

Emma shivered and looked across the table at Joseph. He and
Doniphan were two of a kind, and might be great friends if time and
circumstances would allow.

If a storm was gathering, Emma chose to ignore it. She loved
her home in Far West. The children were happy and well-fed, and she
was content to plant her garden, milk her cow, and await the birth of
her sixth child. Amidst perpetual contention surrounding the church,
Emma maintained a calm, peaceful atmosphere in her home. She had
to. She would take no chances on turmoil and strife affecting her
unborn baby. She would not suffer the other children to quarrel, nor
would she allow complaints of church members to be voiced in her
home. If Joseph had to arbitrate a disagreement, she insisted he take
the discussion elsewhere. She was determined her baby would have
every chance to be born in serenity. She had lost too many little ones,
and this pregnancy had already been fraught with hardship in moving
from Kirtland to Far West. During the months before the birth, she
spent time rocking, humming, and sewing clothing for the baby. In
times past, she thrived on talking over the concerns of the church with
Joseph. Now she allowed nothing to disturb her peace of mind.

Thus it was that Emma missed reports of a meeting her husband had with Sampson Avard of the Far West High Council. Avard
was a man she had passed once on the street, and had instinctively
shied away from his dark, swarthy, narrow-eyed looks. He reminded
her of a rattlesnake, coiled to strike. He constantly carried tales to
Joseph and Sidney of vexatious lawsuits by Oliver and the Whitmers,
as well as reports of petty contentions with non-Mormons. One night
in Sidney Rigdon's parlor, he proposed a secret society committed to
preserving the safety of the saints.

"I agree a military organization is needed. We don't want a repeat of the Jackson County abuses. But I'm not convinced it needs to be secret," Joseph mused.

Avard watched his leader's face like a hungry man. "But it must be! You have enemies all about. You can't always tell who is a friend. Under my plan, real friends will bind themselves with secret oaths and signs. They'll pledge support to the leaders of the church and each other — unconditionally! Together we shall purge the church of evil and help build Zion."

Joseph looked at Sidney. There was a little compound of dissenters entrenched in Daviess County, with McLellin, Cowdery and the Whitmers at its heart. They were turning the older settlers, who had once welcomed the Mormon newcomers, into fearful and belligerent neighbors. Sidney nodded his assent to Avard's plan. Joseph drummed his fingers against the arm of the chair recalling a letter from Doniphan delivered just this week advising him to form a county militia to quell mob activity. Still, Joseph hesitated. He would rather put the militia under the command of a man he trusted. He personally did not like Sampson Avard, but he would rather have him as a friend than an as enemy.

"All right. We'll form the 'Sons of Dan' as a militia, because the prophet Daniel predicted the saints would possess and protect the kingdom forever. However, it must not be said the Mormons came spoiling for a fight."

Avard nodded as if in agreement with everything his leader said. Still, Joseph left the meeting wondering if he had unleashed a tiger.

There was little chance for Joseph to ponder on it. Emma was nearing her time. She was having pains every time she got out of bed. So for the last few days, Julia was Emma's right hand, taking care of the two younger children and waiting on her mother. At age seven, she loved school, but it would have to wait; she was learning to be a woman now.

Early the morning of June 2, 1838, a newborn squall of protestation was heard. A summer storm the night before had cooled the air with hail and refreshing rain, while Emma was in labor. The midwife handed Joseph his baby son, and by candlelight in the pre-dawn, he noted with satisfaction the boy was plump and healthy, his color good, and his lungs strong. He tenderly washed the child himself, and carefully wrapped him in soft bunting. When Emma had rested, he took their son in to her.

Exhausted and weak, she whispered, "Put him in my arms. Is he healthy?"

"Yes, and look how he grips my finger. He's 'hale and hearty'."

Emma smiled weakly. "To honor our friend, Mr. Doniphan, and since there was a true "*Hale* storm" last night, shall we name him Alexander Hale?"

"So you liked my attorney friend," he teased. "Maybe he has stolen my wife's heart."

"Nonsense," she insisted. "I just think our son deserves a distinguished name, and I like the sound of Alexander Hale Smith."

"And so do I. Doniphan will be pleased. Now, get some rest, dear." He kissed her forehead and took the infant.

"Joseph?" she murmured, "Are you happy? Now you have three male heirs. Does that make you happy?"

"Most certainly. But you are my greatest happiness, Emma. You always have been."

It was what she wanted to hear. She smiled and closed her eyes. Joseph left her to satisfied dreams. Then he spent the next few hours walking about, cradling their new son against his shoulder.

Two weeks later, on Sunday the seventeenth, Sidney Rigdon responded to further threats on Joseph's life, demanding the dissenters leave the area forthwith. Emma was still in confinement after the birth of little Alexander, so she didn't hear the caustic speech which became known as "the Salt Sermon." When Rigdon denounced apostates, he compared them to the salt of which the Savior spoke, in the gospel of Matthew. "If the salt has lost its savor, it must be cast out and trodden under the feet of men." Wary of the Sons of Dan secret militia, or "Danites", Rigdon's unnamed apostate dissenters left the immediate area, concerned for *their* safety.

Later that week, Emma's Kirtland friend, Eliza R. Snow, paid an unannounced call. The Snows had just arrived from Ohio. They had made the trip in wet, muddy spring weather. Phoebe and Sidney had opened up their home to Eliza and Lorenzo. Phoebe was glad for female companionship, and Eliza's brother was so ill he required rest and constant care.

"Was Kirtland nearly deserted when you left?" Emma asked.

"Oh yes, all but abandoned. The Whitneys are still there, and I saw Oliver Granger before I left. He has done much toward settling church debts and selling off land, as Brother Joseph instructed him." Eliza wanted to give Emma as much good news as possible. She had been aware of the church indebtedness, which had almost crushed the Smiths before they fled Kirtland.

Eliza continued, "I saw Mr. Harris — Brother Martin, that is — just before we left. We invited him to come with us, to cast aside bitter feelings and renew his faith. He seemed sad. I think in his heart he wanted to go, but he said, 'My house is here, my friends are here. I think I'll stay.' It was hard to leave him behind. I often heard him testify of the angel and the golden plates. He was a great man once. Now he's a lonely man."

"Oh, Eliza, I wish he had reconsidered. I miss Martin. He was our dear friend. So were Oliver and David. I never would have guessed the three witnesses would turn against Joseph. It has nearly broken his heart."

Eliza sought her friend's advice. "My father says Far West is like a powder keg, just waiting to blow. He wants us to go north to the town of Diahman as soon as my brother regains his health. What do you advise?"

Emma repressed her feelings of loneliness. "He's probably right, but selfishly, I wish you would stay. I've missed our long talks. You can't know how many times I have reflected with enjoyment on the parties we had in Kirtland. I consider you a dear friend. However," she sighed, "to be honest, and having your best interest at heart, perhaps you would be better off to settle in Diahman. Just promise you won't be a stranger. Come back to see us often."

Eliza reached forward and squeezed Emma's hand. "Dear Emma, we will always be friends, and I admire you more than I can say. I will visit you as often as possible."

Emma was rested enough to attend the Fourth of July celebration in the town square. Cornerstones for a new temple would be laid. Their military band would play, the militia would demonstrate marching skills and horsemanship, and the liberty pole would bear a new flag — an eagle, as well as the Stars and Stripes. Emma left the younger children home with Emily Partridge, Edward's daughter who frequently came to help with the family.

Emma took Julia and young Joseph to see the festivities, which began at ten in the morning — and festive they were! They marched in a long procession with the rest of the Far West saints, with vigorous band accompaniment, to the excavation site where church leaders laid the new temple's four cornerstones. The children became so excited that little Joseph was jumping up and down, playing soldier. Only Emma's sternest reprimand could quell his enthusiasm.

"Sit, Joseph! I have spread this blanket out on the grass for you to sit right here beside me. No! You may not go to join your father on the stand. Every seat is taken. Look. You can see your father talking to Mr. Doniphan. Look! Can you see them?"

"*I* can see him. Mother, make Joseph sit down," Julia whined.

"I see them!" the boy shouted. "That's my father! And Uncle Hyrum, and Brother Rigdon!"

"Yes." Emma pulled her son down on her lap. "And that gentleman talking to your papa is the man we named your baby brother after."

"I remember when he came to our house!" Joseph's little face was flushed with excitement.

"That's right. Now let's be quiet. Brother Sidney is going to speak."

Sidney stepped to the pulpit as though he owned it. Comfortable as only a good orator can be before a crowd of several thousand, Sidney began his speech with all the flowery, high-minded, idealistic talk of a patriot. Every few sentences brought cheers from the audience. Some were waiting for words concerning the new temple they were to build. Building the Kirtland Temple was a time of extreme sacrifice, but it brought great spiritual blessings. Would it be the same here? The church was even poorer now. Did God really expect them to start another temple so soon? The faithful had turned out en masse to hear the Lord's further directions to them. A sea of humanity spread out across the grass, trying to stay cool in the humid Missouri heat. They came to hear the comforting word of the Lord, but heard instead a shocking warning to enemies of the church from Sidney Rigdon.

Emma sat through the beginning of Sidney's speech, applauding with others his many references to patriotism and liberty. Later, she sat amidst the great hush which fell on the audience as they heard Rigdon's impassioned proclamation:

"*. . . that mob that comes on us to disturb us; it shall be between us and them a war of extermination, for we will follow them, till the last drop of their blood is spilled, or else they will have to exterminate us; for we will carry the seat of war to their own houses, and their own families, and one party or the other shall be utterly destroyed— Remember it then all Men!*

We will never be the aggressors, we will infringe the rights of no people; but we shall stand for our own until death. . . we proclaim our liberty on this day, as did our fathers. And we pledge this day to one another, our fortunes, our lives, and our sacred honors, to be delivered from the persecutions which we have had to endure for the last nine years. . . We this day then proclaim ourselves free, with a purpose and a determination that never can be broken, — no never! no never!! NO NEVER!!!"

Shouts of hosannas began. Individuals waved their hats. Emma looked on in astonishment. People were standing and cheering! She quickly glanced at the stand. Her husband was standing as well, loudly shouting his approval. Even Doniphan and other Missouri officials in attendance, not members of the church, were applauding the speech. Her stomach churned, and she felt sick. How long would it take for Sidney's threatened war of extermination to be turned against the saints? She jumped up, folded the blanket and guided her children out of the crowd, away from the town square and back home to peace and serenity. Julia and little Joseph cried the whole way home. They wanted to stay back with the jubilant throng, but Emma marched them home in haste, fighting off premonitions of danger. She was melancholy the rest of the day.

That night brought domestic fireworks. "It was a foolish speech, Joseph! Could you not stop Sidney?"

Her husband looked at her in surprise. "Stop him? Why, that is exactly what the apostates and the Missourians needed to hear.

We will no longer turn the other cheek. We have been slapped enough. If anyone believes we will continue to suffer without retaliating, they are mistaken. I have given permission to have that speech printed and distributed."

"Oh, no!" she cried.

He didn't respond. He stood immobile by the fireplace, his face set, and his hand in a fist on the mantle. She tried to soften her reproach.

"Joseph," she warned, "Sidney will get us all killed with that speech. And who will blame *him*? Not the newspapers, nor the mobs. They will blame you. You are the church spokesman, not Sidney Rigdon! If anything sounded like a gauntlet thrown down, his speech did. It was an invitation to war."

"It was a simple statement that we have had enough. Surely you're sick of being driven and hounded?"

"I am! I am! That's why we *must not* provoke more persecution. Don't you see that's exactly what Sidney is doing?"

"Today Sidney stated our official position, and rather well, I think. If you personally disagree, *kindly* keep it to yourself."

She stared at him in disbelief. He usually listened to her counsel and valued her opinion. Now he had shut her out, his face unusually stern, his eyes direct and commanding. Intense fear gripped her.

"Joseph," she whispered, "This course will lead to your death. No one will come after Sidney or the others, but someone may murder you! If I lose my husband because of that silly speech, I will *'Never, no, never!'* in this lifetime or the next, forgive Sidney Rigdon!"

"If I am killed, it will be God's will, not because of Sidney's speech. Leave the governing of the church to the priesthood, Emma."

With that, he opened the front door, thrust his hands in his pockets and strode out into the dark. She lay awake all night, awaiting his return. He was not back at daybreak, nor at noon. She was determined not to cry. She was right; she knew it, and he was just being stubborn. Being right, however, was lonely business, and she was desolate over their altercation.

When Joseph finally came home to eat, she breathed a sigh of relief and did not ask where he had been. He sat at the dinner table, smiling and gentle as usual. No word passed between them about the previous evening, and the night passed with the children playing at their father's knee. She felt awkward at bedtime, and delayed her preparations. When she finally slipped under the covers, her husband was turned away from her on his side, asleep.

The relationship between Joseph and Emma was still strained when his extended family arrived in late July. Father and Mother Smith arrived with Sophronia, Katherine, Don Carlos and their families. Mother Smith and Katherine had both been quite ill during the two-month trip. They had suffered through wind and rain, wearing soaked clothing, and traveling on foot to get their wagons through quagmires. Katherine had given birth to a son in a small, abandoned hut by a river. A kind farmer had offered shelter for the mother and child when Father Smith sought help.

Famished and worn down by travel, these Smiths arrived in Far West during the oppressive summer heat. There was no brass band to greet them, and hardly any shelter, for the steady influx of saints had already taxed the resources of Far West. Still, Joseph managed to purchase an inn, and it was turned over to his family until they might build individual dwellings of their own. Mother Smith set about washing and mending her family's soiled and ragged clothing. Her energy seemed endless. Her quick eye caught fatigue on the faces of her daughter and husband. Katherine was young and would recover with care, but Joseph Sr. was showing signs of serious impairment. Lucy kept watch over him like a guardian angel, directing him to rest.

One August day at the Smith inn, Joseph sat writing a letter. Lucy looked out the window, hoping for a sign of a breeze. The summer heat was inescapable. Anyone outside, in the direct sun, dallied with sunstroke. Inside, the cloistered heat made it hard to breathe. It wasn't uncommon to see Lucy with her handkerchief dripping water and tied about her head. Today she had been caring for the children while Katherine, still in delicate health, rested.

Seeing a large company of men advancing toward the city, she queried aloud, "Now who's coming?" The main body came to a halt not far off, and eight officers dismounted and headed for her house.

"How do you do?" she greeted them politely from her front doorstep. "You are welcome to come in and rest. I haven't much to offer, but cool water and pie."

The men glanced at each other warily. They accepted her invitation to go in, but refused to be seated, standing instead in a menacing line across her parlor.

"Gentlemen," she repeated, "Please, won't you be seated?"

"We do not choose to sit down; we've come here to kill Joe Smith and all the Mormons." The shortest man in the line seemed to be the spokesman. His voice was nasal and sharp. The other men looked at the floor in embarrassment, but he glowered as he asserted his mission.

Lucy stood before them, a tiny slip of a woman with white hair and a cheerful countenance. "Then, I suppose you intend to kill me with the rest!"

"If you're a Mormon, yes, we do," the officer growled, but not so firmly.

"Very well, then. I want you to act the gentleman about it, and do the job quickly! Just shoot me down at once, then I shall be at rest, for I should not like to be murdered by inches."

The embarrassed officers looked at each other, and shuffled uncomfortably. The short militia officer struck the floor with his rifle butt. "There it is again," he said. "You tell a Mormon that you'll kill him, and he'll always tell you, 'Go ahead! If you kill us we'll be happy.'"

Just then, Joseph, having finished his letter, pushed back his chair and entered the room. His mother triumphantly announced, "Gentlemen, suffer me to make you acquainted with Joseph Smith, the Mormon Prophet."

The men stared at Joseph as if he were a specter. They had hardly expected to find him, much less in such an innocuous setting. He smiled broadly, stepped forward and offered his hand to each officer. One by one they looked into his shining blue eyes and began to soften.

"Now then, Mother, I heard talk of pie? Let us sit, gentlemen, and enjoy my mother's fine cooking. You are offended by our religion? Well, first you must understand it. We believe in being subject to the laws of this land. We believe our neighbors should also be subject. We do not seek a fight, nor will we run from one. Unless I miss my guess, you men feel the same way."

As they nodded agreement, he continued in his companionable style, explaining the peaceful intentions of his people and his hope that all could find ample room to live together in harmony. Lucy's pie was enjoyed and draughts of cool water consumed, and finally Joseph stood up, kissed his mother's cheek saying, "I believe I'll go home now. Emma is expecting me. Gentlemen, it's been a pleasure. Do come again."

With that he started out the door. Two officers sprang to their feet. "Mr. Smith," one cried, "let us accompany you. Our men came here a little bloodthirsty. You might not be safe alone."

Conversation erupted after Joseph left. "Did you feel strangely when Smith took you by the hand? I never felt so in my life."

"I couldn't move," a tall, skinny officer confessed. "I would not harm a hair of that man's head for the whole world."

The gruffest ruffian of all grouched, "That story about his killing those men is all a damn lie, there is no doubt about it, and we've had all this trouble for nothing! I won't be fooled again. Come on men, let's go home!"

Escorted home by the two talkative militia officers, Joseph learned of the Gallatin election battle the day before. On August 6, 1838, about seventy early Daviess County settlers tried to stop thirty Mormon men from voting in the county elections in Gallatin, a town of seven houses and three saloons. Voting, they declared, was neither for Negroes nor Mormons. When Samuel Brown, a Mormon elder, was felled with a blow to the head, a riot broke out.

When Joseph arrived home, thanking his escorts most cordially, Emma was seated in the parlor with a very impatient John Butler, who had ridden hard to bring the same news to his church leader.

"I picked up a hickory stick and came in swinging! I'm afraid I bloodied a few heads myself, but I don't think anyone was killed. However, two of our men were left for dead on the street. The rest of us went into the polls and voted — it's our right! — then we rode off before there was any more trouble. Brother Joseph, I've been sent to ask you to come straighten this out!"

Joseph acted quickly. "Emma, I'm going to Diahman. I'll return when I can."

Joseph strode to the table, cleared his papers, pulled on his riding boots, and tucked a pistol into his waistband. His face was set like stone. Emma stood holding their baby against her shoulder, watching his every move. Her heart was thumping almost out of her chest. She knew she couldn't stop him, and perhaps even shouldn't, but her eyes begged him not to go. He avoided those eyes and started from the house with never another word to her. His boys, Joseph and Freddy, looking up from their play in the yard, waved and shouted goodbye to their father.

Emma called after him, as he mounted his horse, "Joseph! Take care! Please, be careful."

He nodded, turned his black gelding, and rode off with Butler. Within a half hour, he and Rigdon had a force of fifty men called up, and rode north to Lyman Wight's home beside Grand River. The saints from the surrounding area had gathered there for counsel and safety.

Joseph reprimanded them, "What happened to the truce we worked out with the Missourians last month? I told you then that you had better all move to Far West or Diahman, for there was trouble at hand. Now trouble is here."

After interviewing the men involved in the conflict, Joseph and other church leaders visited Daviess County Judge Adam Black, who lived less than a mile from Diahman. They hoped to persuade him to issue a statement to allay the excitement among Mormons who feared anti-Mormon violence.

Justice Black was hardly the cool head necessary to quiet the furor of the incident. However, when Joseph greeted him civilly, promised there would be no violence from the Mormons, and expressed his concerns about constitutional rights, Black seemed satisfied and wrote out an affidavit stating:

"I, Adam Black, a Justice of the Peace in Daviess County, do hereby sertify to the people, coled Mormin, that he is bound to support the Constitution of this State, and of the United States, and he is not attached to any mob, nor will not attach himself to any such people, and so long as they will not molest me I will not molest them. Adam Black, J.P. - This is the 8th day of August, 1838."

Joseph was content with Judge Black's statement. He and his men rode back to Diahman. However, they had no sooner left Gallatin than William Peniston — now colonel of the Daviess

County militia and an aspiring politician — convinced Black to state that he had been threatened and intimidated into giving the affidavit. The two men drafted a complaint to Judge Austin King, with Peniston swearing that his life had been threatened by the Mormons.

Judge King issued a warrant for the arrest of Lyman Wight and Joseph Smith, and sent a sheriff to apprehend Joseph.

"I have always been subject to the laws of the land," Joseph assured the man, "and will certainly submit to a trial. However, I wish to be tried in my own county. I give you my word, I will remain here in my own home and make no attempt to escape."

The sheriff looked from Joseph to his wife and children gathered around the table. He could see no desperado here, and told Joseph he would return in a few days with Judge King's legal writ. However, when he returned he said that Caldwell County was beyond Judge King's jurisdiction, and left Joseph on good terms.

The following day Joseph convened a special meeting of Missourians and Mormons. He proposed a covenant of peace between both parties, to which they agreed. However, peace was short-lived. Soon a price of three thousand dollars was promised for the head of "Joe Smith." The allegation was that Mormons were conspiring with Indians to make war on Missouri.

Responding to new allegations, Austin King ordered up the militia of adjoining counties to lend aid to the residents of Daviess. Angry citizens, calling themselves militia, gathered. Black and Peniston issued another complaint against the Mormons and sent it to Governor Lilburn W. Boggs.

Joseph, Hyrum, and others met at Rigdon's home.

"It isn't just the Daviess County militia now," Joseph informed the brethren. "Boggs is sending General Atchison with an army of four hundred men. I am accused of raising an army of fourteen thousand men. Well, brethren, you can see the hornets' nest that has been stirred up by Black and Peniston.

"I want Lyman Wight here in Far West. If by submitting to trial we can stave off a war, then both of us will certainly submit. I have sent word to General Atchison requesting a meeting. He's a fair man, and a partner in law with Alexander Doniphan. I have also invited Judge King to meet with us here in Far West. We will prove to the people of Missouri we are law-abiding citizens, and they have nothing to fear."

Joseph's voice was firm as he reasoned it through. "Colonel Hinkle reports the Missourians have heard tales of 'Danite' justice by theft and death, and they are scared. Avard has done us no favors with his secret militia.

"When General Atchison and Judge King arrive, I intend to cooperate with them in every way. In fact, I expect to hire Atchison and Doniphan to represent us at trial. I don't want any trouble from Avard and his men. Is that understood?" Every man in the room nodded his assent.

Lyman Wight came that night to report the countryside was filled with angry Missourians. General Atchison arrived the next day and was treated to a fine dinner. On September fifth, Judge Austin King arrived.

When Joseph arose the next morning and donned his best clothing for the trial, Emma watched with trepidation. She straightened his cravat and smoothed the dark broadcloth coat over his shoulders. "There, you look fine, even respectable."

He smiled wryly, "You mean, even for an outlaw Mormon prophet?"

"I mean, respectable enough for even Judge King. I'll be praying every second you are gone."

Her tenderness was answered with an embrace and a kiss of appreciation. "Don't worry, Emma. God is my protector. My time has not yet come."

Julia wandered sleepily into the room. He picked her up and kissed her curls.

175

"Papa, are the mobs going to burn our homes?" Julia was solemn at eight years old.

Joseph looked over her dark, curly hair to his wife's troubled face. "No, dear. They are not. I'm sure it will all be settled without violence."

"Good," the little girl smiled and kissed him on the cheek. "I'm going back to bed now."

The sound of horses' hooves outside summoned Joseph from Emma's embrace. When Joseph was out of sight, she began a prayer that would last all that day and the next.

The trial was postponed, since Adam Black and William Peniston did not appear. The next day, Peniston swaggered into the rough log house where the trial was set to begin. He had decided to act as prosecutor. Adam Black was his only witness. He swore to everything Peniston asked him, stumbled several times over his words, and concluded with accusations that Mormons refused to submit to his authority.

General Atchison then called four independent witnesses for the defense. Their testimonies refuted most of the details Black had given. Judge King finally leaned across the table, squinting at the defendants and the prosecutors.

"Gentleman, this is a serious matter. If we are not careful, more blood will flow. Black, you're a damned liar, as far as I can tell. Wight, you are foolhardy and spoiling for a fight. Smith, I don't believe most of the so-called evidence against you. Still, I hold you personally responsible for the hostilities in this county. Move your people out of Daviess and Carroll Counties and violence will cease. This court fines you five hundred dollars, and orders you to be bound over to the next examination of a grand jury. That I do in hopes of satisfying the Missourians and averting a war. Now, all of you go home and live in peace with one another!"

Joseph and his entourage walked out of the makeshift courthouse and concluded that they would have no justice in Missouri. Joseph rode back to Emma and Far West, reflecting on the persecutions rising again. He squinted, surveying the wide prairie stretching away on his right hand, lying fertile and quiet in September's golden sun. Suddenly, he was mortally tired. Joseph slumped in his saddle and slowed his horse to a walk. He was still a relatively young man, only thirty-two years of age, but he felt ancient with his history of too much violence past and the prospect of more violence ahead. The election-day trouble at Gallatin was the flame that could erupt into a conflagration. Joseph's hand passed over his brow, not to wipe the moisture collecting, but to brush aside fearful visions of destruction that seared his mind. His soul groaned. All the euphoria of the Fourth of July speech had shifted now to melancholy.

Oh, Emma, his mind turned homeward, you were right. Please forgive my foolishness. . . and Sidney's speech!

Chapter Five

Betrayed

Peace was — as the Apostle Paul described faith — ". . . the substance of things hoped for, the evidence of things not seen."

While Missourians in general grew determined to rid themselves of Joseph Smith and his followers, local farmers reacted to inflammatory assertions by shrewd land developers. Land was valuable — a thing to fight for and die for. Land could be developed and used as a foundation for wealth. A smart man could become a rich entrepreneur overnight if he controlled land. The Battle of Gallatin was quickly exaggerated and distorted by men who calculated an opportunity to oppose the Mormon possession of Missouri land. Public meetings were held denouncing the constantly arriving Mormons, and Missouri settlers met in groups to decide how to expel them.

The citizens of Daviess County wrote an impassioned plea to Governor Boggs for his help with the fearsome Mormons. Alexander Doniphan, commissioned as a general in the state militia, was sent to diffuse the situation. Doniphan found three hundred state militiamen encamped between Far West and Diahman training for battle. Despite his orders, they refused to disband. He then visited the Mormon camp and found Lyman Wight drilling two hundred men.

"I'll disband, General," Wight responded. "I'll send my men home, and if I have men guilty of crimes against the Missourians, I'll give them up. But we won't lay down our arms and allow our people to be butchered."

Doniphan then positioned his troops between the hostile militia forces and waited for his associate and superior officer, General David R. Atchison. He arrived on September fifteenth and held a court of inquiry, then wrote a letter to Governor Boggs outlining the situation.

"The Mormons of Daviess county, as I stated in the former report, were encamped in a town called Adam-ondi-Ahman and are headed by Lyman Wight, a bold, brave, skillful, and I am to add, a desperate man; they appeared to be acting on the defensive, and I must further add, gave up the offenders with a good deal of promptness."

A few days later, it was proposed that the Mormons buy out the non-Mormon holdings and perhaps thus settle the conflict. Joseph approved, and an effort was begun to raise the cash to buy them out.

Times were tense, but with the help of Alexander Doniphan and David Atchison, Joseph and the church leaders were doing their best to deal with one problem at a time. The *coup de grace* came when an apostate Mormon charged Joseph Smith and Lyman Wight with heading a body of men called "the Danites," purportedly organized to plunder, steal, and swear to protect Joseph Smith *above all else*. Pandora's box was opened.

Emma, still stung with Joseph's admonition to stay out of church politics, kept hearing the term "Danites." Finally, one evening, she could hold her tongue no longer.

"Joseph," she began cautiously, "everyone seems to be afraid of the 'Danites.' Exactly what are they?"

Joseph continued eating his dinner. "They assist our regular militia."

"Why are they secretive?"

"There are so many dissenters that Sampson has to hold his men together with secret oaths. They would die for each other or for the leaders of the church."

Emma was silent for a moment. "Is that what you want? I thought you always said *you* would die for the cause of Zion."

He answered quietly, "And so I would. Yet, it is comforting to know that others feel the same about me."

Looking steadily down at her plate, she said, "I do."

Joseph placed his hand over hers. "I know."

A tear formed quickly and rolled down Emma's cheek at her husband's touch. "I'm worried about this Danite society. It is whispered that they will stop at nothing."

"Ordinarily I wouldn't countenance Brother Sampson's secret society, but we need all the men of commitment we can get. If the Danites help us survive the mob, you'll be grateful to him one day."

Emma doubted it, but held her peace.

Alexander Doniphan sat in Joseph's front room. "Withdraw your settlers from De Witt, I tell you. If you don't, you'll be charged with starting a war."

Doniphan was advising Joseph on the conflict that had escalated around the town of De Witt in the southeast corner of Daviess County. He looked from Joseph to Hyrum and around to the other leaders present. Doniphan, the church attorney, could have predicted this conflict — it didn't take a prophet, given the bitter feelings of the Missourians — but it gave him no satisfaction to be right.

"I can't do it," Joseph countered. "You may be right, but I won't allow my people to be driven. There must be another way to avert war."

"So direct *all* your people to move to Caldwell County! That was the intent of the bill passed by the state legislature. If you would only content yourselves to stay in Caldwell, you would all be safe."

Sidney gave a short laugh. "Safe? Don't you mean it would be easier to exterminate us all at once?"

"Sidney!" Joseph's voice was a warning. Doniphan's eyes hardened and narrowed as he regarded the impassioned Rigdon.

"I have not mentioned the word 'exterminate,' sir. You are the only one who has used that term." Alexander was losing patience with Joseph's counselor. The man seemed not to care if blood flowed, nor whose it was. He turned back to Joseph and Hyrum.

"My advice remains the same: gather your people to this county, keep the peace, and appeal to Governor Boggs as law-abiding citizens."

He stood to leave, and Joseph shook his hand, "Thank you for coming and for your advice. I will act on as much of it as I can." He walked his friend to the door and bade him farewell. He watched as his attorney rode off into the night. If only it were possible to follow all of his counsel.

Joseph sighed like a sentenced man and turned back to his counselors. "I agree with Alexander. I'd like to get all our people settled here, even though that means much crowding. If we have to defend ourselves, we can make a better stand in one place than in five or six."

He spoke to Sidney. "Write to Governor Boggs. Make it your best effort. Maybe war *can* be averted."

Sidney nodded. "The letter will go tomorrow, but I don't think the saints will desert the homes they have established. They have said they will die before giving ground."

Frustration overtook Joseph, and he slammed his fist down on the mantle. "I want all the saints here! This is our stronghold and our best chance of defense. If the mobs attack, the angels themselves will come to our aid. I won't see the saints bleeding and dying in the land of Zion. That is not my vision!"

Sidney and all except Joseph's brothers left without another word. Joseph poked the dying embers of the fire, then turned to his dauntless supporter. "Hyrum, what have we done to deserve this? Have I ever urged anything but peaceable means to settle differences? If the saints would just do as I tell them and settle here, they wouldn't be turned out of their homes. They call me a prophet. I like to think they believe it. Then, why won't they listen?"

After a few minutes, Hyrum said stoically, "They're free thinkers, Joseph. It's very plain; the destroyer is at work here. Satan has unleashed his power against us. Only God can protect us now."

Joseph went to sleep that night and dreamed that a great storm was gathering. A heavy downpour outside coincided with the devastating flood in his dreams. After tossing and turning all night, he awoke the next morning with Emma's arms around him.

"Emma, the saints will be murdered if they don't gather to Caldwell County."

"Where can we put them?" the practical Emma asked. "Far West is crowded already."

"I must search for other land we can purchase."

"Oh Joseph! I'm afraid to have you riding about the countryside. It is so infested with mob sympathizers you could be shot!"

"The saints in outlying areas will certainly be killed if I don't find land they can occupy. I have to try…"

Joseph left later that morning with a few trusted friends, and rode out searching for available land to settle. He rode with a prayer in his heart for the scattered sheep of Zion.

At Joseph's insistence, the evacuation of the De Witt settlement began on October 11, 1838. Governor Boggs had answered Sidney's appeal for arbitration with a terse, "Let them fight it out." The governor's attitude emboldened mob forces. General Parks of the state militia found he could barely control his men, even as a pitiable train of wagons started for Far West under a white flag of truce.

Colonel George M. Hinkle oversaw the migration. The desperately poor saints left behind many possessions in order to escape with their lives. Chilly October winds spoke of winter coming on, and most of them could boast no more than a wagon to shield the women and children from the cold. Joseph rode out to meet them, his heart and his eyes smarting with sympathy.

The people of Far West opened their arms when the saints from surrounding counties crept into the isolated settlement, tired, hungry, but safe, and few complained, though they were forced to camp in their wagons or tents. Food was scarce, and the whole town resorted to a diet consisting mainly of cornmeal and pumpkin. No effort was made by the citizens of Missouri to recompense the Mormons for the homes or belongings they were forced to leave behind.

Every day Emma went through the town, picking her way among refugee tents, crying children, and careworn women. Her own home was already packed with two other families. Her small garden was depleted, and she had little to give the new refugees except her encouragement and a few herbs for the most ill among them. Poor, wounded Zion, she grieved! You have no shelter but the arms of His everlasting love! Alexander Doniphan's words ran endlessly in her mind, "Mark my words. A storm is brewing." It now appeared to have broken over their heads with a vengeance. She had rarely seen Joseph in these last few hectic weeks. He was in constant consultation with other church leaders, and had stopped telling her his concerns. She knew he didn't want to worry her, but she also suspected he was still

stung from her condemnation of Sidney's speech, which he had so vigorously applauded. The strength of her objection echoed so loudly, she
needed to add nothing.

Alexander Doniphan had become a familiar and, somehow,
reassuring sight on the streets of Far West. Serving as legal counsel for
the church, he was also a brigadier-general in the Missouri state militia out of Clay County. As an attorney, he did what he could to help
the saints obtain damages from anti-Mormons. As a state militia
leader, pressed into service to preserve the peace, he filled a unique
position as both protector of and liaison to the Mormons. His air of
authority inspired confidence, though the onrushing events did not.
He was in town shortly after the refugees arrived, for he had received
news that mob forces, nearly eight hundred strong, were about to
move against the saints at Diahman.

"Joseph, I'm not sure I can control the militia if they attack.
Many of my own men sympathize with them. The militia is composed
of too many mobacrats. I have released Captain Samuel Bogart, a local
Methodist minister, from duty for his sympathies are so much with
the mob he cannot be trusted. You'd better place Colonel Hinkle's
forces on guard around the borders of your county and town until I
can summon more state troops from Clay to enforce order."

"What can our enemies complain of now that we have withdrawn from the outlying counties? We are on the land the state designated for us."

Doniphan gave a short, humorless laugh. "You still hold land
in Daviess County around Diahman which the Missourians want for
themselves. The government land sales will be finalized soon. If they
can drive you out before that happens, they can secure that land for
themselves. My associate, Atchison, and I have importuned Governor

Boggs to come here. His presence could quell the mob violence. But he refuses. It would seem other matters are more important than the deaths of innocent people."

Joseph's hollow-eyed gaze never wavered. "Are we to be murdered where we stand?"

"Not while I can defend you. But how long that will be, I do not know."

"Then, by Almighty God, blood will flow, for we will die as our forefathers died, for freedom! No unhallowed hand can take that from us! We have tried to appeal to the law, but it is always administered against us. We have given so much; we cannot give more. I care not how many mobacrats come against us."

Following Doniphan's advice, Colonel Hinkle arranged for Mormon militia to guard the Caldwell County borders and the approaches to Far West. These soldiers and cavalrymen went on constant patrol. He called on other men to ride with Joseph at their head to Diahman. The hearty band of defenders traveled with all haste, pressed by a cold wind and light snowfall, in time to see Mormon refugees staggering toward the town center. Women and children had been turned out of their homes into the cold, and their property along the Grand River burned.

At eleven o'clock that night, when temporary shelter had been found for everyone, Joseph settled in at Lyman Wight's home. The leaders sat up planning the defense of the town. Colonel Wight commanded the Mormon militia in the Diahman region, while Colonel Hinkle directed the men at Far West.

Maps were strewn over the table. The men were bending over them, pin pointing where the enemy would likely be gathered. Suddenly, they heard a noise outside and then a faint, hesitant knock sounded on the door. Wight hesitantly opened it, and was dumbfounded at the sight of Joseph's sister-in-law, Agnes Smith, wet and shivering before him. A year-and-a-half old child clung tightly about her neck, and in the crook of her left arm, she held a squalling baby.

"Joseph!" he called, "See here! It's your brother's wife!"

Joseph bounded toward the open doorway where snow was blowing in. Don Carlos had recently been sent to the southeast in an effort to raise money for the church, and Agnes had been left, as many of her sister-saints had, to care for farm and family.

"Agnes! Merciful God in Heaven! You are wet through!" Joseph helped her into the room, took the toddler from her right arm, unclasping the little arms from around her neck. She sank down in front of the fireplace before the men could push a chair under her. Melting snow began to trickle down her neck, and she sat with head bowed while Lyman called his wife.

After Agnes surrendered her baby to the loving care of Sister Wight, she remained sitting with her head still bowed, stunned by the events of the last few hours. Her icy skirt, stiff from wading across the frigid river, began to steam. Joseph knelt beside her, gently rubbing her frozen hands. The young mother seemed impervious to any attentions.

"Talk to me, Agnes," he said softly.

It was that tenderness in the aftermath of all she had been through that turned shock into hysteria. Tears rained down her numb cheeks, sobs shook her body, and her voice broke with the effort to speak sensibly. Her home had been looted that night, and she had clutched her baby and toddler beneath her cloak, hiding in the woods to escape the militia-mob. Huddling in the underbrush and praying for heaven's intervention, she decided her only hope was Diahman, three long miles away.

Joseph was appalled. "How did you cross the river?"

Hiccups now accompanied her answers. "With baby. . . above my head. Little Agnes. . . holding on. . . water up to my waist. . . at midstream. C-c-cold, Joseph. . . so c-c-cold!"

"Dear God!" he cried. "How long?"

"Not much longer!" Lyman strode over to the open maps, jabbed the point of his knife through them, and swore. "Joseph, it's time to make a stand! If Boggs won't control the militia, by the Almighty *we will*."

In the days that followed, several stands were taken to prevent the saints from being driven any farther. Joseph admonished his men never to accept peace at the sacrifice of truth and justice. To punctuate this resolve, three rounds of a cannon were fired off at Diahman. The prophet's troops waved their hats and shouted after each discharge, "Hosanna to God and the Lamb!"

Joseph drew his sword and fierce determination rose up within him:

"I have drawn my sword from its sheath and I swear by the living God that it shall never return again till I can go and come and be treated by others as they wish to be treated by me."

His ardor was infectious, and the Mormon soldiers shouted, "Amen!"

But not everyone remained steadfast. There were several disaffections, including two more apostles, Thomas Marsh and Orson Hyde. Hyde had been ill, and both men decided that they had endured enough. They slipped away from Diahman and parted company with the beleaguered saints. It was another severe blow to Joseph. Still, most men remained staunch, even in the face of terrible odds. David Patten, another apostle, told Joseph he would rather die than allow persecution to continue.

On October 24, Patten took his resolve and more than fifty Mormon soldiers several miles south of Far West to prevent a Ray County militia invasion of Caldwell County. The confrontation which followed became known as the Battle of Crooked River, which brought death and confusion to both sides. The Missourians had one killed and six wounded. The Mormons had three men killed and seven wounded.

Patten was shot, and the mortally wounded leader barely made it back to the house of a friend just south of town. In extreme pain, he begged to be allowed to die, but before giving up his "good fight," he implored his weeping wife, *"Whatever you do else, O, do not deny the faith."* With that plea on his lips, the faithful apostle passed away.

The prophet spoke at a graveside service after the saints buried their dead with military honors. Emma stood with other mourners in the chill October morn and heard her husband exclaim, *"There lies a man that has done just as he said he would — he has laid down his life for his friends."*

Emma prayed fervently that no more such sacrifices would be made, but the Battle of Crooked River continued to fan the flames of hatred into a raging inferno.

Governor Lilburn Boggs had just donned his dressing gown and was sprawled on his brocade settee before a roaring fire. It was early morning, and the governor's roomy mansion was chilly from autumn's cold blast. A black servant in starched and perfect attire placed in the governor's hand a large cup of steaming tea with a dollop of brandy. Boggs didn't favor him with a look as he took the cup. He swore slightly as the hot liquid stung his lips, but it did warm his blood. Morning tea with brandy braced him for the duties of each day. As he began to ruminate the ramifications of the coming government land sale in northern Missouri, two men in heavy winter cloaks were shown in by the servant.

"Gentlemen, as you see I'm having my morning tea! Can't this wait?"

"I believe not, sir. General Clark ordered us to deliver these dispatches immediately, day or night."

Boggs was perturbed. His double chin shook as a flush spread up his face. He snatched the messages and broke their seals, while the two men stood fidgeting. They had ridden all night to get to Jefferson City, and were eyeing the warmth from the fireplace enviously.

Boggs mumbled as he read the first dispatch. Another of those complaints against the damnable Mormons!

"The news. . . reaches us hourly that [the Mormons] are destroying. . . property of the citizens. . . Blood and plunder appear to be their object. . . It is the desire of the citizens that his Excellency. . . put a stop to the further ravages of these fanatics. If some measures are not taken shortly, the whole country will be overrun."

He opened the second message. The dispatch contained an unconfirmed and highly exaggerated report of an entire company of state militia, numbering fifty or sixty men, being massacred by the Mormons in the region of Ray and Caldwell counties. It also ended with an appeal for help.

These Mormon fanatics were a constant thorn in his side. Even as lieutenant governor, he had helped to settle problems with them in Jackson and Clay Counties. He had thought now they would be satisfied with the creation of a whole county of their own, but no, they had to defy the order and settle anywhere they pleased. They had the whole state in uproar, and now this! Open warfare, men killed, property confiscated! He slammed the paper down on the settee. Well, he would not go chasing off to negotiate with some fanatical religious agitators.

His bleary eyes smoldered as his anger kindled. He was sick to death of this Mormon problem. Newspapers around the state had been clamoring for some type of action. He had a continual stream of legislators tromping through his office belaboring the

Mormon issue and demanding that he do something, anything. He received letters from his constituents complaining about Joe Smith and his followers, and more letters from the Mormons pleading their cause. Two militia generals, Atchison and Doniphan, sided with the Mormons. Three other generals, Samuel D. Lucas, Hiram G. Parks, and John B. Clark supported the earlier citizens. The situation was out of hand. He couldn't sort it out, and he wasn't about to try; his patience was at an end!

"Bring me paper and pen!" the governor barked to his servant. "We'll settle this once and for all."

Instantly, the domestic went in search of the items, returning moments later. Boggs had moved from his comfortable seat by the fire to his writing desk in the corner. He unrolled the paper, weighted it down with a large candlestick, dipped his quill, and commenced writing. Not pausing to measure nor weigh words, he wrote an infamous epistle.

Head Quarters of the Militia
City of Jefferson, Oct. 27, 1838
General John B. Clark
Sir:. . . The Mormons must be treated as enemies, and must be extermi-
nated or driven from the State if necessary for the public peace — their
outrages are beyond all description."

With a flourish of satisfaction, he waved the document to dry the ink, folded the paper properly, and shoved it into the hand of the messenger who had edged up to the fire.

"Take this to General Clark. I want him to see that my orders are carried out. I hold him responsible to stop this uprising, even if we have to exterminate *every* Mormon. Is that understood?"

"Yes, sir, Governor!" With a smart salute, the messengers left and began the hard ride back to Clark's headquarters.

Unfortunately, for the Mormons, they made an unscheduled stop along the way.

Captain Nehemiah Comstock, Missouri militia commander, blinked when he learned of the governor's "extermination order." He was encamped with his army of four hundred Missourians just over a rolling ridge south of the Mormon settlement of Haun's Mill. Upon seeing this encampment of militia, the two messengers turned their horses in and shared the message intended for General Clark.

Apparently the menace was worse than he had first thought. These Mormons had declared war on the citizens of Missouri. Rage flared in the commander. He had just promised the Mormons peace the day before. Now this! The couriers to General Clark continued north with the governor's message, while Captain Comstock marched through the camp and ordered his men to prepare for battle.

Ironically, it was an unusually pleasant, sunny day for late October, and the modest Mormon settlement of Haun's Mill was bustling with the work of gathering winter supplies. There was a grist-mill, a sawmill, a blacksmith shop, and about ten cabins built along the banks of Shoal Creek. Joseph had repeatedly warned Jacob Haun and the members of his settlement to gather to Far West, but was met with objections.

"The settlers will lose all their homes and crops, if we abandon them to the mob," Jacob countered.

Joseph shook his head, his dream of the flood coming back to haunt him. "You had much better lose your property than your lives, Brother Haun. If your people will just hearken to me, they will all be safe."

Jacob rubbed his bristly black beard. "I'll tell 'em. But I think we can stay and use the blacksmith shop for protection if we should be attacked. It's sturdy, and I think we'd be safe there."

Emma watched as her husband's shoulders slumped and he turned away saying, "Jacob Haun, you are at liberty to do so if you think best."

Jacob shuffled uncomfortably a moment, then said goodbye and ducked out the door. Joseph shrugged, "That man didn't come for counsel. He just wanted me to tell him to do as he pleased, so I did. If I had commanded the settlers to move here, they would have called me a tyrant. Men have their agency to hearken or not. May God have mercy on them."

Joseph's nightmare became a reality for Emma when she learned from him the grisly details of what had happened October 30 at Haun's Mill. She grew weak in the knees as she sat down to listen to her husband's narrative.

"The slaughter at Haun's Mill was not a battle, it was a massacre. Two hundred and forty men gleefully followed Captain Comstock's command to 'shoot everything wearing breeches, and shoot to kill.'"

Joseph's voice sounded tired and old as he told of the tragedy, "Old Thomas McBride, white-haired and gnarled, a veteran of the American Revolution, appealed for quarter, handed over his pistol, as commanded, and was promptly shot to death with it. His slayer hacked the old man's body to pieces with a corn cutter, then he joined the other men, who were firing into the blacksmith shop." Emma's faced blanched and she could hardly breathe.

"Warren Smith, not even a member of the church, was shot down during an attempt to call a truce. They sent their women into the woods for cover and tried to raise a white flag, calling out, 'Quarter, quarter!' No quarter was given. Anything moving, breeches or not, was fair game. Amanda Smith managed to drag her little girls into the woods to hide. A dress she had been washing fell over a log and twenty bullets riddled it within seconds. 'Oh God,' she implored, 'Save my husband and boys!'

"The blacksmith shop was little more than a shooting gallery. The raiders surrounded it, shrieking like fiends. Through open chinks and cracks in the walls, the mobacrats simply fired at will into the shop where most of the men and boys had gathered. Finally, with all the men inside dead or wounded, the attackers threw open the door. A few small, pitiful boys huddled inside. Sardius Smith was one. While his mother and sisters hid and prayed, a Missourian put his gun to the boy's head and pulled the trigger. Amanda found the boy so mutilated she scarcely recognized him. As she cradled his lifeless body, she heard the moans of her other son, seven-year-old Alma. Her oldest son, Willard, brought the boy to her."

Joseph paused in this horrible narrative. His hand went up to his heart as though to ward off the pain. Finally he choked out, "When Amanda discovered he had been shot in the side, his blood flowing, his hip completely shot away, she cried, 'O God, why did we not listen to the prophet?'"

Emma's sobs expressed Joseph's unfathomable grief. He finished his report, comforted his wife, even while needing comfort himself. He sank beside her chair, his head resting in her lap. When a runner arrived at the Smith cabin to summon the prophet to an emergency council meeting at Sidney Rigdon's home, it was all he could do to tear himself from Emma's calming touch to attend to business.

"General Lucas and two thousand men are marching to Far West with orders to slaughter us all!" Reed Peck burst into Sidney's home where members of a special council had gathered to discuss further repercussions of the Battle of Crooked River.

"Lucas!" they exclaimed with one voice. Samuel Lucas was a bitter enemy. He had been behind the abuse of Edward Partridge back in Jackson County, when Lucas was just a judge. Now he was a commander of militia-mob forces, and his hatred of Mormons had not softened.

Porter Rockwell, Joseph's self-proclaimed bodyguard, jerked his head in affirmation. "Yep. Lucas is on the march here, and General Doniphan and his five hundred men are camped just a mile away. Our own men have been spying on them. They're the same Missouri pukes that drove us out before."

Far away, deep rolls of thunder underscored the dire report. The little band of men looked at one another grimly.

"If Doniphan retains local command, it may not be as bad as we think." Joseph grasped at a straw of hope.

"But Doniphan will shortly be joined by Lucas, and he is superior, both in rank and numbers. I tell you they are here to surround us," Peck stated emphatically.

"Damn Lucas!" Rigdon swore. "They won't kill us without a fight. We will *never — no, never —* give in!"

Joseph fixed a stare upon his counselor. Unlike Emma, he could not blame this on Sidney. All the events that had transpired had brought them to this point — the race for land, the migration of thousands of converts, rash words and rash acts — had stoked the fire. Once again he thought back to the Fourth of July speech, which he had endorsed as a warning to the Missourians. He had been almost as bellicose as Sidney. It had all sounded fine and brave in the bright sunlight of a peaceful July, but it had helped to bring this tempest down on their heads.

"Brethren, we haven't much time. What we do have, we must use in strengthening our defenses. Gather the men. George, Brigham, call up your militia companies. Create defenses with timber and wagons. Bring your wives and children here to Sidney's. It is the most secure building we have. Then gather pistols, muskets, powder and shot. We will make a show of force to General Lucas. The law will not protect us. So we will fight, and what we lack, God will provide. He will fight our battles for us!"

George and Brigham left immediately, and Joseph rode home. Emma came out to greet him as he dismounted.

"I heard there is an army marching on us."

"Yes. Lucas wasn't content with driving us out of Jackson County. He's determined to drive us out of Missouri. There's one ray of hope. General Doniphan is in command of a sizeable army close to Far West. Most of his troops are really mobacrats, but we know he is honorable."

"Will there be a battle?"

As much as he would have liked to spare her, he could not. "Probably."

She drew a sharp breath, her hand at her throat. For a moment he thought she might remind him of the argument they had had months before. But no, she uttered no reproach. Her eyes searched the sky, the trees, the clouds, the ground, then they closed, and she rocked back on her heels. She clutched at her husband's shirt, and he gripped her wrists to steady her.

"Emma," his voice was rougher than he intended. "Can you gather our family to Sidney's house for protection?"

"Yes."

"Then do it quickly. I can't stay. I'm needed elsewhere." He started to remount, but her cry stopped him.

"Joseph! For pity's sake, can you not give us one moment?"

His resolve broke, and he turned back to his wife. Pulling her into his arms, he kissed her forehead, her hair, her neck. Fear and concern gave crushing strength to his embrace.

"I love you so, Emma."

"And I love you," she sobbed." Come back to me. The children need you. I need you!"

"I'll come back."

"Promise?"

"I promise." He tore himself away, remounted his horse, and rode to where the men were mustering into military companies.

Wildfire rumors had already spread, and anxieties had turned to terror. Some women helped in overturning wagons and erecting barricades. Caution became everyone's watchword, and vigilance, the order of the day.

Joseph climbed onto an overturned wagon and looked over the ragged and ill-equipped militia of Far West. These were husbands and fathers who had come to Missouri looking for Zion. What could he say to give them courage?

"My friends," his voice rang out with confidence he hardly felt. "It is our God-given right as citizens of these United States to live on this land as we see fit. If the people of Missouri will not leave us in peace, we must call upon the strength of God and his angels to fight our battles. Show them the broad side of courage, boys!"

Joseph jumped down as a cry of support went up. He infused the band of men with determination, marching at their head. Sidney fell in beside him, his pistol tucked into his waistband, his rifle over his shoulder. They passed Hyrum's cabin, where he lay too ill with fever and chills to get out of bed. Mary saw the army pass by and told Hyrum the saints were going to war as Israel of old. Even at that news, he could scarcely lift his head from the pillow.

Joseph and the militia marched to the open prairie south of the town. They formed a line, single file, spacing out as far as possible. Doniphan's aide-de-camp rode back and told his general the Mormons had fifteen hundred men and they were prepared to fight.

Doniphan barked, "There'll be no fight! Our orders are to keep the peace!"

"Yes sir," his aide replied and retired, muttering, "It'll be a different story when Lucas gets here."

Alexander Doniphan sat in his tent pondering the governor's order of extermination, which he had received. He took up his pen and wrote a quick note to Boggs stating he would respect-fully disregard the latter part of his directive, since extermination was illegal. He had just finished the message when his aide again appeared and asked if he would see a Mormon messenger, Reed Peck. Doniphan sat upon his cot, exhausted with the month-long effort of keeping his men under control. He motioned to bring the man in.

"General Doniphan, I have a note from President Joseph Smith."

Doniphan held out his hand impatiently. He opened the note, which was obviously hastily written. It was in Joseph's own hand, requesting a meeting the next morning to see what could be done to avert bloodshed. He passed a hand over his brow and shook his head. Evidently, Joseph knew nothing of the governor's extermination order. A feeling of cold despair ran through him. Good heavens, what could they do now? The order was a command to murder the man who had become his friend, and slaughter a people besmirched by lies and exaggerations. Boggs knew nothing except the hearsay contained in dozens of letters accusing the Mormons of every heinous crime. Doniphan knew better, but he seemed to be the only one who sided with the saints. He prayed silently that his friend and law associate, General Atchison, would come in command instead of Lucas. If so, bloodshed might be averted.

"Tell Mr. Smith that any idea of giving battle will be useless. I have a sizeable command of thirteen hundred men — all of them spoiling for a fight — and Generals Lucas and Atchison are just a few hours away with armies of two thousand more. We will parley at eight o'clock tomorrow morning. He must send his duly-commissioned, ranking state militia officer, and any other representative appointed to negotiate."

Peck rode back to Joseph's camp. He arrived at the same time Colonel Hinkle did. Hinkle rode alongside the line of men in battle position and cursed under his breath.

"Damned foolhardy stand! It'll be a slaughter!" Then swinging down from his horse in front of Joseph, he accosted the prophet.

"Every available male is positioned here in front of the city! Suppose we are attacked from the rear? This is a position of extreme vulnerability. I protest! I vehemently protest!"

Joseph's face was impassive. "I ordered this show of strength."

"With due respect, sir, you are not a military strategist. I highly advise a position with greater protection. This invites attack and certain massacre."

Joseph stood up. He did not normally use his height to intimidate, however, at six feet two inches, he towered over Hinkle, and in the amber glow of the setting sun the prophet appeared as immoveable as stone.

"With *due respect* to your military experience, I stand firm. You may retire, for I am in command here."

Silence hung between them for a full minute. Hinkle's angry gaze was locked with Joseph's steely resolve. Abruptly the colonel saluted his commander, remounted his horse, and rode back into Far West. If Joseph Smith wants my help, he will have to ask for it, the insulted Hinkle resolved.

Peck approached Joseph. "Sir, I have spoken with General Doniphan. Two thousand more men, mostly mob sympathizers, are approaching under Atchison and Lucas. He has agreed to confer with our military negotiators tomorrow morning at eight o'clock."

Joseph made no response. He seemed lost in thought. Peck paused then added, "Colonel Lyman Wight is also on his way here from Diahman with a company of men."

"How many?" Joseph asked somberly.

Peck scrubbed his sleeve across his brow, looked at Joseph from deep-set eyes, tired from lack of sleep. "One hundred and fifty, sir."

After a moment, Joseph said, "Notify John Corrill, William Phelps, Arthur Morrison that they will meet in the morning with General Doniphan Oh, Brother Peck. . . and yourself."

"President Smith, the general stipulated we must have our ranking, *duly-commissioned*, state militia officer there."

"All right. I'll send Colonel Hinkle as well, and instruct him to sue for peace at *any* cost."

"Yes, sir. I'll notify the men."

Joseph sent Brigham down the line with word to fall back to the town's defense barricade. Details of men were organized to work through the night building up the fortifications and standing guard.

Joseph didn't sleep that night. He lay staring into the overcast sky, praying for revelation. Never had the heavens seemed so dark. No stars winked to reassure him of a heavenly presence. No moon penetrated the foreboding clouds. The only light came from enemy fires down by Goose Creek. The situation looked hopeless. He had the lives of thousands of faithful followers, not to mention his own family, resting on his inspiration from God. And pray as he might, no revelation illuminated his soul. No angels came to answer his prayer. How he yearned to have Moroni's counsel now! Brigham lay close by, and Sidney slept soundly a few yards away, but the prophet knew he needed God to fight this battle, as he had promised the saints.

It would take a miracle to avert disaster. The people's confidence at the moment was stronger than his. There was no voice whispering in his ear that a destroying angel would pass through the opposing camp as it had for the ancient Israelites and strike the enemy dead. All Joseph knew was that Jackson County would house the New Jerusalem at the return of Christ. He had wanted to build up Zion around it. It had seemed so right, but something had gone terribly wrong. He had previously thought nothing could be worse than the collapse of Kirtland. Now, that seemed long ago and far away, though in reality, it was just last January he had escaped the chaos there. The burden of debt and the terrible fiasco of the failed economy still hung over him, a mocking challenge to his seership. Joseph cast about in his mind for reasons, for answers. Where had he gone wrong? What sin had he committed? In any case, why should the saints suffer for his wrongdoing? Would God uphold His prophet, or would this plight spell his death? He heard only the moaning wind and a steady drizzle of rain in answer.

Morning light came all too soon on October 31. The meeting arranged by General Doniphan was brief. The peace committee appealed for clemency. He told them General Lucas' army had finally arrived and surrounded Far West. Lucas would now be taking charge of negotiations, and would meet with them at two o'clock. Lucas was awaiting the governor's official orders. When the meeting ended, Joseph's appointees left with less hope than before.

The day wore on, wet and dismal. The hours dragged by, while guards strained for any sound or indication of Lucas' approaching army. Joseph's loved ones were packed into Sidney Rigdon's home, hungry, restless and terrified of imminent attack. Emma's cornbread and savory soup comforted many of the children. Invariably though, the mothers could hardly eat, beset as they were with fear and anguish. Emma watched in vain for Joseph's arrival. The men remained on guard around the town fortifications. Young boys became runners with information. Sidney's son, John, came charging into the yard anxious to report that there was nothing to report. The peace commission had been sent back. There was rumor that General Clark's troops were on their way from Daviess County, burning and confiscating property, and killing livestock along the way. Hysteria had Far West in its grip.

Every time Emma passed the door she looked longingly toward the south. Where was her husband? What was he thinking? Was he suffering? Knowing Joseph as she did, she knew he was blaming himself for this catastrophe. He would be inconsolable with the reports of atrocities which were pouring from all over the countryside. Her lips moved in constant, silent prayer that he would not do anything so foolish as to turn himself over to the enemy for the price of peace.

"Come back to me," she whispered as she rocked the children. "Oh, Joseph, come back to me."

"Mother," Julia asked, having come from an argument with several other children, "can Father command angels to fight our battles? I say he can. My friends," and she pointed to a group of five other children, "say, he can't. But he's a prophet of God, and he can command angels, can't he?"

Her question ended with a plea. Emma understood that plea. She also wanted to suppose God's prophet *could* call upon the hosts of heaven, and divine intervention would save them all from certain death. But her mind flashed back to the birth of her twins. How she had pleaded with Joseph then to ask for a miracle, and even her prophet-husband could not stay the hand of death.

"He can only do what God wants him to do. We must all try to understand God's will, and be strong, no matter what."

"But can he command angels?" Julia persisted.

"No, darling, he can't *command* angels. Only Heavenly Father can do that. But angels *speak* to him."

The little girl was disappointed. She hung her head and walked back to her playmates. Emma heard her assert, "I know my father will ask God to save us, and He *will.*" The children were soon playing again, and Emma went back to work. She fervently prayed that Julia was right.

An hour before sunset, Hinkle and the other Mormon negotiators returned from their interview with General Lucas and found
Joseph, together with other church leaders, planning strategy for what
seemed a sure battle.

"There is good news! Lucas has drawn up conditions of a
peaceable surrender." Hinkle stood confidently in the doorway and
watched the astonishment on the faces of the leaders. Joseph turned to
him, his piercing blue eyes questioning Hinkle's statement.

"And why has he proposed such a thing?" Joseph was wary.

Hinkle was careful. "He now has the governor's orders in
hand."

"What orders?" Joseph walked toward him.

"The governor has ordered that we must all leave the state
immediately, or. . . " and for a moment Hinkle's heart almost failed
him, *"or he decrees that the Mormons be exterminated!"*

Joseph looked to his faithful friends. The men stared at one
another in disbelief.

"Extermination!" Sidney exclaimed. "I can't believe even Boggs
would dare to decree extermination! Are we sheep, to be slaughtered?"

Brigham answered him bitterly. "No, we're cannon fodder!
We're hemmed in here just as they were at Haun's Mill, and we can
expect no better treatment."

Joseph was somber. "Far West was our only hope for holding
off an attack."

Lyman Wight contradicted him. "There never was hope for
holding off an attack. Not against a Missouri mob of twenty-five hundred men."

Joseph addressed Colonel Hinkle. "What are Lucas' conditions?"

Hinkle cleared his throat, drew a deep breath and read from his notes, "First, we must give up our leaders. Second, we must pay for the damages they say we have done. Third, we must leave Missouri, and fourth, we must give up our weapons." He looked up from his notes and tried to speak positively. "I believe Lucas wants a peaceful settlement. More bloodshed could mar his military record. He swears that you will be treated courteously and honorably. Then too, General Doniphan is there advocating peace."

Joseph searched Hinkle's countenance for any trace of duplicity. His heart had begun to beat faster. His mind screamed, No! Still, it was their only chance for survival. After all, even going to prison was better than having his people murdered. He looked at Parley Pratt. Parley was a brave man, and resolute. He blinked and nodded yes. Joseph looked at Sidney. All his pomp and bluster had collapsed. His counselor ran a trembling hand through his white hair. Finally he nodded yes.

Joseph glanced at Lyman Wight, ever the firebrand who had defied state directives. "I'll go meet the pompous little general! I've got a question or two for him!"

Joseph looked at George Robinson, his clerk and lawyer. "I'll go with you, Brother Joseph, even if you ride into hell."

Joseph took a deep breath. "And we may." He questioned a nervous George Hinkle. "When do we meet? Will Lucas treat us as gentlemen and truly seek a peaceful settlement?"

"He wants to meet now. He is having a hard time controlling his troops, and fears trouble in the morning. And yes, I believe he will behave properly." Hinkle was, by now, perspiring and fingering his sword.

Joseph read the signs, but ignored them. There was no help now — no help, except from Heaven. He said to the little cadre of friends, "Let us go then, and perhaps with God's help, we shall all escape Governor Boggs' death decree."

Colonel Hinkle drew a deep breath and turned to lead the way. The men walked out and mounted their horses. Joseph looked toward Sidney's home and pictured his children playing inside. Was Emma there? He had promised her he would come back. Then his resolve strengthened, his natural optimism asserted itself. He would come back. He would negotiate a *peaceful* surrender. His followers deserved that, whatever the cost to himself.

His men cheered as he rode by. "Brother Joseph, we're with you! Just give the word, we'll stand by you."

His eyes filled at the pledges of their support. The shadows were lengthening. The sun had disappeared in the west and left an eerie, golden light as backdrop for every tree and bush. The horizon appeared black and gold — black as Hades, and gold as the refiner's fire. It would be forever burned in Joseph's memory.

They rode slowly toward the enemy lines. Lucas and Doniphan were on horseback at the head of a considerable company of men. Doniphan sat comfortably in his saddle. Lucas almost stood in the stirrups, striving to be taller than his subordinate general. Hinkle stopped before Lucas and dismounted. Joseph and the others did the same.

Joseph stepped forward to shake hands with Lucas, saying, "We wish to discuss surrender terms. Will tomorrow morning do as well?"

General Lucas sat upon his mount, looking down at the man he saw as the cause of so many problems. With a disdainful glance at Joseph, ignoring his outstretched hand, Lucas barked, "Surround these men! They are now my hostages! This will ensure the Mormon surrender."

"Whoo-ee!" a whoop rang out. Instantly, the air filled with savage laughter and more whoops of glee. Lucas' men, faces painted like Indians on the warpath, closed around Joseph and his party. "Prisoners!" they shrieked, brandishing swords and swinging rifles.

"We'll see if you're a prophet! Call down your angels now!"

Joseph spoke above the melee, his voice ringing clear, "General Lucas, we were assured we would be treated honorably. We came in peace!"

The general, still astride his horse, looked back in arrogance. "Peace? You will have peace, for *you* will be the first to die!"

Chapter Six

Majesty in Chains

The heavens opened up a steady drizzle as Joseph and the other church leaders lay unprotected on the ground in General Clark's militia camp. They were surrounded by devils, disguised as men. They kicked Joseph brutally, poking him and the other prisoners with their muskets.

"Just move, damn you, or try to get up, and I'll blow you to hell!" One of the guards swaggered around the circle, jamming his rifle into the ribs of Lyman and Parley. When he got to Joseph, he kicked him in the head, knelt down in the mud, and cursed in his face.

"Come on, preacher boy! Over yonder lies another Mormon. We dashed his brains out, just like we're gonna do to you. Pray, Smith, pray hard! Call on your angels for help! Ask your God to bring him back to life. If you can do that, we'll believe you're a prophet."

Joseph stared back silently into his tormentor's rum-blurred eyes, knowing he could be shot where he lay. Just as Jesus had refused to speak to Herod, Joseph clenched his jaw and refused to respond.

Mocking laughter filled the camp. This prophet had no power! He couldn't call down God or angels! If he could, he'd better do it now. "Come on, Smith, give us a revelation! Show us a miracle! Save yourself!"

Colonel Hinkle returned to meet with Brigham and the remaining church leaders. They were demanded to surrender all arms. The Mormons reluctantly complied the next day. With their leaders — Joseph Smith, Sidney Rigdon, Parley P. Pratt, Lyman Wight, and George Robinson — in enemy hands, the saints' will to resist dissolved. They were afraid a battle would cause the death of their leaders. Lucas' army formed a hollow square two hundred yards south of Far West, leaving an opening for the Mormons to enter. The Missourians were fully armed and prepared to use cannon, as well as muskets, against the townspeople. Six hundred Mormon men marched into the hollow square, Hinkle at their head. He rode up to General Doniphan, who had been ordered to receive the arms. Doniphan's face was stern, and Hinkle found he could not meet the man's eye.

George Hinkle reasoned with himself: It's not my fault. I had to give Lucas the hostages he wanted or all the people would have been slaughtered.

The colonel unbuckled his sword and detached his pistols. He assumed a haughty look of compliance as he addressed General Doniphan. "Receive these in token of our complete surrender according to your terms."

Doniphan acknowledged the smaller man with just one sentence, "Give them to my adjutant." Then disdaining any further conversation, he turned away and urged his mount to the site where the saints were grounding their arms. At their head stood Alexander McRae, a giant of a man, with not a cowardly hair on his shaggy red head.

McRae, at six-and-a-half feet, appeared as a Goliath next to the cowering man who stepped back when the captive Mormon militiaman slashed the air with his sword, then plunged it deep into the soil.

"Take my sword, damn you! It won't do you any good," McRae bellowed.

The Missourian called out in tremulous voice to his companions, "Shoot that man! Shoot him, I say. He threatened my life!"

Immediately several pistols were raised, all pointed at McRae's heart. He stood up straight in defiance, unafraid of death, but none of the pistols were fired.

"I guess it ain't my time yet, you damned infernal pukes!" With that he turned to stride away.

"Take him," the furious Missourian cried out. "He is to be tried for treason along with his prophet."

McRae stopped and turned back in surprise. Four men stepped forward, their muskets against their shoulders, the barrels pointed at his head and heart. McRae's scowl was followed by a broad smile flitting across the craggy features. "I'll be in good company, fellows. I'll go with the Prophet Joseph willingly." And he did, all the way to Liberty Jail.

Joseph and his friends were soon joined by more prisoners. McRae was brought, bound and gagged and closely guarded by smaller men. Caleb Baldwin, a close friend of Lyman Wight, was brought as well, charged with murder for his part in the Battle of Crooked River. Amasa Lyman was also charged. Hyrum was rousted out of bed, feverish and ill. His wife, Mary Fielding Smith, was ready to give birth soon. She wept as he was torn from their home. He was goaded and prodded by bayonets for nearly a mile before stumbling into camp and collapsing at Joseph's feet. The prophet called for a little water for his sick brother. The captors made great joke of the request, as Hyrum lay unconscious on the ground. Joseph wrapped him in a cloak and sat beside him under a tree. Without informing the prisoners of the charges against them, or even allowing them to be present, a drumhead court-martial convened that night.

Through the trees and the drizzling rain, Joseph saw a light glowing in General Lucas' tent. There were many silhouettes. Officers had gathered, leaving their men to drink and riot as they pleased. Samuel Bogart, along with several other militant preachers who had taken up arms against the Mormons, were present.

The group of prisoners crowded close around Joseph and the delirious Hyrum.

"This is what Hinkle described as 'respectful treatment'?" Parley questioned bitterly.

"Damn him!" Lyman spat out. "He's either a traitor or a fool. Probably both!"

"At least, our surrender saved the town from annihilation," Joseph tried to think reasonably. "If we get through the night and tomorrow, we may yet survive, but that seems almost impossible. Any one of these drunken Missourians could put a musket to our heads, with or without orders. See that tent, yonder. Lucas is meeting with his men. I haven't seen Doniphan yet, but all the other officers are there. They're deciding our fate."

"They won't be satisfied with our blood alone," Sidney calculated. "I imagine they'll also try others. We have committed an unpardonable sin in their eyes — fighting back. Well, nobody blames you, Lyman — or David Patten — for Crooked River. A man can turn the other cheek only so long."

Lyman still mourned for his friend. "David was as true a man as I've ever known. He loved the faith and gave his life for it. Maybe we shouldn't have fought back, but we felt we had no choice."

Alexander McRae raised his voice in protest. "We had to feed our women and children."

Joseph sighed deeply. "It was the sight of Agnes stumbling in, that stormy night, that was the last straw! No, men, none of you are to blame. I thought we could make the mob understand we would defend ourselves. Samuel Bogart will never forgive us for that. His vengeance knows no bounds now."

"I saw him go into the tent, one of the first," Amasa added.

For a time, they sat silently, watching the foreboding shadows in General Lucas' tent several yards away. Only Alexander Doniphan had refused to be a part of an illegal court. General Lucas tried to maintain a semblance of propriety, calling on witnesses against the accused — who were not present to answer the charges — and quickly came to his predetermined conclusion: the Mormon leaders must be shot!

As drunken guards slept, Lyman Wight ventured away from his friends, being naturally a loner, and tried to plan an escape. He would not simply bow his head and be shot.

While he was engaged in looking over the lay of the camp, a raspy voice sounded at his elbow. General Moses Wilson of Jackson County had come seeking a turncoat. "Wight, we have nothing against you, except you associate with that rascal, Joe Smith. *He* is our enemy. You're a right fine fellow. If you'll come out and testify against him, we'll spare your life, but if you don't, you'll be shot with the others tomorrow morning."

Wight sat down on a fallen log, his hair matted and streaming water. He had not had a decent meal in two weeks. He could feel the cold blade of a knife lodged securely in his left boot. He squinted up at Wilson. The general had no idea he could be dead in matter of seconds if Lyman chose — and he might have so chosen, had he not known it would mean certain death to his friends. Wight had been absentmindedly fooling with a twig; now he snapped it with a vengeance and replied to the general through clenched teeth.

"General Wilson, you are entirely mistaken in your man, both in regard to myself and Joseph Smith. Smith is not your enemy. Had it not been for Joseph, you would have been in hell long ago, and I would have sent you there myself by cutting your throat, and no other man but Joseph Smith could have prevented me. You may thank him for being alive. And now, if you will give me the boys I brought from Diahman yesterday, I will whip your whole army!"

The general was silent for a moment, staring down at his belligerent prisoner. He shook his head. "Wight, you're a strange man. But if you do not accept my proposal, you can count on it, you will be shot tomorrow!"

Lyman spat on the ground at Wilson's boot, pointed his twig up at the man's face and growled, "Shoot, and be damned!"

Meanwhile, a few yards away, under the weeping trees, Joseph had seldom been more miserable. His wrists were chafed raw. His clothes were soaked, and little rivulets of water coursed down his face and neck. The rain was so cold he wondered if it would snow before morning. He glanced at Hyrum. His brother was shaking violently from the chilly night air.

"Hyrum is a sick man, brethren. We must all pray for him. He might not survive, even if they set us free."

Sidney was trembling too. The overhanging trees were no protection from the miserable rain. His great outer cloak was wet through, and he spoke through chattering teeth, "We may not have much time left. Pray for your souls and the poor, wretched saints of Zion. We may all meet in heaven tomorrow."

Heaven was not what General Lucas had in mind. While the mock trial convened with raucous enthusiasm, General Doniphan stood just inside his partially-open tent flap, his attention riveted on a distant tent, the headquarters of General Lucas. He had warned

Lucas his mock court-marshal was illegal and immoral, but Lucas had laughed and boasted that Governor Boggs would uphold anything he did to the Mormons.

Doniphan reached for the small flask of whiskey on the table at his side. Liquor was the next best thing to a good blanket on a cold night like this. Still watching the far tent, he wiped his mouth with a handkerchief. Just for a moment, a flash of irritation at Joseph Smith and his followers made Doniphan restless. He pulled down the flap against the rain and paced the small confines of his tent.

Why in the world did Smith lead his followers here? Missouri was the very edge of the frontier. More villains lived in these parts than anywhere else in the country — Washington D.C. excluded. Sure, some progress in education and civilization was coming, but if Smith wanted a tolerant society that would condone his unusual teachings, he had come to the wrong place. Joseph was an extraordinary man, and while Doniphan couldn't accept him as a prophet, neither could he see him killed in cold blood.

Doniphan continued to pace and ponder, but could see no way out. His was the lone voice against a torrent of accusers and assassins. General Atchison had already resigned as commander of his three-hundred-man force and left the field of battle rather than participate in a massacre. General Clark was still two days' march from Far West. Perhaps, there was a way to stall Lucas until he arrived. After all, General Clark was the only one authorized by Governor Boggs to "exterminate" the Mormons; Lucas was only acting on verbal permission. Doniphan shivered suddenly as a blast of wind shook his tent. He shivered, not from the cold, but from a haunting vision of Joseph's bloody and battered body in the mud.

After another sip of whiskey he angrily jerked back the tent flap. Lucas' lantern was still lit, shadows jumbled together on the walls. Laughter peppered with curses erupted from time to time. He knew Joseph and the other Mormon men lay exposed to the weather not far from the tent where their in absentia court-martial was being held. Any sign on his part of partiality to the Mormons would undermine his authority with his own men, so Doniphan kept his exchanges with Joseph to a minimum. But, he vowed, he would never be responsible for Joseph Smith's death. However, that was precisely what General Lucas was demanding of him. By candlelight, he read once more the note just delivered from his superior officer.

Brigadier General Doniphan:
Sir: — You will take Joseph Smith and the other prisoners into the public square of Far West, and shoot them at 9 o'clock tomorrow morning.

> *Samuel D. Lucas*
> *Major-General*
> *Commanding*

Damn! Doniphan thought. I'll have none of this! He thinks, because I am a lawyer, my overseeing the execution would lend it some legality.

He curtly commanded the waiting messenger: "I want you to return my note to General Lucas."

General Doniphan rifled through his trunk for a bit of foolscap, then hastily scratched his reply to the direct order from a commanding officer.

It is cold-blooded murder. I will not obey your order. My brigade shall march for Liberty tomorrow morning, at 8 o'clock; and if you execute these men, I will hold you responsible before an earthly tribunal, so help me God!

> *A. W. Doniphan*
> *Brigadier-General*

Dawn had scarcely touched the sky when Lucas sent Colonel Neil Gilliam to inform the prisoners they were to be shot. Gilliam was crowing and cackling before he even reached the band of captives.

"You'll all be in hell today!" he shouted at them. "Lucas gave the order. It'll tickle my fancy to kill you myself. I'll just watch ol' Joe Smith bleed after I put a buckshot load in his hide. Then maybe we'll feed you Mormons to the hogs. 'Course, that might poison our hogs. Maybe we oughta just chop you up and leave you to the crows!"

He kicked Hyrum's inert body. "This one's too near dead to have any fun killing him. Better get on your knees, Mr. Prophet. Start begging for your life! Not that it'll do any good."

The cowardly Gilliam scurried away when General Doniphan came striding toward Joseph and the other prisoners, his handsome face set and his eyes hard. He stood above Joseph and the others who sat up attentively.

Doniphan reported, "You have been sentenced by the court-martial to be shot this morning, but I will be damned if I will have any of it; therefore I have ordered my brigade to take up the line of march and to leave the camp, for I consider it to be cold-blooded murder."

"Can Lucas order our execution?" Joseph asked. "Has he the authority?"

"He has not! Only General Clark might have that authority. Governor Boggs has charged him with this military operation. Lucas is his subordinate, but he is here and Clark hasn't arrived yet. Besides, you are not a military man. You never have borne arms, you nor your brother, nor Mr. Rigdon. I don't know about the others. Wight, your case is a hard one; you're the head of the Diahman militia, so you might be tried by a military court. McRae, Baldwin, you are under the same peril. In any case, you are all sentenced to be shot in the public square at Far West. It sickens me, gentlemen, and I will not be a part of it."

"Can you do nothing more to help us?" Joseph asked.

"Not more than I have already done. I have stated to General Lucas in writing that I will bring him to justice before the courts if he attempts to carry out your sentence."

"Thank you, Alexander. May the Lord bless you for being an upright man. Pray for us."

When General Doniphan challenged General Lucas by refusing to shoot the prisoners, Lucas backed down. He didn't want to risk losing his commission over the likes of Joe Smith.

After Doniphan marched his three hundred men away in protest, Lucas harangued Joseph, "Smith, there is no reason to be lenient with you or your friends. Your court-martial condemned you to be shot this morning, but I have decided you should be tried before another court in Richmond. We'll leave immediately."

Joseph struggled to his feet, and stood eye to eye with the avowed enemy. "Sir, I am not a military man subject to court-martial. I make a formal request that you release us!"

Lucas spat on the ground, his face impenetrable. Then he grinned, "Request denied!"

Sidney Rigdon's voice boomed out with some of its former strength, "General, as an officer and a gentleman, you must, at least, allow us a change of clothing. We are not beasts."

Lucas regarded the genteel man sitting in filth on the ground. Some spark of decency stirred within him. Hyrum coughed violently, then struggled to speak. "My wife is about to give birth, sir. She has no one to attend her."

Lyman Wight offered the general a reasonable option. "Send an armed guard with us, General, but at least let us say goodbye."

A barred cart — a jail on wheels — came rolling across the uneven ground. The driver pulled up within a few feet of the prisoners. With an impatient wave of the hand, Lucas gave the order. "Put these men under strong guard and take them to their homes. They will have a chance to get a change of clothing. That is all! No farewells!"

General Lucas stomped off, unhappy with himself that he had relented and granted the Mormons a favor. He wanted to display his "trophies" in Independence before he sent them back to Richmond. If he waited much longer, Clark would arrive and take away his opportunity. Lucas had previously chased the Mormons out of Jackson County, and now, by heaven, he deserved the right to dispose of the so-called Mormon prophet as he saw fit. Clark and Smith be damned!

"Joseph! Oh, Joseph!" Emma cried out as he was shoved into their home, his clothes muddy, his hair wet and plastered against his head, his hands shackled in front of him.

"Papa, Papa!" Little Julia shouted and tried to run to him.

"Keep her back, Emma! We're not allowed. . . "

"Yeah, he ain't allowed," the guard growled. "Git back!" he barked, motioning as if to stave off the children with his musket.

Still, the children surged forward, little Joseph catching his father around the thigh and pressing his whole body his against leg. Julia broke from her mother's restraint and threw herself against her Papa. Freddy, two-and-a-half years old, began to scream at the sight of his father in chains, and Alexander, nearly five months, joined in the melee, wailing at the top of his voice.

Joseph was afraid for his family. He had already witnessed women and children butted with muskets and shoved to the ground, so he pleaded with the guard, "Don't hurt them! If you have any decency, don't take your anger out on them. Can't we have just a moment, one moment of privacy, to say goodbye?"

"Say it now!" the guard snarled. "No favors, the general said. This ain't your Sunday prayer meetin', ya know! Git yer clothes, if ya want 'em. Then it's back to your cage."

Joseph pushed forward with children clinging to his legs, found his bedroll in the corner and asked Emma to tuck it under his arm. She gave up trying to keep a brave face. With tears streaming down her cheeks, Emma fixed a knapsack, adding a change of clothes, shaving items, clean socks, and a comb. She turned back toward him, shoving the bundle under his arm.

"Joseph," she choked out. "God go with you! We'll all pray. . . "

"That's enough!" bellowed the guard, while his cohort pushed Joseph toward the door with an unsheathed sword pressed flat against Joseph's chest.

Six-year-old Joseph cried out in fear and caught at his father's coattails as he turned and was thrust through the door. "Oh Father! Will the men kill you?"

Emma screamed as the guard thrust the child back into the house and onto the floor.

"Git back, you little brat! You'll see your father no more."

Emma threw herself over the boy to shield him from the guard. "Joseph! Joseph!" she called out, as her husband stumbled off. Joseph's last glimpse of his wife was watching her struggle to stand erect, clasping two of their children in her arms with the other two clutching at her skirts.

Shackled and caged in the barred cart, the Mormon prophet was a sad sight; his clothes were dirty from sleeping on the ground and torn where bayonets had prodded him. From blows and bruises, his face was swollen on one side, while scraped and soiled on the other. Joseph's hat was impaled on a stake, and displayed to entertain the mob. The cart was surrounded by weeping women and sorrowing men. These sounds only added to his misery as he lay bound hand and foot on the rough floor of the cart. Upon hearing rifle reports, he knew the malicious troops that had scourged him last night were now unleashed on the unprotected residents of Far West.

The cart jerked violently as it pulled him back to the center of town. There he awaited the return of Hyrum, Parley, Sidney and the others. Hyrum finally came stumbling back, so distressed he was almost unable to speak. He conveyed the news that Mary was close to going into labor, and he was allowed to give no word of comfort to her or his children. His guard bloodied his back with a bayonet, forbidding him to utter a word. Parley's wife was also left in a pathetic condition, too sick with fever to get out of bed, a three-month old baby squalling at her side, and a five-year-old child wandering about the house crying for food.

The Mormon hostages were loaded like cattle into the cart. Heavy canvas cloth was stretched down over the bars while on-lookers wept and pleaded for mercy. Just as the last flap was being secured, Joseph heard a familiar voice above the din of the crowd.

"I am the mother of the prophet. Is there not a gentleman who will assist me to that wagon, that I may take a last look at my sons, and speak to them once more before I die?"

The sound of his mother's voice was the last straw for Joseph. Through it all he had maintained his dignity. Now he broke. A sob came from deep in his chest. Hyrum reached his bound hands through the bars and took hold of his mother's tiny one, only briefly. Cursing erupted from the guards, and she was thrust back. But Lucy was not intimidated. She and her youngest daughter, Lucy, pushed their way to the back of the wagon where Joseph was huddled.

"Mr. Smith, your mother and sister are here and wish to shake hands with you," a friend in the crowd whispered to him.

Joseph squeezed his hands between the bars and through a slit in the cover. Lucy caught hold of them and called to him, "Joseph my son, it's Mother and your sister, Lucy!"

Joseph could not answer. Words stuck in his throat.

"Oh, Joseph, do speak to your poor mother once more! I cannot bear for you to go till I hear your voice." Lucy's normally clear, commanding tones were broken by tears.

Finally, just as the wagon jolted and started off, he managed to cry out, "God bless you, Mother!" Then it pulled away, tearing his hand away from his mother and his sister. The two women fell into each other's arms, weeping. Someone in the crowd voiced the fears of all. "They'll be shot before nightfall."

Mother Smith raised a tear-stained face from her daughter's shoulder and looked around defiantly. "They won't be killed, I tell you! I know by the power of God their lives will be preserved!" With that, the elderly matriarch straightened up, regained her composure by sheer will, and taking young Lucy's arm, she turned and marched away, her head high.

Facing the possibility of imminent death, they camped for the night on the bank of Crooked River. Reflecting on the battle that had taken David Patten's life here so recently, Joseph strengthened his brethren the next morning:

"Be of good cheer, brethren; the word of the Lord came to me last night that our lives should be given us, and that whatever we may suffer during this captivity, not one of our lives shall be taken."

With this comforting assurance, they endured the indignities of the next months.

General Lucas paraded his prisoners through the streets of Independence, reveling in the power of his position. Curious citizens turned out in throngs to get a look at "Holy Joe," the Mormon prophet. Some Missourians were surprised to see he looked so much like a decent man. Joseph preached several sermons and convinced one woman, as well as some soldiers, that he was not the devil incarnate. Joseph's detractors anticipated a tirade of cursing. Instead, he taught faith, repentance, baptism for the remission of sins and the gift of the Holy Ghost. It was a sermon encouraging righteousness.

Later, in Independence, Lucas turned the prisoners over to General Moses Wilson to hold until General Clark sent for them. General Wilson treated them better than expected. They stayed, not in a barricaded barn or jail, but in a vacant house near Wilson's home. They had no beds, but they did have their bedrolls and a good deal of freedom. Wilson, having determined they were not desperados, placed only a small guard around them, and they were able to come and go freely. Every day there were people who came to the temporary jail to see what these Mormons looked like. Word traveled around Jackson County that the "Mormon menace" was no such thing. Joe Smith was a patient, cheerful, and humble fellow.

November fifth, Joseph, Hyrum, and Sidney were invited by General Wilson's wife to join them for supper. Joseph thought Mrs. Wilson's curiosity was probably behind it.

"Besides," he jested to Hyrum, "who among her friends could boast of having dinner with such a scoundrel as the 'Mormon prophet'?"

Mrs. Wilson greeted them with much ceremony, wearing her favorite ball gown, and giving her gloved hand to be pressed with gratitude. She complimented them on the many favorable remarks which she had been hearing from local citizens — this, too, in a town that was known for its hatred of Mormons. While General Wilson was understandably reluctant to engage in congenial conversation, his wife — delicately powdered, and properly attired — questioned them incessantly about their religion and the conflict in Far West.

It was a delicious dinner, several courses served by one of Wilson's Negro slaves. Joseph's manners, answers, and gratitude for her kindness completely won her over. When it came time for the guard to escort them back to their temporary jail, tiny Mrs. Wilson stood on tiptoe to place her hand on Joseph's shoulder. Looking deeply into his eyes, she whispered, "God be with you, young man."

General Wilson was amazed. He later told a friend,

"I carried [Joseph Smith] into my house, a prisoner in chains, and in less than two hours my wife loved him better than she did me."

Perhaps in response to his wife's request, General Wilson transferred his prisoners to the Knowlton Hotel, but such privileges were not to last. A few days later, when General Clark and his troops arrived in Far West and found the prestigious captives gone, he sent his personal aide to transfer the prisoners from General Wilson's supervision in Independence to Richmond, Missouri for a hearing.

When the confiscation of arms was complete in Far West, — and with Joseph and the other leaders caged — Lucas' militia rabble went a-plundering. They marauded down each street, entering every home, searching for valuables and food. Some of the soldiers were angry at not finding more to eat, but the townspeople were on the verge of starvation. For weeks, women had been boiling corn or milling it into flour by hand. A little cornbread and milk was their daily meal. The soldiers pushed women and children aside with swords and rifles, ransacking and mocking items that held great sentimental value to the families. A treasured cradle, a porcelain teacup, a mother's shawl — these became the army's pitiful plunder.

The looters eagerly searched out the prophet's home, certain he would have sumptuous surroundings and plenty to confiscate. William McLellin — once an apostle, now an apostate — led them to the Smith cabin. Emma had hitched up the buggy and was bundling up the children to take them to Grandfather Smith's home. James Mulholland, Joseph's clerk, and family lived with Emma. As looters invaded the cabin, Sarah Mulholland huddled with the children in one corner of the front room.

"William!" Emma confronted him as he yanked open the door and stumbled inside. The three soldiers with him immediately began rummaging through the cabin. "William, what has happened to Joseph? We heard the whoops and shouts of the soldiers! And we heard the shots! Tell me he's not dead!"

McLellin looked at her coolly and said. "He's not dead."

Emma fell back slightly against the table, her heart beating frantically. With supreme effort, she held back relieved tears. "Will they let him come home now that we've surrendered?"

McLellin sneered. "*Home?* He is a *prisoner*, along with his friends. I doubt he'll be returning *home* anytime soon." His wide grin was evidence enough of his perverse satisfaction. He followed the others, probing through bureaus and trunks. He found a roll of linen cloth Emma had hoped to make into shirts for Joseph and the little boys. He tucked it under his arm and rifled through her sewing cupboard, scooping up buttons and rolls of yarn. Then, insolently, he invaded her bedroom, found Joseph's small library and took several books he coveted.

Emma watched all this, speechless with amazement. Julia tried to grab for a doll, which hung from a soldier's bayonet. "That's mine!" she shrieked.

He swung it out of her reach. "No, you're wrong! It's mine now!" The grinning thief taunted her.

"Julia, shh! It doesn't matter. Come back here," Emma reached to pull her daughter into the safety of her little circle. The other children clung to their mother's skirts. Freddy was wailing as he pressed his face into Emma's dress. Sarah, behind her, held a slumbering Alexander, who, thankfully, slept through the whole incident.

McLellin tried to clear the doorway with his arms full of goods and bedding.

"William, why are you doing this?" Emma asked, incredulous that a former friend and apostle, who had eaten at her table, enjoyed her pastry, and raised his hand to sustain her husband as prophet, would turn on them.

McLellin paused for a moment, considering. His thin lips worked strangely for a moment, trying to frame an answer. Then he shrugged, nonchalant as a tomcat, and gloated, "Because I can!"

He gave a fiendish grin and jumped off the step. Almost falling backward, he righted himself and strode over to where Joseph's mare and rig stood under a tree. He threw the stolen goods into the light carriage, then headed for the barn where he helped himself to a fine harness and young Joseph's bamboo fishing pole. Then he drove away with the harness, the rig, and the means to make her family's clothes, or a quilt to send to Joseph.

The militia that remained tried to best each other by throwing out her chair, basin, pitcher, kettle, blankets, cradle, and even their mattresses. Sarah sat moaning and wiping her eyes, resting on a child's stool — her chair had landed with the other things beneath the hickory tree in the yard. Emma watched the debacle with no further protests, determined not to beg. Only when the men had hauled off their plunder and ridden away from the Smith home did she give way to tears of desperation. But it was not so much the loss of her household necessities that filled her with despair. Joseph was a prisoner!

One late afternoon, Hyrum's six-year-old son, John, ran up to Emma's door, out of breath and bearing an important message. Father Smith wanted a family prayer meeting that night.

"Thank you, John," Emma responded gravely, grateful for a family gathering. With Joseph and Hyrum gone, the Smith family had a responsibility to give hope to the frightened saints of Far West.

"Mother, can I go with John back to grandmother's?" young Joseph asked hopefully.

A tiny smile touched Emma's lips. Children could still play — thank goodness. "Yes, but don't be late for supper."

That evening, when the sparse meal was over, Emma bundled up her children against the November night air, and walked to Mother and Father Smith's. The burgeoning Smith family crowded into the house, making it seem small. Don Carlos had been home only a short while, and stood by Agnes' side, holding their five-month-old baby. William and Caroline Grant Smith were there with their two little girls. Samuel sat before the fireplace with Mary and their two-month-old baby. They had left their home in Marrowbone, Missouri, outside Adam-ondi-Ahman, and now lived with Mother and Father Smith, helping the older couple with the heavier work. Sophronia and her husband, along with their two girls, were also there.

Katherine and her three children greeted Emma's family when they pushed open the heavy wooden door. The children immediately grabbed hands and ran to the other room where more cousins played. Emma embraced her sister-in-law then went straight to Mary Fielding, now heavy with child, and looking very tired and ill. This baby would soon add to the responsibility of caring for Hyrum's other five children.

"Mary, are you well? How much longer do you think it will be?" Emma asked.

Mary tried to smile, but sighed instead. "Soon, I hope. The baby is very low." Then she brightened, "But I am well enough. We'll be fine."

All the Smiths cared for each other. Samuel usually inquired about their material needs, volunteering to fix wagons, stables or leaky roofs. He was so handy that he could repair almost anything. Don Carlos had news of the church members still in the east, since he had recently come from there. William took an interest in politics and never tired of discussing the illegalities of the Missouri persecution and the imprisonment of his brothers. The women consulted on everything from children to conditions of the saints in Far West. Tonight, the talk centered more around the siege of Far West, Joseph and Hyrum, and General Clark's high-handed treatment of the saints.

It wasn't long before the door opened again, and Uncle John Smith's tall frame filled the doorway. Joseph Sr. brightened considerably as his brother entered.

"John! Is there news of Joseph and Hyrum?"

Every face turned toward this uncle. John worked closely with Brigham Young and often had the most up-to-date reports.

"Joseph and Hyrum are well. There has been no more bodily harm. They are in Independence and would win the whole town over if given enough time. However, General Clark has ordered the prisoners moved to Richmond for trial."

Everyone looked to Father Smith. As patriarch, he guided family matters. Joseph Sr., now a little weak, hair thinning and graying, sat staring into the fire as if seeking light and wisdom there. Finally, he spoke, "Let us continue to pray for our dear boys tonight. Then, we'll hold a special fast and prayer meeting for the prisoners tomorrow."

Jedediah M. Grant, William Smith's brother-in-law and a young stalwart of the church, encountered the entourage of guards and prisoners who had traveled from Independence to Richmond, about twenty-five miles northeast, and listened to the guards talk as whiskey loosened their tongues. Then he crept over to the log house where his Mormon leaders were being held in chains and reported all he had heard.

"Clark has already chosen your firing squad. I saw them readying their rifles. I heard him promise them the 'honor of shooting' you on Monday morning at eight o'clock," young Grant whispered fearfully.

"He can promise what he may," Joseph reassured everyone. "But only God will determine our fate, and I am content in His care."

Monday, November 12, 1838, was cold and damp from days of rain. Eight o'clock came and went while the prisoners sat shackled together in their makeshift jail. General Clark sat in his tavern quarters, scrutinizing a copy of the military code obtained from Ft. Leavenworth. Failing to find a legal way to execute his civilian captives, he finally, reluctantly, remanded them to the civil authorities of Richmond for trial.

Judge Austin King presided at the hearing. It was held to determine which prisoners could be sent to jail, and which must be freed for insufficient evidence. King had already stated in a newspaper article he believed the Mormons to be the aggressors. He went on to urge the state to take action against them. A humorless, religious zealot, his mind seemed to be set from the beginning. District Attorney Thomas Burch, presenting evidence against the prisoners, had already proven his stripes. He had taken part in the court-martial at Far West that condemned the Mormon leaders to be shot.

The allegations were murder, treason, and arson, among others. The charges were linked to ties to the infamous Danites. Joseph sat beside Alexander Doniphan and Amos Rees, the defense counsel. Joseph was aghast when Samson Avard, the Danite general, was called as the first witness for the state. Unknown to the prophet, Sampson had been captured by the militia and agreed to supply the names of Mormon offenders in return for immunity from prosecution.

"Mr. Avard," Burch began, "You are personally acquainted with the prisoners?"

"I am, sir." Avard averted his eyes from his former leaders.

"Do you have certain knowledge they directed and approved the robbing, burning, and murdering committed against the citizens of Missouri?" Burch asked.

"Yes, I do. I have heard Joseph Smith say that the Latter-day Saints were justified in taking back what was theirs."

"Were you the leader of this band called 'the Danites'?"

"Yes, sir."

"Where did you get your authority?" Burch asked harshly.

"From those men," Avard pointed straight at Joseph Smith and Sidney Rigdon. Protests broke out from the other prisoners.

"Order in the court!" King demanded.

"What was the nature and purpose of this band of men?" Attorney Burch continued.

"Well, it was a secret organization, supposed to be the means of building up the millennial kingdom of God by availing ourselves of the wealth of the gentiles. With such an objective, we operated in secrecy."

"And you received your authority from Joseph Smith and Sidney Rigdon?"

"Yes sir, indeed we did," he testified.

"Did Smith teach you and his followers that the prophecy of Daniel - that the Kingdom of God would roll forth like a stone that destroyed all earthly kingdoms and stand forever -referred to your church?"

"Yes, he preached that doctrine, and we all believed it."

Judge King's anger was scarcely contained. He turned to the clerk of the court and roared, "Write that down! It is a strong point for treason!"

Doniphan stood up and quietly reasoned, "Perhaps you'd better rule the entire Bible treason, then. I believe, your Honor, that Christ was tried on similar grounds."

Joseph's attorney stared unflinchingly into the eyes of the irate judge. King, too angry to reply, finally pounded the table with his gavel and gruffly commanded the hearing to proceed.

The state called an additional forty-one witnesses, all Missourians and apostates from the church. Judge King instructed Joseph and his associates to furnish a list of names of their own witnesses. A list of forty names was drawn up, but Joseph was dismayed to see it handed to their old enemy, Samuel Bogart. He took the list, went to Far West, rounded up the men, telling them they would be witnesses for the prophet, and then promptly confined them in prison. They were never allowed to see Joseph or his attorneys.

The courtroom ordeal finally ended after three weeks.

"Gentlemen, we have held this court open for weeks waiting for your witnesses.' King sat back in pompous satisfaction. "We will not hold it open any longer at the state's expense."

Joseph looked at his attorneys and shook his head. Doniphan stood up. His face masked disdain. "I refuse to order the presence of any more witnesses on behalf of the accused. If we continue to do so, all the Mormons will be under lock and key in your prisons. If a cohort of angels were to declare these men innocent, it would be of no avail, for you have decided from the beginning to cast them into prison. This hearing has been a mockery."

King pounded his gavel and ordered the court adjourned. Doniphan slammed his papers down on the table and apologized to his clients. "We'll keep on trying. We'll work on a change of venue, and get you tried in Daviess County."

King decreed that Joseph, Sidney, Hyrum, Lyman, Caleb and Alexander would be transferred to Liberty Jail on the charge of treason. Parley P. Pratt and four others were to be tried for the crime of murder for their part in the Battle of Crooked River and held in Richmond Jail in Ray County.

One morning, during Joseph's time at Richmond, a sharp rap had come at Emma's door, and she left her cooking to answer it. The man who stood on her doorstep was as feared as General Lucas. Samuel Bogart, who had sworn himself an enemy to every Mormon, faced her. His hooknose was red, and his black mustache disappeared into his beard, frosted with snow. Emma drew a sharp breath. Her eyes darted about her barren home. There was nothing more to confiscate.

"Yes?" she stood straighter, facing the enemy.

"Are you Mrs. Smith?" His voice was as rough as his appearance.

"Who is inquiring?"

"Captain Samuel Bogart under General Clark's command."

"Do you have *business* with Mrs. Smith?" Emma could be imperious when she chose. Now she chose.

"I have something that belongs to her."

"Indeed?"

Bogart had already figured out that she was the Mrs. Smith in question. There were rumors aplenty about the prophet's beautiful, haughty wife. He glanced around her home. It had been stripped of furniture and amenities, except for a braided rug before the hearth, a couple of children's stools and a bulky armoire, probably too heavy to move. She herself wore a frock that was faded and worn beneath her apron. Still, despite her impoverished circumstances, she was impeccably groomed. A suggestion of a smile began on Bogart's lips.

"Most definitely, and I believe it's something Mrs. Smith would prize highly."

Emma watched his eyes. She could see a grudging respect. Apparently he had not come to turn her out of her home. He would have pushed his way in if that had been his intent.

"I am Mrs. Smith. May I help you?"

"No, I think not. . . though I might be of help to *you*."

She did not speak the retort that sprang to her lips. She just waited.

"I have a message from your husband. He gave it to me to deliver. Did you know he is to appear before Judge King?"

Emma would not give Bogart the satisfaction of seeing how important any news from Joseph was to her. She remained calm and unblinking. Only one eyebrow rose as she held out her hand to receive Joseph's message.

"It is *kind* of you to bring me his letter."

He reached into an inner pocket of his coat. "I would be happy to carry a letter back," Bogart paused, smiled widely and added, "Or to transport his wife to him."

Emma's voice became as frosty as the November air. "As you may note, sir, with my husband imprisoned, the care of our family falls solely to me."

Now Bogart's eyes narrowed, and his expression became hard again. He handed her the letter, folded over and sealed. With that, he backed up, turned sharply and mounted his horse. He disappeared down the street, and Emma breathed a sigh of relief as she closed the door.

November 12th 1838, Richmond

"My Dear Emma,

. . . We are prisoners in chains, and under strong guard, for Christ's sake and for no other causes. . . Oh God grant that I may have the privilege of seeing once more my lovely family in the enjoyment of the sweets of liberty and sociable life; to press them to my bosom and kiss their

lovely cheeks would fill my heart with unspeakable gratitude. Tell the children that I am alive, and trust I shall come and see them before long. Comfort their hearts all you can, and try to be comforted yourself . . . "

Emma read the words hungrily, like a starving person. It was so like Joseph to think of the children first. She held the letter to her heart and hastily went to find a corner alone.

". . . We are in good spirits, and rejoice that we are counted worthy to be persecuted for Christ's sake. . . "

Here she smiled. This was a man who could not be turned from his friend, his Savior, or from his lifetime motto: God and His Kingdom first.

". . . Tell little Joseph he must be a good boy; Father loves him with a perfect love; he is the eldest and must not hurt those that are smaller than him, but comfort them. Tell little Frederick, father loves him with all his heart; he is a lovely boy. Julia is a lovely little girl; I love her also. She is a promising child; tell her, Father wants her to remember him and be a good girl. Tell all the rest that I think of them and pray for them all. . . little Alexander is on my mind continually. . . "

Did he somehow sense that the baby had been sick? Did he guess the older children asked about him every morning?

"Is father coming home?" Joseph and Julia would question their mother.

"Not today. But one day," she would reply.

They would sigh, look at each other, and start breakfast. Freddy was the one she worried about. He had already seen too much for a little boy. His deep, dark eyes held an inner suffering he could not express. He needed the comfort of a father. And he needed to smile more.

". . . Oh my affectionate Emma," A sob caught in her throat as she stopped trying to wipe away her tears. *"I want you to remember that I am a true and faithful friend to you and the children, forever. My heart is entwined around yours forever and ever. Oh, may God bless you all. Amen. I am your husband, and am in bonds and tribulation. . . Joseph Smith Jr.*

P.S.. . . if possible, come and see me, and bring the children. . . "

Emma held the letter to her bosom and sobbed uncontrollably. She knew she must keep a brave face for the family and the other saints. As Joseph's wife, they looked to her for inspiration and hope. Yet in private moments — which were few and far between — she gave way to the aching hurt that seared her heart. She was separated from her best and dearest friend.

Oh, Joseph, Joseph! Where are you? Are you hurt? Can you feel my love and prayers? How long will God allow you to suffer so? I don't know if I can bear to see you in chains! But I will come. I will come to you and try not to be angry with those who oppress you. I know you do not want me to give in to anger, even against such as Samuel Bogart. Oh, Joseph! Think of me! Remember me when you are low! For "whither thou goest, I will go; and where thou lodgest, I will lodge. . . where thou diest, will I die, and there will I be buried."

One night, before the prisoners were transferred to Liberty Jail, Parley lay shackled next to Joseph. All of the accused were pressed together like so many mackerel in a barrel. The log floor to which they were chained was soiled from spit and soured whiskey. The air was acrid from the stench of many unwashed men. Parley was keenly mindful of his stomach, and prayed it wouldn't turn, thereby adding to the horrendous odors already making all of them sick.

Worse than the putrid air were the disgusting jests and boasts of the guards. In drunken glee, they claimed to have torn children from their mothers, dashed out the brains of babies, and raped helpless women. Joseph and his friends listened for hours to their obscene jokes, curses and stories of mayhem. Parley was incensed, but before he could respond to the flood of filth, the chains on his ankles jerked.

The prophet struggled to his feet. He rose up over their heads like a lion under attack. Standing in chains that chafed his ankles raw, his face unshaven, his hair uncombed, Parley heard Joseph speak with a voice like thunder that seemed to shake the old tavern.

"SILENCE, ye fiends of the infernal pit! In the name of Jesus Christ I rebuke you, and command you to be still. I will not live another minute and hear such language. Cease such talk, or you or I die THIS INSTANT!"

Parley would never forget:

"He ceased to speak. He stood erect in terrible majesty. Chained, and without a weapon, calm, unruffled, and dignified as an angel, he looked down upon his quailing guards, whose weapons were lowered or dropped to the ground; whose knees smote together, and who, shrinking into a corner, or crouching at his feet, begged his pardon, and remained quiet till a change of guards.

I have seen the ministers of justice, clothed in magisterial robes, and criminals arraigned before them, while life was suspended on a breath, in the courts of England; I have witnessed a Congress in solemn session to give laws to nations; I have tried to conceive of kings, of royal courts, of thrones and crowns; and of emperors assembled to decide the fate of kingdoms; but dignity and majesty have I seen but once, as it stood in chains, at midnight in a dungeon, in an obscure village of Missouri."

Chapter Seven

A Prison Temple

O *God, where art thou? And where is the pavilion that covereth thy hiding place?*

In the bone-chilling darkness, Joseph mused over these questions for many days and nights in Liberty Jail. His spirit longed for light — heavenly light. He sought communion with God, pondering the heavenly purpose that had placed him far from the people he loved, while they suffered unspeakable hardships. He ached for freedom, fresh air, the song of a bird, and sunshine on his face, but mostly for the sweet companionship of his children and wife.

He and his five companion prisoners were being detained on a charge of treason until the circuit court could convene in the spring. Since Daviess County had no jail, they had been brought to Liberty. Even in daytime, the dungeon in Liberty Jail was dim, lit only by two small windows, just six inches wide and two feet in length. They were heavily grated with strong bars and allowed the only light and ventilation for the dungeon. When night fell, Joseph could scarcely see his hand before his face.

The small, two-story structure was twenty-two by twenty-two-and-one-half feet. Its four-feet thick walls were combinations of stone, rubble, and log. Joseph and his fellow prisoners were confined in the dank, sour, lower room called the dungeon. The floor was dirt, and straw their only bedding. Occasionally, they were allowed to the upper floor for family visits, or Alexander Doniphan's consultations. The outside of the jail appeared almost as bleak as the inside, with the only door five-and-half-feet high by two-and-a-half-feet wide.

Joseph would never get used to being caged in such inhuman conditions. It was degrading to the soul, designed to humiliate and break the spirit. During the day, he summoned his determination and faith to cheer his friends, but in the still of night, alone with his thoughts, he grieved for all that his family and followers had endured.

Joseph usually sat, because it was more comfortable than standing hunched over or lying in the bug-infested straw. It wasn't possible for him to stand straight, for the dungeon roof was very low. So, when he tried to stand, he was compelled to bow his head. It was a prolonged lesson in humility. His neck and shoulders were stiff and sore with the constant hunching, and no amount of rubbing offered relief.

As he sat below the tiny window, hoping for a breath of fresh air, Joseph kneaded his neck, probing the strained muscles. Then his fingers found something creeping on his back. He rubbed it off against the wall. Immediately a stink filled the air. It was more acrid and bitter than even the stench of men living in close quarters with only a chamber pot for sanitation. Another stinkbug had been killed. He supposed it was better than a spider, despite the odor. The bites of black spiders left huge welts that lasted for weeks.

The stench forced Joseph to his feet. He moved to the barred window, trying to breathe in the cold night air. Sadness made him sigh. There was no moon. Sometimes a wedge of moonlight slipped into their wretched dungeon. That would always raise his spirits a little, but not tonight. Joseph twisted his head and tried to gaze into the heavens. He might at least see the stars.

No? Well, cloud cover bespoke a coming storm. Joseph shivered. He had only a cloak for cover. His bedding, so generously donated by the Far West saints, had been burned after the prisoners were given poisoned food. All of them had experienced violent heaving, their systems wracked with pains of poison. His quilt had been so saturated with vomit that it was unusable. The guards carried it out on a stick, alternately cursing and laughing.

He had sent word to Emma for another quilt, but so far nothing had come. He tried to imagine her moving about the kitchen, preparing breakfast, her dark hair neatly arranged, and their home tidy as she always kept it. Joseph sorrowed over the impatient words that had passed between them at the time of Sidney's speech. Had he acknowledged that she was right? She was usually right. God had given him a wise counselor for a helpmeet. He knew Emma was a valuable ally and a formidable opponent, a woman who could be entreated but not commanded. All at once, alone with his thoughts, Joseph's love for the woman he had married almost swept every other thought from his mind.

How long shall thy hand be stayed, and thine eye, yea thy pure eye, behold from the eternal heavens the wrongs of thy people and of thy servants, and thine ear be penetrated with their cries?

In desperation, Joseph silently pleaded his case with the Lord. How long would he and Hyrum, Sidney, Caleb, Alexander, and Lyman remain locked up in this hole? The forces of earth and hell seemed united to overthrow him and the Lord's church.

What chance had they against the combined military, political and civilian forces of Missouri? If they tried to escape, they would be killed. If they went to trial, they would most likely be condemned and shot. If acquitted and allowed to walk away, they would be tracked down and killed by mobacrats. But worse than their possible fate was knowing of the senseless brutality against the defenseless, leaderless saints.

Yea, O Lord, how long shall they suffer these wrongs and unlawful oppressions, before thine heart shall be softened toward them, and thy bowels be moved with compassion toward them?

Joseph pressed his forehead to the cold bar of the grimy window. His stomach growled, and gnawed ferociously. They lived on greasy gruel and the dregs of coffee and tea, already brewed and used at their jailer's table. What they got was days old and rancid, with only a little water to thin it down, but it was the only nourishment warding off starvation.

More recently, they had other concerns about their food. Twice they had been poisoned, and the effects almost killed them. Their captors mocked them, saying they were feeding them "Mormon beef" — the flesh of Latter-day Saints. Joseph usually disregarded the baseless taunts, but once when they had an infrequent meal with meat, Hyrum had twice tried to cut it, but the knife had slipped from his hand. A sudden chill of alarm passed through Joseph, and the Spirit spoke unmistakably.

"Don't eat that!" he commanded his brother. "It's human flesh!"

A shriek of laughter rang out from the guard atop the trapdoor leading into the dungeon. Hyrum looked up to hear the bearded, bloated sentry slap his knee and rise to go amuse the others with the story.

McRae reared his red head, put his fists against the trap door, and pounded on the wood. "Come down here, you Missouri puke!" he roared. "I'll give you a fistful of 'Mormon beef' right down your gullet!"

How long, O Lord? How long? Joseph pleaded weakly. He had lost twenty pounds from his normal weight. Hyrum was emaciated.

His cheeks were hollow. His eye sockets were prominent, and his eyes were surrounded with dark circles. Even Alexander McRae, tall and normally robust, was rawboned and haggard. The low ceiling was hardest on him, for he stood up straight at six feet six inches. He rarely tried to stand, only to go upstairs for a breath of fresh air when the guard permitted.

Joseph stretched his hand upward through the window slit of the dungeon cell. If he really were God's prophet, shouldn't he be able to reach Him?

O Lord God Almighty, maker of heaven, earth, and seas, and of all things that in them are, and who controllest and subjectest the devil, and the dark and benighted dominion of Sheol — stretch forth thy hand; let thine eye pierce; let thy pavilion be taken up; let thy hiding place no longer be covered; let thine ear be inclined; let thine heart be softened, and thy bowels moved with compassion toward us.

Suddenly he started from his reverie. His eyes sought the heavens beyond his grasp, for something had actually touched his hand. It was a soft, swift brush against his fingers and brought a surprising sob to his throat. Then he felt the flutter of a bird's wing. Was it a dove, a dove from heaven just outside his window? His soul expanded with love and gratitude. God had not forgotten his servants, no matter how desperate their plight.

And the captives were certainly desperate. Frequently, Brigham, Heber, Stephen Markham, Levi Hancock, Erastus Snow, and others visited the captives, bringing them news of the church. Families were fleeing as fast as they could pack and ready themselves. They had harvested all they could gather of the wheat and corn. Hunger and fear helped spur them on. Almost fifteen thousand people became vagabonds overnight. They traveled in small groups, avoiding the well-traveled roads. Missourians were convinced Mormons were criminals, and the saints feared for their lives.

Illinois became the Mormons' new hope. Governor Thomas Carlin of that state extended an invitation for the abused people to make it their home. The saints knew the road to the Illinois border town of Quincy well. Most of them had come through there to Missouri. Now they were homeless again, with their prophet imprisoned and his fate not yet decided. They prayed for Joseph even while they walked — sometimes barefoot — through snow and ice to the banks of the Mississippi River, which separated Missouri from Illinois. They could not know of his constant prayers in their behalf, though he sent words of encouragement to them.

Brigham Young and John Smith, the prophet's uncle, headed a committee dedicated to helping the poor families find means to leave. Brigham drafted a proposal, which the saints adopted, January 29, 1839:

". . . we this day enter into a covenant to stand by and assist each other to the utmost of our abilities in removing from this state . . . we will never desert the poor who are worthy, til they shall be out of the reach of the exterminating order of General Clark, acting for and in the name of the state."

Four hundred men signed their property over to the committee so everyone could be helped in leaving Missouri; none would be left behind. The names of John Smith and William Huntington topped the list. Brigham assumed leadership of the effort, earning the intense hatred of the mobacrats.

Brigham offered his help to Emma's family. "I hate to advise you to leave in this bitter cold weather, Sister Emma, but we can't guarantee your safety here. There are looters still ransacking our homes.

Outside Far West people have been murdered. Our weapons are gone. A woman alone is in danger every day. I have a wagon we could load with your things. A small group is leaving this week."

"You are kind, but I cannot leave my husband behind. As long as he is in prison, I will remain here where I can visit and comfort him from time to time."

Brigham looked down at his hat in his hands. He twisted it, examining an invisible spot. After a minute, he looked at Emma again. "Joseph may be held in prison for some time."

"I know," she said stoically. "But I will stay as long as necessary. He has asked me to remain until I hear from him again."

"I'm sure it is a comfort to him to know you are here."

She turned away. She knew her eyes betrayed too much. "Brother Young, I do need your help in something. I'm hoping to visit him."

"I might be able to help. Dr. Madish of Terre Haute, Indiana, has come to Far West with a carriage and a span of horses he is willing to put at our disposal. Perhaps you. . . "

She turned quickly back to him, her face lit up with hope. "Oh, do you think he might lend it to me? I would be so grateful! I never got to say goodbye to my husband. They wouldn't let me speak a word to him. Brother Young, will you arrange it? And please express my profound gratitude."

Brigham and Emma had never been great friends, as much as he revered her husband. Despite sharing many trials in Kirtland and on the journey to Far West, Emma had always seemed coolly remote to Brigham. Now her anguish was open, her love for Joseph evident on her face. He smiled at her reassuringly. Her eyes held such hope.

"Yes, of course. I'll send word as soon as possible so you can make plans."

"Phoebe Rigdon might like to go. She is distraught about Sidney. He's been quite ill."

"Yes, I know. Sister Emma, do you have enough to eat?" Brigham sensed that she would not mention it to him. "With all you do for other families. . . well, I just wondered if there is enough food for your own children. I could help a little. . . "

"We have what everyone else has, cornmeal, a little salt pork, milk, and a few turnips. Your offer is appreciated, but we will be all right."

As Brigham left, Emma closed the door behind him, then leaned against it, strengthened by the thought she might get to see Joseph soon.

A few days later, Dr. Madish loaned his carriage and team to her and Phoebe. Emma took six-year-old Joseph with her to Liberty Jail. Phoebe took her eleven-year-old son, John. James Mulholland drove the carriage. They got a late start by the time Emma finished arrangements for her other children. Alexander was the hardest to leave. He was still nursing, and she wanted to take him, but the weather was too cold. Mother Smith volunteered to keep Alexander while Julia and Frederick remained with Sarah Mulholland. Young Joseph crouched in the back of the carriage with John, both boys wrapped in an old fur cloak. It was a two-day journey of forty miles.

They arrived in Liberty after dark on the second day. James went immediately to the jailor to ask permission to see the prisoners, but was brusquely turned away by the guards. It was just as well; Joseph and Sidney would want time to make arrangements for their wives. So after leaving the women and children at an adjacent inn, James went to Alexander Doniphan's nearby home, and told him the women had come to see their husbands. Doniphan reassured him he would see to it they were granted that privilege on the morrow. Emma spent a restless night at the inn, sleeping little, praying for her husband, and trying to envision their meeting. However, it was nothing she could have imagined.

Doniphan came to the inn the next morning and accompanied them to the jail. He carried permits for both families to see Joseph and Sidney. The guards were surly, but opened the trapdoor to the dungeon cell as if to admit Emma and Phoebe.

"You brute! These women are not going down there!" Doniphan snapped. "Bring those men up to see their wives. I have visitation permits from the court. Women and children will not be subjected to the inhuman conditions of that dungeon."

Emma steeled herself. She knew her husband would be much changed. Still, she was not prepared. A stench rose from the opening of the trap door, and her stomach turned. Phoebe stood by Emma's side, handkerchief to her nose, with a white, tense face. Little Joseph and John each held his breath. Then there were heavy footsteps on the ladder, and in a moment, a shaggy head appeared through the trap. Joseph's shoulders cleared the opening, and he looked up like a starved man at his wife and son waiting for him. It was all Emma could do not to cry out when she saw his condition. The guards had shackled his hands in front of him. His blond and scraggly beard had not been shaved in weeks. He had managed to wash with a little drinking water. Around his neck was clasped a straw-speckled cloak, bespeaking the cold, damp imprisonment.

Sidney climbed through the opening and looked, if possible, even worse than Joseph. Phoebe fainted dead away. Emma and Doniphan helped the unconscious woman to a chair, while John supported his mother. Sidney finished climbing the ladder and stiffly straightened up in the more spacious upper room.

Young Joseph had thrown himself at his father and Joseph knelt down to fondle his boy's hair with his shackled hands, but his eyes were fixed on Emma. She was the embodiment of fresh, sweet, clean freedom, and she had come through the wind and the snow to be with him! Emma crossed to her men and reached out to embrace them, sinking to her knees as well. Then, dirty cloak, chains and all, they were in each other's arms, and all gave way to weeping.

Doniphan turned away, embarrassed that a man and woman of such refinement should have to meet under these conditions. Sidney gently patted Phoebe's hand and cheek, bringing her back to consciousness. Doniphan could not tolerate the pitiable scene any longer. He spoke to the jailer. "Post your guard outside. These men are not going to escape. . . and I'd like their chains removed."

The jailer shook his head. "Nope. My orders say they're to stay bound."

"I'll get another court order then. Their chains should be off while their families are here."

Doniphan started toward the door and the jailer reluctantly acquiesced, "All right. All right, but just while the women and children are here."

Joseph and Emma didn't notice the guards leave. They were scarcely aware the men's chains had been unlocked. They simply held each other, their hearts too full for words.

Phoebe could not stop crying. Throughout the long day they spent together, she continually wiped tears from her cheeks, until they were soon chapped. A couple of benches, two chairs, a rough desk and a cot were all the furnishings the room provided. Yet neither family complained. The joy of being together was enough for them.

The women and boys stayed three days. They had brought baskets of food, hard to find in Far West, but lovingly donated. They had brought fresh clothing for their husbands, which did a much for their spirits as well as appearance. Emma had some small seamstress scissors, and she became a barber for the men. No straight edge razor could be brought into the jail, but she clipped their beards, hair, and Sidney's eyebrows. The boys grew restless after two days of the prison. They were given permission to explore the town, but were admonished to arouse no suspicion or public notice.

The Rigdons slept on the floor in one corner. Emma made a bed in another corner from a blanket and the old fur cloak. In this prison setting, Joseph and Emma vowed their love for one another. Neither scoffs, scorns, lies, filth, nor threats of death could mar their faith and love for each other. God alone knew the depths they had suffered in His service. They were not young any more. They were not naive dreamers as they were in Harmony. Over the years their love had been tried, and they pledged anew, in this dark hour of their marriage, to be true to each other whatever might befall.

Now, in the late night, Joseph clutched the bar of the window, and the memory of Emma's visit was like a silver splinter in his heart. He put his hand inside his shirt and pressed it against his chest as though to relieve the sharp constriction. He must escape! After all, they had never really tried him, never actually proven anything against him, nor formally sentenced him. He and his fellow prisoners were simply being held without bail until the Daviess County circuit court convened for their trial in the spring. Doniphan told Joseph that Judge King was weary of the Mormon problem, and he wanted to be rid of it. He couldn't simply execute them. He would probably find a way to let him and the others escape after all the Mormons had vacated the state.

Joseph and his friends had tried to escape twice, but their first effort was ill timed, and failed. Their jailer had been too alert for them, and successfully bolted the trap door, confining them in the dungeon. Their second effort, which also failed, was attempted once when they were unchained. This fiasco brought jailer, Samuel Tillery, with new shackles. Their dungeon was so dank and foul smelling by that time that those confined could hardly stand it. Joseph's cellmate, Caleb Baldwin was reckless. "Tillery," he said, "if you put those chains on me, I'll kill you, so help me God."

The jailer stepped back, shocked to be so threatened. Then he looked around the dungeon. It was fourteen by fourteen feet square. If he had had to endure this evil place for months, he might be ready to kill someone too. So he decided to throw the chains upstairs and leave the prisoners to their misery. It was dreadful enough.

Their distress was relieved only by letters and visits from friends and family, and baked goods occasionally brought to them. Porter Rockwell's mother lived in Liberty, and she sent food with Porter to the prison. Joseph's bodyguard was deeply offended to see his friends under such wretched conditions and was intent on helping them escape.

Emma had come to see Joseph again on December 20, just before his birthday. Her third visit was made January 21, 1839 with her son, Joseph, Mary, Hyrum's wife, who brought their two-month-old son and her sister, Mercy Thompson and her baby daughter. It had been raining, a cold, chilling drizzle, and Mary lay beneath a makeshift cover in the wagon bed, too ill to sit up. Even Emma's usually potent poultices and herb tea had little energizing effect on her. Mercy looked after her sister with deep concern for her and the baby. After forty miles of sleet and wind, the little inn at Liberty was a welcome haven. When Mary finally rallied enough to go into the jail to see Hyrum, the results were almost disastrous.

Don Carlos Smith escorted the women and children on this journey. At the jail, he knocked on the heavy oak door. No answer. Again he rapped. Still no answer. So with the icy wind blowing and Mary shivering, leaning against him for support, Don Carlos lifted a heavy boot and kicked at the door, raising a terrible ruckus.

Emma, cradling Mary's baby protectively, was distressed by the noise and the vicious response it might evoke from the guards. She was ready to plead with her brother-in-law to be more civil when the door groaned and opened a crack. The jailer's rheumy eyes peered out at them.

"Go away!"

"No!" Don Carlos rebuked him. "We are here to see your prisoners, and I have a legal writ that says we can. Open up!"

The skinny little man who held the dungeon keys looked out at the strapping giant of a man kicking at his door. Don Carlos was six feet four inches tall, and inherently commanded respect. The jailer grumbled, but swung open the door on its creaky hinges.

Emma and young Joseph knew what to expect, but Mary and Mercy were clearly dismayed by the tiny, foul smelling room, littered with rubbish and dirty spittoons. A guard unlocked the chain on the trapdoor and yanked it up.

In the dungeon below, the men had heard the commotion above and knew they had visitors. When the tender sounds of women's voices drifted down to them, Hyrum's hand found his heart, and he drew a ragged breath.

"No!" he whispered hoarsely to Joseph. "It's my Mary! She mustn't see me like this! It will break her heart."

Joseph stepped to the ladder and called out, "Send down our brother! We'll need preparation time!"

Hyrum and Joseph could hardly wait to embrace their brother. They stood locked in each other's arms, heads bowed, yet still touching the low ceiling. Caleb, Alexander, Lyman and Sidney all sat on the floor, looking on. Once the brothers had greeted each other and Don Carlos had reported family news, the other men also made inquiries.

"How's your wife?" Lyman asked Don Carlos.

"She's all right. Not strong, but all right."

"How's my missus?" the terse frontiersman wondered.

"Sister Wight is at Far West helping the saints gather means to leave. She's doing fine."

Rigdon asked for word of his family. Sidney's face was pale, the skin sagging under his eyes. His white hair was thinner than ever before. To Don Carlos, he looked as if he couldn't live another month, but he spoke bravely, "Tell Phoebe I am well enough off. I have hope of obtaining freedom if I can get the ear of an honest judge."

Don Carlos nodded, "I'll tell her." He returned to his brothers. "Mary's been ill, Hyrum. She probably shouldn't have come. It rained and snowed the whole way."

Hyrum cleared his throat. He waited a moment then cleared it again, hoping to gain some measure of control. "Don Carlos, I. . . I can't go up looking like this."

His brother pulled a comb, brush, and washcloth from his cloak. "I don't know if anything can really help much," he grimaced, "but we'll try."

Hyrum wiped his face and neck while his brother brushed his shaggy hair. Joseph also dipped the cloth in water to wipe his own face and hands. His hair was still vaguely presentable, for Emma had clipped it just a few weeks earlier. He was too anxious to wait for Hyrum, so he started up the ladder.

The visitors were waiting impatiently above. When Joseph's blue eyes appeared at the opening, the sound of anxious laughter bubbled up from them. He clambered up the last few rungs and rushed to embrace his wife and son, then more reservedly, to hug his sister-in-law, Mary.

"You're all a godsend!" he gratefully addressed them. "You are ministering angels!"

"If we were truly ministering angels," Emma sadly responded, "we would have brought more than ourselves."

"A quilt, at least, I hope!" he said longingly. Then he wished he could take back his words when he saw the hurt in Emma's eyes.

"No," she said. "I *did* make you a quilt. I begged the scraps and sat up nights to make it, but it was stolen."

"Never mind," Joseph tried to console her. "My cloak is enough. But Mary, Carlos says you've been ill. It's so good of you to come. And Mercy, a true 'angel of mercy' to visit your brothers in prison!"

Emma regained her composure and silently vowed to ask their friend, Alexander, for a blanket for her husband. She was proud, but not where Joseph was concerned.

Soon, Hyrum's eager face emerged from the dungeon cavity, followed by Don Carlos. He crawled up into the room, filled with anticipation, despite the dank, dim surroundings. He crossed the few feet that separated them and gathered his travel-weary wife and infant son into his arms.

"Oh Mary, you've brought our son!" He laughed out loud as he drew her closer. "And here's Mercy with our little niece. And Emma! Oh, my heart is full. . . " he faltered.

"I'm not. . . looking so well, I think." Mary's hazel eyes bespoke her frail health, seeming too large for her wan face. "Since the baby, I've been. . . ill."

Hyrum could detect weakness he had not noticed before. Her pale countenance and trembling hands revealed the courage it had taken for her to make this journey. "You look like an angel to me," Hyrum assured her, his gratitude reflected in shining eyes. "How is the baby?" he asked anxiously.

"Well enough. Mother Lucy gives me her share of pork for nourishment far too often, but still the little one cries. It's the way of all the children of the saints now," she said somberly looking down at her baby, while Mercy also examined her little one. They seemed content and peaceful for the moment, and their serene spirits did much to lift the anxiety of the adults.

Joseph looked at Emma. "Is Alexander well?" he whispered.

"Yes, Papa," young Joseph answered eagerly, "He can even crawl!"

Mary rallied, seeing her husband. Refined and reserved as a proper English woman, she was embarrassed to show much emotion, so she urged Hyrum to a corner where they could visit in private. Joseph, Emma, and their son did the same. Joseph sat with his arms encircling Emma and his boy as each savored the nearness of the other. On the other side of the room, Hyrum and Mary sat talking quietly. Hyrum cradled his small son with all the tenderness of a loving father.

Eventually, Don Carlos and Mercy began to distribute the meager items of food sent by the Far West saints. The contented families ate their fill, while Don Carlos took a basket of food to the grateful prisoners in the dungeon below.

During the meal, Joseph watched his young son with deep satisfaction. He was a good boy, polite and serious — maybe too serious — and Joseph felt a strong desire to bless him. When they had finished eating, they held a simple prayer meeting, giving thanks for life and for the Holy Spirit, which sustained them.

Then Hyrum took his infant son in his arms and gave him a name and a father's blessing. "Joseph Fielding Smith" was a combination of cherished family names, which the father hoped would help mold his son's character.

"I also wish to bless my son," Joseph said, smiling down at his namesake. "Come, Joseph. The Lord has a blessing for you."

The boy stood, a little self-consciously, then suddenly ran to his father and beamed with delight at being singled out. Joseph took a moment to instruct his son on the importance of his heritage, his honorable ancestors, and bearing their good name well. Then he placed his hands on his son's head and bestowed an inspired blessing. Young Joseph and his mother would never forget that occasion or God's blessing under his prophet-father's hand, which promised the boy that he should have power to carry out all that his father should leave undone.

Emma watched and listened earnestly, trying to remember every word of the blessing. Her heart overflowed with gratitude; the blessing was replete with eternal import. When Joseph finished speaking and his eyes met Emma's, a pain shot through her heart with the realization that the promise to her son foreshadowed her worst fear for her husband.

The visitors stayed overnight, but no one slept. Time was too precious, so they sat up and talked softly until dawn lightened the dim room. All too soon, it was time to begin the two-day return trip. Mary and Emma clung to their husbands, reluctant to see them go down to the foul smelling dungeon. The men held their wives protectively, as if to shield them one last moment from the bitter cold of the trip homeward. In each heart was the unspoken fear that this goodbye could be their last. Still, these few days together had been so refreshing, as Joseph waved farewell and looked around the jail, he could still feel Emma's presence.

Finally, at the end of January, Brigham and Heber both advised Joseph and Hyrum that the Smith family should leave Missouri. There were weekly threats on their lives. Their homes had been ransacked not once, but several times, until they were nearly picked clean. Emma and the children had no beds to sleep on, and very little to eat. The Mulhollands had already left for Illinois, so Emma was alone with the children in the house. If the Smiths waited much longer, they would have to ford the swollen rivers of spring.

So, despite intense depression at the thought of being left behind, Joseph and Hyrum sent word to their families to accept asylum in Illinois. General Clark insisted he would carry out the extermination order if the saints did not evacuate by spring.

Emma left before the rest of the Smiths, fearful that her children might be at risk from the mob. She traveled with the Markham family, and others. It was nearly two hundred miles to Quincy, and it was February, 1839. She had no illusions. She had made this trip before and knew what an ordeal it would be. Every day she prayed to be able to feed her children and to keep them warm. When the clouds gathered and shrouded their way with snow, she tucked little Freddy in the wagon with Julia, and cuddled Alexander against her breast, protected by her great cloak. Thankfully, she wasn't with child for this journey, but she was without a husband. Young Joseph often held Emma's hand as they walked, looking up with eyes mature beyond his years. She was painfully aware that with every step she left Joseph farther behind. It was only his command, and Emma's sense of duty to her children, that persuaded her to leave him.

Mother and Father Smith and their daughter, Lucy, traveled with their married daughters' families, the Salisburys, and the McClearys, and with Don Carlos' family. Twice they had given up wagons so others might leave first. They had all agreed that Joseph's family was in danger and had urged Emma to leave ahead of them. Father Smith was ill and had been ever since his sons were captured. His fear of their murder was so strong it affected his own will to live. Mother Smith continued to encourage them all to find joy and comfort in being together. A few days out of Far West, rain scoured the land. They walked for three days in constant downpours, seeking shelter at several farms, but were turned away, except once when a kindly farmer gave them a dry place to sleep and hearty food to nourish them. Mother Lucy fervently thanked him for his goodness.

The weather grew colder as they approached the great, swollen border river. The rain continued, and those on foot began to sink up to their ankles in mud. Upon arriving on the bank of the Mississippi River, they found hundreds of small, hastily pitched camps — a city of miserable refugees, frostbitten, destitute, and waiting their turn to cross the swift river to safety on the Illinois shore.

February, while their families were departing, was the hardest month for the imprisoned Joseph and Hyrum. They anxiously awaited news of their families, remembering the previous year when they had traveled those same primitive roads between Quincy and Far West. Now they could do nothing to help, and they were being left behind to face an uncertain fate.

Meanwhile, despite the prayers and blessings of fellow prisoners, Sidney's health deteriorated. He was delirious much of the time. His stomach would hold little of the disgusting prison food. The inmates faithfully held evening devotionals, but Sidney's spirits still sank.

In their confinement, the church leaders sang songs, preached to one another, and bore testimony of their faith in a living, loving God. The guards eventually became almost respectful of those times and even enjoyed the singing. Word subsequently went through Liberty that the Mormons had the sweetest hymns ever heard. But, try as he would to respond to the encouragement of his brethren, and even with the ministrations of his wife, Rigdon began to fail so dramatically that Joseph was afraid this dungeon would become Sidney's death chamber.

The frequent visits from Alexander Doniphan provided Joseph with valuable information about their legal entanglements. He also brought blessed relief from the sordid, mind-numbing conditions of prison. Together with Doniphan, Heber C. Kimball and Theodore Turley formulated several petitions to the state legislature and the county judges for the prisoners' release, since they were being held without formal charges. These petitions to the authorities were denied. Still, Kimball and Turley continued to petition the judges. Then, in late February, Judge Joel Turnham agreed to hear their complaints. Doniphan went to the jail with Heber and Theodore to arrange the release, and to have them arraigned before the judge. The news was a ray of hope to the jail-weary prisoners.

Doniphan opened the door, and the men stepped outside into the frosty February weather. They hardly cared whether it was winter or spring. The sky was overcast and cold, but they could breathe sweet, pure air! Curious townspeople stood at a distance, watching the Mormon menace. Brothers Heber and Theodore were there to greet them.

If the prisoners had thoughts of escaping, they were sorely disappointed, for they were kept under heavy guard and taken immediately to Judge Turnham's chambers. Doniphan represented all of the men except Sidney, who wanted to plead his own case. He was right to do so. His eloquence, combined with his sickly appearance while reclining weakly on a cot, moved the judge to grant him bail.

"It's difficult, gentlemen, to confine you under these circumstances. Possibly — even probably — you are innocent men, but the people of Missouri will not stand for Mormon domination of their state."

"We have not been charged, your Honor," Sidney pointed out. "Yet, we are being held without bail, in circumstances you would not allow *your dog* to endure. Our wives have visited from time to time, but if *your* wife could see us in the filthy circumstances of that jail, she would rally the women of this state to overthrow the courts and free us. My wife has spent considerable time with me there, fearful that I might die in Liberty's chains. Have you inspected the dungeon, your Honor? Can you imagine a mother, an educated, genteel woman, enduring those conditions in behalf of her sick husband? Would you let your wife or mother stay one day, nay one hour, in such a place? Please, let conscience your guide, your Honor."

Turnham heard him out, soberly pondering his questions and knowing the justness of his complaints. The judge leaned forward, speaking low, "If it were simply up to me, frankly I would release you all. . . but I cannot! The governor would have my job. He wants all Mormons out of the state before any of your petitions are considered."

The judge sat back, looking over the petition for release, and finally gave his decision.

"Mr. Doniphan, your request for a speedy and impartial trial for the prisoners is not within my power to secure. Your petition for a change of venue is a just one, considering it is unlikely your clients will obtain an impartial trial anywhere in the immediate counties. But, again, this is a matter I cannot rule on. There is, however, one thing I will do. That is to grant bail and immediate release to Mr. Rigdon, lest I have his death on my head."

When the Mormons and their attorney emerged from the judge's chambers, the streets were thronged with angry citizens, violently and vocally opposed to freeing any of them. The local sheriff, Samuel Hadley, and the guards returned all the men to the hated Liberty Jail, Sidney included, for they were safer there than on the streets of the town.

"Don't be too brought down," the sheriff spoke quietly to Rigdon. "Make arrangements to post your bail, and when everything has settled down by and by, well. . . there's a fast horse tethered out back. That's all I can say."

Sidney set about contacting Phoebe with the good news, and sure enough, in the days following, the clamor in town quieted. No more pounding on the jailhouse door. No more threats shouted through the bars of the tiny windows. Meals were a little heartier than usual. Finally, ten days after Judge Turnham's ruling, Phoebe Rigdon came to Liberty and quietly posted her husband's bail. Later that evening, she and Sidney said goodbye to Joseph and Hyrum.

"It's farewell then, brethren," Sidney spoke hoarsely and shook hands all around. "If Hadley is true to his word, I'll be off to Illinois. If not, it's my dead body you'll view next, for they'll have to shoot me to bring me back."

"God bless you," Joseph said softly, clasping arms with his friend and counselor. "We'll see you both in Illinois. Tell the saints that God is our friend and our scriptures are true."

Joseph's voice gained conviction as he continued to speak, "God hath said He would have a tried people; that the righteous, like gold, must be purified seven times in the fire, so we will yet be victorious! Tell them that a man might as well stretch forth his puny hand to stop the Missouri River in its course, as to hinder the purposes of the Almighty!"

Joseph embraced Sidney, pressing his bony shoulder in expression of deep affection. How long ago, how very long ago it seemed, since Sidney had delivered his fiery "salt sermon." Lightning had forebodingly struck the flagpole that same day and Emma had vowed never to forgive Sidney if Joseph was harmed as a result of his speech. But Sidney had been Joseph's voice for that sermon. If it had precipitated the horrendous events that followed, Joseph knew the blame lay at his own feet. Responsibility ultimately rested with him.

Abruptly, the jailer and Sheriff Hadley entered the jail from the outside door, leaving it unlocked as planned. Tillery opened the trap door to the dungeon, and directed Joseph and Hyrum down the ladder to join the others, then stood to one side while Sidney and Sheriff Hadley engaged in a mock scuffle. After a few moments, Hadley shoved Sidney out the unlocked door, and the prisoner made a pretended escape, as neither jailer nor sheriff wanted the responsibility of having released him.

Rigdon stumbled toward the carriage kept by his son-in-law, George Robinson, then exclaimed, "I've forgotten my *wife*!" He hurried back, as Phoebe emerged from the jail. The two of them hastened to the rig. Sidney helped Phoebe into the carriage, then hoisted himself up onto the getaway horse, and under cover of a dark, cold night, they struck out for freedom in Quincy.

"Let thine anger be kindled against our enemies; and, in the fury of thine heart, with thy sword avenge us of our wrongs. Remember

thy suffering saints, O our God; and thy servants will rejoice in thy name forever."

Joseph yearned for the glorious manifestations that had lifted him to the heavens in times past. He summoned up the memory of his resurrected Lord standing on the breastwork of the Kirtland Temple. The experience had been so profound, so splendid! The glories of eternity had swirled about his head. He and Oliver had seen the wounds in their Savior's hands and feet as He stood before them in glory.

Where was Oliver now, once a devoted friend, now an avowed enemy? Where was their glorious light now? Where were his angel comforters? He could strengthen others when the Lord gave hope to him. But now it seemed that hope had fled.

How tediously the days had passed after the final visit of Emma and Mary. Caleb's and Alexander's wives had since come to see their imprisoned husbands. Lyman's family still waited for him in Far West, despite the order to evacuate. Finally, a letter came from Don Carlos in early March that the Smith family was safe in Quincy, living in temporary shelter. He was relieved to read of his family's arrival, but there were times alone in the dark when Joseph wept, thinking of his sixty-four year old mother's ordeal.

Within a few days he also received a much-anticipated letter from Emma. She wrote carefully, sparing Joseph the full account of her ordeal.

Quincy, March 7, 1839

"Dear Husband,

". . . I shall not attempt to write my feelings altogether, for the situation in which you are, the walls, bars, and bolts, rolling rivers, running streams, rising hills, sinking vallies, and spreading prairies that separate us, and the cruel injustice that first cast you into prison and still holds you there, with many other considerations, places my feelings far beyond description.

"Was it not for conscious innocence, and the direct interposition of divine mercy, I am very sure I never should have been able to have endured the scenes of suffering that I have passed through. . . but I still live and am yet willing to suffer more, if it is the will of kind heaven that I should, for your sake.

". . . No one but God knows the reflections of my mind and the feelings of my heart when I left our house and home, and almost all of everything that we possessed except our little children and took my journey out of the State of Missouri, leaving you shut up in that lonesome prison. But the reflection is more than human nature ought to bear, and if God does not record our sufferings and avenge our wrongs on them that are guilty, I shall be sadly mistaken.

". . . You may be astonished at my bad writing and incoherent manner, but you will pardon all when you reflect how hard it would be for you to write, when your hands were stiffened with hard work, and your heart convulsed with intense anxiety. But I hope there is better days to come to us yet. . . and am ever yours.
Affectionately, Emma Smith."

That night, after reading Emma's letter, Joseph fell into a deep sleep, and dreamed of his wife and children walking beside a wagon. They were bent against a snowstorm, their cloaks and heads covered with white. Behind them was strung out a long train of ragged men, women and children. Many, very many, of them walked barefoot, with only rags to wrap about their feet. Some left bloody prints in the snow. Babies too weak to cry, children numb with cold and constant hunger, made up this pilgrim band. He saw them pass warm, comfortable homes, but they were never taken in. He saw them camp beneath the overhanging trees, clearing snow to build a fire. This procession of grief stretched far ahead of Emma and the children, into the misty horizon, and far behind them to the deserted settlement of Far West.

In his dream, Joseph saw his beloved sleeping beneath tattered robes, four children curled up around her, seeking her warmth. When she arose in the morning, snow had fallen and frozen her blankets. She held them before an open fire to thaw so they could be rolled up and put into the accompanying wagon that carried a few family possessions. He heard his children cry from hunger. He saw Emma's brow furrow with deep lines and her eyelids droop from weariness. He sensed the chill of numb feet. He heard her prayers for endurance and strength to go on, and he heard her sob his name in the unpitying night.

Joseph dreamed a wide and fearful river rolled before Emma. Ice chunks had flowed downstream and crushed against each other until the waterway jammed with icy boulders. He saw Emma start across the slippery ice with two children holding to her skirts and two babies clinging to her neck. Beneath the heavy skirts, she was girded with deep, canvas pockets, carrying next to her body his private journals and papers, including his inspired revision of the Bible. These precious papers were preserved for him by his wife, even in her time of greatest tribulation. The manuscripts pulled on her and added weight, but they also comforted her in a way. It was all she had of Joseph, besides the children. She pulled her great cloak around them all, bowed her head against the biting wind, and picked her way between the great frozen ice chunks.

Joseph saw her stumble, but she righted herself and forged on. She wedged one foot at a time between the ice chunks. Joseph saw the lowering clouds gleam with silvery beings of another world. They hovered just above her, unseen by Emma, but guiding her footsteps. The hovering mists that cloaked the river upstream and down, and the piercing sound of ice cracking seemed endless!

When he saw her finally reach the other side, just before she stepped onto the bank, a sharp report rang out as the ice broke and the river rose to claim her. Run, Joseph called out to her in his sleep.

Run, Emma, run! She made a dash toward the bank, dragging the children. Then friendly hands reached out to help her to safety just as frigid waters flowed over the ice.

Joseph awoke with a start. "O Lord, my God," he pled, "Spare my family; keep them safe and well! Will I ever hold them again? How long must we endure these afflictions, O Lord?"

Now he sat in the squalor of the dungeon, imploring the Lord he tried so valiantly to serve. He prayed not just for Emma and his family, but for all the Latter-day Saints. "Have they not suffered enough?" he beseeched his Maker. In the dense blackness of the night he needed his Father — his Heavenly Father — to speak, or his soul would surely die. With his back against the wall, his knees drawn up, his forehead resting on them, he gave himself over to despair.

A still, small voice whispered to him. It was tender, patient, and indescribably sweet. It came as a shaft through darkness, flying straight to his tormented heart.

"My son, peace be unto thy soul; thine adversity and thine afflictions shall be but a small moment; and then, if thou endure it well, God shall exalt thee on high; thou shalt triumph over all thy foes. Thy friends do stand by thee, and they shall hail thee again with warm hearts and friendly hands."

Joseph's breath caught in his throat as he listened to the familiar voice. He had heard it many times before and had lately longed for the reassurance that it brought. Now it penetrated the blackness, bringing light, sounding soft and low — and for his ears only — carrying promises and counsel from a loving Father in Heaven.

"If thou art called to pass through tribulation; if thou art in perils among false brethren; if thou art in perils among robbers; if thou art

in perils by land or by sea; if thou art accused with all manner of false accusations; if thine enemies fall upon thee; if they tear thee from the society of thy father and mother and brethren and sisters; and if with a drawn sword thine enemies tear thee from the bosom of thy wife, and of thine offspring, and thine elder son, although but six years of age, shall cling to thy garments, and shall say, My father, my father, why can't you stay with us? O, my father, what are the men going to do with you? and if then he shall be thrust from thee by the sword, and thou be dragged to prison, and thine enemies prowl around thee like wolves for the blood of the lamb; and if thou shouldst be cast into the pit, or into the hands of murderers, and the sentence of death passed upon thee; if thou be cast into the deep; if the billowing surge conspire against thee; if fierce winds become thine enemy; if the heavens gather blackness, and all the elements combine to hedge up the way; and above all, if the very jaws of hell shall gape open the mouth wide after thee, know thou, my son, that all these things shall give thee experience, and shall be for thy good.

"The Son of Man hath descended below them all. Art thou greater than He?"

"No, Lord," he wept, "no! I am but a poor, unprofitable servant for a Master to whom I owe everything. Forgive me, Father, for I am weak. Forgive my faults, my sins, my complaints that weary Thy divine ear. Give me, I pray thee, strength to endure all, so I may be counted worthy of Thy smallest utterance. O Lord, my God, forgive Thy servant Joseph!"

Joseph fell prostrate on the dirty straw, but knew not the filth nor stench, for now he was wrapped in arms of everlasting love. Once again the experience of communing with God lifted Joseph to another world. The Daystar had arisen within him. The prison suddenly became a temple! It was the sanctification and sweetening of his soul.

The next day, Joseph began to write the word of God which had comforted him, painstakingly recalling his answered prayer on that darkest of nights.

A few days later, Alexander Doniphan came to the jail and informed the prisoners they were to be tried in Daviess County. They would soon be transferred to Gallatin for a hearing before a grand jury. After five months of imprisonment, the men were almost too weakened to care what happened next. Joseph wrote one last letter to Emma.

Liberty Jail, Clay Co., Mo. April 4th, 1839
Dear and affectionate Wife.
". . . just as the sun is going down. . . we peek through the grates of this lonesome prison. . . It is I believe now about five months and six days since I have been under the grimace, of a guard night and day, and within the walls, grates and screeking of iron dors, of a lonesome dark durty prison. With immotions known only to God, do I write this letter. . . This night we expect; is the last night we shall try our weary Joints and bones on our dirty straw couches in these walls. . . Ther is great thirsting for our blood, in this state; not because we are guilty of any thing: but because they say these men will give an account of what has been done to them; the wrongs they have sustain if it is known, it will ruin the State. So the mob party have sworn, to have our lives, at all hasards, but God will disappoint them we trust. We shall be moved from this at any rate, and we are glad of it let what will become of us we cannot get into a worse hole than this is. . .

"Thank God, we shall never cast a lingering wish after liberty in clay county Mo. we have enough of it to last forever. . .

"My dear Emma I think of you and the children continually. . . I want to see little Frederick, Joseph, Julia, and Alexander. . . I want you should not let those little fellows, forgit me. Tell them Father loves them with perfect love. . . tell them Father says they must be good children, and mind their mother. My dear Emma, there is great responsibility resting upon you, in preserving yourself in honor, and sobriety, before them, and teaching them right things, to form their young and tender minds, that they begin in right paths. . . And as to yourself if you want to know how much I want to see you. . . I would gladly walk from here to you barefoot, and bareheaded, and half naked. . . and never count it toil. . .

"I suppose you see the need of my council, and help, but a combination of things have conspired to place me where I am, and I know it is not my fault. . .

"I find no fault with you att all I know nothing but what you have done the best you could. . . remember that he who is my enemy, is yours also, and never give up an old tried frien, who has waded through all manner of toil, for your sake, and throw him away because fools may tell you he has some faults. . . "

On April 6, 1839, the remaining prisoners — Joseph, Hyrum, Caleb, Lyman and Alexander — were released from Liberty Jail by Jailer Tillery to the custody of Sheriff Hadley.

"Don't be sad, my boys, you'll soon be free, and that on order of Austin King, hisself." His gnarled face was alight with enjoyment of the drama he had taken part in. He sucked on a toothpick, his eyes dancing with pleasure. "This whole affair wasn't nothing but the governor's scheme to punish you. Reckon you wouldn't git free now except the newspapers in the state took up the cry of 'liberty' since you Mormons ain't a threat no more. Boggs told Tom Burch, yer ol' prosecutor, to fix it so's you could go free."

The men listened to him with more doubt than relief. They believed if tried in Daviess County, they would surely be murdered by the mob that still howled for their blood. King had his reasons for ordering them to Gallatin. Heber C. Kimball and Erastus Snow had been petitioning the courts for a change of venue to Boone or Marion County. Despondently, the prisoners rode under guard by Sheriff Hadley and his men, forty miles to Gallatin. Easter had been the preceding Sabbath. Were they being offered up as Christ had been, before a judge and jury of enemies? This was a fateful time, and Joseph awaited what God had planned for them.

The trial commenced on April 9. The Honorable Austin King presided. It appeared to Joseph that he and the jury were inebriated through most of the proceedings. The jury, composed completely of men who had carried out the Haun's Mill massacre, sustained charges against Joseph and the others of "murder, treason, arson, larceny, theft, and stealing."

Before the jury could actually hear the matter they themselves had defined, something miraculous occurred. Stephen Markham risked his life and came to Gallatin with a writ from the state legislature authorizing a change of venue. The efforts of Heber, Theodore, and Erastus had paid off. When Stephen tried to introduce the writ to the court, he was restrained.

"Your Honor," Markham insisted, "This is *official*, a change of venue, courtesy of your *state legislature*. These men are to be tried in Boone County."

"Order! You are out of order, you damned rascal! These prisoners have been assigned to me for trial," said King, "and I mean to carry it out."

"It's an illegal jury!" Markham shouted. "Not one man here can be said to be impartial!"

"'Impartial,' is it! I'll give you 'impartial,'" Mr. Blakely, one of the jurors, called out. "Meet me outside this courtroom, and we'll see to your 'change of venue.'"

Before Joseph could stop him, Stephen, tall and powerful, strode out the door followed by Blakely cursing at every step, and before Stephen could turn around, the man struck him with a club. Possibly stunned, but undaunted, Stephen quickly jerked the club from Blakely's hand. Robert Peniston, father of Daviess County militia Colonel William Peniston, and one of the most vicious of the jury, jumped on Markham's back and began raining blows with both fists on his head and shoulders. Stephen shook the assailant off like a bug, then grasped the club with both hands and faced the rest of the jury, who had rushed out to join their comrades.

"Come on! Come on! I'll take you on, you Missouri pukes! Try and get me, and I'll kill the whole lot of you with one blow apiece."

The crowd was calling for Markham's blood. Judge King watched the fracas from the doorway. Joseph and the other prisoners looked at each other. Stephen could easily be shot. Joseph and Hyrum prayed silently for an end to the violence. Lyman Wight was itching to get into the fray along with Stephen and go down fighting, if that were to be their lot. However, King called a halt to the fighting and announced the court would reconvene the next day.

Stephen slept under the trees with the prisoners that night, willing to share their fate.

Joseph awoke with a start. "Stephen," he whispered, "You must leave now. There is a plot against your life."

"There's always a plot, Joseph," he answered.

"I've seen it in a dream, and you are a dead man unless you leave immediately."

Stephen got up and rolled up his bedroll. "I hate to leave you in this condition," he protested to his beloved prophet.

"I'll see you in Illinois, Stephen. God bless you. You're a true friend. *Go, now!*"

Markham disappeared into the shadows. The sound of his horse's hooves was followed almost immediately by a howl of disappointment from a band of would-be assassins headed for the prisoners. William Morgan, the sheriff responsible for the prisoners' safety, jumped to his feet and turned the mob back at gunpoint.

By April fifteenth, the change of venue was obtained, and they were ordered transferred to Boone County, where they hoped to have a better chance at a fair trial. They were loaded into a jail wagon and set out again.

After a day and a half of travel, bone-weary with all the harassment and months of imprisonment, they stopped for the night in a grove of trees. With a little money Stephen had passed to him, Joseph purchased a jug of whiskey from a farmer for his captors. The guards got drunk and fell asleep by the fire.

About midnight, Sheriff Morgan stood above the Mormon prisoners and shoved the toe of his boot into Joseph's ribs.

"Smith, see here, I've got orders that you must never get to Boone County. I have the writ for a change of venue, but I'm not to show it, nor deliver you over. Now, I could accomplish that in more than one way. If I gave my men their head, we'll be digging shallow graves. But, instead, here's what I'll do. I'll take a drink of grog — maybe two, maybe *three* — and get a good night's sleep."

The captives looked knowingly at each other. The sheriff, new to the county and the Mormon conflict, smiled and continued. "Yonder are a couple of horses. They're good 'uns, and I recommend you two Smith brothers mount 'em and head for Illinois. That-a-way," he pointed. "The rest of you. . . well, you've got good legs and a head start. *We* won't sober up 'til mornin', and by then it'll be too late to go huntin' for you."

Was the sheriff serious? Would he shoot them in the back if they started off? It was a chance. Still, it was a chance worth taking! With the briefest of salutes, the band of "prisoners for Christ's sake" split up and soon disappeared into the shadows of the Missouri night. They gave themselves another change of venue. . . to the state of Illinois.

No gunshots or shouts signaled an escape. Nine days of hard riding, sleeping in the woods, brought Joseph and Hyrum to the bank of the Mississippi River, across from Quincy, Illinois. The men sat on their horses, watching the current. Joseph remembered his terrible dream of Emma and the children. Now, however, he was not dreaming, and his family was safe, just beyond the surging river! He and Hyrum clasped hands and raised them high in the triumph of their deliverance. Across the "Father of Waters" lay their hope for happiness and a new beginning!

Chapter Eight

Beside the Mighty Mississippi

The gate creaked as a vagrant leaned against it. Emma looked up from her work, and the children stopped playing to watch the stranger. He was emaciated and bearded, with a wide-brimmed, black hat pulled low over hollow eyes. He resembled a lost soul, pulled back from the jaws of death.

Emma screamed, dropping the candles she had been dipping, and flew out the open doorway, straight to the arms of the wanderer. Freddy began to cry. Julia screamed too and ran to pick up Alex. Only young Joseph stood up straight and watched. He saw his mother throw herself into his disheveled father's arms. His siblings might wonder if this stranger could really be their father, but young Joseph had seen him this ragged in Liberty Jail. Emma had talked of little else since they had left Missouri. She reminded him daily to pray for his father — as if he could forget!

"Oh Joseph! Joseph!" was all Emma could say. Joseph once again leaned back against the gatepost, his wife securely in his arms, the two of them swaying, laughing, and sobbing all at once.

Now the children came running when they recognized their father. They threw themselves at his legs, and Joseph and Emma almost lost their footing with the onslaught. Julia carried little Alexander and thrust the boy toward Joseph. A long howl of fright came from the baby. Emma laughed and took him from her daughter. Joseph's long arms encircled the three squealing, laughing children, and he lifted them all up together.

Dimick Huntington stood by, holding the horses' reins. He had welcomed Joseph when the prophet and Hyrum came off the ferry after their river crossing. Dimick directed Hyrum to Father Smith's house and guided Joseph to Judge Cleveland's home, where Emma and the children had been living for two months.

While a prisoner in Liberty, Joseph had written to his friend, the judge, and asked for refuge for his family. Judge John Cleveland and his wife, Sarah, had spent weeks watching for Emma. She finally arrived with the children, faint and almost frozen after her trek from Far West. Sarah and Emma became fast friends, for Sarah Cleveland was truly a friend in Emma's time of need. The Clevelands were members of the church and owned a comfortable farm on the outskirts of Quincy. They had done much to influence the citizens of the area in favor of the Mormons. When Emma settled her little children into a warm, dry bed that first night, she lingered at the doorway, exhaustion near the surface. She went downstairs intending to briefly thank Sarah once more for her generosity. Trying to find words, Emma broke down, and Sarah held her while she wept. That moment created a lifelong bond between them. Sitting before the warm hearthside, Emma rehearsed the last disastrous year in Far West and her three visits to Joseph. Last of all, she retold the numbing experience of trudging over two hundred miles across Missouri to Illinois, knowing she had left her husband farther and farther behind with every footstep.

"He will come to you," Sarah soothed her friend. "I am certain. It can't be far off. The Lord has more work for His prophet, which can't be done in prison. We pray for him every day. Meanwhile, you need some rest. I want you to spend at least a week recuperating, with your children close by."

Emma started to protest, but Sarah wouldn't hear it. "Now, off to bed! Tomorrow we'll sit and talk while our children play and get fat on my chicken stew."

Now, two months later, Sarah's words of comfort proved true. Joseph was reunited with his wife and children beside the mighty Mississippi.

"Papa, we've been praying for you all this time," Julia informed him importantly.

"Thank you. I needed it."

"Papa, you haven't taken a bath! I can tell!" Julia's nose turned up. She was a little lady in most every respect.

"How do you like my beard?" Joseph asked Freddy whose tiny fingers had entwined themselves in the rough stubble.

"It scratches!" The boy was solemn.

"A little bit," his father agreed. "It really scratches when I decide to chew on ears, or necks, *like this!*" He dove at each child, his whiskers bringing more squeals of delight and protest.

"Papa, how did you get out of that jail?" young Joseph asked.

"I walked out, climbed on a horse and rode away."

The boy's eyes popped wide open. "Honest?"

"Of course, there were guards with me."

"Well, how did you get away from the guards?"

"I bought them a jug of good ol' Missouri whiskey — which they drank — and when they went to sleep, I took a horse and just rode off."

"That was easy."

"Yep! I guess they were tired of guarding me, and just as glad to be rid of me as I was them."

Emma broke in, "Is Hyrum here too?"

"He is, and on his way to Mother and Father's house to find his family."

"Are you both well?"

"As well as can be expected after five and a half months in jail and a hard ride here."

"You look like you're starved! Come inside. There is plenty to eat — fresh bread and honey, salt pork and beans. How does that sound?"

"Like heaven! But first — I *might* need a bath," he smiled.

"We have a kettle heating for the wash. You can use that, and I'll heat more. A bath first *might* be a good idea," Emma agreed. "Your horse smells better than you do!"

"He wasn't in the dungeon!"

It was April 22, 1839, and the weather was mild, so Emma prepared the bath for Joseph out in the carriage house. Chasing the children away, she scrubbed his back, shaved his beard, and washed and clipped his hair. Then she helped him slip into clean clothes she had sewn for this very day.

"I feel human again. Do I smell better?"

"Um hmm," she murmured against his clean neck. "Better than before."

"Better than in jail?" She knew he was smiling as he held her tight.

"Even better than that." Her voice took on a severe tone. "Joseph Smith, don't ever go back to Missouri! It's bad for your health!"

"Yes, ma'am! I promise!" He kissed her forehead, her cheeks, even the tip of her nose, and her sweet mouth. After several long delicious minutes, he said, "I have missed my bride!"

The light laughter of the children rang outside the door. "You have children and friends waiting for you."

"Let them wait. I feel as though I have died and am in heaven," he murmured against the nape of her neck.

He was teasing, but she was wounded. "Don't say that! Don't ever say that! You don't know how many times I dreamed that you were dead. When they captured you in Far West, when they sentenced you to be shot, when they tried to poison you at Liberty — Joseph, I saw you die a thousand times! And I died with you. Don't ever tease me about dying!"

Months of anguish and fear ravaged her. She clung tightly to her husband, sobbing uncontrollably. Joseph simply sat down on a box and held her on his lap. It was a long while before her tears washed away the hurt and fear of the last year. They held each other until Emma's emotions finally calmed, and she rested her head on his shoulder. It wasn't long until they heard excited knocking at the carriage house door.

High voices called out, "Papa? Papa, are you finished?"

"Yes, children."

". . . Because you have visitors. Lots of visitors."

Joseph kissed his wife one last time, and they both stood up. Emma washed her face in a basin of water, smoothed her hair, and tried to smile.

"You are beautiful, as always," he reassured her, taking her hand as they walked to the door.

Yes, there were lots of visitors. They came in a steady stream to the Cleveland home. Joseph greeted everyone with the joy of a man returned from the dead. Rumor was running rampant in town that the prophet and Hyrum had escaped jail and were here in Illinois. As the rumor was confirmed, and word spread that Joseph was at Judge Cleveland's, the oppression and hopelessness of the Far West experience completely lifted from the destitute Latter-day Saints.

Still, with thousands flooding in from Missouri, there was not enough housing, and many of the saints slept in tents along the river. Joseph was no better off than they. He was weak, almost broken from lack of decent nourishment. He was also a beggar, as they all were, with no home, no property, no money of his own. The horse he had ridden from Missouri was the only thing of material value he possessed. As members of the church came to the Cleveland home, Joseph shook their hands, embraced all, and assured them of better times ahead.

That night, after Sarah Cleveland had graciously but firmly said goodnight to the straggling visitors, Joseph and Emma retired to their bedroom. They stood locked in a silent embrace for several minutes after closing the door. The candle flickered, and outside the window, the moonlight silvered the tops of the trees. Joseph drew his wife toward the moonlight to watch the leaves shimmer on the trees.

"Emma, you will never suffer the likes of Missouri again. I promise you a home of your own — soon — and I will be there with you. No more being impoverished and dependent. Your father would say I've neglected you. Maybe I have. . . or maybe God has seen fit to try you, as He has me. If I had anticipated all this when I asked you to be my bride, I'm not sure I would have asked, but I'm glad I did. Without you, I could not have endured. You possess every attribute of Christian charity. I have never known another woman so fine! I love you with all my soul. You must never doubt that."

Joseph's unsolicited words brought joy to Emma's spirit. This moment, so sweet, so quiet, as they basked in gentle moonlight and each other's love, was even more precious because she had wondered if it would ever really come. Walking away from Liberty Jail was the hardest thing she had ever done. She had tried to prepare herself for the possibility that Joseph would be killed there, and she might never see him alive again. Now she knew she had not been prepared at all. Without him, she knew she was not strong. She was not brave. She endured it all for Joseph, and would do it all again, just to come to this quiet moment in his arms.

The next day they went to visit Mother and Father Smith. Lucy said she had been watching for her two sons.

"How did you know we were on our way, Mother?" Joseph asked.

"I saw you and Hyrum two nights ago in vision." Lucy beamed with satisfaction. "Ask Brother Partridge, here, if I didn't. I told him yesterday you would be arriving soon. He didn't believe me until Hyrum walked in. Brother Partridge and Brother Morley thought I was a false prophet. Isn't that right, Edward?"

Edward Partridge acknowledged her accuracy. "That's right, Mother Smith. I'll never say it again. I humbly beg your pardon."

Lucy beamed, "Now see! They were wrong and I was right! Joseph, in my vision I saw you and Hyrum crossing a wide prairie. You boys had nothing to eat. I saw you sleep on the cold ground. I saw Hyrum so weak, and it was so clear I walked the floor all night, worried, wishing I could give you something to eat. But I was confident I would soon have you both back."

Joseph grinned at his mother. "Who could doubt you, Mother? I never have."

Just then, his father appeared. "Joseph! I thought I would never see you again! God has delivered you from the Philistines!" The older man choked with tears as his son crossed the room in three strides to embrace his father. Joseph felt the trembling weakness of his father and realized what a toll the last few years had taken on him. When the older Smith could speak again, he roundly denounced Governor Boggs, General Clark, Liberty Jail, and the entire state of Missouri in general. Joseph's presence calmed him somewhat, but his father saw beyond his son's clean clothes and clean shave.

"You're skin and bone, my boy," he mourned.

"Well, you're not any better. Have you been ill, Father?"

"I certainly have. We've *all* been sick. Fever, chills, shaking; I thought your mother would die a month ago. Little Lucy came down with it. Samuel's family got sick. Your mother tried to nurse everybody through it, but she got down worse than any of us. We're all feeling better now, but still shaky."

"You look wonderful to me, all of you. And look! Here's my Lucy-girl!" Joseph greeted his youngest sister with a long embrace.

"Have you been caring for Mother?"

Lucy shook her head. "She's been caring for me."

"Are you better now?"

"Better," his mother affirmed. "At least no one in our family died. That's more than I can say for others. We've all been a little weak because of the Missouri ordeal, especially your father. He has suffered even more since we left Far West, and hasn't talked of anything but you boys. If word had come that you had been killed, he would have died too."

Soon Hyrum and Mary came in with their family. Hyrum sat holding his five-month-old son, who snuggled contentedly in his father's arms. Mary was quiet, glowing with the warmth of this reunion. She was still pale, for her trek from Far West had been very taxing to her already weakened constitution, but her English determination was anything but weak, and had won out.

The saints needed a new place to settle, so a few days later, Joseph, accompanied by Hyrum and a committee of church leaders, rode north to look over land offered them by Dr. Isaac Galland. He was selling property in Commerce, Illinois, a small town of one stone house, three frame houses, and two blockhouses.

Joseph rode his horse up to the edge of the bluffs overlooking the river. Spring wildflowers of lavender, pink and yellow grew alongside thick prairie grass that waved for miles all around. Below the bluff, plentiful woods stretched down to the riverbank in a shady thicket of ash, chestnut, dogwood, and hickory trees all interwoven with a dense tangle of underbrush and honeysuckle vines. The wide Mississippi waterway bent in an open horseshoe around the land, and small, green islands dotted the blue ribbon of water. It was a warm spring day. A pleasant expression came over Joseph's face. He remembered his promise to Emma.

"Hyrum," he said, "have you ever in your life seen a more beautiful spot for settling?"

"Can't say I have."

Joseph returned to Emma at the Cleveland's home, excited to tell her what they had discovered. When he arrived, he found Heber C. Kimball waiting with a letter in hand. It was from Orson Hyde begging Joseph's forgiveness for having turned against the church during the conflict in Missouri. Joseph sat and read it while Heber stood, twisting his hat in his hand. Joseph finished the letter without uttering a word.

Heber stammered, "He's miserable, Brother Joseph."

"No doubt. I've never seen a happy apostate, especially one who will turn on his brothers and help put chains on their feet."

Heber nodded.

Joseph's normally forgiving eyes were now uncharacteristically hard. "It was Orson's testimony, along with Sampson Avard's and Thomas Marsh's, that put us in Liberty Jail! Orson swore to things he knew were not true, and he conspired to drive the saints off their lands. Boggs and his lackeys believed him, since Hyde was one of our leaders. . . Now he wants to be rebaptized?" Joseph was visibly agitated.

Heber looked mournfully at the floor. "Joseph, Orson is a broken man. He knows he has done a despicable thing, and if he doesn't make restitution he — and his posterity — could be cut off from the Lord. He begs to be allowed to appear before the next conference to seek forgiveness."

Joseph controlled his feelings with great effort. Finally, he turned back to his compassionate friend. "Heber, if you will speak for Orson — and if Hyrum concurs — I will not stand in the way of his return."

Heber looked into his prophet's eyes. His own were filled with sympathy. "I thought I would always hate the men who put you and the others in that dungeon. I've tried to hate Orson, but now when I see him so humble and penitent, I just can't. I guess I still love him."

Joseph softened. He squeezed his friend's shoulder. "You're a Christ-like man, Heber," he sighed. "Notify Orson to attend conference. We'll settle it then."

That night, Joseph lay awake beside Emma, staring into the darkness. After a long time, long after he thought she was asleep, she spoke lowly, "You're still awake. What's bothering you?"

"Orson wants to return to the church."

"Orson Hyde?" Emma asked incredulously. "It was just seven months ago he deserted us. Next thing you know, Thomas Marsh will be wanting his membership back."

"Heber is pleading for Orson to be reinstated. I can't get my mind free of the testimony he gave before Judge King. All the while he was swearing to the most damnable things, his countenance was like a whipped dog. He was even more miserable than I was, and I had been in jail two months. Even then, I couldn't hate him. I pity anyone so subject to fear that he turns against everything he holds dear."

"Oh Joseph, think of what he put you through!"

"I am, but it was a refiner's fire and it gave me perspective I never had before. Emma, God told me in Liberty Jail that I had about five years to accomplish my work. I wish I could say we will grow old together, but we may not. You will live a good, long life, but I may not be by your side."

He looked soberly into her questioning eyes. "Emma," he said forcefully, "Whatever God requires is right! His kingdom must roll forth. The earth and all that's in it is Christ's, and He will reign. My task is to bring forth and establish the cause of Zion. I am only mortal and imperfect, but I have been chosen for this time."

Joseph rolled onto his back, his hands clasped beneath his head as he contemplated. "I love the saints, and I love the Lord. All my life I have tried to discover His will and to obey it. I listen for His voice, and sometimes I hear it. I heard it in Liberty. One night I pleaded and cried. I begged for His voice, and it came to me. He told me trials were necessary for my experience, and that He had passed through them all."

Joseph's voice grew intense with emotion. "Emma, I'm an ungrateful fool. Orson helped give me the very experience the Lord wanted me to have. And now, my brother wants my forgiveness. How can I begrudge it?"

Joseph's voice broke. After a moment, he said, "I am the one to repent. Who am I to deny him, what Christ never denied me — blessed forgiveness?"

Orson made his plea before the conference and was rebaptized into the church. His brethren forgave him all the hardship he had helped to bring on the church. Joseph gave him the right hand of fellowship and reinstated him as an apostle.

"Oh Joseph! Commerce is a beautiful place! Look, a fresh spring, right behind our house. I can get my water here instead of going down to the river. And these beautiful willow trees! They are huge. So much shade! And we have a perfect view of the river. What do you think, children? Will you like it here?"

The boys chorused, "Yes."

It was early May 1839. Joseph and Emma opened the door to their newly acquired home on the Mississippi River.

"Will our friends move here too?" Julia asked.

"I think they will," Joseph answered, winking at Emma. "I imagine quite a few of our friends will want to live right here with us."

"And no Missouri pukes will come and make us leave!" young Joseph chimed in.

"Joseph!" Emma scolded.

Joseph smiled, "I don't think so."

"Good, 'cause I didn't like them. And I especially didn't like walking all the way from our last home. I was cold, and my shoes got ruined."

"Papa," Julia interjected, "why did those people hate us so much?"

She was maturing beyond her years. She would never forget the tragic events of her early years. She was only eight, but spoke as though she were much older, and Emma had come to treat her as if she were already grown.

"They hate because they don't understand. That is the root of most hatred — that and selfishness. Misunderstanding can be overcome, selfishness rarely."

The little girl considered his answer for a moment, then broke away and called to her brothers, "Let's go play by the river."

"Be careful," Emma called after them.

"They'll be all right," Joseph reassured his wife. "We can see them from here. So, do you like our new home? We could wait and build a new house, but I want to get my family settled before the saints begin to gather here."

"I agree. Besides, we're into May now, and I need to plant a garden. It'll be up and growing in no time."

"I'm afraid the house isn't big. Just one room down and one room up."

"We can build on. I would like a summer kitchen back here. That will keep the heat out of the house during the summer. It'll be just fine. We don't need a large place right now. We're a small family."

"Of course, that might change," he said lightly.

"You mean your parents are coming to live with us?" she avoided his meaning.

"Well, actually, yes. . . until I can build them a house of their own."

"We'll make room for them. After all, we've lived together many times."

"The Rigdons have purchased a house just a stone's throw away, by that grove of locust trees yonder. It is a beautiful site as well. In fact, everything is beautiful here."

His wife took his arm and smiled up at him.

Midnight on the Mississippi was magic. With the children bedded down, Joseph and Emma stood looking over the flowing water. Islands were dark spots far out in the current. Fish jumped near the shore and frogs croaked. They walked without speaking, enthralled by the music of night birds. The stars were like scattered diamonds in the night sky, and thousands of fireflies danced above a small tributary, turning it into a living river of light. Emma had loosened and brushed her hair. It hung far down her back, heavy and thick, still as dark as when Joseph had first seen her almost fourteen years before. In the moonlight he couldn't see the lines of care that bespoke the ordeals she had surmounted. Joseph was quickly regaining his strength, nourished by sufficient rest and Emma's good cooking. He was once again filled with the energy of the Lord's work. Emma rested her head against his shoulder and sighed with contentment.

"Will there be many nights like this?" she asked wistfully.

"I hope so."

"What will you do tomorrow?" Emma absentmindedly slapped at mosquitoes.

"Plant a garden with my wife, and go exploring with my children."

"You'll soon be building houses and laying out a new city. Zion will reclaim you. But, I'll always savor this night, having you to myself."

Joseph knew she was right, for as much as he cherished his time with his family, his mind was already racing ahead to the city in his imagination.

"I think we'd better go in," he said. "There is a chill off the wetlands, and the mosquitoes are beginning to find us."

Just before they closed the door of their new home, Emma looked back for one last sight of the silver-streaked river, murmuring promises as it lapped the shore. It was a dream come true.

In the days following, Mother and Father Smith came to Commerce, along with Hyrum and Mary, accompanied by Don Carlos' family. After them, the Theodore Turleys, Lorenzo Brown and family, the Whitneys, the Partridges, the Rigdons arrived, and so on, until Emma's solitude was completely gone. Other families came and camped in tents or wagons on the Smith property while they built houses of their own. Joseph and Hyrum sold town lots as fast as land could be surveyed. They planned a neat, orderly, quarter acre division of the lowlands. Another prime site was up on the bluffs overlooking the city. It was owned by Squire Daniel H. Wells. Wells was an industrious, capable young married man, and sympathetic toward the persecuted saints. He met Joseph Smith under a towering oak tree where many treaties had been made with local Indians. When Smith asked him about terms for purchasing additional acreage, Wells considered the plight of the penniless church, the honest, humble look of the Mormon prophet, and named a conservative price with liberal terms.

"I imagine you could use a little good will about now," Squire Wells observed. "I think you and your people will make good neighbors."

One evening, Joseph and Emma watched the sun set from the bluff above the flats. To the southwest, the river barges and steamboats passed each other on the Mississippi. Commerce had the prospect of developing into a great city, though at that precise moment, with acres of marshy wetlands, dotted only with a few houses and a sea of tents, it hardly seemed to live up to its name.

"Joseph, no one else would dream of settling this swampy place, it's such an enormous task."

"That's why we are just the people for it. We have willing hands and vision." He continued sublimely, "And here we will build another House of the Lord."

She looked over the spot he indicated, while savoring the deepening gold and salmon-colored clouds. She replied, "Perfect. Just perfect!"

The next weeks and months saw much change and growth in the little settlement. Water was drained from the land, more and more saints gathered, and Joseph proposed to change the name of the city.

"Nauvoo. It's a Hebrew word," he explained to his friends. "It means 'beautiful habitation,' and connotes the idea of rest. That's exactly what we are planning for."

When comments were favorable for the change, he went ahead and printed it as a caption on a published plat of the city. It would take a little time before the change became official, but the new name became a favorite immediately.

During the summer of 1839, change and growth were accompanied by sickness and death. The ague — fever, chills, and sweating — reached epidemic proportions among the new settlers. The Smith family was not exempt from the disease.

"Father," Joseph called out jubilantly as he bounded through the doorway of his home. "Father! We have found exactly the right materials for the temple! Where is Father?" he asked Emma.

"Lying down. He's sick, Joseph. Fever and chills. I'm afraid it is the ague."

"And Mother?"

"She's beside his bed, fanning him to keep the flies away. Neither of them is strong. Your father has suffered from all that has happened the last few years. Word came today that the Rigdons have also come down with swamp fever. We had better send someone over to watch over them."

"How many are sick now with the fever?"

"I've lost count. Every family has someone down. I believe it is the hot weather and the unhealthy mists from the swampy areas. Lately the stench is so bad I cover my mouth and nose with a handkerchief."

"How are you feeling?"

"Tired, but otherwise all right. How about you?"

"Fine. You know me. I rarely get sick."

"Joseph, I'm worried. Should we try to stop more saints from coming in, at least until the weather cools and the disease abates?"

"Might as well try and stop water from flowing downstream. Everyone on the river banks at Quincy is already on the move here."

Emma shook her head. "Well, they'll all get sick. Dozens fall ill everyday. I have gathered herbs until the plants will soon be stripped, and nothing is helping. My little store of medicines and poultices is entirely gone."

By evening, there were more calls for help. Emma left her household chores to attend many of the sick people now lying out in her yard. They camped in tents under the trees, by the spring, and in the shade of the smokehouse. She brought one elderly sister, who moaned continually, into their home and gave her their bed. Soon she had three more cases, so sick she was afraid to leave them outside. They all had welts from mosquitoes. Emma made poultices to soothe

the itching, and fed her patients mild tea. That night, she and Joseph slept outside in a tent hastily made of bed sheets. The swamp gases nauseated her, and she wondered if she was coming down with the sickness; but no, Emma awoke in the morning weary but well. On the other hand, Joseph tried most of that day to conceal his fever from her. By evening, he was as ill as the others.

There had already been several deaths, and Joseph's fever ran so high, Emma worried incessantly that he might die. Sidney's aged mother had died, and the whole Rigdon family was so sick they were unable to care for each other. Emma left her duties with her own family members, saddled her horse, and rode to the Rigdons' home to minister to their needs — cooking, emptying chamber pots, sponging down feverish faces and limbs. At the end of the day, miserably tired, she returned to hear young Lucy tell her that most of Hyrum's family were down with the ague. By now she had developed a regular routine: wash this sister; feed that man soup; give another one tea; rock a child and sponge him down; check on Father Smith; check on Joseph — and so on it went unrelentingly. Sarah Cleveland arrived to help and found Emma so fatigued, she put her friend to bed and took over her nursing duties. That day of rest saved Emma from complete collapse.

Next, young Lucy fell sick, and Mother Smith was beside herself with worry. Every hour she would ask Emma, "Do you think she is worse?"

"No, Mother, she's not worse. She's sick, but I'm sure she'll be all right."

"Is there anything else we can do for her? And I fear for my husband. He is so unwell. It's been weeks, and he is no better."

"I know Mother. Father Smith is no better, but he is no worse."

"Are you worried about Joseph? I saw Brother Johnson tending to him yesterday. Joseph was delirious, quite delirious."

Emma sat down heavily in the rocking chair. "Benjamin has volunteered to take over his care. I have so many patients to help I can't give any of them the attention they need. Thank heavens for the Huntington sisters and the two Partridge girls."

"Well, it's a wonder you haven't come down with it yourself, tending all those sick folk."

"It's God's blessing for my service. Stay inside, Mother. I believe you are better off to suffer the heat in the house than the swamp gases outside. Those inside seem to do better than those outside in tents and wagons. So many are sick, we scarcely have men well enough to dig graves for the dead."

Then she regretted mentioning graves, for the older woman's face went white, and she hurried back to the bedsides of her ailing husband and daughter.

Most of July passed with little relief for the sufferers. It had been several days since Joseph had fallen ill. He showed no sign of getting better. Emma tried not to fuss over him, but coming and going, tending to the needs of dozens of other people, she watched over him anxiously.

One morning Joseph awoke and said, "By all that is holy, I have endured prison, poison, three death sentences, hatred by my enemies, and betrayal by my friends. I have seen the faithful suffer and grieve until I can stand it no longer. I now call on the promises of God to this people! He has promised us the blessings of heaven if we but live His commands. We may not be perfect, but we are trying to live God's word, and today we shall be healed!"

He rose from his pallet on the floor, walked on shaky legs to the springhouse, doused himself with cool, refreshing water, and pleaded for the healing power of Jesus for himself and his people. Then, filled with faith and determination, he returned to Emma. She gave him a clean shirt and a silk bandana.

"With the Lord's good pleasure, I am going to heal the saints. This siege has gone on long enough."

"Good!" she responded. "I hope you'll begin with your father and sister. Mother Smith is almost beside herself."

And so he did. He laid his hands on their heads and rebuked the disease. Young Lucy rose from her bed immediately, and Joseph's father sat up and asked for food. Then the prophet went among the sick in his yard, blessing them and asking some to go with him to bless others. He went to Hyrum and called him forth from his sick bed. Hyrum arose, and together the brothers walked the riverbank and continued the work of healing. They went to Sidney's, then to Heber C. Kimball's and Parley Pratt's homes.

The band of men crossed the Mississippi in a skiff to Brigham Young's house. He had been sick for days. Surrounding Brigham's bed, the brethren joined in prayer as Joseph called down healing powers from heaven. Brigham opened his eyes, smiled at the men and rose up to join in ministering to the sick. They passed Wilford Woodruff's home, and Joseph called, "Brother Wilford, follow me." It was all the apostle needed. He immediately joined the group.

Then they came to the home of Elijah Fordham. "It's too late, Brother Joseph," his daughter mourned. "My father is on his deathbed. The rattle of death is in his throat. He hasn't eaten in days and a glaze is over his eyes."

Joseph paused in her tiny parlor. Then he looked beyond the doorway to the bed where her father lay, and a smile came over his features.

"We'll see, Sister Fordham."

He ducked going through the doorway into the cramped bedroom, took off his hat and held it. Certainly Elijah was at death's door. His skin had a waxy look, and his breathing was irregular and faint. Joseph stepped up to his bedside and took the man by the hand.

"Brother Fordham, do you know who this is?"

No answer, no response — the man lay perfectly still.

"Brother Elijah," Joseph spoke more intensely, "Don't you know me?"

A light of recognition flickered in the sick man's face. With difficulty he whispered "Yes."

"Do you have faith to be healed?"

"I'm afraid it's too late, Brother Joseph. If only you had come earlier."

"Do you believe in Jesus Christ?"

"I do."

Joseph stood erect, holding the hand of the afflicted man. His face took on the luminous quality his friends had seen before. When he spoke, his voice rang with power and authority. "Brother Fordham, I command you in the name of Jesus Christ, to arise from this bed and be made whole!"

Fordham's whole frame convulsed. He sat straight up, leaped to his feet, and was immediately made well. His face took on a healthy color, and he looked at the poultices about his feet. He kicked them off and requested his daughter to bring his clothes and shoes. Pausing only to eat a bowl of bread and milk, he called after Joseph's departing band, "Wait brethren. I'm coming with you." He left his daughter, astonished and weeping, while he went out rejoicing and rehearsing his story to all he met.

It was July 22, 1839, a hot, muggy day that would be remembered as the day Joseph and his companions walked the riverbanks, healing the sick. He gave Wilford his silk handkerchief to wipe the faces of sick children. The handkerchief became a token of healing to the youngsters Wilford ministered to, and a bond of unity between himself and Joseph. It was a miraculous day, and when it was over, the saints had learned much about the healing power of faith in Jesus Christ.

At summer's end, with the long siege of sickness past, Emma had one more brush with death. One particularly sultry day, just as she finished her chores and rested briefly in the shade of the over-hanging trees, a vaguely familiar figure walked up the incline from the river landing. As the man drew nearer and removed his hat to wipe his brow, she recognized her sister Elizabeth's son, Lorenzo Wasson. A sudden burst of joy swept over her at seeing a family member, and she spontaneously stood up, excitedly waved to him. He responded in kind and a moment later was in her yard. She hurried to meet him.

"Lorenzo! What an unexpected pleasure!"

"Aunt Emma!" Her tall, slim nephew greeted her with an affectionate smile, put down a small satchel he was carrying, and pressed both her hands in his. "I am well, and am especially glad to see you so 'Hale' and hearty! I hear the ague has taken its toll in these parts. You must have had much sickness this past summer. Is your family well?"

"Yes, right now we're all well enough. Come, bring your bag and sit out here where it is cool. Joseph will be delighted to see you."

They sat in the shade, chatting amicably for a few minutes. After Emma's introduction of the children and a brief rehearsal of how the Smith family had come to settle there, Lorenzo finally disclosed his unhappy news.

"Aunt Emma, I have come to tell you of the death of Grandfather Hale. During the first few days of this year, he took sud-denly ill, and before any of us could discover why, he passed from this earth. Grandma Hale has been none too well herself. I'm sorry. . . sorry to be the bearer of bad news, but I wanted you to learn of it from family, not someone else."

Emma's pleasant expression had frozen. Her brown eyes lost their luster, and she looked away, staring out across the river. Her hands, typically busy with needlework, rested in her lap, while she was lost in reverie. Her nephew sat quietly, respecting her grief, turning his hat over in his hands. It was several minutes before she spoke.

"Was the family there?"

"Most everyone."

"Did he. . . ask after me?"

Lorenzo hesitated, then responded softly, "No."

Emma had been sitting stiffly upright. At that quiet answer, she sank back into her chair. Her face lost all expression. The years that separated her from her father seemed but moments. She no longer remembered him as he had been at their last goodbye, hard, cold, and angry. That was not the father she cherished. No, Emma remembered her papa, the man who swung her up into his arms, the man who tickled her cheek with his bushy whiskers, the powerful hunter returning with food for their winter supply, the patient instructor who had taught her to paddle a canoe and ride a horse. She remembered someone who felt out of place in a pew of the Methodist church, but went, just the same, to be with the people he cared for most — his daughter and family. She tried to stifle her sobs as she hurried into the house to regain her composure.

Her nephew waited quietly under the trees. He had known the news would be hard on his aunt. He wished he had been able to truthfully tell Emma that his grandfather had died speaking her name, but it was not so. Isaac Hale had asked for each of his children and given them instructions, but his favorite daughter's name had not crossed his lips. Only Elizabeth, her mother, had considered Emma, and pleaded with her family to carry the news to her in person. Lorenzo had always admired his mother's sister and wanted to understand what had caused her to follow Joseph Smith. So he had taken up the charge to find Emma and bring her news of the death. Observing the new houses and looking across the river, Lorenzo thought he had never seen a lovelier spot. He considered staying a while to judge this new religion for himself.

When Emma returned, sad but under control, they talked a bit more of family matters, but the joy had gone out of their conversation. For Emma, it was a deep blow to realize that even on his deathbed, her father had not forgiven her for choosing Joseph. With a sigh, she reflected over the past few years and all she had endured. As hard as it had been, it was harder still to learn her father had died without so much as a word for her. That wound went straight to her heart.

Emma knew the days of having her husband at home could not last, but it was so satisfying, seeing him at work on his history, writing, dictating, and consulting with associates about building up the settlement. He had asked his brother, Don Carlos, to start a newspaper for the town. Mary Smith's brother-in-law, Robert B. Thompson, helped him set up the press in the cellar of a warehouse by the river. After weeks of working in the damp, both men became ill with fever and chills, and Don Carlos' co-publisher, Ebenezer Robinson, brought out the first edition of the Times and Seasons in November 1839.

Joseph worked hard collecting hundreds of affidavits from the saints regarding the persecution in Missouri. He wrote a lengthy petition to the United States Congress rehearsing those wrongs, insisting on their constitutional rights, and asking for two million dollars in reparations. Almost one year to the day of his Missouri incarceration, he set out for Washington D.C. with Sidney Rigdon, Elias Higbee, his attorney, and Porter Rockwell, his faithful bodyguard. They left in a two-horse carriage, October 29 1839, heading for Quincy on the first leg of their journey to obtain redress.

"Do you really have to go?" Emma protested when he told her of the intended trip. "Isn't it enough to send Sidney and Elias?"

Joseph had known she would protest. Emma clung to him more now than she ever had before.

"I'm afraid I must go. It is the feeling of the high council that I need to go in person to dispel the lies about us and to importune the President and Congress. I hope Sidney will be well enough to contribute to the effort. When we go before Congress we will need his eloquence. Don't worry, Emma, I'll be all right."

"How long will you be gone?" Emma asked, sick at heart.

"No longer than necessary. I have hopes that when the members of congress hear the truth and read the affidavits, they will be outraged. It is only right that Missouri recompense us. Not that they can bring back our dead, or give back our property, but if we had a monetary settlement, it would help finance our city's development."

"You know I'll pray for your success. The sooner your petition is granted, the sooner you'll be home."

"Not tired of me yet?" he kissed her forehead.

"I don't get much of a chance. When you're home, you're not home. You're writing, consulting, preaching or planning. But. . . " she continued over his protest, "I'll take that over your being gone."

"Do you have enough supplies?"

"I can send to Quincy if need be. One day, maybe Nauvoo will have a ferry of its own to bring goods upriver to us."

"A very good idea! Now, we must be off. Wish us well."

"I do! Oh, I do! Hurry home."

Hurry was not the order of the day in Washington. Even getting there proved more difficult than they had anticipated. Sidney became ill even before they reached Springfield. They were referred to a new convert and well-to-do physician, Dr. Robert Foster, a friend of Isaac Galland. Foster attended to Rigdon overnight, packing his feet with poultices and bleeding him, but Sidney was no better in the morning. Still, he refused to be left behind. He wanted desperately to speak before Congress and assist Joseph as his counselor. Foster packed quickly and joined the group. Despite his constant attention, however, Sidney's condition worsened. It was now November, and the open-air carriage was hard on them all as they continued across Illinois, Indiana, and into Ohio. Joseph and Porter sat on the driver's seat while Sidney reclined in the back of the carriage, tucked between blankets, quilts, and heated stones. Foster and Higbee idled away the time debating the points of the petition. After ten more days of travel, Sidney's health fell so low he was in danger of total collapse, so Joseph arranged for him, Porter, and Dr. Foster to stay at an inn in Columbus, Ohio, while he and Elias continued on by stagecoach.

It was more comfortable for them in the enclosed coach, and Joseph, as was his inclination, made friends with the other occupants, some members of Congress and two women, one of whom had a babe-in-arms. At first they were reluctant to converse with the notorious Joseph Smith. Tales of the "Mormon prophet" had spread throughout the country. One of the ladies studied him continually to catch any evidence of horns beneath his beaver hat. After all, Smith was reputed to be the devil incarnate!

The congressmen were cautious. They didn't want to be drawn into conversation about the recent Mormon troubles in Missouri. They would, however, discuss the financial plight of the states. That was uppermost in everyone's mind. Ohio's economy was struggling, and Illinois was among several states, including Missouri, on the verge of financial collapse. A congressman asked about Joseph's political leanings. Joseph supported Illinois Governor Carlin, who had promised the Mormons permanent protection in his state and support for their petition against Missouri on constitutional grounds.

After a week, the prophet had won the respect of his fellow travelers. One day, on mountainous terrain, a little distance from the capital, the stagecoach driver stopped at a public inn for a grog of ale. The passengers, all anxious to go on, remained in the coach. The horses were unattended.

"Mr. Smith, do you actually intend to sue Missouri?" one of the gentlemen asked. He was cut off by a sudden jolt. Panic broke out as the horses bolted and the coach rocked precariously as it began a headlong plunge down the steep road at full speed.

"Aaah," the mother screamed. "My baby, my baby!"

"Sit still," another passenger commanded, "We'll be all right."

"We're tipping!" she screamed again.

"We won't tip," Joseph shouted above her. "Elias, keep this woman calm. I'm going to stop the horses."

With that, he threw open the coach door, and clinging to the upper side of the vehicle, inched his way to the driver's box. "Whoa-o-o-o," he shouted to the frantic animals. "Whoa, now. Whoa. . . !"

They ran on, out of control, with the stage swaying dangerously. If he didn't get the horses under control soon, they might be killed. He grasped the reins tightly and began to gently pull back, with a long, steady, careful pressure, all the while calling to the animals.

"Whoa, whoa! Steady, boy!" Joseph's voice was low and comforting. The reckless descent began to slow. The horses still snorted and tossed their heads, but they slowed finally to a walk. When he had reined them in completely, jumped down, and soothed the frightened animals, he checked on the terrorized passengers.

The mother had fainted, and Elias held her baby. The other young woman was speechless and wide-eyed. No more did she look at Joseph as though he were the devil incarnate. When he helped her out of the coach, she gave him her heartfelt thanks. The Mormon prophet, it seemed, had influence over animals as well as people. After their parting the next day, however, Joseph would hear no more from his traveling companions of praise or gratitude.

Joseph and Elias wasted no time. They found a boarding-house, and the next morning prepared to enter "the lion's den." They took a coach to President Martin Van Buren's White House residence, presented themselves at the door, and asked politely to speak with the President of the United States.

"Whom shall I say is calling?" the servant asked.

"Tell him that Joseph Smith, and Judge Elias Higbee of Illinois wish to speak with him of our petition to Congress." Joseph handed his papers to the servant.

Minutes later the servant returned, took their hats, and showed them into the President's study. Van Buren was at his desk, reading. He did not look up. Joseph and Elias took the chance to look around. It was an elegant room, heavily draped to keep out cold and heat. The furniture was all dark mahogany, polished until it shone. Thick, plush, imported carpets covered the hardwood floor. In the corner, a grandfather clock chimed the hour.

After a few moments, Van Buren laid down the petition papers, turned to the visitors and grimaced in a kind of smile.

"So you're the Mormon prophet. You're causing quite a commotion out West, sir. What do you want of me?"

Joseph handed him a letter of introduction from Illinois Governor Thomas Carlin. The President took it with a bit of a frown, broke the seal, and scanned the letter. The frown deepened. He pulled at his earlobe, then folded the letter, and handed it back to Joseph.

"See here, I respect your letter from the governor, and have reviewed your grievances with the state of Missouri. They may even be just, but what can I do? If I step into the middle of this, I'll come up against the whole state. Besides, Missouri can't pay its current indebtedness, much less two million dollars to you. Be reasonable man, these are hard times for all."

Joseph would not be put off. "Sir, surely you are an honorable man, or you would not hold the position you do. I know you have sworn an oath to protect our constitutional rights. If you had seen the violation of those rights, as I have, the abuse of women and children, the murder of innocent men, the theft of land, the looting and burning of homes — well, I can't help but think you would be moved to restore our rights and the means to start over."

"But two million dollars!"

". . . For fifteen thousand homeless people!"

Van Buren took off his reading spectacles and shook his head. "Gentlemen, your cause is just, but I can do nothing for you. I'm sorry for your people, I really am. No doubt they have been wronged. However, I believe that is primarily your responsibility, Mr. Smith. You have introduced a religion in our country that causes agitation. Everywhere you go, citizens rise up against you."

He squinted at Joseph, then at Elias sitting quietly nearby. "You don't look like scoundrels. What in the world do you preach that turns people against you?"

Joseph looked about him at the expensive trappings of power. He looked back to the President. Joseph had learned to assess a man by his eyes, but this man avoided eye contact. Van Buren squinted and shifted his gaze frequently. He smelled of cigars and aged wine. Any prolonged religious discussion would be lost on him.

"We desire to preach to all people the great plan of salvation, which was devised in heaven, as made known to the saints of God. We wish to expound the everlasting gospel of Jesus Christ, as laid down in the *revealed word of* God. We stress the necessity of embracing it with full purpose of heart to usher in the great day when Christ himself will reign upon the earth and rule Missouri, Illinois, and even

Washington D.C.! Therefore," said the prophet, as he stood up, "we shall deliver copies of our petition to Congress, that they too will be left without excuse to uphold the Constitution and our God-given right of religious belief."

Van Buren did not rise. With an expression of distaste, he watched them leave, then settled back into the settee and called his servant for a glass of wine.

Joseph and Elias set about delivering other letters of introduction to various representatives and trying to get commitments from congressmen to consider their petition. The representatives from Illinois were, understandably, the most receptive. Still, the wheels of the government turned slowly. Delays and more delays prompted Joseph to write to Hyrum.

". . . There is but little solidity and honorable deportment among those who are sent here to represent the people; but a great deal of pomposity and show. . . There is such an itching disposition to display their oratory on the most trivial occasions, and so much etiquette, bowing and scraping, twisting and turning, to make a display of their witticism, that it seems to us rather a display of folly and show, more than substance and gravity, such as becomes a great nation like ours."

U.S. Senator from Illinois, Judge Richard M. Young, however, was a refreshing exception, and eventually agreed to take their plea to the Senate. While the machinations of government wore on, Joseph went to Philadelphia by rail during the Christmas recess to preach to the local saints. Elias and Porter met him there a few days later with his carriage. When Sidney's health allowed travel, he and Dr. Foster followed Joseph and the others to Washington D.C., and then to Philadelphia. Although Dr. Foster accompanied Joseph and the others when they returned to Washington on January 27, 1840, Sidney remained behind to recuperate.

The Missouri delegates did all in their power to lessen the claims of the petition. Senator Young arranged a public meeting so Joseph could preach and try to win favor for it. As usual, he spoke so convincingly that many representatives, as well as newsmen, were temporarily swayed.

However, when no real progress was made after February 6, Joseph spoke to Elias, "I know it's hardly fair. You have been away from home as long as I have, but with Sidney also absent, Emma expecting and Hyrum bearing the load of the church alone, I must hasten my return. Will you stay and present our case?"

"Of course I will."

Joseph left for home with Porter and Dr. Foster a few days later. He had scarcely departed when Missouri's ex-Governor Boggs sent his own report to Congress refuting Joseph's claims and charging him with high treason, having conspired to circumvent existing authority and take control of north-central Missouri by force. The ire of the Missourians was raised anew at the very public Mormon petition for redress. There were questions put to Higbee about the activities of the Danites, and the testimonies of once-trusted friends, such as Thomas Marsh and William W. Phelps, were used to damn Joseph. Public opinion went against the Mormons, and their petition was dismissed. Resentful Missourians were still not content. They would not rest until they had the thoroughly discredited and utterly destroyed the Mormon prophet.

After long months, Joseph arrived back in Nauvoo bone-weary. He had endured extreme weather — snow, mud, wind, and rain. Astride his horse, he paused on the bluff above Nauvoo, marveling at what he saw; the busy, burgeoning town. A lone eagle soared above the expanse of the Mississippi River in wide, silent sweeps. It was Wednesday, March 4, 1840. A beehive of activity was in progress, and so many new families had moved in, he could see why Hyrum needed his help. Joseph soon discovered that Hyrum wasn't well. He had recovered from the ague, but had not fully regained his strength.

Joseph made his way down the narrow main road toward his little cabin on the riverbank. Spring rains had washed out part of the road. Mud sucked at his horse's hooves, but wagons pulling timber cut from the northern pineries and bricks from local kilns, delivered load after load all around him. The booming town was alive with activity. He was enthusiastically hailed by many friends, so enthusiastically, in fact, he could go only a few rods before being stopped by their hearty welcomes. As he drew closer to home, he pulled away from each encounter more quickly.

Then a tug came at his boot, and a high voice called, "Hey Mister, you look just like my Papa!"

He took off his black hat and grinned down at the young face staring up. "Hey boy, I am your Papa! Come on up here." He hauled young Joseph up to sit with him on the saddle.

"I thought you were never coming home," his son exclaimed.

"I'll always come home, son. Don't you know that?"

"Mother said you had to see the president."

"I did. But he isn't as important to me as you and the family. Have you been taking care of your mother?"

"She's expecting a baby. . . "

"I know." Joseph spurred his horse, and they galloped the rest of the way, young Joseph grinning from ear to ear. When he glanced about the Homestead, Emma was nowhere to be seen. Joseph pushed open the door, expecting to see her at the hearth or the oven. She was not there. He climbed the stairs to the bedroom. She was not there either. His high spirits tumbled. Where was she? From the back door he called, but there was no answer.

"Joseph, do you know where Mother is?"

The boy went to the corner by the hearth. Her leather bag containing medicine and herbs was gone. He answered his father, "Her bonnet is gone, and her medicine bag is gone. I guess she's visiting the sick."

"And where are Julia and your brothers?"

"At Grandma's."

Before Joseph could walk the short distance to his mother's home, Hyrum came to meet him. Word that the prophet was back had spread quickly. Joseph embraced his brother and asked about his illness, which Hyrum quickly dismissed. He had more important news, for he carried a letter for Joseph with word that their petition had been dismissed. The whole effort had been in vain. Hyrum also handed him a letter from a Mr. John C. Bennett, soon to be confirmed quartermaster general of the Illinois militia, and a professed doctor. He was offering his services in ridding Nauvoo of the fever.

"I'll respond to Mr. Bennett in due time. Right now, I want to see my wife. Do you know where she is?"

"One of our new families sent for her. Their baby is due, so she took the buggy at dawn and has been gone ever since. Julia and the boys spent the morning at our house, but they went with Mother and Father to the Kimballs' a few hours ago. Julia is wonderfully responsible for such a young girl."

Joseph was no longer listening. He had spied a rig coming down the road, bouncing over the ruts. His wife was driving the horse as fast as she dared. She reined in, climbed down, and tossed the reins to her brother-in-law. Then she was in Joseph's arms. So eager was he to embrace his expectant wife he hardly realized she was chastising him.

"I have looked for you everywhere," she said breathlessly. "Everyone in town has seen and spoken to you, with the notable exception of your wife. Don't you know the way home, Mr. Smith?"

"Me? I've been home alone, looking for my wife, and she was gone!"

"You look fine! Travel must agree with you."

"I'm hoping you'll agree with me most!"

Emma spoke over her shoulder. "Please excuse us now, dear Hyrum. My husband is home, and for a little while at least, he's all mine!" She smiled as she took Joseph's arm, and guided him firmly toward the house. "Joseph, son, go back to Grandma's and help Julia tend the little ones."

Together after months, they couldn't bear to be any place but in each other's arms, even when discussing Joseph's disappointing trip or the local news. Most distressing of all were Emma's reports of a band of thieves hiding out along the river bottoms. Visitors had been robbed, and blamed it on the Mormons. The neighboring *Warsaw Signal* newspaper published every rumor about the matter and people in the area were blaming everything on the Latter-day Saints.

"Be patient, dear," Joseph soothed her concerns. "The church is petitioning the state for incorporation, and once we obtain a charter, we'll be empowered to govern and regulate affairs here. Nauvoo will become the most orderly city in the world."

However, Emma was not the only one who was worried about crimes being blamed on the saints. Hyrum presented a report that very evening. Joseph listened to him, then laid plans to eradicate the band.

"Most important is for Nauvoo to be incorporated. We must insure that we have *all* legal rights to protect ourselves from any more attacks, official or otherwise, and a charter will grant us the ability to raise a militia. It will also empower us to establish a university."

By June 1840, Nauvoo, as Commerce was officially renamed in April, had spread across the flat and the bluffs, and more settlers came every day. The need for a city charter became more and more urgent. However, church leaders delayed work on petitioning the Illinois legislature for a city charter until Elias Higbee returned from Washington.

As the days grew longer and the weather warmer, Emma's pace slowed, for her seventh child would soon be born. In the late afternoon, she would sit outside in the shade of the trees, which overhung her yard. With a basket of mending beside her, she plied her needle and savored the long, cool shadows of approaching twilight. Joseph's voice drifted out from the open doorway as he labored over the charter petition. Children raced along the riverbank collecting berries, sticks, polliwogs, and sometimes a few cuts and bruises, as reckless youth will do.

Emma had accumulated a good supply of clean linen and healing herbs, as she cheerfully anticipated the baby's birth. June 13, 1840, their next son was born. Even through the effort and pain of childbirth, it was a joyous occasion, and Emma remained calm. Likewise, the child was even-tempered, with watchful eyes and a placid nature. His personality was so like that of Joseph's younger brother, the babe was named for his uncle, Don Carlos Smith.

"Are you sure you like that name for our son?" Joseph asked Emma solicitously.

"It's perfect," Emma murmured, her lips against the soft, downy hair of her newborn. "With such a name, perhaps he'll surpass even his father in height."

"With such a mother, he'll no doubt surpass me in many things."

Little Carlos — as he was often called — provided a happy relief from business and government concerns, for Joseph loved to push away from his desk, stand, stretch, and gather his son in his arms, taking a much needed respite. Don Carlos was the easiest birth of all Emma's children, and he was sturdy and healthy. Still, she watched carefully for any signs of the swamp fever, so prevalent in their settlement, a dreaded companion of the hot weather.

Joseph's parents lived just a few rods away from the Homestead. Emma enjoyed her privacy, but she prized wonderful afternoons of visiting with Mother Smith and her sisters-in-law as the women snapped beans, shelled peas, baked bread, made candles, spun wool or hooked rugs. An almost constant breeze from the river cooled her summer kitchen. The Smith children played between family homes, and Emma took on the task of teaching them their letters. Joseph was preparing the *Book of Abraham* for publication, as well as a reprint and update of the *Doctrine and Covenants* — a compilation of latter-day revelations — and a revised hymnal. He also began dictating a detailed history of the church to Howard Coray.

Joseph's energy seemed to know no bounds. He went with Emma to visit the sick, laying hands on their heads to bless them. He oversaw the sale of lots in Nauvoo, along with the paperwork required. Church leaders met with him weekly to discuss draining the swamp, ordaining officers, and purchasing more land. Political visitors also became more commonplace, seeking Joseph's favor in upcoming elections. Through all this, Emma moved efficiently, making provisions for her home and family, gardening, nursing the sick, and guiding her children with a firm hand.

Joseph seldom held a grudge. He readily gave his forgiveness to anyone if they simply asked, and in June, William W. Phelps wrote asking forgiveness for his apostasy in Far West. Joseph sent a heartfelt response.

"When we read your letter, truly our hearts melted. . . It is true we have suffered much in consequence of your behavior. The cup of gall, already full enough.. . . . was indeed filled to overflowing when you turned

against us. . . However, the cup has been drunk. The will of the Father has been done, and we are yet alive, for which we thank the Lord. . . Believing your confession to be real and your repentance genuine, I shall be happy once again to give you the right hand of fellowship and rejoice over the returning prodigal. . .

Come, dear brother, since the war is past.
For friends at first are friends at last.

Yours as ever, Joseph Smith, Jun."

Frederick G. Williams earlier sought reinstatement, after having broken fellowship with Joseph in Kirtland. When he joined the saints in Quincy in March 1839 and discovered his excommunication, he pleaded for restored membership. Once again — and to Emma's unbounded gratitude, for she loved Rebecca Williams as a sister — Joseph happily extended the hand of fellowship to a friend.

In August, 1840, a high councilman and good friend, Seymour Brunson, died. The next day, Joseph spoke at his funeral. The heat and humidity were unrelenting. There were handheld fans fluttering throughout the outdoor assembly gathered to honor this good man. Joseph spoke with feeling about his longtime friend, and assured them Seymour Brunson would come forth in the resurrection a whole man, made perfect in Christ. Then he held up his Bible and quoted from First Corinthians, 15:

"If in this life only we have hope in Christ, we are of all men most miserable. But now is Christ risen from the dead, and become the firstfruits of them that slept. For since by man came death, by man came

306

also the resurrection of the dead. For as in Adam all die, even so in Christ shall all be made alive. . .

And when all things shall be subdued unto him, then shall the Son also himself be subject unto him that put all things under him, that God may be all in all. Else what shall they do which are baptized for the dead, if the dead rise not at all? why are they then baptized for the dead?

. . . All flesh is not the same flesh: but there is one kind of flesh of men, another flesh of beasts, another of fishes, and another of birds. There are also celestial bodies, and bodies terrestrial: but the glory of the celestial is one, and the glory of the terrestrial is another. There is one glory of the sun, and another glory of the moon, and another glory of the stars: . . . So also is the resurrection of the dead. It is sown in corruption; it is raised in incorruption: It is sown in dishonour; it is raised in glory: it is sown in weakness; it is raised in power. . ."

The prophet's voice carried across the grove as he spoke with all the energy of his soul.

"Brothers and sisters, do not fear that our friend will languish in the grave. He will be raised up by Jesus Christ, in due time with a celestial body, which is to say, a body like Christ's, glorious, everlasting, and heir to the highest blessings God can give! But what of those beloved ones who have died without hearing the gospel? You all have those. There are good people all over the earth, in all ages of the earth, who have never in this life heard of the gospel of Jesus Christ. Shall they languish eternally in hell, as the Christian churches preach? I tell you the love of Christ extends to all, and they must be baptized in His kingdom. How will this be accomplished? You will be the saviors on Mount Zion who will be baptized in their stead, so they may be saved in the Kingdom of God."

Emma sat up straighter. She looked around. The fans stopped, the air was still. This was new doctrine! To be baptized for loved ones who were dead — it was unheard of! As usual, Joseph taught with power, never hedging, and never minding whom he offended. Others looked around as she did. Some were confused, but on many faces a new light of hope shone. All at once, Emma realized she could participate in this new ordinance. She had loved ones who had died without receiving the truth! She would be baptized for them! Perhaps in the next life her father's eyes might be opened, and he would accept the teachings of the restored gospel!

Word of the new doctrine spread rapidly. Baptisms were performed for deceased parents, children, and other beloved family members. Emma's nephew, Lorenzo Wasson was among the first to participate in the new ordinance. Soon thereafter, Emma waded out into the cool river water and was baptized for Isaac Hale, with a prayer in her heart that God would heal the rift between them in the great hereafter.

Eventually, the charter petition for the Nauvoo Charter was refined for submission to the state legislature. Though Joseph was the inspiration behind it, the finished product was derived from the contributions of many men, including the expertise of Dr. John C. Bennett.

Bennett had corresponded with Joseph many times and finally met him in Hyrum's parlor in early September 1840. He was determined to befriend the saints, and in particular, their prophet. He was almost a head shorter than Joseph, slim, dapper, and given to pomp and ceremony. He had a Roman nose, and dark hair which curled about his face as prettily as any woman's. Still, his handshake was firm, and he was a man of great energy and talent.

Though very different in temperament, he and Joseph struck up a friendship. Bennett seemed to be able to contribute on so many fronts, and Sidney and Hyrum were both in ill health. Although Elias Higbee was Joseph's principle legal counsel, Bennett had considerable influence in Springfield, where the legislature would meet to consider the petition for a charter. He had taken care over the years to acquaint himself with people of political and social prominence. Now a duly commissioned quartermaster general, and new member of the church, he promised to use all his influence to help push the petition through.

Whether or not there was any real purpose or reason, Bennett consulted with Joseph almost daily. Soon he was Joseph's right-hand man, another counselor, and indispensable. While cultivating his position with Joseph, Bennett was offering his services as a doctor to the ladies in a most solicitous style.

Bennett displayed knowledge in many areas, and had an idea for a cure of the swamp fever. He and Joseph went riding together through the marshlands. In places the trees and vines were so thick their horses could hardly get through.

Bennett gestured at the trees. "Cut them down. You need the timber, and the trees provide so much shade, the sun can't dry out these swampy areas. I tell you as a qualified doctor, the swamp gas carries disease and infects your people. Tell them to sleep on the second story and to drink quinine. Also, there is a beautiful red fruit that is beneficial to the health. It is called the 'tomato.' I highly recommend it."

"We don't have quinine."

"But, as it happens, I do. I will be happy to sell my stock at a loss if necessary, to alleviate suffering in Nauvoo. Our people have suffered quite enough!"

"Brother John, we haven't money to pay for your services or your medicine right now. I had hoped the United States Congress would recognize our afflictions and recompense us for our losses. That hope is gone."

Bennett shook his head regretfully as he listened to Joseph's disappointment. "I want no compensation, Brother Joseph. Your regard and the opportunity to be of help is enough for me."

Joseph studied the sincerity of the new convert. "If you want to share the poverty of the saints, you are welcome to do so," Joseph said. "And by doing thus, you may rely on the approval of Jehovah."

"Poverty will not be your lot for long," Bennett remarked shrewdly. "You're a man who would come out victorious, though they should pile the Rocky Mountains on top of you."

Emma was not amused by Dr. Bennett. He knocked at her door one evening in autumn, introduced himself, and asked for her husband. As was customary, Joseph invited his new friend to dinner, and Bennett spent the evening flattering his hostess. He quickly saw that the Smith home was ruled by the capable hand of Emma Smith, for her touch was everywhere, from the cunning little highchair for her baby, to the glazed window glass she had purchased from Brigham Young. Rag rugs tied by her own hand covered the wooden floor. Apparently, the way to Emma's favor was through her home and family, so he complimented her cooking, noticed her fine stitching, and even played with her children. Emma was wary. She sensed a hidden purpose in his flattery.

That evening when the Smiths retired, she warned her husband, "He's a small man, Joseph, in more ways than one. He has a sneaky look, and he's jealous of you."

"Now why should he be jealous of me? I'm a pauper, with a big job on my hands."

"But you have authority. He obviously aspires to authority. He enjoys the title, "Dr. Bennett," though he's no more knowledgeable than I am. . . and he is an officer in the state militia. He wants more power. One day, he'll want *your* power."

Joseph contemplated his wife words. She was astute. He was pleased she wanted to protect him from others who would use him.

"I won't have the man near me, Joseph. You may find him a useful friend, but I don't trust him."

Her husband laughed. "You are certainly one of the few women who feel that way. Other ladies find him rather charming. He is polished, dapper — altogether a gentleman, don't you think?"

Emma was uncharacteristically scornful. "He's a charlatan."

"Emma, that is uncharitable."

"If I'm wrong, I'll repent!"

Joseph's sister Lucy ran to his house a few days later. "Joseph, Mother says to come quickly! Father is coughing blood again." She was out of breath from running.

Joseph was at work on the charter petition, but he shoved it aside. Joseph Sr. had been ill for a long time. Mother Lucy had tended him day and night for months. He knew his father would not live much longer, but now that a crisis had arrived, Joseph could not bear the thought of losing him.

It was September 14, 1840, and the summer heat had cooled. His parents' cottage was opened to breezes from the river. Joseph found his mother holding her husband's hand. She patted it now and then, and wiped his dry lips with a wet handkerchief.

Lucy looked up at her son. "I believe something has burst inside. Your father's been in terrible pain all night. I can't get him to take any nourishment. He keeps saying he wants to give his children blessings. Please talk to him, Joseph," and she quickly left, wiping her eyes.

Joseph took up the vigil at the old man's bedside. "Father, the Lord revealed a new doctrine for the kingdom. We are to have the privilege of being baptized for our kindred dead who never had the chance in this life."

His father's face brightened for a moment. His sunken eyes shone as he smiled at his son. "Alvin! You can be baptized for Alvin! Do it soon!" After a moment, the old man asked, "Where are my other children? I shall not live much longer, and I want to bless them."

They started arriving within the hour. Joseph, Sophronia, Hyrum, Samuel, Don Carlos, William, and Lucy gathered in his little room. Father Smith gave each of them his last blessing. He even pronounced a blessing for Katherine who was home with her very sick husband. The dying man was perfectly calm as tears streamed the faces of his wife and children.

"Mother," he whispered to Lucy, "do you know you are one of the most singular women in the world?"

Lucy shook her head and wiped her eyes on her apron, but the patriarch would not be denied. "You've brought up my children and comforted them in every circumstance."

She stroked his frail hand. Her heart was too full for words.

"Remember how we always said we wanted to die together? But we can't! You must stay and comfort these children now."

Sorrowful sobs came from a shattered Lucy. She had lived with this dear man and loved him for forty-four years. How could she live without him now?

He whispered a final prophecy to Lucy. "Your last days shall be your best days, and you will have more power over your enemies than you have had. Again I say, be comforted."

Presently he looked up, and with a tone of surprise he said, "I can see and hear as well as I ever could. I can see Alvin!" He paused a moment, then said, "I shall live but seven or eight minutes."

Feebly, their patriarch and father straightened his wasted body on the bed, joined his hands together, and while his children and wife watched and wept, his spirit calmly took leave of the old temple. His breath stopped without a struggle. A father in Israel was gone!

Chapter Nine

Adversaries and Allies

ohn C. Bennett was surrounded by the important men of the state, and was on a first name basis with many of them, which, he thought, could not fail to impress Joseph Smith. Bennett was smugly satisfied that he had been chosen over Sidney Rigdon to lobby for the church petition. The older man, and counselor to Joseph, had been ill for two years, hardly well enough to attend his church meetings. Bennett was more than willing to fill the vacuum left by Sidney's absence, yet the role of assistant president was not the one he coveted. He had something more in mind, something on an equal footing with Joseph. First, however, he must exert his influence to see that the charter was approved.

"These poor, persecuted people have suffered unmentionable atrocities at the hands of so-called good citizens of these United States," Bennett had lobbied prominent legislators. Then he went on to mention the abuses with as inflammatory rhetoric as possible, following up with a glowing account of Nauvoo's orderly settlement and

Smith's expansive vision for the town. Bennett had secured many promises of support. Of course, the vote by a lower house representative, Abraham Lincoln, was questionable.

Lincoln had run for office as a Whig, against Democrat James H. Ralston. Ordinarily, Joseph would not have promoted a Democrat, for it was the party of Boggs and Van Buren. However, Ralston had come to Nauvoo and befriended the prophet, pledging his support for land development. Joseph had voted for him, and the saints had done likewise. Now, Joseph wondered if he had done the right thing. Abraham Lincoln was mild as a lamb, but shrewd as a fox. Lincoln's honesty was as legendary as the political ambitions of his colleague, Stephen A. Douglas. Douglas, now Illinois Secretary of State, supported a broad charter for Nauvoo, but Lincoln and his associates had the vote to approve or deny it.

The vote for approval of a charter for Nauvoo was taken on a bleak December day in 1840 and passed easily, along with other proposed legislation. Joseph breathed a sigh of relief, when he heard Lincoln had voted for it after all.

Governor Thomas Carlin signed the approved legislation into law on December 16, 1840, effective the first Monday of February 1841. When city elections were held in January, John C. Bennett was the only name on the ballot for mayor of the newly chartered Nauvoo. The plum position fell like overripe fruit into his hands.

Emma's concern was not diminished by the victory. "Now that Mister Bennett is mayor, I suppose he will be even more insufferably important, if that's possible," Emma commented as she served her husband's breakfast.

"Emma, I don't like the way you talk about John. He is extremely capable. He's the best choice for mayor. Would you rather I had taken the position?"

"No." She sat across the table from Joseph. "You have enough to do. Why not Elias Higbee? I don't understand the fascination with Mister Bennett."

"You can't deny he was instrumental in getting the petition passed. Without his lobbying, we would still not have a charter. John is energetic, ambitious, and as anxious to build up Nauvoo as I am. We need him."

Emma finally backed down, as she usually did in an argument with her husband. "Be careful, Joseph. Don't trust him."

"Well, so far, I do."

Bennett went to work establishing the university the legislature had approved. He appointed himself chancellor, as well as head of the Agricultural and Manufacturing Association, and Major General of the Nauvoo Legion. For university trustees, he appointed capable men such as Orson Pratt, Orson Spencer, and Sidney Rigdon, but a structure was never built. The plans languished in the shadow of a more important undertaking.

For Joseph the victory of obtaining a city charter was overshadowed by more death in the Smith family. Samuel's wife, Mary, died January 25, 1841, another victim of the Missouri persecutions. Hyrum was especially grieved, remembering his own loss when Jerusha died. Now his brotherly bonds with quiet, dependable Samuel deepened.

At April Conference, Joseph directed the laying of cornerstones for the Nauvoo Temple. That day began with a call to arms. It rang out across the flat, and fourteen companies of the Nauvoo Legion were joined by two adjunct units from Iowa. John C. Bennett had worked hard building a militia from several adjoining towns. Every man was required to serve, and all were willing, for the memory of Missouri was still vivid in their minds. Even boys were trained in a youth organization. Bennett loved to don his splendid uniform and ride his horse in front of the farmers, many of whom practiced formation drills in bare feet. He managed to acquire three cannons for the Nauvoo Legion and a plentiful supply of state-issued rifles. The militia drilled three times a week. On April 6, 1841, they made an impressive debut. The men formed companies, wearing their best appropriate clothing, while their officers appeared in full military dress.

Joseph had already determined to lay the temple cornerstones and wanted this to be a day of ceremony and celebration, so weeks of planning resulted in a showy drill by the Nauvoo Legion, followed by a parade. Joseph's dark blue, military uniform was topped by a hat with a pure white plume. He carried a dress sword given to him only weeks before. Emma wanted to escape public attention, but her husband would have none of it.

"You shall ride in the parade beside me," Joseph insisted.

Emma donned the new riding habit her husband had purchased for her, and rode next to him, her voluminous skirt neatly draped, and the veil of her fancy hat thrown back.

The day marked the first of many such celebrations. The saints of Nauvoo were a dedicated people, but not stodgy. They enjoyed a social gathering, as did their prophet. He left oration to Sidney, and as soon as the ceremony and singing were over, Joseph descended the speaker's stand to mingle with his friends. He shook hands with gusto, and carried children about on his shoulders. He danced to the strains of the Nauvoo band, and in the afternoon, he helped serve a feast, which the women had prepared. While Emma observed her husband with satisfaction, not everyone admired him.

Thomas Sharp was among the Illinois neighbors invited that day. He was the editor of the influential *Warsaw Signal*, a newspaper published in nearby Warsaw devoted to county affairs. Sharp was a lawyer, and his interest was in stirring up proper attention to politics. He used his newspaper to that end, endorsing candidates, examining issues and exposing fraud. He had heard much of Joseph Smith, and considered him an imposter. He was there to meet the man and disclose his deceptions. In Sharp's opinion, Smith held far too much power as the military, political, and spiritual head of Nauvoo, without regard for separation of church and state. Sharp studied the men surrounding Smith. Surely one of them had reason to turn on a leader with so much influence and power. He decided to find that man and learn about the real Joseph Smith.

Emma noted Thomas Sharp standing out from other visitors. He had a pale complexion, long hands and fingers, and he frequently said, "What was that? Can you speak louder?" He took her hand as if holding a snake by the tail.

What a strange man, Emma thought. He has spent the whole day determined not to dance, not to eat, not to socialize. Why did he come?

She tried to engage him in conversation, but his answers were terse and evasive. He asked nothing about her or Joseph, but scrutinized the prophet. And Emma watched *him*. An uneasy feeling warned her he would be trouble in the future. Some weeks later, it became clear he had come for editorial ideas. Everything was fodder for his writing. Apparently, the only person he approved of was Mayor Bennett.

The main event of the conference was the laying of the temple cornerstones. The Nauvoo Legion encircled the temple lot in proud formation. Military procedure was strictly observed, and the citizens of Nauvoo thrilled to the pomp and ceremony, as well as the challenge to again build a house of the Lord. The saints who had lived in Kirtland noted the new structure was to be larger than the one they had built. It would rise nearly sixty feet from the bluff lot Joseph had selected. Baptisms would be done in the basement. There would be two main floor assembly halls with pulpits at the east and west ends, similar to the Kirtland Temple. There would also be rooms for offices and special ordinances. Oil lamps would light the interior where instruction in gospel ordinances would be given. The beautiful, arched windows and colorful, circular ones would adorn the new temple.

Conference in April was scarcely over when construction began on the holy building. The saints donated one tenth of their income or their time, and in many cases, both. The ladies of Nauvoo started a penny collection to buy nails and glass. A limestone quarry down by the river was brought into full production. Great blocks of stone were dragged up the hill for the foundation.

The city of Nauvoo now boasted two sawmills, a tool factory, graded streets, a flourmill, many commercial shops, and extensive gardens. In less than two years, they had drained and transformed the swamplands into productive fields and were currently trying to harness the power of the Mississippi River to help industrialize their city.

"Why is it so imperative we build this temple right now, Joseph?" John C. Bennett protested. "We'll bankrupt the city trying to pay for materials. I would rather see a university built. The temple is too ambitious an undertaking to start right now." Bennett and Joseph sat on a large block of stone, observing the foundation being laid.

Joseph was unmoved. "You'll understand when it is done. It is imperative because I cannot effectively teach the fullness of the priesthood any other place. There are binding covenants this people must make with the Lord, and it can't be properly done elsewhere."

"Like baptism for the dead? That's already being done in the river. I'm not sure I fully accept that principle yet. Still. . . " he quickly changed his tone when Joseph looked at him reproachfully, "still, I admit it does make sense from a scriptural standpoint, and it relieves the mind about loved ones who die without the gospel."

"There's more," Joseph said simply.

Bennett was silent, wondering what Joseph meant. After a bit, Joseph remarked, "John, I have already taught you about plural marriage. Beyond that, there is a great covenant of eternal marriage to be revealed in this temple — sealings that will create celestial kingdoms with a man and his wife at the head, and their posterity joined in an unbreakable bond. There is a divine order you know nothing of as yet. The world knows nothing of it."

The prophet looked sternly at his new counselor in the church first presidency. "To be worthy, your eye must be single to the glory of God, and all your relations founded on that. Tell me, in all the time you've been with us, have you not found a woman suitable for a wife?"

Bennett stumbled over his words. "I, uh,. . . well, I've, uh, . . . thought of several."

"But you haven't approached any of them?"

"No! Oh, no! I want to know the mind of the Lord in this matter, before I do."

Later, Joseph was to learn that wasn't exactly true. Bennett was already married — a fact he concealed from Joseph — yet every pretty face caught his attention. As a doctor, he enjoyed something most men did not: personal, private time with the ladies. He began to make serious advances to young women. Some were Emma's friends, and she soon confronted Joseph.

"The lord mayor is working on more than the town's business," Emma commented one night as she prepared for bed.

"Meaning?"

"There has been considerable talk."

Joseph did not pause, but went right on removing his boots. "There is always talk."

"Priscinda Huntington is a discreet woman, but even she has complained that Bennett has made improper advances."

"Priscinda?" Joseph frowned. "I'll have to ask John about it."

"The sooner the better. How does it look, Joseph, for the lord mayor — your personal friend, and now your counselor as well — to be improper with women? If he comes under criticism, you will too."

Joseph sighed, "I've always been criticized."

Emma faced him directly. "Why does this man feel he can come here and behave inappropriately?" Her voice was uncharacteristically hard.

Sitting after he took off his boots, Joseph looked up at his wife. He knew what she was thinking. Joseph had taught Bennett the principle of plural marriage a month before, and she suspected him of twisting it to his own purposes. Joseph had already warned him. This was a holy principle, not to be entered into at will, but entirely dependent on revelation. That was the only way it was to be practiced. So far, Bennett had not actually taken wives, but had flitted from one pretty lady to another.

Joseph knew to what she referred. "Yes, I have told him about plural marriage."

Emma immediately turned away, her mouth closed tightly. Joseph went on, "I have emphasized the spiritual nature of the commandment, but it's plain he doesn't understand it."

"Yes, that is certainly plain. I hoped that after you obeyed that law back in Kirtland, we could put it behind us."

"Emma," he spoke carefully, "we cannot 'put it behind us.' It is God's law. Full obedience to God's commandments is the only way to eternal life. For your sake, and because of the unsettled condition of the church, I have hesitated in teaching full compliance . . . but I can't delay much longer."

She waved him away. "I don't want to hear this," she shook her head, finished fastening the buttons on her nightdress, and changed the subject.

"Emma, why won't you discuss this with me rationally?"

"I only wanted you to be aware of the talk about Bennett."

He sighed, "I know about the talk. Until I know more, I must give him the benefit of the doubt."

In June, Joseph visited Governor Carlin at his home in Quincy. Carlin had so befriended the church that Joseph sometimes sought his advice on municipal matters. They had taken dinner together and sat in the parlor talking for an hour. When they parted, Carlin did not shake hands, but turned quickly to his desk for some papers. Joseph thought it strange at the time, but took his leave and started off. June was pleasant in western Illinois. It was sunny and clear. The fields and gardens were blooming. Joseph was not expected back in Nauvoo immediately, so he stopped at Bear Creek where a small community of the saints lived. He was pondering Governor Carlin's odd behavior when he heard the thunder of horses' hooves behind him.

"Smith, I have a warrant here for your arrest!" shouted Thomas King, the Adams County sheriff, riding at the head of a small posse and accompanied by Constable Jasper of Quincy and another officer from Missouri.

"On what grounds?" Joseph startled.

"On grounds of treason in Missouri," answered another officer. "We've come from Governor Boggs with an extradition order!"

"Under whose authority?"

"Governor Thomas Carlin! He sent us to bring you back to Quincy."

"I don't believe it. I just dined with Governor Carlin."

"Here is his signature," the sheriff said roughly. "Now, come along quietly, and there will be no trouble."

"I will go with you to Quincy, but I won't go back to Missouri! I insist on a hearing in my own state!"

Joseph sent for his friends and his lawyers. O.H. Browning, along with Elias Higbee and four other attorneys, after obtaining a writ of habeas corpus in Quincy, met Joseph in Monmouth five days later for the extradition hearing before Judge Stephen A. Douglas. The charges had been printed in the local newspaper, and people in

Monmouth were hostile to the Mormons. It was a crowded court-room, and the case had no precedent. Judge Douglas listened patient-ly to an impassioned plea from Browning, who cited the fact that no charges of treason had been substantiated against Joseph Smith while in Missouri. Douglas considered the extradition papers at length and finally declined to rule. The case involved important relations between states, relations not yet clearly defined, and he did not want to set precedent. Joseph was freed, but he never forgot Governor Carlin's duplicity.

Members of the Quorum of Twelve Apostles began arriving home in July, 1841. They had been in England preaching the gospel, baptizing thousands and organizing branches and districts. Brigham Young, Heber C. Kimball, John Taylor, Orson Pratt, Willard Richards, and Joseph's devoted cousin, George A. Smith, all came home at Joseph's request. It was time to teach them concerning the new "endowment" and "fullness of the priesthood".

Joseph had put it off as long as possible. Since Kirtland, the commandment of plural marriage had been like a rock in his boot. It worried him constantly. He received prompting almost daily to live and teach the principle as being necessary to establish the cause of Zion, which would usher in the millennial reign of Christ. One night, after retiring, Joseph woke from his sleep, and immediately sat up in bed, for the room was alight with an unearthly radiance. An angel stood at the foot of the bed, and was not smiling. It was his mentor, Moroni, who held a blazing sword in his hand. Immediately, he instructed Joseph in all solemnity that if he refused to teach the commandments of God, he would be removed as head of the church and cut off *eternally* from God's presence. Joseph's heart was pound-ing as he looked down at Emma who had sleepily pulled the covers over her head. Joseph's soul was balanced precariously on the precipice of eternity. A dark eternity yawned beneath him. Salvation depended on obedience to a principle he knew would be his earthly downfall. By the time his vision of the angel ended, he knew what he must do.

Since April, he had taught the principle to a few, select men but felt it had been misunderstood. None of the Smith family, including Hyrum, was ready to accept the principle. Bennett, however, was another story. Joseph sent Hyrum to Pittsburgh to gather information about the good doctor. He soon received a letter from Hyrum confirming that Bennett had a wife and children in Ohio. They had left him after charges of domestic cruelty! Joseph had finally seen enough of John C. Bennett to believe him capable of duplicity. Joseph was determined to confront him about rumors of inappropriate relations with women, but he needed to teach the spiritually rooted principle of plural marriage to trusted members of the Quorum of Twelve before he could properly explain Bennett's deception to them.

When the last of a special joint council arrived, Joseph addressed the meeting. He rehearsed to them the commandment he had received in Kirtland concerning plural marriage, as well as the angel's recent declaration. Then he challenged them to adopt the ancient principle the old prophets had lived, for as long as God saw fit. It would be for the good of their posterity and the church. Their seed would be a great leavening as the church expanded.

Heber C. Kimball was overwhelmed by the commandment. Orson Pratt was despondent. Brigham Young said he would rather be dead. The very idea of taking plural wives, went against every moral belief they had. Joseph turned to Brigham.

"Tell me, Brigham, which wife will you claim in the resurrection? Will you claim Miriam, your first wife, or Mary Angell, your second? Which of those women and their children will you cast off in the next life?"

Brigham shook his head. "I. . . I don't know. I hadn't considered it."

"Well, consider it. God's order provides for family life beyond the grave. Your family is your personal kingdom. You must treat your wives and children with the utmost tenderness and care, or they will be given to another. On the other hand, if you enter into this covenant relationship with singleness of heart, following the prompting of the Holy Ghost, you will have God's blessing. Only righteous women will be willing to live this principle, and the posterity thereby created will provide a great, wide foundation for the growth of the church and the kingdom of God."

They all looked crestfallen. Many of them shook their heads in disbelief. Heber actually burst into tears when Joseph called him by name.

"Heber, am I a prophet?"

"I can't deny it," the plain, gentle man confessed, wiping his eyes.

"Orson? Have you preached this restored gospel, to deny me now as a prophet?"

Orson sat as if in a stupor. Joseph turned to another. "Cousin George, am I a liar? Have I ever lied to you?"

"No," George A. replied somberly.

"The world will say I am a liar. It will say that I am a wicked man, but I am not lying. . . or asking you to sin. Did Abraham sin when he prepared to sacrifice his own son? But Abraham had no choice; he was commanded to do it. And he would have done it, except God intervened and declared it a necessary test.

"God will have a tried people, and we are being tried. Obedience, after all is the great test. My love for Jesus Christ is so strong I will do *anything* He asks. So, will you be obedient, even when you don't understand the reason for the commandment? Will you live

326

by the world's standards, or by God's word? This I know: God has clearly spoken to me, and I have hesitated. He has prompted, and I have delayed. I have sinned by not obeying a clear command from the Lord. I cannot delay any longer. I must teach you eternal principles and assure your salvation, whatever the consequences.

"Now, I have done my duty. My conscious is clear. The responsibility falls on your shoulders. Don't take my word for it; I don't want you to obey *me*. Seek confirmation on your own. You must know God's will for yourself. That is your privilege and your responsibility. Inquire of God, and you will know what to do!"

Joseph stood up a lighter man. He looked happy for the first time in months. To his close friends in that council, he looked as though the weight of the world had been lifted from his shoulders. However, it had fallen on theirs.

Less than three weeks later, when Joseph confronted Bennett about his clandestine relations, Bennett broke down in a dramatic show of repentance. He swallowed poison; he begged Joseph not to expose him. He wept; he pleaded; he swore his allegiance to the church. He cited ignorance of the true principles, and Joseph gave him another chance.

"It doesn't seem like the fever," Agnes Smith said, wiping beads of perspiration from Don Carlos' neck and forehead. "But he has been sinking so fast lately, I'm afraid he won't recover." She turned to her brothers-in-law. "Can't you do something? A blessing, a prayer?"

Joseph and Hyrum stood at the foot of their brother's bed. He was twenty-five years old, the youngest brother and the family favorite. He had devoted his time and energy of late to his calling as editor of the *Times and Seasons*. Mother Lucy sat with Agnes beside Carlos' bed. Emm a had taken their two little girls to her home so

Agnes could spend the last few days with her husband, for Carlos was clearly dying. A month earlier, he had begun coughing, often so violently that blood showed on his handkerchief. He tried to conceal his fatigue, but soon pounds melted from his large frame, and night sweats kept him from restful sleep. Agnes grew more and more concerned by his shortness of breath. Finally, he collapsed, unable to rise from his bed. His voice was barely above a whisper, and he coughed continually, unable to hide the bright red blood. In the oppressive heat of August 7, 1841, Joseph and Hyrum laid hands on their brother's head, but words promising recovery did not come to them. Instead, with tears coursing down their cheeks, and in the name of God, they blessed their beloved brother with eternal life, and he soon breathed his last.

Agnes sank down at the foot of his bed, washing his feet with her tears, sobbing her grief. Neither Hyrum nor Joseph could comfort her. So recently she had lost her dearest friend and sister-in-law, Mary Bailey Smith, and her second little girl, Sophronia. Now, she faced a bleak future without these three treasures of her heart.

Mother Smith sat staring into the set features of her youngest son. She had washed that face when he was a child and patted it lovingly as he grew to young manhood. Her heart was broken. Her sweet husband had died a year earlier, now her darling son was gone. Anguish enveloped her soul. Hyrum and Joseph comforted the women all they could, but finally left, to spare their mother seeing the sorrow they, too, suffered. People had gathered at a respectful distance, awaiting the news. Joseph announced that Don Carlos was dead, and mourning became universal, for he was loved by all.

That blow was scarcely over when one week later, Emma's darling toddler, little Don Carlos, took sick overnight. She found him burning with fever in the morning. Frantically, she sponged him with cool water. She rocked him all day long, while he grew steadily worse.

Night fell. Her precious fourteen-month-old was unresponsive, his breathing shallow, his skin flushed and clammy. Dread clutched Emma's heart. Not little Carlos! Not her angel boy, Don Carlos! "Oh no, Lord, not him?" Emma lamented. She and Joseph sat with him constantly, sleeping only briefly, praying constantly. Joseph could not console his wife, for he was as stricken as she. Nothing had any effect. Their darling Carlos looked up with red-rimmed eyes, tried to reach out to them, and died on August 15.

That blow was followed by the death of Mercy's husband, Robert C. Thompson — Mary Fielding's brother-in-law and Don Carlos' co-editor of the *Times and Seasons*, on August 27. A month later, Hyrum's seven-year-old namesake son by Jerusha died as well. The entire Smith family mourned profoundly. Almost every branch had lost precious leaves.

While Emma gave herself over to caring for her other children, Joseph threw himself into construction of a unique store just down the road from his home. It was built of brick, painted red inside, and finished with wood counters and pillars painted to look like marble or mahogany. He had a private office and sleeping room upstairs, adjoining a large assembly room, where a local order of Masons met, at times school instruction was given, dances were often held, and most significantly, the new temple endowments were instituted. From his office, he could see the river with its passing boats. He opened it January 5, 1842, stocking it with goods brought in from St. Louis. His mercantile venture in Kirtland had not been successful, but in Nauvoo, a barter system was established in preference to a bank. Then too, the saints were more prosperous, and the Red Brick Store became a favorite place to gather.

Sometimes he slept at the store. Life with Emma had become difficult the past few months. Her emotions were on edge from little

Carlos' death, as well as the passing of so many other family members, and she was expecting again. Chills sometimes shook her so badly she simply huddled beneath her quilt. Chores still had to be done, but Julia and young Joseph III bore greater responsibilities as their mother's strength waned. When Joseph expressed his concern over her health, Emma tried to dismiss his worries.

She became sad and uncommunicative, refusing comfort. Joseph knew the true basis of her melancholy was more than the losses in the family, it also stemmed from rumors about plural marriage. He had had several plural wives sealed to him already, abiding by Emma's wishes that she not be forced to know or approve. Many of the church leaders had also taken at least one other wife. Some women were beginning to learn the principle from parents, siblings, or sometimes friends whom they trusted, though the principle had still not been preached publicly as revelation. Most of the women who entered into the order of plural marriage did so under personal revelation that it was a God-given commandment. Joseph admonished each woman to pray for confirmation of the principle. Others not participating in the practice spoke about it in whispers.

Emma was in the embarrassing position of having to look past what she suspected was true and to protect her husband from gossip. There were days when she was just plain angry and would not speak to him. Those times he often spent at the store. The next day she would come to him, loving as a young bride, and beg him to come home. The seesaw was wearing Joseph down. He knew she must become converted to the principle, but she would not allow him to talk to her about it.

Snows blanketed Nauvoo that winter — heavy, wet snow that fell like a shroud over a town still grieving from so many losses. Christmas in the Smith home had been subdued, and marked only by reading the Bible and a day of peace and quiet.

January passed, and Emma's activities were more curtailed as her term drew near. Mother Smith visited almost every day, noting Emma's determined show of cheerfulness and uncharacteristic slow pace. Emma and Joseph's cozy cabin seemed bleak without the prattling of little Don Carlos. Lucy tried to cheer her daughter-in-law with talk of the babe to come. She sewed baby clothes for the infant and wove a new blanket, but Emma's dutiful attempt at gratitude was hollow.

On February 6, 1842, Emma and Joseph's seventh son was born but never breathed. A perfect little boy, tiny and frail, he came into the world without a whimper or a breath. She needed a baby so desperately to assuage the grief of losing little Don Carlos! After four successful births, this one brought back the sorrow of her first bitter losses. Emma closed her eyes — and her heart — at the pronouncement by Mother Smith that the little one was not strong enough to survive. For the first time, she wondered if she was.

Joseph approached her one day at the beginning of March. "Emma, we need an organization of women to minister for the salvation of the souls of women and men." She had come back from visiting her friend, Elizabeth Ann Whitney, who had recently given birth. Snow still clung to her cloak. She rubbed cold hands before the fire.

Emma looked up at Joseph. His words seemed to please her. "We *have* talked about an official society of our own. In fact, I've spoken with both Sarah and Elizabeth Ann about it. The ladies like getting together to work. Under a well-organized plan we could get twice as much accomplished."

Joseph mused, "It should be patterned after the manner of the priesthood, although you ladies would run it. You should have a president and counselors, as we men do."

On the morning of March 17, 1842, Joseph and John Taylor met in the room above Joseph's Red Brick Store with a still fragile, but now enlivened, Emma and her closest friends. The ladies had dressed in their best gowns. Elizabeth Ann Whitney had brought her month-old baby, which Emma delighted to hold. They were elated at being asked to head up a women's organization. After brief discussion, Joseph invited them to name a president, and asked her to call two counselors. Then the gentlemen left the room, being reluctant to influence the choice.

"Of course, it should be Sister Emma," Sarah Kimball said at once. "She *is* our leader, as Joseph leads the brethren."

Bathsheba Smith said on a practical note. "She also knows the new converts. They all come to her door, looking for a place to stay."

"One of our efforts should be finding shelter for the arriving pilgrims," Eliza proposed. "There are scores coming daily."

Emma was demurely silent as her friends discussed her quali-fications. Within minutes, Eliza R. Snow officially proposed Emma as president, and a vote was taken. Pleased that they had confidence in her, Emma paused before naming her choice of counselors. She loved all the women. Two women, however, had endeared themselves to her by taking her in and sheltering her when she was destitute. Emma selected Elizabeth Ann Whitney and Sarah Cleveland as counselors.

"Eliza, speaking for the presidency, would you consider becoming secretary of this organization? We will need to keep precise records," Emma said, addressing to her trusted friend.

"Yes, of course. I would be a privilege."

Bathsheba Smith called the men back and presented the pres-idency. Joseph was not surprised.

"And have you decided on a name for the organization?"

"It shall be the Female Relief Society of Nauvoo, since our mission is to provide relief to the souls of the needy."

"Good. Now, we will ordain your presidency for their callings by the laying on of hands from the priesthood." By way of explanation, Joseph informed the ladies, "Sister Emma's promised ordination of 1830 is now confirmed, for she was officially commissioned to expound the scriptures and exhort the church in her role as 'elect lady.'"

Joseph smiled at his wife with obvious pleasure, then proceeded, "Brother Taylor, would you administer these ordinations?"

John Taylor laid his hands upon Emma's head, blessing her to preside and to dignify her office by teaching other women gospel principles.

In the days following, Joseph taught the sisters charity, mercy, harmony, unity, the exercise of spiritual gifts, and the blessings of forthcoming temple ordinances. This having been done, he declared:

"I now turn the key to you in the name of God, and this Society shall rejoice and knowledge and intelligence shall flow down from this time."

"I don't feel good about the drill today." Emma worried aloud as she helped Joseph button up his uniform for the May 7, 1842 *programme militaire* starting soon.

"Why not?" Joseph was curious to see if they felt the same prompting.

"John Bennett is up to no good. You said he wants you to be a part of this little sham battle he has arranged to show off the militia's skill. Well, what if you were 'accidentally' shot during the battle? It could happen easily, since you'll be without your guards. Joseph, don't go! You know he is not to be trusted!"

"I will handle John in my own way, in my own time. Don't worry. I have already determined to stay out of harm's way. I am investigating him. I want to verify all the evidence before I take any action."

Emma did not like the sham battles the Legion sometimes staged, yet they were entertaining, and most of the people enjoyed them. Such demonstrations made the citizenry feel safe and protected. However, it didn't sit well with outsiders, and Nauvoo had a constant stream of visitors. Riverboats docked at the Nauvoo landing daily, and sightseers wandered the town. Mock battles had been reported in the *Warsaw Signal*, instilling fear of the Nauvoo Legion in its readers. Lately, the unfavorable reporting was turning public sentiment against the Mormons.

Emma confided to Eliza Snow her most intimate fears and concerns. Eliza had come to live with them just a few months before, and it was a most welcome companionship for Emma. She sometimes wondered if perhaps her reserved nature was misunderstood as pride. Eliza was just as private as Emma and they both cherished their friendship. She had opened a school and was busy with that, but many nights when Joseph was away, the two women conversed at length.

Eliza came rushing to the house one evening just after dark. She had been late at the school preparing lessons for the next day. Walking the uneven dirt road along the river, she was passing near the Red Brick Store. She didn't realize, until she drew quite near, that an important drama was being played out on the steps. She drew back under the trees, and listened to Mayor John C. Bennett plead for his public life.

Joseph was on the steps when Bennett dashed up and grasped his hand as though for benediction. Joseph stood like a stone in the moonlight, Eliza thought, more stern than she had ever seen him.

"Brother Joseph!" Bennett implored, "don't cast me off! Perhaps I have been too hasty, too subject to my emotions. I repent of that! I swear I meant no offense. I was only trying to live the principle you taught us. I was wrong, clearly. I admit it! I repent!

My intentions were never dishonorable. I thought I was doing what you wanted."

Joseph's face was set. "John! Why are you using my name to carry on your hellish wickedness? Have I ever taught you or any of the men such lustful behavior?"

"No," Bennett shook his head. "No!"

"Have you not been forgiven once?"

"Yes! You have been generous. Could you not be so again?"

"If I fail to cut you off now, I could not teach that holy principle to the saints in the proper way. Your behavior with women is an embarrassment. You have threatened some with drugs and death. You have even threatened the life of a righteous husband, in order to have your way with his wife. This is not obedience to God's command. This is despicable behavior, done under the cloak of priesthood authority. I will not let it be used this way!"

Eliza had been accustomed to seeing the prophet as a husband and loving father. His feelings for his children were so tender he sometimes failed to discipline them, leaving that for Emma's sterner rule. She had seen his face awash with love and concern for his family, and had seen it haggard and weary, or alight with inspiration and laughter. She had never seen his features as they were this moonlit night, set and hard with disapproval. Bennett groveled before his church leader.

"I will resign, Joseph, if you will just spare me exposure. I will resign as mayor and as your counselor. Leave me my good name. It is all I have to take with me."

Joseph looked into the man's eyes. Even that was a lie. In his several professions as doctor, quartermaster general, and mayor, Bennett had amassed moderate wealth during his stay in Nauvoo. Besides property, he had gold and silver, livestock, fine furnishings for his home; however Joseph let him have his sniveling lie.

"Come with me to Alderman Wells and sign a statement that I did not authorize your behavior with women, and I will accept your resignation. You can leave town and we will let the matter drop."

"Yes, yes, of course. Daniel Wells. . . but he, uh, he's a personal friend, Joseph. Do I have to go on record?"

Joseph's look was even more severe.   "Squire Wells knows something of the scandals you have raised." Joseph said coldly, "but I shall not record it all, only what is necessary."

Eliza backed up, quietly, carefully, until the two men entered the store to get Hyrum as witness, then she struck out for the Homestead, where light flickered a short way off. In her haste to tell Emma, she stumbled once, but hurried on to tell her friend that at last Joseph had confronted Bennett.

"I'm relieved," was Emma's satisfied comment. "Joseph has felt indebted to the man for helping to get our charter passed. Then, too, my husband is more inclined to trust people than I. After so many betrayals, I trust no one completely."

Emma set her needlework aside and grasped Eliza's hand impulsively, "Do you think the *former* lord mayor will leave Nauvoo?"

"I believe so."

A shadow of concern passed over Emma's face. "He could make even more trouble away from Nauvoo. Joseph doesn't need another enemy."

Eliza was openly scornful. "I think he's too much of a coward to risk it."

Emma shook her head slowly.

"Your husband is the mightiest man on earth! God is his defense and protection. As long as he does the Lord's work, no one can hurt him."

Emma responded thoughtfully. "That's what he says too, but I am worried for him." She seemed tired lately. She spoke in measured tones, and it wasn't merely because of her position as head of the Female Relief Society. The loss of little Don Carlos and the stillborn son had torn her soul. She had put the precious wooden high chair away. Every so often, Eliza would catch her gazing out over the river with a faraway look, and when she spoke, Emma seemed distant and melancholy.

Emma patted Eliza's hand. "Thank you, my friend. Your report is the best medicine I could have had." She paused, then concluded, "We'll see how fast he leaves Nauvoo."

They didn't have to wait long. Bennett left the next day, leaving his home and furnishings to be sold at auction, taking his gold and silver and the title to his land. He went straight to Springfield where he began writing letters to the editors of the *Sangamo Journal* and the *Warsaw Signal.*

"Mr. Sharp, you once invited me to tell you the true story of Joseph Smith."

Thomas Sharp looked over his shoulder as the bell above his workshop door jingled. The voice and face were familiar. This was the man who had ridden at Smith's side that day in Nauvoo. Sharp was leery. He slid a book back into its place on the shelf before facing his visitor.

"Are you here at Smith's behest?" Thomas Sharp's lips had a way of curling when he faced a distasteful task.

Bennett grimaced wryly. "I am my own man; you may be sure of that. I made Joseph Smith what he is today. He had not the slightest notion of how to obtain a charter for Nauvoo; he knew less about governing it. He built his city with my expertise and now wants to get rid of me, garnering all the glory for himself. He has taken my position as mayor, since running me out of town. He will be satisfied with nothing less than total control in Nauvoo. . . and eventually the state. You should hear him talk about 'building his kingdom.'"

"I've heard him and read his editorials." Sharp warmed to his favorite subject, the excesses of Joseph Smith. "The man doesn't just talk with God; he thinks he is God. All this military pomp and ceremony is ridiculous. You don't see Baptists and Methodists raising an army of zealots to fight for them. The Mormons have earned the persecution they've suffered, and they're going to enjoy the 'fruits of their labors' again, if they don't learn to live as the rest of us do."

Bennett smiled. He knew he would find an eager ear in Thomas Sharp. "Smith has completely duped the simple Mormon folk. They believe every word he says, and now he has revived the notorious Danite organization, so even you could be in danger, Mr. Sharp!"

"Oh, I'll be careful, all right! I'm sure Smith would like to silence me. But surely you did not come here simply to warn me."

"Well, certainly your personal safety is my primary concern. . . " Bennett broke off his speech as scratching at the window alarmed them both. Sharp jumped up and rushed to the window, only to discover a tree branch brushing against it.

John Bennett sat, still uninvited, on a bench near the newsman's press and smiled at Sharp's too obvious panic. "But I can see you're not a man to be easily daunted. Your paper has accused of Joe Smith of plural marriage. Well, I can give you names and dates."

Now he had Sharp's undivided attention.

The publisher growled. "Bennett, I don't trust you any more than I do Smith, if you're gambling on my support."

Bennett's expression was impassive. "I do not gamble. I am in earnest when I say I want to see Joseph Smith stopped before he gains any more power."

He responded to Bennett suspiciously. "What do you want for this information?"

Bennett turned up his palms and spread his hands, shaking his head. "Nothing, sir. I am not here for money."

"Aren't you afraid for your life?"

"No, I shall be beyond their reach. I will carry on my work against that imposter in more civilized cities, for there is more, vastly more, information I alone possess." Bennett then wrote down several accusations against Joseph Smith calculated to serve his purpose. When he finished and turned to go, Sharp was glad, even though the man had provided him with sensational news for several issues.

Bennett also went to Simeon Francis, editor of the *Sangamo Journal* in Springfield, carrying lurid tales of Nauvoo. Many of the vile and despicable things he had done himself, he attributed to Joseph Smith. His accusations against Nauvoo's leaders were calculated to stir up sentiment against the Mormons, and they did!

Joseph knew he had lost the backing of Governor Carlin, and he began looking for other politicians who would be fair with his people. They were not easy to find. Elections were won on denunciations and promises. It was convenient to denounce the Mormon threat. Joseph had underestimated Bennett's influence.

Emma was most affected. What was once whispered about her husband, was now in bold print, and she was frequently confronted by visitors. With her cool reserve, they never knew how it cut her to the quick. Eventually, anger began to build in Emma. She felt publicly shamed and pitied by her friends.

One afternoon, Emma and Eliza overtook a group of ladies as they walked to the Coolidge home for herbs and molasses. The two women had finished their own conversation and were silent as they approached. A young voice rang out, "Well, I would rather die than live that principle. Just imagine, sharing your husband with other women! I am so sorry for Sister Emma. It must be awful!"

Emma stopped stock-still. Suddenly aware of her presence, the young women who had been gossiping saw her stricken face.

"Oh, Sister Emma!" the girl cried, "I could bite my tongue off!"

"I was taught that one should bite her tongue before uttering gossip," Emma spoke reprovingly.

"But it's not gossip, it's in the newspapers!" the girl spoke under her breath.

Emma's eyes were cold. "Newspapers can be the devil's tool! Though you can't help being young women, take care not to be silly women as well!" Emma's quickened her stride, leaving the thoughtless young woman to her embarrassment.

Instinctively, Eliza knew she should offer neither sympathy, nor counsel. Emma Smith would suffer any privation for her husband, but she could not abide pity.

To clarify the sanctity of marriage, Joseph gave lectures before the Relief Society. It was plain he was broaching the issue of plural marriage. On one such occasion, when he finished speaking, the room was deathly quiet. The women hardly dared look at one another until he left. Then one of the younger women asked naively, "Sister Emma, where did the doctrine of polygamy come from?"

Hotly indignant, with eyes flashing fire, Emma answered, "Straight from hell, madam! *Straight from hell!*"

She stalked out of the room, and after a moment of stunned silence, Sarah Cleveland spoke softly. " Now, ladies, let us finish our work on the missionary shirts. How many can we have ready this week?" The women took their cue from her and went back to their needlework.

Emma walked right past her house. She went down to the water's edge, anger boiling within. If Joseph thought she would have to accept it because he was now teaching it to other women, he was wrong! She didn't have much in this life. Since marrying her plowboy prophet, she had lived off the charity of friends, spending scarcely more than four years in a home of her own, had shared her husband with visitors, sick friends, angels, mobs, and politicians, had overseen his business and reared their family alone for months on end while he traveled, preached, tended church business, or was in jail or hiding.

Just look at me, she thought. Prophet's wife or not, if I can't retain my dignity, I have nothing at all!

She marched back home, put supper on the table with scarcely a word. William Clayton and Willard Richards, Joseph's scribes, joined them for the meal. They were planning to work on the history of the church, but Emma had other plans. She took her husband aside when supper was over.

"I want to talk tonight."

"But we're planning to. . . "

"Do it tomorrow!"

Joseph stopped, dead still. Emma had become more demanding lately. He looked straight into her brown eyes. They were flashing. He knew what that meant. He sighed, nodded, and rejoined his friends.

"Gentlemen, our plans have changed. We'll meet tomorrow at my store."

Willard and William looked at one another and quickly nodded. When they took their leave, Emma removed her apron, folded it neatly, smoothed her hair, and called her daughter.

"Julia, your father and I are going out for a walk. Watch the little ones, dear, and don't let Freddy and Joseph bicker. We won't be too long."

Joseph waited for her outside. It was a pleasantly cool evening. The stars twinkled brightly in the windswept darkened sky, but this night Emma was in no mood to admire stars.

"If you think I will stand to be publicly humiliated, you are very much mistaken. I have endured whispers long enough, and now I blush to read a newspaper! I actually have strangers stop and ask me if I am Joseph Smith's *first* wife *and* if I give my approval to his *other* marriages. How do you think that makes me feel? How would you like it if the shoe were on the other foot? I've had enough of this! I can't stand it, Joseph! I *won't* stand for it! You either stop or I will leave you!"

"Oh, Emma, I'm so sorry that. . . "

"I don't want an apology! I *want you to stop teaching this principle!* Can it be more important to you than my happiness, our marriage, our family? Don't you know it will destroy me? Don't you care?" Her voice rose until quite shrill, then broke on the word "care."

He tried to take her in his arms. "Of course, I care. I love you, Emma."

She pushed him away. "Stop telling me you love me, when you are marrying other women." She changed her tactic and her voice fell into a terrified whisper, "Don't you know it's dangerous? You could be killed because of it!"

His words were somber. "I've known that since Kirtland, but I have no choice. If this were my choice, I would choose to live out my days quietly with you and our children. But I've always known it would not be so. I have not simply started a new church, God has *restored* His old one, which means the restoration of all things. God has chosen me to be prophet of the Dispensation of the Fullness of Times. What does that mean, the '*fullness* of times?' It means we have all the keys, power and authority of the priesthood restored."

Stubbornly she retorted, "You haven't restored animal sacrifice, so it isn't the restoration of *all* things, is it?"

"The blood of Jesus Christ fulfilled animal sacrifice."

"Then why restore *polygamy?*" Her voice rose hysterically.

"Because God commanded me, and *whatever* He requires is right. Trust me, Emma, trust me, and trust God."

She put her face in the curve of his shoulder and stood shaking in his arms. When she finally spoke, she balled up her fist and pressed it against her chest.

"It hurts. . . so much!"

"I know, but I can't put off compliance any longer. The angel told me I could set aside the Lord's commandment only at my peril. If I continue to refuse, I will be cut off, perhaps forever. Only the Lord can help you, for it is He who commands us. Go to Him — not with an angry spirit, not with a protest — but in humility and ask if the principle is true. Everyone must do that. If you doubt me, ask Him! But I tell you, I am no fallen prophet."

"But I *can't* share you!"

"You have to."

She looked past his shoulder at the peaceful, flowing river, and wished she could give herself up to its rushing current.

"Why can't we simply enjoy marriage as others do?"

"Because God requires something else. But my enemies will use it to condemn me. If you want to protect my life, you must swear never to reveal to anyone that I practice this principle. Can you do that?"

"Is God punishing me?"

"No, my love." He kissed her forehead, "Not punishing you. . . rather, testing you."

Emma threw herself into her husband's arms and pressed him fiercely to her. "I will swear to anything, *anything* to protect you. Whatever may happen, whoever may question, remember that on this night I gave you my solemn oath that I will *never* speak of it to anyone."

On the sixth of May 1842, Missouri's ex-governor, Lilburn W. Boggs survived an assassination attack. He was shot through an open window at his home in Independence with a blast of buckshot, which hit him in the back of the head. The act was at first believed to have been committed by a political opponent, but subsequently, John C. Bennett publicly accused Porter Rockwell of doing the deed under orders from Joseph Smith. Porter had recently brought his wife to Independence to be with her parents, as she was expecting a child.

"It's a damned lie," said Porter. "I never did an act in my life I was ashamed of. I have done nothing criminal." Then he added simply, "Them that accuse me, don't know me. Boggs would have been dead if I had shot. I never miss."

Bennett influenced the recovering Boggs to swear out a warrant in mid July for Joseph's arrest on conspiracy with Rockwell to commit murder. Illinois Governor Thomas Carlin signed an order for their arrest and surrender to agents from Missouri, so Joseph and Porter were arrested in Nauvoo on August 8, 1842, but were immediately released on a writ of *habeas corpus*, which infuriated Governor Carlin. Joseph went into immediate hiding, and Porter rode out of town, hell-bent for the east.

"Mrs. Smith, Governor Carlin has promised a two hundred dollar reward for the arrest of your husband," tall, lanky Sheriff Thomas King of Adams County Illinois told Emma, as he stood with one boot wedged in the Homestead doorway. "He cannot escape the justice he deserves."

"I hope not," Emma replied coolly. "If he gets the justice he deserves, the state of Missouri will return him several hundred thousand dollars which it stole from him."

"Well, he won't escape, no matter what you may think."

"I haven't personally seen my husband in days. I know no more than you where he has gone. There are riverboats coming and going every day down at the dock. He may be somewhere far away by now."

The sheriff's black eyes narrowed to slits. He obviously did not believe her, though she had spoken the truth, strictly speaking.

"I'll be back. He won't get away." The sheriff warned as he walked away.

It was the start of a long, protracted game of hide-and-seek. Joseph moved from place to place, staying with various families in and around Nauvoo. Wilford, Heber, Brigham and others visited him, seeking his guidance on spiritual and civic matters, but they had to be careful, for everyone was being watched. When he grew too lonely for his family, he would creep into town late at night. Friends and family placed food on their back doorsteps for him. More than once he was nearly detected and hid in the tangled, dense woods where every rustle of leaves startled him. The weather was hot and sticky and the mosquitoes unmerciful. The sheriff quickly conducted a systematic and relentless hunt for him. Joseph moved one night by a small skiff to one of the islands in the Mississippi River. A few families lived on this island, and he stayed with John Walker's family, cementing a lifelong bond of friendship.

During August 1842, Emma visited her husband every few days, wherever he stayed, with news of the family, the missionary work, the progress of the temple, as well as news of his mother and family. Wilson Law, the new major general of the Nauvoo Legion since Bennett's dismissal, ferried her to the island, reported the latest news then rowed the skiff back after the couple had spent a few hours together. Days turned into weeks, and the manhunt dragged on. Joseph passed his time writing letters and recording reflections of his dearest friends. He wrote tributes to Hyrum, to his mother and late father, to Joseph Knight, Newel K. Whitney and others.

"These I have met in prosperity, and they were my friends; and now I meet them in adversity, and they are still my warmer friends. These

love the God that I serve; they love the truths that I promulgate; they love those virtuous, and those holy doctrines that I cherish in my bosom with the warmest feeling of my heart, and with the zeal which cannot be denied. . . they shall not want a friend while I live."

One night, the waves lapped up on the shore, beaching a rowboat. As was his habit, Joseph watched from the underbrush. He saw several close friends disembark. Then Hyrum stepped from the boat, helping Emma out. She wore a dark cloak over her clothing to keep the moonlight from glinting off her hair and dress. The passengers looked around, dragged the boat into the bushes, and Joseph parted the dense brush, pushed through the honeysuckle vines, and grasped hands with his friends even as he pressed his wife to his heart. After heartfelt, affectionate greetings with each faithful visitor, the men discussed legal maneuvering and future plans. George Miller suggested Joseph might want to move even further from Nauvoo, as the sheriff might eventually follow someone to the island. Dimick Huntington recommended the northern pinewoods, near Wisconsin. Lyman Wight and George Miller had been operating a sawmill there, hauling tons of lumber for temple construction. Even William Clayton and Newel K. Whitney agreed it might be his best refuge. Joseph was so tired of hiding; he liked the idea. A trip upriver, especially if he could take his wife and children, would be a welcome change.

As the hour grew late, Joseph stood, and taking his wife's hand, gently drew her to her feet. "Gentlemen, Emma and I will take a short walk," he said, and the couple was soon out of sight in the thick foliage.

The moon was high in the sky, and a wind had picked up across the water. Joseph's heart was so tender with emotion, he trembled as he held his wife. More than anything he longed for a day at home with her and the children, free of anxiety, enjoying the simple activities of family life.

"I shouldn't have asked you to come," he apologized.

"I would have come anyway."

"It is dangerous, you know."

"More so for you than any of us."

"Sometimes, when I reflect on all you have suffered because of your plowboy, I feel guilty. You deserve better. . . "

She kissed him to stop his melancholy reflections. Then she murmured "There is no one better for me than you. I have never wanted anything but to be your wife, the mother of your children."

"Kiss them for me, my love. I miss them terribly."

When at last they returned to the group, Joseph's heart ached as he watched them settle into the skiff and start back across the dark water. The day following that visit he was overcome with feelings of gratitude. In the hot afternoon sun, he scratched a loving tribute.

"How glorious were my feelings when I met that faithful and friendly band, on the night of the eleventh, on Thursday, on the island at the mouth of the slough, between Zarahemla and Nauvoo: and what unspeakable delight, and what transports of joy swelled my bosom, when I took by the hand, on that night, my beloved Emma — she that was my wife, even the wife of my youth, and the choice of my heart. Many were the reverberations of my mind when I contemplated for a moment the many scenes we had been called to pass through, the fatigues and the toils, the sorrows and sufferings, and joys and consolations, from time to time, which had strewed our path and crowned our board. Oh, what a commingling of thought filled my mind for the moment, again she is here, even in the seventh trouble — undaunted, firm, and unwavering - unchangeable, affectionate Emma!"

Emma read his letter anxiously the next day when Law delivered it to her. He had signed it, *"your affectionate husband until death, through all eternity; forever. Joseph Smith.* " She pressed it to her breast. The choice of his heart! Yes, she believed that, even though he might take other wives as commanded, she was comforted by that simple phrase, "the choice of my heart." She sat down at her writing desk. She took up pen to reply and answered with her heart.

"Dear Husband, I am ready to go with you if you are obliged to leave. . . "

She paused a moment, looking around her snug home. She loved this place. It had been her home for three years. It would be almost unbearable to uproot again, leave all her comfortable things, and move the children to live in hiding with her husband. Then she thought of Joseph as she had seen him, lonely and dejected, yet maintaining hope. What hope had he? Once sympathetic, Governor Carlin now obviously believed the accusations. If he gave himself up to Sheriff King, he would be sent back to prison in Missouri straightaway and he would die there. His only hope was to wait this out until a new governor could replace Carlin, one who might see the illegality of extraditing a man against whom there was no evidence. She thought back to her last parting with Joseph. He had lifted his hand in farewell while the moonlight cast long, sad shadows across his face. She could not let him go north alone.

Emma finished the letter quickly, including information on taxes and land. Then she took another piece of foolscap and composed an eloquent letter to Governor Carlin. It urged him to have Joseph tried in Illinois instead of delivering him back to sworn enemies. She reminded him persuasively of past friendship and appealed to him as she would to a father:

"And now may I entreat your Excellency to lighten the hand of oppression and persecution which is laid upon me and my family, which

materially affect the peace and welfare of the whole community; for let me assure you there are many whole families that are entirely dependent upon the prosecution and success of Mr. Smith's temporal business for their support; and, if he is prevented from attending to the common vocations of life, who will employ those innocent, industrious, poor people, and provide for their wants?

". . . And now I appeal to your Excellency, as I would unto a father, who is not only able but willing to shield me and mine from every unjust persecution. I appeal to your sympathies, and beg you to spare me and my helpless children. I beg you to spare my innocent children the heart–rending sorrow of again seeing their father unjustly dragged to prison, or to death. . .

Respectfully, your most obedient, Emma Smith"

It was late and the candle had nearly burned out as Emma finished her letter to the governor. She folded it neatly, then opened it again to pen one final line: *"Sir, I hope you will favor me with an answer."*

When she closed it the second time, she sealed it with wax and placed it atop the desk. The next day, William Clayton personally carried the letter to Governor Carlin in Quincy. Though Carlin seemed impressed by Emma's eloquence, he later wrote that he could not help her.

Emma roused, sat up in bed and looked for her husband. It was Joseph's voice in the darkness. Then she heard it again, her name spoken softly. She threw off the light cover and hurried to the narrow stairway. Just as she reached the top stair, she paused, shaken by a racking cough. It was September 9, 1842, and she had been very ill for days, unable to go to her husband.

"Emma?" Joseph bounded up the steps; then she was quickly in his arms. She continued to cough. "This is why you haven't come. I told Brother Taylor something must be wrong. You've never gone a week between visits. Do you have the chills?"

"Yes, and something has settled in my chest. It makes me weak." She coughed again, but waved away his concerns. "It's worse at night. During the day, I'm not so bad. I don't sleep with the window open anymore. The children are all sick as well," she whispered.

Joseph was alarmed. "How sick?"

"None of them are dangerously ill. They ask about you all the time. Freddy is afraid you are 'back in that nasty jail.' I tell them you're camping and fishing. I don't want to alarm them."

"That's all true."

"Sheriff King has been here several times asking for you. Once I found him sneaking around the property. He obviously hopes to find you here."

"Let's go to the children's rooms."

Emma knew her husband missed their children as much as he missed her. Joseph was rejuvenated from playing with the youngsters. He could listen to their prattle for hours and not grow irritable as she often did. The concerned parents tiptoed to where the children lay restlessly asleep. Julia's sweet, maturing face was wreathed in moonlight.

"She's growing up so fast," Joseph mused. "Soon she'll be a young woman."

Emma allowed her husband his reverie.

"I think Joseph looks much as Jesus must have as a boy."

Emma's hand moved to her chest as she looked down at her sleeping son. "Really?" she whispered.

"Yes, sometimes I look at Joseph's face, and his eyes have that same tender melancholy."

He paused with his hand on his son's head and blessed him. Then he went on to Alexander.

"He reminds me so much of you," Emma observed. "His coloring, his wide cheek bones, the way his lips curve."

They stopped at the last child, dark-haired Freddy, now six. He was in a fitful sleep, tossing and turning. Joseph knelt beside him and put his cheek against his son's. The boy quieted immediately. Joseph stayed several minutes, whispered a blessing, and left a kiss on his son's forehead.

"Emma, you have given me the sweetest children in the world. How could I help loving their mother? I wish I could take you back with me." He sighed, then tried to find a more cheerful subject. "I went shooting with John Taylor's little brother, William, on the island the other day. We made rabbit stew. It was much better than cold salt pork."

"How long do you think this will last?" she asked. "You can't hide out the rest of your life. I'd rather go into the wilderness again, if it meant we could be together. I'll go anytime you say."

"Hyrum advises against leaving. He says we must be patient until Carlin is out of office. Thomas Ford seems most impartial of all the candidates for governor. I've met the man. He's not exactly a friend, but I believe he is fair."

"How many times have we thought that of people who turned against us?" Emma said bitterly. Then she threw her arms around his neck. "Oh Joseph, I'm tired of all this persecution. I could be happy if people left us alone. I'm weary of the legal entanglements, the newspaper harangues, and everyone who wants a favor from you. I think I might actually enjoy going with you to Wisconsin."

Joseph was touched by his wife's devotion. Her face was thin and drawn. Her dark eyes were sunken. He kissed her cheek. "Emma, darling, you may be willing but you're in no condition to go anywhere.

Besides, I believe Wilson Law is right when he says I must be acquitted of these charges filed by Boggs. If I left, it would solve my problems only momentarily. Eventually, the law would find me, and it
would go harder on me. No, I must find the right time to stand trial
and be cleared."

That opportunity came in early 1843. Governor Thomas Ford
had won the election in Illinois. He was known as a fair man, honest
and hardworking, but no particular admirer of Joseph Smith. Judge
James Adams of Springfield, a loyal friend, wrote Joseph a sympathetic note urging him to stand trial, promising it would be fair and unbi-
ased. By then, Joseph had spent five months in hiding. Sheriff King
still tracked him, and Joseph felt he put his friends at risk by staying in
their homes. He was even more concerned about Emma. She had
taken so ill he feared for her life. Her cough had worsened, and fever
and chills took a heavy toll. Joseph sneaked home so he could sit with
her and try his best to comfort the children who were convinced their
mother was dying.

When Governor Ford took office on December 2, 1842,
Joseph felt he could risk a trial at last. So, just after Christmas, he
took Orson Hyde, Willard Richards, John Taylor, Hyrum, William
Marks, Levi Moffitt, Peter Haws, and Lorin Walker with him and
started for Springfield in the custody of his Legion major general,
Wilson Law. A light snow had fallen the night before, but as soon as
they started out, the snow began again in earnest. The men rode
silently, with snowcaps piling up on their shoulders, and their horses huffing little clouds of frosty air. By nightfall all were exhausted
and grateful to stop at Plymouth where the prophet's brother,
Samuel, was taking care of the inn usually operated by their brother,
William, who had been recently elected to the state legislature. An
evening around a warm fireplace, a hot meal with Samuel and
William's families — temporarily living under the same roof — was

a welcome respite. Samuel's comforting prayer gave Joseph the courage to face a trial, the outcome of which he increasingly feared.

Shadrack Roundy, Edward Hunter, and Theodore Turley joined them on the trip. The prophet arrived at the state capitol surrounded by good friends. They took rooms at Rushville Bell Tavern in Springfield. Immediately, Joseph conferred with his legal counsel, Justin Butterfield. Judge Adams had set the trial for Wednesday, giving them four days to prepare their defense. The next evening was New Year's Eve and a celebration ball for the new governor. Most of the important people of Illinois were invited. An invitation was delivered to Joseph's hotel room that morning. The prospect of festivities appealed to his normally sociable nature. Besides, he reasoned with his legal counsel, Law and Butterfield, the people he would meet at the party were the very individuals he wanted to win over.

Joseph made his entrance late. The ballroom of the hotel was already filled with gentlemen in splendid attire, and ladies in satin and lace dresses of the day. Lamps threw a golden glow over the room, and black waiters in black suits with white cravats moved gracefully, threading their way between guests. Joseph waited in the open doorway to be announced.

"Mr. Joseph Smith, of Nauvoo, Illinois."

Conversation ceased. Joseph had worn his fawn-colored breeches with a cream-colored broadcloth suit coat. A satin cravat and beaver hat called attention to his imposing height. There was more than one lady who caught her breath upon looking at the infamous Mormon prophet. When the silence became prolonged, another taller, leaner figure, firmly guiding his wife, broke through the throngs toward Joseph.

"Didn't know if I'd see you here, Mr. Smith. You're certainly welcome. 'Spect it will give these good ladies something to gossip about for a spell." Abraham Lincoln extended his long arm to shake Joseph's hand.

"Thank you, sir, for your hand of fellowship." Joseph smiled congenially. "It may be the only one I shake tonight."

Lincoln then introduced his wife. She was a tiny woman, dwarfed by her extraordinary husband — that is, until she spoke. Mrs. Lincoln gazed up with unabashed interest in the young prophet. As he was presented to her, he recognized her cultured manners. "Your lady looks like a governor's wife."

"My lady is Mary Todd Lincoln of the Virginia Todds, and I have no doubt she is the first lady, even if I never get to be governor."

Mary quizzed Joseph. "Have you political ambitions, Mr. Smith?"

"No, ma'am. I am busy building a city, rearing a family, and writing my history."

"Will you tell everything in your history? I understand it includes angels, a mysterious golden bible, and a long residency in jail. Just how do those very different things combine in one man's lifetime?"

"Ahh," Joseph replied, "thereby hangs a tale! Perhaps you'll read it when it is finished. Mr. Lincoln, your wife is as intelligent as she is lovely."

That pleased Mary, and Lincoln nodded his assent. "Now, Mr. Smith, I'm going to throw you to the wolves." Lincoln gestured to the room behind him. "Come; I'll introduce you around. Some will like you; some will hate you, but they'll all want to say they met the Mormon prophet."

Lincoln made a few introductions before the music started. Couples paired off, and Joseph stood conversing with the other men. He did not imagine for a moment that any woman there would dare to dance with him. He was mistaken. When the first cotillion ended, Abe Lincoln had completed his duty, so Mary turned to Joseph, and with perfect self-confidence, indicated she would like to dance.

With an air of triumph, she paraded her prize out onto the floor. If Mrs. Lincoln expected the Mormon religious leader to be uneducated in the social graces, she was mistaken. Joseph could dance until the band went home. Mary Lincoln later recorded in her diary that Joseph Smith, the Mormon prophet, had the most remarkable blue eyes.

Governor Ford's secretary, an austere, pale man, just past youth, could not resist questioning Joseph.

"Mr. Smith, it is said you will be tried before Judge Pope. Does that concern you?"

"Not at all, sir. After all, the pope and I occupy similar positions, as spokesmen for the Lord." Laughter rustled through the group. "I'm sure *Judge* Pope will be fair. You are all welcome to attend this Wednesday, if you desire."

Many did so. The courtroom was packed, with the gallery filled with prominent ladies of Springfield, including Mrs. Lincoln. Attorney Justin Butterfield rose to address the court, and offered a humorous observation, "Please understand, your Honor, I have been placed in a most precarious position today. We are met in Pope's court, where I will be expected to defend the Mormon prophet, before a bevy of angels in our gallery."

After the laughter subsided, he then succinctly stated the defense. Joseph Smith had been in Nauvoo, nearly three hundred miles from the scene of the crime. Boggs' affidavit did not purport Smith was personally culpable of this crime committed in Missouri; additionally, there was no precedent to transport Joseph back to a state without evidence, since he had not fled the state *after* charges were made.

The verdict was rendered Thursday, January 5, 1843 before a crowd of prominent Illinois citizens, including Mary Todd Lincoln.

Pope freed the prophet, declaring an unwillingness to set the precedent of extraditing a man based on unsupported accusations.

Joseph and his attorneys drew up copies of the court proceedings and decision. Joseph took them to newly elected governor, Thomas Ford, the next day, for his certification. Ford was a handsome man, nearly forty-three years old. He was a lawyer, and known for his simplicity and economy. He had, fine, wavy hair and long lashes. His manner was refined, and at this meeting, civil but cool.

"I have one piece of advice for you, Mr. Smith. Refrain from all political electioneering."

"Sir, I have always acted upon that tenet. Only persecution has dictated my recent political involvement. Thank you for your certification. I hope to see you under better circumstances in the future."

Ford pushed back his chair, and gazed up at the younger man. "Yes," he replied, rather unconvincingly, "I hope so too."

Joseph and his friends left the next morning for home. The weather was still snowy, and the horses' sweat froze on their backs, but now hearts were so light the men sang as they rode. Joseph felt a burden lifted. Just let me be, he thought, and I'll do great things for the Lord and for my people. The kingdom of God on earth is only in its infancy. Great things are to come.

Joseph's renewed vision encompassed the church spreading across the world. He knew that one day, this fledgling church — now struggling with malaria, poverty, and persecution — would triumph. . . whether he was there to see it or not.

Chapter Ten

Promise of Eternity

oseph helped his wife from beneath heavy robes in the sleigh. He wrapped his great cloak about her, enfolding her next to his warmth as they stood at the front of the temple and looked out across the burgeoning city they had established. From the windswept bluff, they had an unobstructed view down to the landing where a steamboat had just docked. People swarmed over the platform and along Water Street, heading for the comfort of the Red Brick Store or other shops, where they would be warmed by hot drinks beside roaring fires. It was the morning of January 18, 1843, and the restless Mississippi River was a mass of white-capped waves, and in places, ice chunks clogged the shoreline. Bare tree limbs were frosted silvery white.

Joseph had laid out a fine city, with wide, parallel streets. Each square block had four acres, with one house per acre, providing space for outbuildings, gardens and livestock. In spring, women cultivated roses and lilacs, colorful black-eyed Susans, forget-me-nots, and foxglove along their garden paths. Gardens featured herbs such as thyme and lobelia, along with vegetables: cabbage, turnips, onions, and carrots.

Recently, with the ever-increasing gathering of new converts, some large lots had been subdivided. Farming was done outside of town, and expensive land on the flat boasted new houses made of logs or brick. Joseph was concerned that too many people crowded the flat when they should have been expanding the town outward. He had made tracts of land to the east available for reasonable prices, but the preferred lots were still in the heart of Nauvoo. Emma's dreams of solitude were far behind.

Their times of seclusion came like this, a few moments alone when they escaped the demands of councils, committees, disputes, and decisions.

"I want to be buried here, in the vault named for my father," Joseph mused then added quickly for Emma's sake, "one day."

"Up here on the bluff?"

"Yes, next to the temple."

"I want to be buried beside our little house. . . if I go first, that is."

"You just want to be buried outside our window so you can keep track of me," Joseph teased her.

She chuckled. "That's right. Someone has to. Men and boys always need good, adult supervision."

"Look what we have done, Emma! This is the most beautiful city anywhere. And behind us the temple of the Lord is rising! It will be as fine as Solomon's temple when it is finished."

"Progress seems slow."

"It will be done sooner than you think."

Joseph drew her closer and kissed her hair, savoring her nearness and warmth while the wind buffeted them. "Sixteen years! Today we have been wed sixteen years. I am always amazed that you would love me when the world believes me to be a scoundrel. Only an angel could marry a scoundrel and make of him a king."

"I've never cared what the world thinks of you. I know your heart."

Despite Emma's private agony over plural marriage and the growing public scandal, she still believed in Joseph's love — for her as well as the church. She drew a deep breath of frosty air and nestled closer into her husband's arms.

Soon, however, her practical mind turned to daily problems, which never seemed to gain Joseph's full attention. "We have been entertaining as though you were a king. Joseph, we need the extra space the Mansion House will provide, and guests need an inn where they can stay. They are overwhelming our means. I can hardly accommodate the politicians, merchants, clergymen, and others who demand your time."

"I know. Other cities this size provide a hotel for guests. Sometime I'll have to assert myself as mayor, since Bennett left the office to me, to see that the Mansion House gets finished."

"Now that you have been tried and released, I'm hoping to concentrate on other important things."

"We certainly will! Today, we will host our friends, to celebrate our wedding anniversary, the start of a new year, and the goodness of God in preserving my life."

Emma sighed. It was over, this precious moment of privacy. Guests would soon arrive, and she must oversee it all. Much had already been done. Neat rows of pastries and popovers lined the kitchen sideboards. A pig was prepared and roasting, and the great pot held a tasty stew, seasoned with onions and herbs that Emma had saved since last fall. The Homestead was filled with mouthwatering smells, but there was more to be done in the way of cooking and cleaning.

Some of Emma's household chores had been lessened since the four eldest Walker children had come to live at the Smith home. When Sister Walker died, Joseph and Emma extended their help to John's family. Catherine and Lucy Walker were young girls, healthy, strong, and anxious to help. They took over much of the burden of cleaning and cooking. Still, today there was more to be done before the party.

Guests began arriving at ten o'clock and continued throughout the day in shifts. Carriages lined up around the house and down the river road. Many friends who lived nearby simply walked. They arrived with much stomping and shaking of snow from boots and coats, frosty clouds of breath hovering over their heads, and exuberant greetings to each other. Daniel H. Wells — a close friend, though not a member of the church — came with his wife, Eliza, in their fine carriage. Sidney and Phoebe came, though there lately seemed a false heartiness in Sidney's greeting. Brigham and Mary Angell Young came despite Brigham's recent illness. Hyrum came early to help with last minute arrangements, but Mary was too ill to attend. Stephen Markham and his wife greeted Joseph enthusiastically, while John Taylor came carrying a New Orleans newspaper for Joseph's perusal. Throughout the day, more than seventy guests crowded into the Homestead and the addition built to accommodate the Smiths' growing family. One table was set up. Guests and children were all served around the same table in four shifts.

Emma took extra care to dress in a gown of midnight blue. A string of gold beads, which Mother Lucy had given her, glowed as they lay against the rich fabric. Her hair was still dark brown with few silver threads, and she had arranged it with ringlets brushing her shoulders. She moved gracefully in her humble log home and more than once Joseph squeezed her hand with approval. The long ordeal of hiding was over. He had been cleared of charges. He could live as any other man, his children on his knee and his loving wife at his side.

After welcoming their friends, Joseph exulted, "It is a day of jubilee! A day to give thanks to our God for His blessing and protection! There are similar parties of thanksgiving going on all over Nauvoo, and I wish to express my gratitude for your friendship. A man can endure anything with friends such as you."

He looked about the room fondly, a catch in his throat. Only four years ago he had been languishing in the Liberty Jail, the church in tatters, his dear ones huddled on the snowy banks of the Mississippi River. Just a few months ago he had been in hiding. Now, after the trial of their faith came the blessings.

"Sister Eliza R. Snow has written a jubilee song celebrating my recent exoneration from false charges coming out of Missouri. I have had it printed on these cards. Please, Sister Snow, would you kindly lead us in singing the words?"

Eliza stood a little self-consciously and began a familiar tune with her words of rejoicing:

> *"That deed — that time we celebrate,*
> *So rife with liberty;*
> *When the official pow'rs of State,*
> *Pronounc'd the Prophet free.*
>
> *When foul oppression's hand was stay'd —*
> *A feast of Liberty,*
> *The Prophet and his Lady made,*
> *To crown the Jubilee."*

Emma smiled upon her friend, pleased by the accolades Eliza received and so demurely turned into praise of the prophet. She was a friend Emma trusted implicitly. A delicious sensation of well-being flooded Emma's heart. She was grateful to the Almighty for watching over her husband once more.

Joseph insisted on helping Emma serve. He brought in the roasted pig, still sizzling and steaming on a large board. Mouths began to water while expressions of delight echoed through the home.

"The first slice for you, Brother Hyrum — in remembrance of the months we spent together, hardly at "*liberty*" in Missouri! We overcame, thanks to the kindness of Heaven! Now if only Brother Porter were here to rejoice with us. May he also be blessed and speedily exonerated so he can rejoin the saints here in Nauvoo."

"Today, dear friends, Emma and I rejoice, not only in my legal victory, but in our sixteenth anniversary as well." Joseph looked at his wife and thought she looked especially beautiful. Her countenance was carefree and her eyes danced.

Public declarations were rare for Emma, but she spoke in praise of her husband on this occasion. "I share with you the association of a remarkable man, my companion, the Prophet Joseph Smith. It is a triumphant day, and despite his persecution, he remains patient, loving, and an inspiration to us all."

Emma's remarks were accented by the guests, "Hear, hear!" She went on to her conclusion. "May his welfare be as close to your hearts as your well being is to his, for you know how he loves his friends! And those who are his true friends, will always be dear to my heart."

It was a long, satisfying day with some political talk, a sermon, and many jokes. Joseph and Emma felt unburdened for the first time in months, and went to bed that night still talking over the events of the day. The months of hiding now seemed long ago. Joseph slept soundly and well. Emma snuggled closely under a goose down quilt, relishing his warmth and the sense of security that came from just being next to him.

After the acquittal, Joseph lived in his own home, unharassed. The children claimed him as their prisoner at night, climbing all over him, begging for stories. Joseph loved not only his own, but children of all ages. He would roll hoops and wrestle with children or friends, and he never refused a contest of pulling sticks, chopping wood, jumping to a mark, or shooting pistols.

Emma was happy as long as she could distance herself from any facet of plural marriage. She knew Tom Sharp of the *Warsaw Signal* was still printing salacious articles, trying to turn public sentiment against the "Sultan of Nauvoo." Joseph shrugged off the mounting tide of accusations. He loved a good theological debate, physical contests, or shocking stuffy visitors with unorthodox behavior. He wielded an axe with powerful strokes, and swung a scythe faster than many younger men. As physical as he was, Emma noted the tenderness with which he watched over his mother when she fell ill. For several days that spring, he tended her himself.

One afternoon as he and Emma were coming home from Mother Smith's, Joseph confided to his wife; "Lately I have received reports that Sidney is corresponding with Bennett. He denies it, but Brother Orson Pratt has also had letters from Bennett, which he brought to me. Sidney is definitely getting correspondence from Bennett, but hasn't shown me the letters. I'm afraid Bennett's influence is undermining Sidney's devotion to the cause."

She looked at her husband astutely. He was the picture of health, robust and energetic. Emma reminded him, "Sidney is simply not well, and he has not been himself since the tarring and feathering in Ohio. He has periods of terrible headaches and other episodes approaching insanity. Is it time to call another counselor? You and William Law are carrying the first presidency."

"Hyrum, as Associate President, is my right hand. But, yes, I will have to replace Sidney if he is conniving with Bennett."

Rigdon's value to Joseph and the church had been greatly diminished since he had been corresponding with John C. Bennett. Now, both Sidney and Ebenezer Robinson, his son-in-law, seemed on the verge of disaffection. Joseph became convinced Sidney must retire as postmaster general when letters addressed to him had obviously been opened. As trust in Sidney waned, other more dedicated men had gained Joseph's confidence and become the driving force of the church and Nauvoo.

Joseph was surrounded by many capable men, but none surpassed him in accomplishment. In addition to the demands of spiritual matters, he had recently been sustained as mayor by the city council and assumed those civic responsibilities as well. He guided the growth of the city through land sales and approval of commercial activities, while still finding time for receiving and recording revelation.

Emma was concerned. "I wonder what Governor Ford thinks. Scarcely two months after his warning about politics, you have become the mayor. People in and out of Nauvoo watch you, Joseph. Please don't give any of them cause to fear you."

"Ford can give me advice, but I must answer to God. Besides, how long can we count on the governor's good graces? If he turns against us, I want Nauvoo to be able to defend itself; that's why the Legion drills regularly; that's why we lobbied for a charter, granting enough power to protect us from our enemies."

The first of May, Emma returned from a riverboat trip to St. Louis to purchase supplies and furniture for the Mansion House. Joseph had said their spacious, new home would be ready in early August, as part of a new hotel. Her family needed six of the twenty-two rooms. The rest could be rented out to Nauvoo visitors. Going to St. Louis should have been a wonderful adventure; she was instructed to order new furnishings, rugs, a chandelier, dishes and silverware to furnish the riverside inn.

She made arrangements with several merchants to deliver her purchases to Nauvoo, and then she took the steamboat, *Maid of Iowa*, back upriver. The May air was balmy, so she spent much of her time standing at the bow of the boat watching the scenery. Trees were budding, flowers brightened the grassy banks, and lily pads lined the waterway. Eagles were nesting along the riverbank near Keokuk, and Emma watched them hover over the fields near the river. Another time, Emma might have cherished this peaceful ride with time to contemplate moving into a splendid new home. Today, however, disquieting thoughts plagued her.

A few months previous to the trip, she had lost her dearest friend. Rumors abounded that Eliza R. Snow was secretly married to Joseph. When Emma confronted her, it was a deeply painful encounter.

Eliza confessed the truth of the rumor and tried to assure Emma her relationship with Joseph was one of deepest respect. Nothing could assuage the betrayal Emma felt, that such a trusted friend had deceived her was so cruelly. She resolved that no one would ever be allowed to hurt her again. The last few days, such a premonition intruded on her activities, that instead of enjoying her trip, she rushed to get back to Nauvoo to be with her husband.

When the steamer docked at Nauvoo, Emma was first to disembark. Hurriedly giving instructions for her luggage to be taken to her home, she headed straight for the Homestead, where she hoped to find her husband. She did, and spent hours in more discussion with Joseph about plural marriage. Emma was tormented by a consuming need to be reconciled to a principle she completely abhorred.

However, her willing compliance had become crucial, when Joseph explained they could not receive the promise of eternal sealing until she accepted *all* that God had revealed. Moreover, Emma was required to administer the preparatory sealing ordinances to the sisters, as Joseph did to the men. The pressure to comply had become overwhelming. It was then Emma recalled her mother-in-law's advice, "When all else fails, try obedience!"

Emma reflected at length on that advice, washed her face, changed her dress, and recombed her hair. Apprehensively, she started for the Red Brick Store. At first, each step was torture, but as she proceeded, conviction grew. Unaccustomed assurance and excitement began to rise in her heart, until divine confirmation brought her to her husband.

William Walker was helping customers in the store. When Emma entered, he simply pointed up the stairway. She stopped at the top of the stairs and looked through the doorway. Joseph sat at the drop leaf desk by the window, and waited for her to speak.

"You've always said I would do the right thing. Do you still believe that?"

"Yes."

Emma was curious. "How do you know?"

"I know my wife's heart."

Emma entered the room. "And I know my husband's. I know his heart is good. I know he is determined to obey God's commandments, even at the peril of his life. It's an admirable and terrifying quality. I have always loved you for it, but resented it, as well. However, I have my testimony of your calling as a prophet."

She caressed his face. "I cannot deny that calling. I can't say I have had my own revelation; perhaps I never will, but Joseph, I want to be faithful. By God's grace, I am ready to take that step. I *must* take it to be sealed to you forever."

Joseph rose and reached for his wife's hand. Raising it to his lips, he kissed her gentle hand, reverently. He knew of her pain and the courage it took for her to obey. Until God saw fit to reveal more to Emma, her test was simple obedience, and it would be counted a blessing to her. Joseph was overjoyed that she understood this at last! Now she could be sealed to him for eternity! Only one more hurdle remained — perhaps the most difficult.

"Emma, dear, we can be sealed immediately. . . but God requires one thing more."

She searched his eyes and knew. "I must choose your wives. That's it, isn't it? Very well, then. If you must take other wives, I *will* choose them for you." Two bright young faces seemed to flash through her mind. "I choose Emily. . . *and* Eliza Partridge. Those sweet girls are like daughters to me, and they need your protection since their father died."

Joseph already knew these two young women were destined to be his wives. He knew them as children, knew their humble natures, and for some time understood they must be sealed to him eternally. The event was accomplished in the Red Brick Store, May 11,

1843, when Emma placed Eliza Partridge's hand in Joseph's, to be married to him. Then Emma led Emily forward, and she was married to him. It was an Abrahamic test for all parties. The Partridge sisters were young, but revered Joseph as a prophet, knowing their father had been utterly devoted to him. When the participants had finished their vows, they returned to their daily chores. Emma had faced the proceedings with dignified calmness, but an inner numbness. She could not be certain God was testing her commitment, but she did know this exercise in obedience was the hardest thing she had ever done. Only faith in God, her undaunted spirit, and the promise of eternity with Joseph sustained her.

On May 28, 1843, it was raining and cold. The day before, a thunderstorm had drenched Nauvoo. At five o'clock that Sunday afternoon, Hyrum came to dinner at the Homestead. It was a simple meal. While Emma and Julia cleared the table and cleaned up, Joseph and Hyrum sat talking and bouncing the boys on their knees. As soon as chores were finished, Emma asked Julia to take the boys to Grandmother Smith's for a visit. Julia herded them out the door despite their protests. Emma went upstairs to change her clothing. Joseph and Hyrum lingered below.

Dressed all in white, with a veil covering her hair, Emma stood in her bedroom, looking at herself in the mirror. Her years were beginning to show. Shadows in the darkening room made her cheeks appear hollow. Her hand went up as if to brush away the wrinkles settling in about her mouth and eyes. Did he still love her? Did he recognize all she did to serve him and the children? Did he count her hours of tireless service in the church? It was all for him, all for Joseph. Then the hoped for words came to her mind: Joseph still loved her and wanted her forever, and she certainly wanted him! To be Joseph's wife for eternity, she could bear all trials and persecutions.

Emma fixed her veil and rubbed her cheeks to bring a little color. Why, she almost looked young again. There, she was ready. While surveying her appearance one last time before calling to her husband, another face appeared in the mirror behind hers; Eliza Partridge, young, pretty, and innocent, had come to assist Emma.

The reverie was broken. For a moment, she wondered if it was an omen. Emma might like to imagine herself still youthful, but Eliza's fresh face reflected reality. Putting such thoughts aside, Emma patted her collar and turned away from the mirror.

She walked to the middle of the bedroom and called for her husband. She saw her husband's eyes light up when he first glimpsed her, all dressed in white. Then, he went to her, took Emma by the right hand, and the two of them faced each other. After a long satisfied gaze at one another, Joseph and Emma knelt, to look up at Hyrum, the Patriarch and Associate President of the church, as their witness, Eliza, stood nearby.

Emma was gently coached through priesthood promises. She kept hold of Joseph's hand, and he clasped hers securely. He looked into her eyes with tender and devoted love, seeing no one else, neither Hyrum nor Eliza. At that moment, Emma saw herself mirrored in his eyes, forever young and beautiful. This look of love was the image she would cherish through many long years to follow.

Though the promise received was conditional, they were assured if they continued "true and faithful," the day would come when the eternal nature of their relationship would be confirmed upon them.

Joseph was her heart's devotion, even after all she had suffered. In maturity, he seemed handsomer than ever. His unwavering blue eyes could still move her, and the force of his spirit lifted her beyond herself. This was what she wanted, and if it truly could be for eternity, it was worth any price.

For a month, life was sweet, as Emma dreamed of eternity with Joseph. Then she fell desperately ill, and Joseph would not leave her side, tending her for weeks. Her normally vigorous good health had declined these last few years in Nauvoo. The saints kept her continually in their prayers. Joseph was a devoted nurse, and when she finally rallied, he was determined to give her a change of scenery.

During this time, Elias Higbee — longtime friend and legal counsel — succumbed to swamp fever and passed away. With his friend's death on his mind and concerned about Emma's recovery, Joseph decided it was time for a family vacation. He loaded up a carriage, put his wife and children inside, and started north to Dixon, Illinois, several days away, where her sister, Elizabeth Wasson, lived. Elizabeth had invited Emma and Joseph to visit whenever possible. The children were in high spirits on the trip, and Joseph had to constantly remind them to settle down, for mother was not completely well. In fact, Emma looked dangerously pale to Joseph. It was evident he had been right to get her away. The June weather was warm, but not oppressive. Joseph pointed out different wild flowers and birds, indicating noisy blue jays and cardinals. Stopping at inns along the way was a special treat for the children. By the end of the journey Emma was in better spirits and interested in the scenery. She told the children about her family in Pennsylvania, answering a hundred questions about their Aunt Elizabeth's family. They were especially interested, since they liked her son, Lorenzo, who had come to Nauvoo to visit them and had decided to stay. Elizabeth's daughter, Clara, was engaged to William Backenstos, whose brother Jacob was the sheriff of Hancock County, in which Nauvoo was located.

"Do you suppose they'll like us?" young Joseph asked anxiously.

"Of course, they'll like us," Julia responded in her mother's stead. "They are family."

"Mind your manners, and you'll be well received," Emma cautioned.

They arrived before supper on the third day while Elizabeth was churning butter. She hurried out to embrace her sister and assured Emma she had looked forward to this moment since Joseph's letter arrived. Then she gave her hand in greeting to Joseph, and exclaimed over the polite children standing by the buggy.

Elizabeth's youngest son peered shyly around the side of the house, while Emma's and Joseph's boys stood shoulder to shoulder, presenting a unified front to their cousin. Finally he came forward, introductions were made, and soon the children were rolling hoops, chasing squealing piglets around the pen, and testing each other's agility. Julia, very much a young lady, stayed with the adults and moved indoors, then took out her needlepoint and earned glowing comments from her Aunt Elizabeth.

Three days passed in peace and delighted reminiscences. The Wassons were well aware of the talk and inflammatory newspaper articles about Joseph Smith, the "King of Nauvoo." Lorenzo was such a devotee of Joseph's that he had tempered his family's potentially bad impressions. Now, with more opportunity to observe Joseph as a concerned companion, Elizabeth breathed a sigh of relief. Her sister's notorious husband was quite congenial, even humble when she had expected arrogance. He entertained them with lively stories and paid as much attention to her children as to his own.

Emma grew stronger every day. She sat for hours under the massive oak that shaded Elizabeth's yard. She was grateful Joseph had insisted on coming. Elizabeth's approval was important to her, since she'd had little personal contact with her family after marrying him.

About two o'clock on the afternoon of June twenty-first, a rap came at the door. Elizabeth answered and two rugged men tipped their hats, saying they were Mormon elders. They asked to see the prophet.

"He is out at the barn, I believe," Elizabeth told them, "just around the side of the house."

The men quickly overtook Joseph heading to the barn to hitch up the buggy for a midday ride. Before he knew what was happening, Joseph felt a hard metal gun barrel shoved into his ribs.

"What is the meaning of this?" he demanded.

Joseph H. Reynolds, sheriff of Jackson County, Missouri, belonged to that gun barrel. He had wanted to get his hands on Smith since the previous year. Now he was vindictive. "I'll show you the meaning. If you stir one inch, I'll shoot you, damn your hide!"

Joseph pulled back his shirt and bared his chest. "Shoot away! Do you think you can frighten me? I'm not afraid to die." He met the vicious look in Reynolds' eye with boldness. "I am a strong man, however, and with my own natural weapons could soon level both of you. But if you have any legal process to serve, present it and I'll go peacefully. I am at all times subject to law and shall not offer resistance. Harmon Wilson, is that you?" he asked the second assailant.

Wilson was a constable from Carthage. Joseph had met him many times. The man looked shamefaced but ordered him into their wagon. The door to the Wasson home flew open and Stephen Markham came out at a dead run. He and William Clayton had ridden hard for two days to warn Joseph a warrant was out for his arrest. When Joseph learned it was old charges by Boggs, of which he had already been acquitted, he had been sanguine about the news, believing the Missourians had no claim or jurisdiction over him.

But jurisdiction or no, gunpowder speaks, and Sheriff Reynolds of Missouri now had Joseph in his power.

"Get back! Get back, you damned Mormon! If you come closer, I'll kill him. I swear I'll kill him before your eyes!" Reynolds was so hot under the collar, he was fairly dancing, grasping Joseph's shirt and pushing him, his pistol beating against his prisoner's ribs.

Markham seized the horses' bits and held their heads. "No law on earth requires a sheriff to take a prisoner without his coat!"

Reynolds now leveled the gun at Markham's chest. "Get away!" he roared. "Or I'll shoot you where you stand!"

Emma and the family had heard the commotion. The children came running, mouths agape. Young Joseph hollered at the men to let his father go. Elizabeth shushed the children and tried to head them back into the house, but the Smith boys would not budge. Emma came running out of the house with her husband's hat and coat. By that time, Reynolds and Wilson had Joseph in their buggy.

"Now, let go of my horses, damn you!" Reynolds turned his pistol point blank on Stephen. He reluctantly backed away. Wilson flicked the whip and the horses jumped to a trot. Reynolds held Joseph's arm, while his gun bruised his prisoner's ribs. The buggy jerked, careening out of the yard.

"Ride into town and tell the sheriff I'm being kidnapped!" Joseph called back to Stephen.

Elizabeth thought her sister would faint, and she ran to put an arm around her waist.

"Sheriff Campbell is the sheriff here in Lee County. He'll treat Joseph fairly," Elizabeth said to comfort her.

"He may never even see Joseph," Emma cried. "They might murder him before anyone can stop them! The Missourians have wanted to kill him for years. They've tried every legal means. These men won't give him due process. They probably don't even have a warrant. I knew it could be dangerous for Joseph to leave the protection of Nauvoo. But he insisted, for my sake." Emma was inconsolable.

Emma could see Elizabeth didn't understand. How could she? She had not lived through the siege of Far West, or the horror of Liberty Jail. She had not seen Joseph sentenced to death, thrown into a wagon, and paraded before bloodthirsty Missourians. She had not lived the last year with constant threats on Joseph's life. Emma had, and she was petrified.

Reynolds and Wilson locked Joseph in a back room of the tavern at Dixon and went to arrange for fresh horses. They had a writ for Joseph's arrest all right, signed by Governor Thomas Ford. Stephen and William went immediately to Edward Southwick, a lawyer living in Dixon. They brought him to the tavern to see Joseph, but Reynolds denied them access.

"You can't do that," Southwick indignantly informed him. "This man has a right to counsel."

Reynolds spat on the floor, narrowed his eyes and shoved his bearded face in Southwick's. "Oh, ain't that too bad? Nobody sees the prisoner. Smith ain't gittin' away this time. He's goin' to Missouri. And I'll shoot any man who tries to free him!"

Then Stephen surprised Reynolds and Wilson. He left and went to the justice of the peace and swore out a complaint that the Missourian had threatened his life as well as Joseph's. With complaint in hand, Sheriff Campbell marched back to the tavern and put the two kidnappers themselves under arrest. That dampened their fire a little. William Clayton started back to Nauvoo by riverboat, seeking help from the Nauvoo Legion.

The next day, Joseph was released on a writ of habeas corpus and taken by county officers to another town. Again, he was kept in seclusion. Cyrus Walker, a noted lawyer and political hopeful, came to exert his influence in Joseph's behalf. Plans were made by Joseph's lawyers and friends to get him to Quincy, over two hundred miles away, so Judge Stephen A. Douglas could arbitrate the matter. Douglas had freed Joseph from extradition before regarding this very charge; hopefully, he would again. They started out by stagecoach.

Emma stayed with her sister, getting frequent reports from friends as long as Joseph was held in Lee County. When her husband left for Quincy, Emma left Elizabeth's home with her recently arrived nephew, Lorenzo, and started for Nauvoo. It was a somber journey, especially after young Joseph's fingers were crushed in the carriage door. Emma bandaged them as best she could, agonizing as only a parent can with her child's pain. Then they went on. It had been raining for days, and the dreary dampness further oppressed Emma. With every jounce and jolt of the carriage, her heart felt bruised. She couldn't banish from her mind the vision of Joseph dead.

She had not counted on help from Hyrum. He issued a public announcement for the men of Nauvoo to ride to the aid of their prophet. Three hundred men volunteered and rode out in search parties, scouring the countryside, looking for Joseph. Two days later, mid-morning, Joseph saw Nauvoo Legionaries riding hard up over a ridge of waving grass. William and Wilson Law led the search party, which came charging down to the convoy on its way to Quincy. Some of the militiamen jumped from their horses, surging around Reynolds, Wilson, and the lawyers who accompanied Joseph.

Joseph slipped from the coach into the hearty embrace of his friends. After many claps on the back and shouts during their joyous reunion, Joseph turned to his captors, his face shining. "I'm not going to Missouri this time. These are *my* boys!"

Reynolds and Wilson looked around. They were completely surrounded by members of the renowned Nauvoo Legion. They went frozen with fear, and Reynolds began to shake. Any thought of gunplay left their minds. They would be dead before they could cock their pistols.

Joseph was jubilant. "Mr. Wilson, Mr. Reynolds, Quincy is still over a hundred miles away, whereas Nauvoo is much closer. I think we should have this matter heard by Squire Wells of Nauvoo. He is not a Mormon, if that sets your minds at rest."

His two captors looked at each other, frustration plain on their faces.

Reynolds answered gruffly, eyeing the Nauvoo Legionnaires, "We'd best git on to Quincy."

Joseph smiled broadly. "I disagree! Don't be afraid, Sheriff, you'll get better treatment than I did in Dixon. . . or Liberty! Come on boys, I'm lonesome for Nauvoo, the Beautiful!"

They turned their horses and started for home, Reynolds and Wilson already having concluded their lives were not worth much. The strange party, with prisoner Joseph — a captive of Reynolds and Wilson — and prisoners Reynolds and Wilson — captives of Sheriff Campbell of Lee County — accompanied by incidental lawyers — all escorted under guard by a contingent of the Nauvoo Legion — was welcomed by strains of a brass band the next day.

Emma had arrived earlier. She and Hyrum, flanked by hundreds of the Nauvoo saints, went out to meet them, and Joseph gratefully exulted, "I am out of the hands of the Missourians again, thank God. I thank you all for your kindness and love to me. I bless you all, my friends, in the name of Jesus Christ."

Joseph invited the entire party back to his home, to the amazement of Cyrus Walker, the Illinois lawyer who was electioneering for U.S. congressman. Reynolds and Wilson had no choice but to follow. Reynolds spent the entire ride glancing about, watching for the glint of a pistol that might spell his death. On reaching the Homestead, Joseph led the way inside. He turned cordially to the surprised pair. They were even more ill at ease now in the lair of the lion. Clad in dirty clothes and shod with dilapidated boots, they were a bit thunderstruck, being in the Mormon prophet's home.

Joseph's countenance beamed. "Sheriff Reynolds, Constable Wilson, please do me the honor tonight of taking seats at the head of a table set for my friends."

Unfamiliar with mercy, Reynolds suspected a trick. Wilson blushed furiously and tried to refuse. "We'll just take our meal in the stable."

"What? I won't hear of it! You are my guests." Joseph included the accompanying lawyers with the sweep of his hand. "I want you to meet my friends. My wife — whom you refused to let me see when you held me captive in Dixon — tells me dinner is ready. She will serve you with the best our table affords."

That evening, Joseph thought he had rarely enjoyed a meal more. Many of his closest friends joined them. Emma oversaw the entire party. As gracious as she was, she couldn't resist a final word to Sheriff Reynolds.

"Sheriff, last August, Sheriff King told me my husband could not escape the justice he deserves. He was right. Judge Pope *freed* him, and tomorrow I'm quite sure justice will be done again!"

Reynolds scowled, while Wilson fidgeted. Emma simply smiled benignly and retired from the room.

The Nauvoo municipal court met the next morning, examined the writ of habeas corpus, heard the matter out, and ordered the release of Joseph Smith. Sheriff Reynolds and Constable Wilson left Nauvoo immediately and went straight to Governor Thomas Ford, urging him to raise the state militia to take Joseph Smith.

A day of celebration throughout Nauvoo followed. Joseph was in a joyous mood when he spoke from the stand, making light of the incident and declaring the municipal court had all power to free him. There was cheering and a great deal of grandiose talk. Then, as evening came on and the crowd finished dancing to the rousing music from Isaac Allred's fiddle, Joseph called for the singing of his favorite songs. They were melancholy tunes: "Wife, Children and Friends," "Massacre at the River Raisin," "Soldier's Tear," "Soldier's Dream," and ending with the poignant melody, "Last Rose of Summer."

Later that night, as Emma lay by Joseph's side, she breathed a sigh of relief. "For a time at Elizabeth's, I feared you were a dead man," she murmured wearily.

Joseph stared into the darkness. His mind flashed back to the barrel of the gun aimed pointblank at his chest. He gingerly touched his bruised ribs. This hadn't been his time. One day, there would be no escape, no friendly militia to protect him, no sympathetic lawyers or townsfolk to insist on due process. One day, there would be no joyous homecoming. His arm tightened protectively around his wife.

"Don't worry, Emma. No matter what happens, our love is forever."

Chapter Eleven

Purified in the Fire

The *Maid of Iowa* slipped from her moorings and started lazily upriver on a late afternoon pleasure cruise. Joseph had become half owner of the steamship in May of 1843 after a previous riverboat, Nauvoo, purchased from Lieutenant Robert E. Lee, of the United States Army Corp of Engineers, had been wrecked on river shoals. The *Maid of Iowa* was useful to the Nauvoo settlement in delivering goods to and from St. Louis, in transporting immigrants, for pleasure cruises for the saints, and sometimes as a patrol boat protecting Joseph from arrest. Its original owner, Dan Jones, had developed a great friendship with Joseph and delighted in putting his vessel at the prophet's disposal.

Two men sat side by side on a split rail fence watching the steamboat. From a distance it seemed a peaceful scene, just two comrades talking over homey details of their lives. Children played along the fence line, chasing rabbits, scaring up flocks of wild geese, and playing tag. The men were unmindful of the summer sun or the shouts of children, for the conversation that passed between them was anything but casual.

"I feel I have lost my brother's confidence. But where have I offended him?" Hyrum Smith spoke from a saddened heart. "I know there is something or other, which I do not understand, that is revealed to the Twelve. Brother Brigham, tell me what to do."

Brigham cleared his throat and considered his answer. He knew it would hurt. "Hyrum, Joseph feels he has lost your confidence. He would tell you everything the Lord reveals to him, if he could."

Hyrum was chagrinned. "What things can he not tell me?"

"You profess him to be a prophet. You hold up your hand to sustain him as such. Yet you refuse to obey the Lord's commandment — the very one that tests a man's real commitment to the restored gospel."

Hyrum knew to what Brigham referred. "Plural marriage."

The senior apostle nodded in affirmation.

Hyrum mused. "That is why there is a sudden halt to conversation when I enter the room." He turned to Brigham. "Surely he doesn't mistrust me!"

Brigham answered carefully. "These are perilous times for Joseph. There are brethren in the inner circle who evidence signs of betrayal. He must be very careful with his confidences now."

Hyrum sighed and stared out across the busy waterway, where a barge was headed downstream even as the *Maid of Iowa* headed upstream. They sat silently for several minutes.

Brigham continued, "Brother Hyrum, I will tell you about this if you will swear with an uplifted hand never to say another word against Joseph and his doings, and the doctrines he is preaching to the people."

Hyrum replied, "With all my heart. I want to know the truth and be saved."

As Brigham recounted his own experience with the doctrine, the Spirit bore witness to Hyrum's soul that the doctrine was of God, and conversion was instantaneous. He swore to Brigham, "I will never again argue or work against Joseph in any way."

Later, Hyrum went to find Joseph in his office above the Red Brick Store. Joseph was dictating to his scribe, William Clayton. He looked up in surprise as Hyrum came in. Something in his brother's face told Joseph there had been a "mighty change."

"I have come to ask your forgiveness, Joseph."

"It is yours. Whatever offense you imagine, I freely forgive."

Hyrum placed a chair next to his brother's, sat down and grasped Joseph's hand. "You have never told a falsehood, and I now know you have spoken the truth regarding plural marriage. I doubted because I didn't want to accept it."

"That is the crux of a man's salvation," Joseph said, "To live God's word, even when he doesn't want to." He threw his arms around his brother and put his head down for a moment. "Hyrum, my soul can now rest knowing you have a witness."

"And has Emma finally accepted it?" Hyrum asked.

"Logically, yes," Joseph shifted in his chair, "but not emotionally! She still struggles with it. I think she feels she has done her duty and she can accept no more." He shoved a hand through his hair, frustration evident in his gesture.

"Perhaps it's because you haven't written this revelation down as you have the others," Hyrum ventured.

"If I write it down, it will be all the evidence my enemies need."

"If you don't write it, other saints will doubt too. Emma cannot deny the evidence of her eyes."

Joseph weighed this advice. He knew he would be signing his own death warrant by setting this down for the world to see. But he also knew the truth of Hyrum's counsel.

"If we record it, it must be only for the most faithful."

"I agree," William interjected.

"Dictate it, Joseph, and I'll take it to Emma. She'll listen to me. I'll testify of my own struggle with the doctrine and of my conversion. She loves you too much not to suffer jealousy, but she may accept the principle if I witness to her."

Joseph shook his head. "I hope you're right."

Turning with determination to William Clayton, Joseph directed his scribe to get fresh ink and paper. Resolutely and with great care, he began to dictate.

Once the process began, the words came to Joseph in a constant flow, unremitting and relentless. William had often seen Joseph under the influence of heavenly inspiration, but this was extraordinary. The revelation itself required complete suspension of social customs, expanded one's perception of eternity, and would be the ultimate test of obedience. Yet, Joseph had always known that putting these words to paper could seal his fate.

Hyrum watched William put the final marks on the manuscript. Joseph gave William permission to make one copy of the revelation. When that was done and the ink completely dried, Joseph gave the original to Hyrum.

"It will be all right, Joseph," Hyrum tried to reassure him. "I'll reason with Emma."

Joseph smiled slightly. "You don't know Emma as I do."

It was a short distance from the store to the Homestead. Hyrum soon entered the back door of his brother's home.

"It's Uncle Hyrum," Julia called out to her mother.

"Ah!" Emma dried her hands and came from the kitchen to greet him. "Hyrum, I'm glad to see you! Joseph isn't here, I'm afraid. You may find him at the store."

"I'm here to see you, Emma. I have something for you."

"Really? What is it?"

Hyrum made no move to give her anything. Instead he went to stand by the fireplace, seeming to measure his words.

"It is a great prize, Emma. Something of inestimable worth." As she looked at him curiously, he plunged ahead. "I have with me a document from the Lord. Joseph has just had it recorded. I have no doubt of its validity."

He stopped there, still reluctant to put the revelation into her hands. She prompted him. "To what does it pertain?"

"To the principle you and I have struggled with so long."

"He has caused it to be written down?"

"Yes. I urged him to, for there are others who will also wrestle with this principle. I believe that once they see it formally set down as a revelation, they will receive it."

Emma's eyes widened. "Hyrum! Do you know what you are saying? Joseph must not commit that doctrine to writing! His enemies would use it to kill him!"

Hyrum unrolled the manuscript, scanned the beautiful penmanship and read aloud that righteous men were commanded by God to take righteous women as plural wives. It ended with an admonition to Emma to fully accept this principle and support her husband in its practice. Her blood began to boil. She *had* accepted it. She *had* given Joseph other wives. And she would not be publicly chided in this document! Their private life was sacred, and Joseph had no right to reveal it to the world.

Emma directed her brother-in-law to put the revelation on the fireplace mantle.

"Now Emma. . . " he began.

"Don't!" she commanded him furiously. "Do not reproach me!"

"I'm not. I simply want to talk reasonably."

"Reasonably?" Her voice rose. "Reasonably? I'll give you reasonably! Joseph is mad to write this down. It will bring the whole world down on him." She grabbed the fireplace tongs and snatched up the document. "And he is mistaken to think *this* will win me over." She brandished it in his face. "I am *shamed* by it!"

Hyrum was embarrassed by the raw emotion Emma displayed, and mortified that he had not anticipated the disgrace she would feel.

She rushed on, almost breathless. "My *children* will be shamed by it! How will they respond to whispers behind their backs? What is wrong with you men? Can't you see the position it puts us in?"

"Emma, it's not a censure, believe me, it is. . . "

She cut him off with a scathing dismissal. "Out! Get out! I thought I had a friend in you. I trusted you. Who persuaded you to accept this?"

"God gave me my answer."

"Well, let me give *my* answer!" She thrust the tongs gripping the revelation into the fire. "Tell my husband I would not look upon, not even touch such a document!"

As flames leaped and licked up the document, Hyrum backed out of the room, and headed back to the store. Emma watched his departure from the doorway, and furious with the recklessness of men, she slammed the door behind him.

Days later, William Clayton asked Joseph what he wanted recorded in the official church journal. Joseph quietly replied, "Just write that I spent much time in conversation with Emma." He paused. "Be sure to keep the copy of that revelation in my safe. Emma burned the original."

William's mouth opened, but he refrained from comment. "What will you do?"

"I'm tired of fighting over this. It has come between my wife and me too long. If she can't live it, I won't either. If she goes to hell for refusing it, I'll go after her and bring her back. I can't do any more. I am weary to the bone."

When word got back to Emma that Joseph had said he would give it up for her, she could hardly believe it. Characteristically, she softened, begged his forgiveness, and once more faced the world, her head high, her hand in his.

In August 1843, the Mansion House was finally ready for the Smith family. A majority of rooms were finished, and the six-room residence was furnished with items Emma had purchased in St. Louis. A great chandelier hung in the dining hall where a hundred people could be accommodated. Marble-topped tables and plush carpet created the fine atmosphere Emma wanted for a home that would receive renowned visitors. The new linens and dining cutlery had been delivered. The adjoining stable could accommodate a number of horses. The Mansion House had already become a showplace.

Had Emma been in better health, she might have enjoyed the move more. As it was, she was quite ill in August, so William Walker oversaw the relocation from the Homestead to the Mansion House. At last, Emma had means to properly house her family. Not only the Smith children, but the Walkers, Emily and Eliza Partridge, Maria and Sarah Lawrence, and Lucy Mack Smith, all lived with Joseph and Emma at the hotel. Since her husband had died, Mother Smith had stayed from time to time with her children, but her favorite place was in the thick of things at Joseph's residence. There was always something happening, and Lucy loved being part of it all. She had her own room and maintained a little museum for her Egyptian curiosities. Joseph was publishing his transliteration of Mother Lucy's papyri in the *Times and Seasons* under the title "Book of Abraham."

Joseph's devotion to Emma was not diminished by their shared heartache, the principle of plural marriage, and he spent days tending his wife. Emma had too often been ill lately. She was thirty-nine years old, and had she had suffered countless trials. As she watched her husband serving her, attentive to her every need or wish, her heart remained soothed, and they discussed many of her concerns, drawing closer than ever in their spiritual communion.

It was a hot summer, accompanied by suffocating humidity, mosquitoes, and large, black swamp flies. From frequent excursions on the *Maid of Iowa*, combined with much rest, Emma's health gradually improved.

The weather finally cooled in late September as rain showers brought welcome relief. After one such cool, wet day, a few friends met with Joseph and Emma at seven o'clock in the evening on September 28, 1843, in an upper room of the Mansion House for the highest and holiest order of priesthood blessings. The previous promises concerning "the fullness of the priesthood" were confirmed that night upon Joseph Smith and his wife, Emma Hale Smith. Joseph dictated the procedure, and Hyrum assisted in conferring the ordinances upon his brother and sister-in-law. It was the first time in latter-day history that the fullness of the priesthood was received. The Prophet and his Elect Lady became the first couple of the restoration to have their blessings so confirmed and to stand as witnesses for the men and women who would follow them in seeking to have their "calling and election made sure." The prophet explained to his gathering of friends that these blessings were the "highest powers available to mortals."

The ceremony always remained perfectly clear in Emma's mind. This time there were no shadows of other, more youthful faces to diminish the joy she felt. This time, all the conditional promises of her earlier sealing were pronounced secure in the fullness of the priesthood.

Joseph and Emma shared tears from the fountain of joy that sprang from deep within their souls. They found themselves crying and laughing at the same time. Joseph clasped her hand tightly until the end of the ceremony, and as the final words were spoken, he drew his wife into his arms. At long last, their souls were irrevocably bound for eternity.

"I seal upon you your exaltation, and prepare a throne for you in the kingdom of my Father. . . "
(Doctrine and Covenants 132:49)

The Mansion House was dedicated on October 3, 1843, with flags flying, speeches given, and a day of festivity enjoyed by the entire city. Emma and Joseph entertained two hundred guests that day and a constant stream for days afterward. Nauvoo had come of age. It boasted a concert hall, a dramatic arts society, two symphonic bands, two newspapers, a fine library, a ferryboat, hundreds of homes — brick, as well as snug, log cabins — mercantile shops, mills, and an ambitious, hardworking citizenry.

Tourists came by the hundreds on steamboats to form their own opinions about the Mormons. Nauvoo, Illinois, had become perhaps the busiest city in the western part of the United States. These achievements had come about in four years, though the saints had started with nothing. The day of dedication was a watermark of their accomplishment.

That autumn Emma and Joseph entertained politicians who courted the Mormon vote. Joseph met with close friends Willard Richards and John Taylor.

"Gentlemen, it is obvious we have the numbers to influence elections." Our support gave John C. Calhoun enough votes to win a congressional seat and to put Thomas Ford in office as governor — a fact which, nevertheless, does not seem to win his favor. Whether that influence helps us or hurts us, I cannot say, for it certainly seems to infuriate our enemies."

John shook his head. "Mob action is starting again. Robert Foster and George W. Thatcher attempted to take the oath of office in Carthage last week and were threatened with violence."

Willard continued the report. "Leading citizens of Carthage met the next day and drafted a resolution asking Governor Ford to extradite you to Missouri on the old charges." He paused then went on, "Walter Bagby has gone to Missouri to drum up support against us. Already some of our men have been beaten and their farms burned."

Joseph shook his head wearily. "The mobacrats will not rest until I am dead."

John and Willard looked at each other across the table. Plainly they agreed.

"How does Governor Ford reply to our warning of a border war with Missouri?" John asked.

Joseph observed. "He doesn't believe it. . . or so he says. The truth is, he doesn't care," He brought a fist down on the table. "Our best defense is strength. We must put men into office who will support and defend us. I want to know what Henry Clay will do for us if we vote for him as president. Willard, write to Clay, to Calhoun, and to Lewis Cass. Ask each man this question: What will be your rule of action relative to the Latter-day Saints?"

Emma came into the room just then bearing her fragrant, delicious fritters, hollow balls of pastry served with cream and sugar. The men paused in their political conversation while they enjoyed her offering. Richards beamed up at her, his round face alight with appreciation of good food.

"Sister Emma, I declare these your best effort yet. Tell me, what do you call them, and may I have the recipe for my wife?"

Emma smiled at his obvious enjoyment as he ate a fourth pastry. "I call them 'candidates'," she wryly answered, "for they are all puffed up and full of hot air."

The candidates for the presidency of the United States responded to Joseph's question and unwittingly fulfilled Emma's metaphor. They offered words of sympathy, prattled about rights, then declared they must make no commitments to any group. In short, none were anxious to identify themselves friends of the unpopular Mormon sect.

Joseph spent weeks musing over a political decision. Christmas, 1843, at the Mansion House was a grand celebration with carolers, parties, and guests. None was more welcome than the ragged, unkempt visitor who crashed the party. Joseph was entertaining in the dining hall. A wayfarer stopped at the old Homestead, poked around inside, and determined that the Smiths had moved. Across the street, light radiated from a beautiful, new structure. A holiday party was in full swing. He left his horse tied to the old hitching post, crossed the snowy street and pushed open the door to the Mansion House. He stopped in the front parlor, taking in the finery, and to the indignant questions of several guests, he insisted, "Git Joseph. He knows me."

"Brother Joseph has room in the stable if you wish to stay there. This is a hotel. . ."

"Yep, and a mighty *fine* one too."

"Sir, you'll have to leave. This party is by invitation only."

"Git Joseph!" the disheveled drifter raised his voice and fist simultaneously.

The confrontation turned into a scuffle as several men tried to put him outside. Then, from the next room, Emma summoned her husband.

"Joseph, you are needed in the parlor!"

Joseph peered through the open doorway, gave a whoop, and rushed to the front room.

"Porter!" he shouted. "Porter Rockwell, you're a sight for sore eyes! Boys, this is my friend! He gets the best we have to offer."

Rockwell glowered at the numbskulls who had tried to put him out of Joseph's home. "I told 'em to git you. 'Pears you moved to better diggins, Joseph!"

Joseph beamed and threw an arm over Rockwell's shoulder. "Not good enough for you, Port, but I guess you'll sleep better tonight than you have for a while."

"I could sleep in the snow under yer window and rest better'n I have for a year. They had me in a dungeon like Liberty. Couldn't hardly eat the food. Tried to bribe me to turn traitor on you." He grinned up at his boyhood friend. "But I damned 'em to hellfire. Told 'em I'd die first. Pert' near thought I would, too."

Joseph looked into the emaciated, hollow-eyed face. Porter had aged ten years in the time he had been gone. His hair and beard were long and tangled. He had been treated like an animal, based merely on accusations. Without a trial or formal hearing, Porter had been beaten, starved, and threatened with death. He had only to renounce his friend to be freed. He spit in his captors faces and took their abuse.

Joseph choked up, embraced his friend, and then blessed him:

"I prophesy, in the name of the Lord, that you — Orrin Porter Rockwell — so long as ye shall remain loyal and true to thy faith, need fear no enemy. Cut not thy hair and no bullet or blade can harm thee!"

Following this pronouncement, Joseph escorted him into the dining hall, and exultantly presented him to Emma, then to everyone else. Porter was a wonderful Christmas present.

Early in January 1844, Joseph made an announcement over breakfast. "I've decided to run for president."

Emma put down her fork. "President of *what*?"

"Of the United States."

His wife smiled and passed the plate of steaming eggs. "Oh!"

"I'm not joking. None of the current candidates has more to offer than your 'candidates.' I can't in good conscience cast my vote for any of them. None has the slightest notion of what we've suffered or the will to redress our grievances."

"So, you will take matters into your own hands and run for president?" she was incredulous.

"Yes. Why not?"

"Do you think you could possibly win?"

"I don't have to carry Missouri to win. I think I can carry Illinois with the Mormon vote. I'll send missionaries to the other states, and my campaign will promote national recognition of gospel precepts."

Emma pondered his reasoning. After a moment, she responded. "It could raise more opposition than ever."

He finished his breakfast, pushed back his chair and went over to her. "Emma, you can't keep me in a glass case, you know."

"I want you to be sensible! Your enemies won't stand for it. You'll be off campaigning and some wild-eyed Missourian will shoot you."

"I don't intend to leave Nauvoo. We have plenty of volunteers to present my platform for me."

"What is your platform?"

"It will address issues from slavery to the economy. I've looked at every problem facing our country, and I know God has the answers. I'll be the only candidate who isn't full of hot air."

Joseph wrote out his political platform with the help of W. W. Phelps and John M. Bernhisel, his trusted attorney. He completed and signed it February 7, 1844 under the title, "Views on the Powers and Policy of the Government of the United States." True to his word, Joseph addressed social, economic and constitutional concerns:

"'Since the fathers have fallen asleep,' wicked and designing men have unrobed the government of its glory." The platform advocated a reduction in the number of congressmen by two-thirds, and a pay reduction for the representatives, putting them on a more equal footing with farmers and other constituents. He also proposed giving the president full authority to send troops to protect citizens where local authorities refused to uphold constitutional rights. He recommended a system of freeing slaves, while recompensing slaveholders through the sale of public lands. He outlined prison reform, which would abolish court-martials for desertion, employ prisoners in public works projects, and restrict the death penalty to murderers only. He advocated expansion of the United States into unsettled western lands, and he argued for a national banking system to stabilize the country's economy. He urged more economy and fewer taxes, greater equality and less distinction among the people.

The next evening W.W. Phelps presented a public reading of Joseph's platform, at a political meeting in the assembly room of the Red Brick Store. At the conclusion of this reading, Joseph addressed his audience:

"I would not have suffered my name to have been used by my friends on anywise as President of the United States, or candidate for that office, if I and my friends could have had the privilege of enjoying our religious and civil rights as American citizens. . . "

Joseph's views were published in a lengthy pamphlet and mailed to two hundred national leaders. It called for nearly fifty conferences to be held around the country, culminating finally in Washington, D.C. Three hundred and thirty-six missionaries were appointed to conduct those conferences. Enthusiasm caught fire and swept Nauvoo. The saints felt Joseph was more fit to be president than any man living, considering his extensive accomplishments.

Eastern newspapers were then printing accolades of his translation of "The Book of Abraham," and national critics praised his scholarship. Joseph's letter of 1842 to John Wentworth, publisher of the *Chicago Democrat*, setting forth his personal and the church's history, was respectfully acknowledged. Now it seemed possible to teach the gospel alongside politics issues.

Elder King Follett was killed in a well cave-in, March 9, 1844. This early church member was one of Joseph's personal favorites, for he always spoke the truth, even when it wasn't popular, and was a cheerful worker on the temple. His passing set a solemn tone for the upcoming conference on April 6-9, in a grove east of the temple.

A speaker's stand was erected and conference mornings were ushered in with the ringing of bells. Families came carrying picnic baskets, and bringing blankets to sit on. On April 7, the grove filled with the largest congregation ever seen in Nauvoo. It was estimated that between fifteen and twenty thousand people gathered. Seated on the stand, Joseph looked out over the assembly, then beyond to the river noting an eagle's wide, sweeping course, finally his gaze returned to the congregation before him

These were good people, Joseph thought, the best on earth. Would they understand the advanced principles he wanted to teach them? He wanted to impart precepts to unravel a lifetime of false, religious superstition. But could they receive it? He still had not taught plural marriage publicly. Only a select few knew of the principle.

Every plural or celestial marriage had to be approved by Joseph, lest John Bennett's accusations prove true and a righteous principle flare into an unholy flame. Even the elect scarcely understood eternal exaltation and the sealing ordinances. Yet, he felt polygamy would be the means of establishing a widespread righteous posterity who would form a broad, firm foundation for the fledgling church.

Joseph stood and faced the crowd. He prayed for his voice to be strengthened and to carry across the multitude. Murmuring quieted. Here and there a baby fussed. A cool breeze fanned the congregation. Joseph's eyes found Emma's. With her encouraging smile and a wave from exuberant Freddy, the prophet's voice rang out unprecedented doctrine:

"Beloved Saints. . . I address you on the subject of the dead. The decease of our beloved brother, Elder King Follett, who was crushed in a well by the falling of a tub of rock, has more immediately led me to that subject. I have been requested to speak by his friends and relatives, but inasmuch as there are a great many in this congregation who live in this city as well as elsewhere, who have lost friends, I feel disposed to speak on the subject in general, and offer you my ideas, so far as I have ability, and so far as I shall be inspired by the Holy Spirit to dwell on this subject.

". . . I want to ask this congregation, every man, woman and child, to answer the question in their own heart, what kind of a being God is? . . . Does any man or woman know? Have any of you seen Him, heard Him, or communed with Him? Here is the question that will, peradventure, from this time henceforth occupy your attention. The Scriptures inform us that 'This is life eternal that they might know Thee, the only true God, and Jesus Christ whom Thou hast sent.'

". . . I will go back to the beginning before the world was, to show what kind of being God is. What sort of a being was God in the beginning? Open your ears and hear, all ye ends of the earth, for I am going to prove it to you by the Bible, and to tell you the designs of God in relation to the human race, and why He interferes with the affairs of man.

"God himself was once as we are now, and is an exalted man, and sits enthroned in yonder heavens! That is the great secret. If the veil were rent today, and the great God who holds this world in its orbit, and who upholds all worlds and all things by His power, was to make Himself visible, — I say, if you were to see Him today, you would see Him like a man in form — like yourselves in all the person, image, and very form as a man; for Adam was created in the very fashion, image and likeness of God, and received instruction from, and walked, talked and conversed with him, as one man talks and communes with another.

". . . These are incomprehensible ideas to some, but they are simple. It is the first principle of the gospel to know for a certainty the Character of God, and to know that we may converse with Him as one man converses with another, and that He was once a man like us; yea that God Himself, the Father of us all, dwelt on an earth, the same as Jesus Christ himself did; and I will show it from the Bible.

". . . The scriptures inform us that Jesus said, As the Father hath power in Himself, even so hath the Son power — to do what? Why, what the Father did. The answer is obvious — in a manner to lay down His body and take it up again. Jesus, what are you going to do? To lay down my life as my Father did, and take it up again. Do we believe it? If you do not believe it, you do not believe the Bible.

". . . Here, then, is eternal life — to know the only wise and true God; and you have got to learn how to be gods yourselves, and to be kings and priests to God, the same as all gods have done before you, namely, by going from one small degree to another, and from a small capacity to a great one; from grace to grace, from exaltation to exaltation, until you attain to the resurrection of the dead, and are able to dwell in everlasting burnings, and to sit in glory, as do those who sit enthroned in everlasting power. And I want you to know that God, in the last days, while certain individuals are proclaiming His name, is not trifling with you or me."

The upturned faces before him looked stunned. The vast audience was amazingly quiet, listening to the Prophet Joseph Smith reveal principles that none before him in this age had ever imagined, or dared explore. As he spoke, he seemed to expand with an enormous power. Emma watched her husband. She knew his determination to present immortal doctrine to people who had come to be spiritually fed. Well, here was not milk, but meat!

He spoke on, using Latin, German and Hebrew, for the unlearned plowboy had gained a remarkable mastery of languages, philosophy, and logic. Emma thought how very far he had come since she had reassured him that Jerusalem had a wall.

". . . We say that God himself is a self-existent being. Who told you so? It is correct enough; but how did it get into your heads? Who told you that man did not exist in like manner upon the same principles? Man does exist upon the same principles. God made a tabernacle and put a spirit into it, and it became a living soul. How does it read in the Hebrew? It does not say in the Hebrew that God created the spirit of man. It says 'God made man out of the earth and put into him Adam's spirit, and so became a living body.'

"... I am dwelling on the immortality of the spirit of man. Is it logical to say that the intelligence of spirits is immortal, and yet that it had a beginning? The intelligence of spirits had no beginning, neither will it have an end. That is good logic. That which has a beginning may have an end. There never was a time when there were not spirits; for they are co-eternal with our Father in Heaven."

The prophet took from his finger a thick gold ring, which gleamed in the sunlight, and held it up for all to observe.

"... I take my ring from my finger and liken it unto the mind of man — the immortal part because it had no beginning. Suppose you cut it in two; then it has a beginning and an end; but join it again, and it continues one eternal round. So with the spirit of man."

Joseph seemed to gain strength as he spoke. His voice rose and carried across the thousands who stood or sat in the warm sun of April. Those within earshot relayed the speech back to those farthest away. Some in the audience had heard whispers that Joseph was a fallen prophet. Rumors of polygamy had shaken the faith of others. He was aware of these murmurings and now went on to teach with power about man's relationship to Deity, knowing it would prove he was no fallen prophet.

"... You mourners have occasion to rejoice, speaking of the death of Elder King Follett; for your husband and father is gone to wait until the resurrection of the dead... Your friend will rise in perfect felicity and go to celestial glory... Don't mourn, don't weep. I know it by the testimony of the Holy Ghost that is within me; and you may wait for your friends to come forth to meet you in the morn of the celestial world. . . I have a father, brothers, children, and friends who have gone to a world of spirits. They are only absent for a moment. They are in the spirit, and we shall soon meet again. The time will soon arrive when the trumpet shall sound. When we depart, we shall hail our mothers, fathers, friends, and all whom we love, who have fallen asleep in Jesus.

He faced the audience, and spread out his arms as if to envelop everyone. His voice filled with emotion

". . . I have intended my remarks for all, both rich and poor, bond and free, great and small. I have no enmity against any man. I love you all; but I hate some of your deeds. I am your best friend. . . if I reprove a man, and he hates me, he is a fool; for I love all men, especially these my brethren and sisters. I rejoice in hearing the testimony of my aged friends.

"You don't know me; you never knew my heart. No man knows my history. I cannot tell it: I shall never undertake it. I don't blame any one for not believing my history. If I had not experienced what I have, I would not have believed it myself. . . When I am called by the trump of the archangel and weighed in the balance, you will all know me then. I add no more. God bless you all. Amen."

There was complete silence. Mother Smith wept. Samuel Smith's face reflected Joseph's light, as he, too, wiped away tears. Henceforth, Emma's testimony that her husband was God's true prophet was shared by many, and placed beyond doubt. Most of the comfortless had been strengthened by Joseph's sermon of love and hope.

Not long after conference, when Joseph was passing William Law's home, William's spirited wife, Jane, beckoned to him to come in. Joseph paused in his errand and congenially stepped into her parlor for friendly conversation. She wanted to be sealed in the eternal covenant to her husband, and asked Joseph why that request had been denied. Joseph tried to spare her feelings by concealing certain facts he knew to be true about William's worthiness. Jane was not to be put off, so she then coaxed and begged to be sealed to Joseph as a plural wife, if she could not be sealed to her husband. Cautiously disengaging himself from the conversation, Joseph politely refused and quickly left the Laws' home.

Spurned and humiliated, Jane immediately sought out her husband, accusing Joseph of attempted seduction. William believed his wife, and immediately a rift developed between Joseph and his counselor. Certain immoral behavior on William's part had already come between him and the prophet. When private rebuke failed to stop William, and a similar situation involving Robert Foster had surfaced, Joseph eventually reprimanded them both publicly. Anger and embarrassment was soon followed by their total apostasy from the church.

Memories of Kirtland and Far West, combined with this agony of being at odds with former friends, challenged Joseph anew. Brigham Young was the one to articulate the reoccurring paradox, *"Joseph Smith had the gift to make use of the talents and ability of someone short on integrity, rather than use his other leaders who were more sterling in character, but had appreciably less administrative ability and political influence."*

Brigham always marveled at "that ability which Joseph possessed to see and understand men as they were." That ability caused defensiveness and belligerence in those who were "weighed in the balance and found wanting."

"I'll have Joseph Smith's life or die trying!" William Law swore before a group of sympathizers. All had rejected Joseph's teachings on plural marriage, the character of God, and the mixing of religion with politics. At first, both Joseph and Hyrum had tried to counsel with them, hoping these close friends might avoid excommunication. However, no exhortation could heal the rift. Joseph's former counselor rushed on vehemently. "I put pistols in my pockets the other night and went to his house, intending to blow his infernal brains out, but I couldn't get the opportunity to shoot him."

There was a chorus of admiring approval. Numbered among the antagonists were William Law, counselor in the first presidency, his brother, Wilson Law, second in command of the Nauvoo Legion, Chauncy and Francis Higbee, Joseph's attorneys, and Robert and Charles Foster, his business partners — all recently excommunicated from the church.

Having given up Mormonism completely, the alienated men began conspiring to kill Joseph. At a secret meeting, they bound themselves together in a dark covenant: "You solemnly swear, before God and all holy angels, and these brethren by whom you are surrounded, that you will give your life, your liberty, your influence, your all, for the destruction of Joseph Smith, so help you God!"

The apostates then set up their own church and named William Law their leader. They immediately began soliciting members from among Nauvoo citizens who were disgruntled for any reason.

"Willard, the hounds are on my trail," Joseph confided to his friend and scribe one afternoon in May. "They haven't done their worst yet. I wish we had better reports of the West from our scouts. The time will come when the church is established in the Rocky

Mountains. I have seen those majestic mountains in vision, with their clear, flowing streams. Out West we could have greater freedom to practice our religion as we see fit."

"This Gadianton band of apostates has no evidence against you. It's all speculation," Willard reassured him.

The accusations turned into official charges of adultery when William and Wilson Law went before the circuit court and grand jury in Carthage and swore out an affidavit against Joseph Smith. The grand jury issued an indictment against him.

"Don't go!" Emma pleaded early Monday morning, May 27, 1844, as her husband prepared to face the charges against him.

"I must."

"They won't come here and take you, not with the Legion protecting you."

"As a candidate for United States President, I must clear myself."

Emma was not even listening. "I can hide you here in the secret closet."

Joseph was unyielding. "I must be subject to the law."

"Porter warned us there were traitors in your circle of friends," Emma worried.

Joseph sighed. "I wanted William Law to repent. He was my counselor, and a valuable ally. I was not surprised to find the Higbees turn against me — they have been friends of Bennett from the beginning."

"At least, have Legionnaires escort you." Emma's eyes were swollen.

"My friends would give their lives to protect me."

"If you must go, then I want to go too. No one would shoot a man in front of his wife."

"Emma, you are not going. You must think of the child you carry."

Emma was now three months into her eighth pregnancy, thin and continually tired. She was nearing her fortieth birthday.

"Besides, I'm just going to file an answer to the charges. Don't worry; I will be fine."

A throng of friends rode to Carthage with Joseph, determined to protect their prophet. In Carthage, they found that William Law and the prosecution were not ready to proceed. The courthouse was filled when Judge Thomas finally set him free on bail, since witnesses against him failed to appear. But worry and dread had taken their toll on Emma by the time her husband returned home that evening.

"I am more in danger from some dough-heads in this city than from all my enemies abroad." Joseph told the police force that guarded Nauvoo. "There is far greater danger from traitors within than enemies without. We have a Judas in our midst."

When Wilford Woodruff left on a campaign mission to the east, he embraced a somber prophet as he said goodbye.

"Brother Joseph, I am sorry to go and leave you in these circumstances. Would to God there was something I could do."

Joseph shook his friend's hand. "I have been in perils before, more often than anyone in this generation." He smiled wryly. "I should be like a fish out of water if I were out of persecutors. God bless you. Let's hope we meet again in better times."

Better times were hard to envision. On June 7, a newspaper was distributed throughout the city. Emblazoned across the sheet was the name, *Nauvoo Expositor*. It was published by erstwhile friends, the Laws, the Higbees, and the Fosters. It contained lurid accusations of against both Joseph and Hyrum. The prophet was portrayed as "pernicious and diabolical," and referred to his doctrines as "heretical and damnable." They accused him of abusing political power and being a common seducer of women. If the dissenters couldn't indict Joseph before a court of law, they would indict him publicly before all Nauvoo.

Emma was shaking when she presented Joseph with the scandalous sheet. He had come home after an early morning walk and had already seen the paper.

"Now the accusations spring from our midst!" She was furious.

"They spring from the traitorous hearts of William Law and the Higbees, promoted by John C. Bennett." Joseph was tired. He knew he had more than one battle on his hands. "More than that, they accuse me of their own crimes. It is an old trick."

"But, Joseph. . . Jane Law? Is her accusation entirely false?"

"Yes," he responded, "*entirely.* I spurned her when she asked to be sealed to me, and she is seeking revenge."

"I'm tired, Joseph," she whispered. "I want it to stop. I would give up the Mansion House and all our conveniences to return to the happy time in Kirtland."

"There were problems there too, Emma."

"But I was younger." Her voice carried a desolate tone. "I am so weary of plural marriage, politics, and persecution. . . "

He knelt beside her chair, stroking her hair. Usually so carefully combed, this morning it was unkempt. "Emma, you do need more rest. Don't worry. I will take care of everything."

He went straightway with Willard Richards to consult Hyrum. It was decided to call a meeting of the Nauvoo City Council.

The city council met Saturday, June 8, and the next Monday, June 10, 1844, to discuss and debate the problem of the Nauvoo Expositor.

"It's a public nuisance!" Hyrum denounced the publication.

"Yes," William Phelps agreed. "And if the definition of a nuisance is disturbing the peace, this inflammatory rag qualifies! It must be silenced!"

"Smash it and scatter the type!" Hyrum was unusually vehement.

Nauvoo's Marshall, John P. Greene, warned, "Francis Higbee thinks he has caught us in a snare. He told a friend that if we should lay a hand on his press it would mean our downfall. We must find other ways to silence it."

"Such as what?" Joseph asked.

"We could sue for libel."

"Just the spectacle our enemies want! I don't think it would be good for us." Hyrum rejected the proposal.

Jonathan Holmes mused, "We could forbid any further publication upon pain of personal punishment."

"These men are far beyond such a threat," Joseph argued. "They are already convinced our city police are trying to intimidate them."

Councilor Warrington, not a member of the church, was the lone voice for leniency. "I think it rather harsh to declare the paper a public nuisance. It may be a nuisance to Mayor Smith — and certainly it is scandalous — but prudence dictates lawful means to silence it. I propose a three-thousand-dollar fine for every libel, and if they don't cease publishing, carry the matter to the courts."

Joseph considered all comments. "These are vipers in our midst. They care nothing for truth or honor. We *must* remove their ability to disseminate lies."

Warrington shook his head. "The constitution guarantees a free press."

"That guarantee applies to government not dictating what a press will report. It does not uphold a press dedicated to reporting lies as fact and destroying our society!" Joseph was adamant. "If we do not destroy it, it will destroy us."

After the three days, the council took a vote and declared the *Nauvoo Expositor* a public nuisance, endangering the safety of the city by eliciting a spirit of mobacracy. In short, they applied paraphrased principle, obtained from the Book of Mormon: "It is better that one printing press should perish than an entire city dwindle in unbelief."

The council directed Mayor Joseph Smith to "cause said printing establishment and papers to be removed without delay, in such a manner as he shall direct." Joseph immediately issued an order to Marshall John P. Greene, to destroy the press, mix and scatter the type, and arrest anyone who might attempt to intervene. By eight o'clock that night, the fateful deed was done.

Thomas Sharp of the *Warsaw Signal* responded to urgent knocking at his door late the night of June tenth.

"Who the devil is it?" he growled.

"I have a message from Nauvoo," Charles Foster had ridden hard and fast. He handed over a simple handwritten letter to the newspaperman.

Sharp took it from him, grumbled his thanks, and closed his door. By lamplight he read Francis Higbee's message, "The *Nauvoo Expositor* printing press, type, printed papers and fixtures have this day been destroyed by order of Joseph Smith! Our constitutional rights are denied. Tyranny reigns in Nauvoo!"

A whoop of joy burst from Sharp. He stamped his foot and held the missive aloft. "Now he's done it! We've got him this time!"

He turned up the lamp and went to work feverishly. The next day, the *Signal* printed a denunciation of Joseph, following sensational headlines:

"Unparalleled Outrage at Nauvoo! War and Extermination are Inevitable! Citizens Arise One and All!! Can you stand by and suffer such infernal devils to rob men of their property and rights without avenging them. . . "

Sharp's continual assault against Joseph Smith and the Mormons now took on an incendiary tone as he called for their expulsion from the state. The Higbees and the Laws rode to Carthage to swear out another complaint against Joseph for denying their constitutional rights. Joseph, Hyrum, and the other city council members dutifully appeared before the Nauvoo Municipal Court, were tried and discharged on grounds that Joseph had acted on proper authority.

Joseph went home for supper. He was ready to retire for the evening when two brethren from farms outside Nauvoo came with a message for him.

"What is it, Joseph?" Emma asked from the top of the stairs.

"Oh. . . nothing much. Some news from the farmers. Mr. Hamilton is paying one dollar a bushel for corn."

The two messengers wore damp clothing from a steady rain. Their hair dripped water and their boots were muddy. Emma thought it strange they had come on such a night with crop news, but she went back into her bedroom, grateful to retire, as she was still unwell.

Joseph listened intently to the two brothers' warning.

"Three hundred men, including Missourians, are forming a mob in Carthage, Brother Joseph. They intend to come against Nauvoo."

He gazed into the two worried faces before him. "Stay here tonight, boys. I'll address this tomorrow."

Joseph didn't know that Thomas Sharp was masterminding a meeting in Warsaw that very night, an anti-Mormon meeting that produced a hauntingly familiar resolution:

"Resolved, that the time, in our opinion, has arrived, when the adherents of Smith, as a body, should be driven from the surrounding

settlements into Nauvoo. . . and if not. . . a war of extermination should be waged to the entire destruction of his adherents."

The next day, Joseph wrote to Governor Ford outlining the events of the past week and asking for his presence in the county to restore order. Joseph ordered the Nauvoo Legion placed at the disposal of Marshal John P. Greene as a precaution against attack.

The following day, Isaac Morley sent word that Colonel Levi Williams from Carthage had ridden into Lima, Illinois, a Mormon settlement, and demanded all Mormon arms. He also reported fifteen hundred Missourians crossing the border into Carthage and men training for battle. Joseph sent Porter Rockwell and Samuel James to Springfield with his letter to Governor Ford.

When Hyrum came to his brother's office, Joseph and Willard were examining the minutes of the city council meeting, which had resulted in the destruction of the press.

Hyrum pulled up a chair. "We must keep cool heads. The situation is looking bleak. The rumors of attack bring back memories of Missouri."

"Everyone must stay calm. The city is safe," Joseph responded.

"Yes, the Legion is the best trained force in the state, but it must not come to that."

Willard muttered, "I hope Ford is not another Boggs."

Joseph appeared in military dress the morning of June eighteenth. He was unusually solemn as he descended the Mansion House stairway. Emma watched her husband with dismay. Normally Joseph was in high spirits in his lieutenant general's uniform.

"Why is the Legion assembling?" She was determined to know.

"Preparation."

"For what?" When he didn't answer, she guessed. "It's this business about the Expositor, isn't it?"

Joseph paused in his preparations and faced her. "Are you strong enough to travel?"

Emma kept her face impassive with great effort. "You're thinking of a trip?"

"I think perhaps the church should move to the Rocky Mountains. The Indians pose no threat; they have more honor than the white man."

Emma felt a chill come across her heart. "Are you going to fight?"

"I hope not. . . but I will if I have to."

"That's what all the midnight meetings have been about?"

"Yes."

Emma gathered up a quilt and methodically folded it. "I'll move if you want me to. I've always been willing to go with you wherever you go."

He smiled bleakly, remembering the Lord's earlier command to her. "I know. It would be my last resort. You are in no condition to travel. . . but if my presence here endangers the city, *I* may have to go, at least temporarily."

"Is all this Sharp's doing?"

"His and all those who willingly believe his mischief."

Emma laid the throw quilt down on the chair and went to her husband. She meant only to adjust the gold braid on his uniform, but found herself clinging to him, her head on his shoulder, her heart beating an intense staccato.

"Be careful! Please careful! Don't speak so boldly. It could be used against you."

"I'll be careful. . . but I won't be a coward. Stay indoors today, Emma. I do not want you outside; there may be danger."

She watched from the window as he went out and mounted his horse. All day she listened to sounds of the Legion, as riders patrolled the city. Mother Smith was impatient with the noise and uproar.

"Can't folks stay home? I turned away a dozen people last hour, and told them to go about their business. Do they listen? No, they like to worry. Well, I intend to get my afternoon nap and you'd better too. You still look a little peaked to me."

There was no nap for Emma, however. In the afternoon, the Legion was drawn up in front of the Mansion House. From her bedroom window, Emma, looked down, and watched her husband climb the scaffolding of a new building nearby and address the troops. During his lengthy and passionate speech, she saw him draw his sword and thrust it toward the heavens. She drew a shaky breath as she heard his voice ring out:

"I call on God and angels to witness that I have unsheathed my sword with a firm and unalterable determination that this people shall have their legal rights, and be protected from mob violence, or my blood shall be spilt upon the ground like water, and my body consigned to the silent tomb.

". . . You are a good people; therefore I love you with all my heart. . . You have stood by me in the hour of trouble, and I am willing to sacrifice my life for your preservation."

No! Emma cried within herself, not again! Don't speak of your death! I could not bear it! A roar went up from the Legion, as Emma closed the window. She could no longer bear to listen, but she could not take her eyes off the man she loved.

That night, all alone, Joseph wrote a letter to a friend in the east. In foreboding tones, he poured out the musings of his soul, contemplating the path that had taken him from the Sacred Grove to the bluff above the river:

". . . I have long felt that my present work was almost done, and that I should soon be called to rule a mighty host, but something whispers me it will be in the land of spirits where the wicked cease from troubling and the bands of the prisoners fall off.

"My heart yearns for my little ones but I know God will be a father to them and I can claim face to face the fulfillment of promises from Him who is a covenant keeping God, and he sweareth, and performeth, and faileth not to the uttermost.

"The wolves are upon the scent and I am waiting to be offered up, if such be the will of God, knowing that though my visage be marred more than that of any, it will be unseared and fair when archangels shall place on my brow the double crown of martyr and king in a heavenly world.

"In the midst of darkness and boding danger, the spirit of Elijah came upon me, and I went away to enquire of God how the Church should be saved. I was upon the hill of the temple and the calm father of waters rolled below, changeless and eternal. I beheld a light in the heavens above and streams of bright light illuminated the firmament, varied and beautiful as the rainbow, gentle, yet rapid as the fierce lightening. The Almighty came from His throne of rest. He clothed Himself with light as a garment. He appeared and the stars and moon went out. The earth dissolved in space. I trod on the air and was borne on wings of Cherubims. The sweetest strains of heavenly music thrilled my ear, but the notes were low and sad as though they sounded the requiem of martyred prophets.

"I bowed my head to the earth and asked only wisdom and strength for the church. The voice of God answered, 'My servant Joseph, thou hast been faithful over many things and thy reward is glorious, the crown and scepter are thine, and they wait thee, but thou hast sinned in some things and thy punishment is very bitter. The whirlwind goeth before and its clouds are dark, but rest followeth and to its days there shall be no end.'"

Early the next morning, Joseph instructed his scribe, "Willard, send letters to the Twelve and the rest of my campaigners. They must return as soon as possible. I received word Governor Ford is in Carthage. His recent letter condemns the destruction of the press, and he wants me to stand trial there."

Willard stared at his friend and prophet. "Carthage! With apostates, Missourians, and the Carthage Greys! How can he assure your safety?"

Joseph answered with regret, "I don't think that is his concern. He wants to break the political power of the Mormons, and this is his chance."

"Sharp and his anti-Mormon league have raised over three thousand men from surrounding counties."

"I know. I have already put the city under martial law." Joseph went on. "I could not assure our safety as mayor, but I will as lieutenant general."

Joseph went to the window and stared down at the river. After a moment he continued, "Willard, I want Hyrum to succeed me. If I go to Carthage, he must not go with me. He must take his family and leave Nauvoo. . . tomorrow, if possible."

Hyrum came at Joseph's summons, but refused to desert his brother.

"*Joseph, I will not leave you!* Let's write to President Tyler. We deserve protection and a fair trial, and Ford has obviously thrown in with the mob at Carthage."

Joseph had become morose. "The governor has written again demanding that I come to Carthage to answer further charges, yet he knows I'll be walking into a trap."

"Write and request his personal protection. He should come here and escort us back to Carthage."

"If we are to be tried, it should be in Springfield, where some law and order prevail. For him to insist on a Carthage trial is to sacrifice me to my enemies." Joseph handed his brother the governor's latest letter.

"If you, by refusing to submit, shall make it necessary to call out the militia, I have great fears that your city will be destroyed, and your people, many of them, exterminated. . . excitement is a matter which grows very fast upon men when assembled. The affair, I much fear, may assume a revolutionary character, and the men may disregard the authority of their officers."

Hyrum put down the letter in disbelief. "Well, so threats instead of assurances!"

Joseph shook his head. "There is no mercy — no mercy here."

"No," Hyrum agreed, "Just as sure as we fall into their hands, we are dead men!"

The men sat in doleful silence for a time. Eventually, Joseph's countenance brightened and he said, "The way is open. It is clear to my mind what to do. They only want us. They won't harm anyone else. Hyrum, we will cross the river tonight and go away to the West."

"Leave our families?"

"They can take the *Maid of Iowa* to safety and meet us later."

"Emma can't bear to travel right now," Hyrum reminded his brother.

412

At that moment, Emma slipped into the room. She had been listening to part of their discussion just outside the doorway.

"I will bear whatever I must," she said with determination.

Joseph turned to her, his eyes bright with pride. "Emma! You are my constant comfort in the face of trouble." He went to her and took her hands in his, raised them to his lips and kissed them.

"I must leave tonight," he said. He was reluctant but determined.

She was afraid her voice would break, so she simply nodded.

"You understand?" Joseph asked.

"Do what you must. I need you safe," Emma consoled him in shaky tones.

"We'll be safe. Don't worry." He turned to Willard, whose presence he had almost forgotten. "Go get Porter. He will get us across the river."

"I'm going too," he declared. "Your chief scribe goes where you go. History requires it."

Joseph smiled. "*If* you can get Porter to fit four of us in a skiff."

Hyrum stood looking out the window. The weather had been stormy the last few weeks, and tonight was no different. It was raining – not hard, but a steady drizzle. The air was sultry. Crossing the Mississippi at night in a small skiff was not a pleasant thought — however, neither was a journey to Carthage.

Emma went to fix a knapsack for them. When she came back, her resolve had weakened. Joseph was ready to go, his cloak thrown about his shoulders to brave the rain. He held his wife and kissed her tenderly, then started down the stairs.

"Don't go!" Emma sobbed and ran after him.

"It will save many lives if I leave," he tried to reason with her. "It won't be for long."

Emma was weeping, wiping her tears with the back of her hand. "We could go back to Kirtland. No! Let's go to Cincinnati! It's a civilized place. Mobs can't come in and kill you there. Please, Joseph, don't go!"

"I *must*," his voice was gruff as he tore himself away. "I can't delay any longer. My life depends on it. I'll write, I promise!" He descended the stairs, his face in his handkerchief, not daring to look at Emma's face.

It was June 23, 1844, two o'clock in the morning and so black they could scarcely see one another, when they finally secured a boat. It was hardly large enough for Joseph, Hyrum, and Porter. Still, Willard would not be left out, and he entreated them to take him. Porter clamped his jaw tightly and finally motioned the scribe into the boat. With four men, the craft rode low in the water. They started upstream and began to row. The water was choppy, and half way across, the boat began to leak. Willard and the Smiths took off their boots to use for bailing, while Porter rowed. The wind blew furiously. The swift current pushed them downstream. The pitching boat wallowed through the dark, choppy water. All he held dear was receding into the darkness — his city, his people, his children, and his eternal companion.

With Porter's tireless help, they made the opposite shore and sought refuge with William Jordan in Montrose. After a few hours rest and a little refreshment, Hyrum, Willard, and Joseph began to discuss the next leg of their journey.

"You'll need horses." Rockwell assessed practically. "I'll go back for 'em, and bring 'em on my ferry. Just sit tight."

With that he left, walked back to the shore, pulled the leaky craft from the bushes, and started back across the cold water.

The sky was barely light when a posse of men thundered down the road to Joseph Smith's home. Constable Bettisworth from Carthage rapped sharply on the front door. When no one answered, he pounded, then forced his way in, followed by a half dozen men. Emma had thrown a shawl over her nightgown and started downstairs.

Bettisworth spoke haughtily, "Joseph Smith is summoned to meet Governor Ford in Carthage. We are his escort."

Drawing on her considerable self-discipline, Emma answered calmly. "Mr. Smith is not at home."

At that, the men separated and began searching the house.

"He cannot escape, Madam! The governor has troops at his command who will search forever, if necessary, to find Smith and make him answer for his crimes."

Emma stared into his ruddy face. "I know of no crimes — except for your trespassing."

Bettisworth was furious. "He's here men; I have it on good authority. Search every room!"

Emma's voice was icy. "Sir! These are my private quarters! My children and aged mother are asleep here. I forbid you to enter their rooms, and I give my word of honor, Mr. Smith is not here!"

Reluctantly, Bettisworth left. His parting words cut her like a whip. "Rest assured, we'll find him, and hell will see him before you do!"

Emma closed the door after the last man departed, then sat down carefully. She did not doubt the constable's threat. The Missourians still pursued Joseph after five years. On the Iowa shore he had no protection. Once the state militia got word of his departure, they would start a search, and they would not give up until they found him. How could she and Joseph ever have peace? If he didn't answer these charges, he would be hunted forever. East, West, it would not matter. He would always be in danger. Perhaps if she appealed to Governor Ford to move the trial to Springfield where mercy was possible.

Emma almost convinced herself that Joseph would be all right if he returned. She washed her face, dressed herself properly, and tried to eat a little. Then people of Nauvoo began arriving. . . and questioning.

"Some of us are dreadfully tried in our faith to think Brother Joseph would leave us in our hour of danger. The last steamboat was completely loaded with people leaving Nauvoo. What will we do if the mob comes?"

"The mob is not coming," Emma assured them gravely. "That's why Mr. Smith left. He knows they only want him, not the rest of us. He is trying to save the city from assault."

Someone else interjected, "Sister Emma, I can not have my family in danger."

And another, "If Joseph could just bring himself to meet with the governor at Carthage, I believe the furor would die down."

And so it went. . .

Emma finally walked over to Hyrum's home where Mary was packing. "So you are going?" she asked Hyrum's wife.

"Of course; aren't you?"

"I'm not sure it's necessary. People are begging me to ask Joseph to come back. Oh, Mary, I must confess, I wish they would come back."

Mary continued her preparations. "So do I. Our Lovina is to be wed to Loren Walker tomorrow, and her father was to perform the ceremony. Still, I must have everything ready to go on the steamboat tomorrow."

Emma sighed. "It's not easy for me to leave. I have a hotel to run, a child due soon." She had found no support here.

Later that afternoon, Porter came to her. Always reticent in Emma's refined presence, he pitied her frazzled appearance. "Here's a message from your husband. I'm taking Joseph's and Hyrum's horses across the river, and would be glad to take him your reply."

"Do not despair. If God ever opens a door that is possible for me, I will see you again. I do not know when I shall go, or what I shall do. . . May God Almighty bless you and the children, and mother, and all my friends. My heart bleeds. No more at present. If you conclude to go to Kirtland, Cincinnati, or any other place, I wish you would inform me. . . "

Emma held the note for a long time, poring over the hasty handwriting, remembering her husband's face when he had left her.

"What are you hearing around town, Porter?"

Rockwell leaned on the doorjamb. He cleared his throat. "They say he's a coward. They say he's running away."

Emma took up pen and paper and answered Joseph's letter. She reported the accusations of cowardice, but reaffirmed her willingness to go with him wherever his safety could be assured. She had moved before; she could do so again. No hardship would be greater than separation from Joseph. The thought of him a fugitive again, far away and alone was insufferable. Exhausted and ill, she needed him more than ever. . . and she knew he needed *her*!

Porter left that afternoon, along with Reynolds Cahoon, Lorenzo Wasson, and Hiram Kimball. They arrived across the river at William Jordan's and found Joseph consulting with Attorney John M. Bernhisel. Porter handed Emma's letter to Joseph.

All were silent as he read it. When he put it down, his face was grim. Emma would forsake her home with its comforts, but could he ask it of her? He shook his head.

"What say you?" he asked his wife's nephew, Lorenzo.

Lorenzo and Hiram both criticized his plan to leave. Hiram finished with, "Just last Sunday you said if the church would stick with you, you would stick with the church. Now how does it look having the shepherd desert the flock, Joseph?"

Reynolds added, "William Law's supporters are gloating over your retreat."

Joseph turned then to his tried and true boyhood friend. "What shall we do, Port?"

Porter spit his chaw on Reynolds' boot. "You're older, Joseph, and ought to know best. As you make your bed, I will lie with you!"

Joseph sought more counsel. "Brother Hyrum, you are the oldest, what shall we do?"

Hyrum's thoughts flashed to his family, to his daughter Lovina, about to be married. "Let us go back and give ourselves up, and see the thing out."

Joseph heaved a great sigh, walked about the room in deep contemplation, and presently the words seeped from his heart.

"If you go back, I will go with you, but we shall be butchered."

"Let us go back and put our trust in God. . . The Lord is in it. If we live or have to die, we will be reconciled to our fate."

An alarm sounded in Joseph's mind. He was about to go against divine revelation; God had shown him a way out. He had seen in vision the beautiful mountains where he and his people could live in peace. If he ignored that instruction, he would forfeit the Lord's protection and inspiration.

Finally, Joseph spoke, his voice low, *"If my life is of no value to my friends, it is of none to me."*

During his lifetime, some had looked upon him as a scoundrel; some had looked upon him as a seer, but he would not be looked upon as a coward. Knowing fully that this decision would seal his fate, Joseph laid aside his prophetic mantle and, meek as a lamb, started back across the river to his rendezvous with destiny.

Chapter Twelve

Eternal Triumph

Emma, can you train my sons to walk in their father's footsteps?"

Joseph's lap was full of children. He looked up at Emma over the tousled heads of their three sons. Julia leaned over his shoulder, her slender, young arms around her father's neck. At thirteen, she was becoming a woman, and was aware of the perilous times her father faced. Young Joseph, eleven, had rallied to the excitement of Legionnaires around Nauvoo, but now, understanding it meant danger for his father, his face was sad, his head on his father's shoulder. Freddy sat on Joseph's knee, his face pressed against his shirt. He was eight years old that June, trying to copy his older brother, thriving on adventure and assuming a daredevil air.

Right now, all he knew was that his father was leaving again, and he didn't like it. Six-year-old Alexander sat on the other knee, every few minutes straining to kiss his father's cheek. His little voice was lost in the hubbub of activity. No one heard him repeat in his lilting tones, "Papa, don't go. Please stay home, Papa." This he repeated many times until Joseph had to finally remove them all from his lap and take the coat Porter handed him.

"You will come back," Emma tried to assure her husband, though assurance was the last thing she felt.

Joseph buttoned his coat and put on his hat. His eyes had not left Emma's. He repeated his question, "Can you train my sons to walk in their father's footsteps?"

Emma began to tremble. She was certain his best course of action was to seek the governor's protection, but that certainty was crumbling, and with it, her resolve to bear up bravely. "But, you're coming back, Joseph!" When he didn't answer, bending instead to kiss his children, Emma tried to be cheerful.

"I'll attend the court hearing," she said. "Governor Ford has pledged to protect you."

"The governor didn't bother to send military protection like he promised." Porters's scorn of state authority was born of hard times in Missouri. "But, I'm a better bodyguard than all his militia."

Unconsciously, Joseph's hand went to his pocket where he kept a recent letter from Ford. Far from sending a militia escort, the governor now ordered Joseph and Hyrum to come to Carthage before ten o'clock, or Nauvoo and its citizens would face retaliations. It was already six in the morning, and a party of seventeen friends had gathered outside.

"A moment alone," Joseph spoke quietly to Porter and Willard as they started downstairs. The two men nodded and left the sorrowing family. Hyrum had already said goodbye to his wife and children and now tried to reassure his elderly mother. The rest of the traveling party only awaited the signal to ride.

Emma cast herself into her husband's embrace. "Oh Joseph, Joseph, come back to me!"

He stroked her long hair, which fell loose down her back. The depth of sorrow that burdened his heart made it almost impossible to talk. He wanted to reassure her, to comfort her, but false words would not come.

"Never doubt my love, Emma. We have come far from Harmony. I don't regret any of it."

"Nor I," she choked out.

He kissed her tenderly, taking precious time to enjoy the touch of her lips. Then he asked for the final time, "Can you train my sons to walk in their father's footsteps?"

She broke into sobs then, and the children, hearing their mother weeping, began to wail. He tore himself from their arms, and Emma followed him to the door. "You're coming back!" she cried with determination.

He didn't answer as he took her face in his hands, kissed her slowly and passionately one last time, then descended the stairs.

Joseph embraced his mother, kissed her cheek, then looked for the last time into the eyes he had loved as long as he could remember, and bid her adieu.

The children gathered around their mother. Julia's youthful arms encircling her as she tried to give her comfort. Mother Smith moved back to the doorstep and stood with the children. That was the image of his family Joseph carried with him to Carthage: his mother, his wife, his daughter, his sons. . . a flutter of small hands.

He turned ol' Charley toward Carthage. Up on the bluff, he paused as his party rode past the unfinished temple. By dawn's light, the walls reflected a spectrum of red. He seemed to see the finished structure in his mind's eye, the bell tower overlooking the city, the windows all alight, mighty doors open to receive him.

"This is the loveliest place and the best people under the heavens," he said to John Taylor, who rode at his side. "Little do they know the trials that await them," he predicted. And they rode on.

Porter and Stephen Markham led the way, frequently riding ahead to scout the road for unexpected attack. Only a few miles from Carthage, they met a company of sixty mounted militiamen riding toward them. As the parties met, the militia commander, Captain Dunn, addressed Joseph.

"General Smith, I am instructed by Governor Ford to collect all state arms in the possession of the Nauvoo Legion."

The announcement came as no surprise. It was obvious Ford meant to reduce Nauvoo's ability to defend itself. Porter cursed Ford, spurred his horse and rode up protectively beside Joseph.

"May I see your orders?" Joseph asked the captain.

He and Hyrum looked over the papers Captain Dunn extended.

"Would you oblige me, General, and countersign these orders, so your people will know I am acting with proper authority."

Joseph and his friends bristled. To a man, their thoughts flashed back to the surrender of Far West, grounding their arms, and then submitting to the abuse of a mob slavering for their blood, and here they were, once again at the mercy of their enemies. Joseph hesitated. Was there any recourse? Could his people adequately defend themselves? The Nauvoo Legion was the best-trained militia in the state. There was no doubt they could put up a good defense, but at what cost? How many friends' lives?

"General Smith. . . " the officer prompted.

Joseph called for pen and ink. John Taylor supplied it. "I trust you will go about this task peaceably," Joseph said, as he signed away his best defense.

Coldly, the governor's man replied, "Only your people can determine that."

It wasn't an answer that satisfied Joseph. He consulted with Hyrum, then finally resolved, "All right then, Captain, we will return with you to Nauvoo to see that no provocation, from either side, causes an altercation."

The men of the Nauvoo Legion were dismayed when their prophet rode back into Nauvoo under militia guard, especially when they learned of the order to surrender their state-issued arms. With much trepidation, they complied, recognizing the tension in the moment, and taking care to retain all their personal arms and ammunition.

While the order was being enforced, Porter was still at Joseph's side. It soon became apparent to Joseph that one more good-bye would be necessary before he continued on to Carthage. He also knew his boyhood friend would be reluctant to relinquish his position as bodyguard, but it had to be done.

"Porter, I need you to oversee the collection of the state arms in my stead. It will take some time. You are the only one I can trust to stop an altercation! Do not fail me, or the saints in this trust, and keep the peace, no matter what."

"No matter what, Joseph. . . no matter what, my friend."

Joseph's decision to have Porter stay behind was clearly the prudent path. The city needed men of his courage and experience. So, leaving his bodyguard behind, Joseph's party started once again for Carthage, with a loss greater than the state arms.

Shouts of encouragement sounded from his men on every side. Joseph sat astride ol' Charley and spoke out, loudly enough for all the gathered troops to hear:

"I am going like a lamb to the slaughter, but I am calm as a summer's morning; I have a conscience void of offense towards God and towards all men. If they take my life, I shall die innocent, and it shall be said of me, 'he was murdered in cold blood!'"

Just outside Nauvoo proper, the tidy farms were greening up after weeks of almost daily rain. Joseph stopped one last time, looking out over his own acreage. The pungent odor of rich, loamy soil was sweet in the warmth of the late afternoon sun. How he loved to spend his hours here. Those hours had been few and far between lately, as other matters consumed his days. Now there was no more time.

Stephen Markham urged the party on. Joseph excused his reflective moment: *"If some of you had got such a farm and knew you would not see it any more, you would want to take a good look at it for the last time."*

It was melancholy talk, but no one contradicted him, and the mood of the entourage became even more somber. It was midnight when Joseph's party reached Carthage. The town was in an uproar; crowds of men brimming with liquor and anger roamed the streets. More than fourteen hundred unruly militiamen from six counties swarmed around the Mormons, demanding Joseph's blood. Captain Dunn and his men, arriving back from Nauvoo, pushed their way through the crowds and escorted their detainees to the Hamilton House, where the governor was staying. Joseph and Hyrum rode proudly, certain of their innocence, tall in the saddle and apparently unintimidated by the show of violence around them. Side by side, they faced the predicament as they always had, together, through every trial of life.

At the Mansion House, Emma tried to keep calm. It was no use. No matter what Mother Smith said to reassure her, Emma was inconsolable. She dressed in a black skirt and blouse, twisted her hair into a bun and put on a cap to hide it all. By nightfall, her emotions were so raw she could not eat, sleep, nor care for her children. Mother Smith gave up trying to encourage Emma and took supper in her room. Julia was, once again, left to watch the boys.

Mansion House guests left on the *Osprey,* a steamboat going upriver, for Nauvoo did not appear to be a safe place. Word had blazed across town that the Legion had surrendered their arms, and a great mob was gathering in Carthage. Many families began packing to leave; some tried to secure passage on steamboats, while others loaded wagons to escape whatever onslaught might be coming.

Emma sat in her rocking chair in the bedroom, twisting and untwisting her handkerchief. She stared through the open window as though she might see her husband riding into Carthage. The child within her womb was restless. Without realizing, she put a hand on her stomach, attempting to soothe the movement.

As the hours dragged on and the lamp burned low, Emma eventually gave up her chair and lay down on the featherbed. She curled up on her side, but sleep would not come. Her imagination teemed with thousands of mobacrats. When she finally fell into exhausted sleep, it was in the wee hours of the morning.

While Emma slept, Tuesday morning, June 25, Joseph and Hyrum reviewed the state militia assembled in the Carthage Square. Governor Ford had ordered their presence, apparently to show the angry Carthage Greys he had the Mormon leaders in hand. The militia had been drinking and brawling for days, anxious to wreak havoc on the Smiths. Joseph and Hyrum walked beside the governor. John, Willard, and W.W. followed behind. There was a frenzy of shouting and pushing among the hostile men. Swords were drawn. Hissing and verbal abuses challenged the Smiths at every step, and the governor made no attempt to curb it. The strain of the last few days, no sleep, little food, and constant anxiety were taking their toll on both brothers, and every minute ticking by confirmed what he already knew.

By noon, Emma had received more visitors, all inquiring after Joseph. Had she heard anything? "No," she patiently replied. "Not yet." After several encounters, she automatically met them at the door and gave the answer. Her dearest friends, Sarah Cleveland and Elizabeth

Ann Whitney, came to sit with her and offer comfort. Emma, however, could not be comforted. She knew she would cry if she talked about Joseph. Instead, she did the wash, but stood over the washboard staring toward Carthage. Julia and Joseph III had to finish the project.

In the afternoon, Emma walked over to the Red Brick Store. It had never been so empty. She climbed the steep stairs to Joseph's private office, and sat at his desk, picturing him there, then put her head down and wept.

Meanwhile Joseph stood before his avowed enemy, Robert F. Smith, local justice of the peace and captain in the Carthage Greys. He had not been slated to hear their plea. Ford had promised it would be heard by Justice Morrison. Nevertheless, Robert Smith charged the defendants from Nauvoo with riot in destroying the *Nauvoo Expositor*. Joseph, Hyrum, and the other members of the Nauvoo City Council were ordered to stand trial in the Hancock County Circuit Court. Most of the accused posted five hundred dollars bail and returned to Nauvoo. Joseph and Hyrum, remained at the Hamilton House, for a morning interview with the governor.

At eight o'clock in the evening, a sharp rap at Joseph's door came from a constable carrying a writ of conveyance remanding them to jail on proposed charges of treason. Although this was a new charge with no preliminary hearing, protests were all to no avail. Governor Ford backed up his captain, insisting he could not interfere with the courts. Robert Smith's troops pushed their way through the clambering rabble outside the hotel, and marched their captives to the jail. Eight of Joseph's friends went with them. Stephen Markham was among them, carrying a walking stick which he called a "rascal-beater." Willard Richards counted more than a few rascals that needed the edge of those sticks. Hundreds of glowering militia crowded around to catch a glimpse of the man they considered a menace.

The solid stone jail looked more like a house, and indeed, the jailer lived there with his family. Jailer George W. Stigall was nervous as he took charge of the captives and shut the door in the faces of the Carthage Greys. He directed the prisoners into the main floor debtor's room, which was furnished with a bench, some blankets, and a night bucket.

The men held a prayer meeting before settling down on the floor to sleep. The jailer and his wife could hear the singing of hymns and the murmur of voices hushed in prayer. A calm spirit spread over the jailhouse, though in other parts of town soldiers sat up late, drinking and cursing the Mormon prophet.

At home in Nauvoo, Emma also called for evening prayer. True to custom, the Smith family started with a hymn. Emma's sweet soprano voice started bravely enough,

"Blest be the tie that binds our hearts in Christian love;
the fellowship of kindred minds is like to that above."

When they got to the fourth verse, bravery faltered:

"When we asunder part, it gives us inward pain;
but we shall still be joined in heart, and hope to meet again."

It wasn't easy to get through the melancholy words. Her voice failed her, but Julia picked up the tune and sang out. Mother Smith wanted to pray, and Emma was grateful. Her own emotions were too overwrought. Lucy prayed so long the younger boys fell asleep, and when the prayer was finished they were tucked lovingly in bed.

Normally, the Mansion House was full of activity until late at night. Now, without Joseph's presence, their home was quiet as a tomb. Emma went from room to room, securing windows, and most carefully of all, bolting the doors to the outside. She reminded her stableman to watch for prowlers. No looting or burning had happened thus far in Nauvoo, but there were rowdies about who might take advantage of the times.

Emma then retired to her bedroom for another sleepless night. She tried to start a letter to her husband, but gave up when she could think of nothing hopeful to write. If only she knew the governor would protect him as promised! When at last she slept, it was a fitful rest. Wind and rain drove against the house, rattling windows and buffeting the structure. She was awakened several times by the moaning wind, which eerily echoed her own thoughts.

Early the next morning, a messenger rapped on the Mansion House door. Emma was already dressed and going about her chores. A letter from Joseph! She almost fainted from relief. She took it gratefully, offering the rider breakfast for his efforts. He declined, tipped his hat, and rode in search of his own family. Emma broke the seal, and her eyes devoured the writing.

"Dear Emma
. . . when the truth comes out we have nothing to fear. We all feel calm and composed. . . Governor Ford has just concluded to send some of his militia to Nauvoo to protect the citizens, and I wish they may be kindly treated. They will co-operate with the police to keep the peace."

Keep the peace! The only thing *disturbing* the peace was the threat of the governor's militia! Without that threat, the atmosphere of Nauvoo could remain calm.

Emma's fears momentarily gave way to hope. That's right, she thought, we have nothing to fear. Joseph simply removed an inflammatory newspaper, a nuisance to the citizens of this city. Surely any fair-minded judge will see that. The governor will see that the people of Nauvoo are law-abiding and civil.

Knowing her husband wanted his instructions given to the saints, Emma turned the letter over to William Marks, Nauvoo Stake

President and close family friend. Soon the entire city knew the governor's troops were coming, and terror swept the community.

Meanwhile, Wednesday, June 26, came in drizzling rain. After the prisoners' meager breakfast, the jailer, out of consideration for the prisoners' comfort, relocated them to his own upstairs bedroom, furnished with a bed, mattresses for children in the family, a writing table and chairs, a chest, and a wardrobe. Curtains hung at the windows, which were open for ventilation. Governor Ford put in an appearance at the jail, presumably to reassure Joseph of fair treatment. He spent some time with the prisoners, as Joseph stoutly defended the actions against the Expositor.

"Governor Ford, we could not suffer that newspaper to vilify and calumniate not only ourselves, but the character of our wives and daughters, as was impudently and unblushingly done in that infamous and filthy sheet. . . deliver us from this place and rescue us from this outrage that is sought to be practiced upon us by a set of infamous scoundrels."

Thomas Ford was unmoved. His pale eyes were cold when he replied, "There is a great deal of truth in what you say, and your reasoning is plausible; yet. . . it is so contrary to the feelings of the American people to interfere with the press."

"We are desirous to fulfill the law in every particular," Joseph assured him. *"You say the parties ought to have had a hearing. Had it been a civil suit, this, of course, would have been proper; but there was a flagrant violation of every principle of right, a nuisance, and it was abated on the same principle that any nuisance, stench, or putrefied carcass*

would have been removed. . . Furthermore, let me say, Governor Ford, I shall look to you for protection. I believe you are talking of going to Nauvoo; if you do, sir, I wish to go along. I do not consider myself safe here."

Ford agreed, seemingly swayed by Joseph arguments. "I am in hopes that you will be acquitted; but if I go, I will certainly take you along." He stood up and straightened his cravat. "I do not, however, apprehend danger. I think you are perfectly safe, either here or anywhere else."

Looks of doubt showed on each Mormon face. As the governor started for the door, Joseph made his last appeal. "Governor Ford, I ask nothing but what is legal. I have a right to expect protection, at least from you. . . You have pledged your faith, and that of the State, for my protection, and I wish to go back to Nauvoo."

Ford seemed annoyed, but assured them of his protection once more and started down the stairs. Outside the jailhouse, Ford was mounting his horse when an officer of the militia guarding the jail confided in him. "Governor, the soldiers are determined to see Joe Smith dead before they leave."

Ford jerked around to look the man in the face. His eyes narrowed. He looked at the ground in deep contemplation, then gave his command, "If you know any such thing, keep it to yourself." He sat astride his horse, looking up to the second story window where Joseph and his friends waited, completely defenseless. Then he rode back to the Hamilton House.

As the day wore on, unconvinced by the governor's impotent assurances, Joseph remained anxious, in the crowded upstairs room.

In an effort to comfort his brother, Hyrum said, "I cannot think that the Lord will suffer any harm to come to you. He will surely spare you once more for the sake of the church."

Joseph placed his hand on his brother's shoulder. "It would not matter so much about me, if you could just be liberated. As for myself, I don't mind being killed, if only I'm not hanged like a common criminal."

Willard interrupted and said, "Brother Joseph, you did not ask me to cross the river with you — you did not ask me to come to Carthage — you did not ask me to come to jail with you. . . But I will tell you what I will do; if you are condemned to be hung for treason, I will be hung in your stead, and you shall go free."

Compassionately the prophet replied, "You cannot." Whereupon Willard insisted, "I will!"

The prisoners spent that rest of the morning trying to cheer each other. Willard kept copious notes. John Taylor read passages from the Book of Mormon, and Joseph preached to the guards who were left to protect them. It was late before the men went to sleep and even later when gunshots outside roused them. Joseph had been sleeping on the only bed with his brother. He lay down now, instead, on the floor between his friends, John S. Fullmer and Dan Jones, offering his arm to John for a pillow. Both men were ready to protect him at all costs.

In the darkness, with the smell of campfires and gunpowder drifting on the warm night breeze, Joseph and his friends whispered one with another. Joseph was nostalgic. *"I would like to see my family again,"* and *"I would to God that I could preach to the saints in Nauvoo once more."*

"I think you will often have that privilege," John attempted to cheer his beloved friend.

In the darkness, Joseph sighed, wishing it could be so. Presently he turned and whispered to Dan Jones, "Are you afraid to die?"

"Has the time come, think you?" Dan considered only a moment. "Engaged in such a cause I do not think death would have many terrors."

Uttering his last recorded prophecy, Joseph said, "You will yet see Wales, and fulfill the mission appointed to you before you die."

After the others slipped into uneasy sleep, Joseph lay awake in the darkness. God's prophet! The Prophet of the Lord! He had grown used to the appellations. He reflected on the years since he had been a callow youth in upstate New York. What was mortal life supposed to be? If it were a time for man to be tested and tried, to prove himself before God, then his life had been one continual fulfillment of that divine purpose, for surely he had been tested.

Joseph sensed that Hyrum was also awake, and long forgotten boyhood scenes they had shared began to stir other reverberations in his mind. He found some comfort in Emma's recent promise concerning the child she was carrying. If the babe were a son, she would name him David Hyrum; David after her own brother, and Hyrum after this loyal brother who would not desert him.

Joseph continued to reflect over the events of his life. If death came tonight, he would not fear it, but, oh, how he hated to leave the church, his friends, and his precious family.

Joseph's heart ached especially for Emma; the young girl he had spied through the trees along the Susquehanna River, so beautiful, so innocent! *Wife of my youth!* Have I failed you? Too often you suffered, because you chose me after God did.

As Joseph lay awake on the Carthage Jail floor, Emma was clinging to the hope of the governor's promised protection. But there was no hope. Now, alone in the "seventh trouble," Emma went to her knees and pleaded with God for her husband's life. No longer "undaunted, firm and unwavering," she poured out her soul: "I want nothing but his safe return. My Joseph is innocent before Thee. O Lord, let him live! . . . Or take me, for I cannot live without him!"

The next morning, Thursday, June 27, 1844, Joseph dispatched his friend, Dan Jones, to Quincy to secure the services of attorney, Orville H. Browning a highly renowned defense lawyer. As he left the jail, Dan discovered the governor's militia mustering nearby. Concerned at their presence, Dan went to the Hamilton House to find the governor.

"Sir, I fear that when you leave for Nauvoo, assassins will murder the Smiths!"

Coldly, Ford replied, "You are unnecessarily alarmed. The people are not that cruel." Governor Ford dismissed Dan, and left for Nauvoo with upwards of fourteen hundred troops. Riding west from Carthage, he never looked back.

At the same time, Joseph was dictating another letter to Emma, trying to reassure her, saying he was certain some of the troops would defend him in case of mutiny among the troops. Taking up the pen himself, he added a postscript,

"Dear Emma,

"I am very much resigned to my lot, knowing I am justified, and have done the best that could be done. Give my love to the children and all my friends. . . ; and as for treason, I know that I have not committed any, and they cannot prove anything of the kind, so you need not have any fears that anything can happen to us on that account."

During this ignominious day, one source of comfort came: a letter from his old friend, Oliver Cowdery. Though it had been years since their last meeting, coming as it did in this time of peril, Oliver's letter brought Joseph a measure of peace.

A little later, Cyrus Wheelock came to the jail to see Joseph and Hyrum. A steady rain had given him an excuse to wear an overcoat, even in late June, and he smuggled a loaded six-barrel pistol, called a "pepperbox " in a side pocket. He quietly slipped the gun into Joseph's pocket. The prophet pulled it out and, after examining it, kept it. He then handed Hyrum a single-shot pistol given to him earlier by John Fullmer.

"I hate to use such things or see them used," Hyrum said.

"So do I," Joseph answered, "but we may have to defend ourselves." After thanking Cyrus, he gave him messages to deliver to his family and friends. "Tell them not to make any kind of military display. This is no time for bravado. Let every man and woman keep a calm spirit and perhaps avoid disaster."

A guard opened the door and pounded the floor with the butt of his rifle. "All visitors out!" Joseph asked John Fullmer to return to Nauvoo with Cyrus and obtain witnesses for the promised trial. They left reluctantly, then hurried downstairs, mounted their horses, and headed for Nauvoo.

As the day of treachery wore on, the summer sun beat down on sodden earth. After the midday meal, Stephen Markham went out to get some medicine for Willard. John Taylor and Willard Richards were left alone in the second story bedroom with Joseph and Hyrum. The men sat in shirtsleeves; the windows were thrown open for the chance of a breeze.

After an hour the men began to wonder what had become of Stephen. They could not know he had been barred from reentry and had been run out of town. He refused to leave, but the Carthage militiamen prodded his legs with their bayonets until blood ran into his boots, and he was forced at gunpoint to leave. Meanwhile, the remaining four men in Carthage Jail grew more dispirited.

Entering Nauvoo, Governor Ford and his men rode past members of the Nauvoo Legion, mostly disarmed but still encamped along the eastern boundary of the town. Nauvoo was shut down, tight as a drum, its streets nearly empty. No one wanted a confrontation. He rode down the main road to the new hotel, Joseph Smith's Mansion House. It was the only place that could accommodate his staff. An astonished Emma opened the door to a sharp rap from Governor Ford's captain of the guard.

"Governor Thomas Ford and his staff desire to dine." the captain informed her.

Past his shoulder, Emma could see Ford's face. His handsome features were stiffly set. Her heart raced. If Ford were here, Joseph had no protection in Carthage! She steadied her nerves to welcome her visitors.

"Governor Ford is welcome in the home of Lieutenant General Joseph Smith." Emma used her husband's official, military title purposefully. "You may stable your horses in our carriage house."

Ford dismounted and approached her. She nodded slightly in deference, but neglected to extend her hand, as she once would have. "Dinner could be served within the hour, sir. I trust we can make you comfortable. My husband would want nothing less." At that she looked fully into his eyes.

Ford dropped his gaze and murmured thanks. His men crowded in around him. Mother Smith came down the stairs, curious about the noise, and found the parlor filled with uniformed militia and Governor Ford. Anger boiled within her. She started to speak, but Emma signaled a warning to her.

"Sir, I would be most pleased to wait upon you and your men, if it weren't for my concern for my husband's safety in your absence. What assurance can you give an anxious wife?" Emma was polite, but direct.

Ford cleared his throat and banged his riding crop against his boot. He responded, "I have left him in the competent hands of Jailer

Stigall with a guard posted and my direct orders to the captain of the Carthage Greys that no harm should come to him or his friends in my absence. I do not suppose they would do anything rash which might endanger *my* position here. I intend only a brief respite here," then as Emma's eyes betrayed her dismay, he went on, "after which I shall address the populace of Nauvoo on their duty to remain law-abiding."

Emma's heart raced so fast, she was almost lightheaded. She clamped down hard on the bitter words that sprang to her lips. They would not help Joseph's cause.

"Mother Smith, this is Governor Thomas Ford," Emma introduced Joseph's mother, hoping to soften his heart. "He and his men will be dining with us presently. Will you please see to it that everything is right in the kitchen, and I will try to make the governor's party comfortable."

Ford noted the reddened eyes of Joseph Smith's mother, her white hair and feeble frame. His conscience twinged, and he drew a deep breath. Emma directed him and his men to the dining hall, where they lounged and muttered about the events in Carthage. Emma went to the kitchen with Lucy and prayed for strength to be civil. Then she returned to the governor's side, determined to plead her husband's case.

Ford was embarrassed when Emma delivered her appeal. "Governor, I'm sure you have been well apprised of the events which led to my husband's hearing. I'm not sure you place as much weight upon the affront to genteel sensibility as the *Expositor* publication warranted. The city council *directed* Mr. Smith, as mayor, to remove the blasphemous work. This he did, quietly, with no undue violence or unnecessary loss of property to the offenders. Even if you consider the action illegal, it is still inappropriate that he be subjected to threats and intimidation at Carthage. Reprimand the council as a whole, moderate the authority of our city charter if you must, but do not hold my husband solely responsible."

He listened to her impassioned plea, then answered guardedly, "Mrs. Smith, your husband is the one responsible, by virtue of the sway he holds over the minds of the Mormon people. I do hold him — and his brother — responsible, and consider his action an offense to the Constitution of the United States of America."

She responded quietly, "And the Constitution is not offended by the illegal confinement of men untried and unsentenced?"

The icy look in Ford's eyes gave way to fury. "Madam, I will not be censured! Your husband has placed me in a very difficult — almost impossible — position. I am constantly harangued by men clamoring for Nauvoo's destruction. He brings trouble to any region in which he resides. He is involved in schemes and practices which offend the sensibilities of our country, and then he calls upon me, or others of my station, to defend his rights."

He slammed his fist on the table. "I am doing my best to maintain law and order, and I *will* have peace, if it means expelling every Mormon from my state."

Emma and Ford were locked in a combative gaze. The officers seated at the long table had fallen silent. Emma nodded briefly and replied as quietly as Ford had violently. "I appreciate your dilemma, sir. But, if you intend to purchase peace at the price of my husband's life, your conscience will never be clear."

As she left the room, the governor muttered gloomily, "I'm afraid she is right." That thought soured his disposition and his stomach. He scarcely took a bite of the fresh bread and roast duck served them.

Emma prepared the bill for services rendered. It cited service for sixty men and stable fees for their horses. As the governor and his men prepared to leave, she presented it to the captain of the guard with the request that it be paid promptly, for she needed the money.

Emma stood at the door and watched the governor's entourage ride northward, past Lyon's Drug and the Masonic Hall. When they were some distance away, she dragged herself wearily upstairs to bed and fell upon it in deep despair.

John Taylor's clear melodic voice began a tender hymn, a favorite of Joseph's from the new English hymnal:

"A poor wayfaring man of grief,
Hath often crossed me on my way,
Who sued so humbly for relief
That I could never answer, 'Nay.'
I had not power to ask his name;
Whither he went, or whence he came;
Yet there was something in his eye
That won my love, I knew not why."

For Joseph, it called back bittersweet memories of an evening at home with his family around him, when he had first heard it. Then, as John went on to other verses, which spoke of loving service to the "man of grief," he allowed himself reflection on the many kindnesses done him by loving friends, and his heart ached with foreboding and a fullness of gratitude.

In a lyrical tenor, Taylor continued:

"In pris'n I saw him next, condemned
To meet a traitor's doom at morn;
The tide of lying tongues I stemmed,
And honored him 'mid shame and scorn.
My friendship's utmost zeal to try,
He asked if I for him would die;

The flesh was weak, my blood ran chill,
But the free spirit cried, 'I will!'"

Joseph wept, for surely the notes were "low and sad," as he had described them days ago, as "the requiem for martyred prophets." When John faltered, Joseph's choked voice urged him to finish the final verse of the song:

"Then in a moment to my view,
The stranger started from disguise;
The tokens in his hands I knew;
The Savior stood before mine eyes.
He spake, and my poor name He named.
'Of me thou hast not been ashamed;
These deeds shall thy memorial be;
Fear not, thou didst them unto me.'"

At five o'clock, Jailer Stigall came into the bedroom and suggested to the men that they would be safer in the iron cell. The talk of violence he heard outside the jail had persuaded him to send his family to safety. Now he was worried about the prisoners in his care. Joseph thanked the jailer and told him they would go into the cell after supper. After the jailer left the room, John sang *A Poor Wayfaring Man of Grief* a second time.

Suddenly Joseph heard a loud commotion outside, the shuffling of many feet on the stairs, and escalating voices. Quelling the tumult below, calming words from his angel-mentor, Moroni, reverberated in his mind:

". . . I prayed unto the Lord that he would give unto the Gentiles grace, that they might have charity. And it came to pass that the Lord said unto me: If they have not charity it mattereth not unto thee, thou hast been faithful; wherefore, thy garments shall be made clean.

And because thou hast seen thy weakness thou shalt be made strong, even unto the sitting down in the place which I have prepared in the mansions of my Father. And now I. . . bid farewell unto the Gentiles, yea, and also unto my brethren whom I love, until we shall meet before the judgment-seat of Christ, where all men shall know that my garments are not spotted with your blood."

Heavy pounding shook the outside door. The jailer shouted then was silent; angry voices rose to a loud pitch, gunfire sounded below, and heavy boots pummeled the stairs! Hyrum threw himself against the closed door. The others jumped to their feet as a volley of shots rang out. One bullet ripped through the wooden door, hitting Hyrum in the face. He fell backward, exclaiming, "I am a dead man!"

A cry of anguish broke from Joseph. For a brief moment, he knelt and cradled his brother's head in his arms.

"Oh, dear brother Hyrum!"

But there was no time for anguish. The mobbers on the landing threw themselves against the door, as others shot through the open windows from outside. A shower of bullets poured into the room. Joseph grabbed the pepperbox, jerked open the door, and pushed his pistol through the crack. One, two, three barrels discharged, surprising the mob and causing them to momentarily retreat down the stairs.

With this brief respite from the mob at the door, John Taylor rushed to the east window. A ball from behind struck him in the thigh, and he fell against the wide sill, smashing his watch, which stopped at precisely five o'clock sixteen minutes and twenty-six seconds. He collapsed backward into the room, and rolled under the bed as more bullets riddled him. Willard took up their defense with Stephen Markham's heavy "rascal-beater," poised to bat down muskets stuck through the door entry.

Although Willard was a very large man, he completely escaped serious injury. In the midst of a hail of balls, he stood unscathed, except for a ball that grazed the lobe of his left ear. His escape fulfilled literally a prophecy which Joseph made over a year before, that the time would come that the balls would fly around him like hail, and he should see his friends fall on the right and on the left, but that there should not be a hole in his garment.

The mob below, no longer fearing more gunfire from the prisoners, charged back up the stairs to the bedroom. Joseph knew he was the one they wanted. If he could draw the assailants' fire, perhaps Willard and John might yet be spared. He dropped his revolver and ran to the window. The casement was wide.

"Oh Lord, my God! Is there no help for the widow's son?" He gave the Masonic distress cry. Joseph and Hyrum were both Masons, and any fellow Mason hearing him was obligated to come to his defense, but there was no help! In his hour of need, there was none to defend a brother. He determined to save his two friends with a last act of love. In deliberate sacrifice, Joseph dived from the window to the ground, twenty feet below.

A shout went up from the mob within the jail, "He's leaped the window!" Then they rushed from the building to join the multitude below. Joseph lay crumpled and defenseless beside the well. A makeshift firing squad propped his body against the well casing, and several riflemen shot him pointblank.

Finally Joseph and Hyrum Smith — "the best blood of the nineteenth century" — were beyond hatred or harm! At ages thirty-eight, and forty-four, the Prophet Joseph and Patriarch Hyrum Smith were dead.

Far across the rolling hills, green and beautiful that summer of 1844, news of the pernicious deed was carried on an ill wind. Joseph Smith was murdered, and with him his brother, Hyrum! Samuel Smith, their younger brother, had ridden hard to get to Carthage after hearing his brothers were in danger there, but he was too late.

Members of the same mob that had killed his brothers, ambushed him. After a furious pursuit, he escaped and eventually made his way to Carthage. He claimed the bodies of his brothers, and the next day bore them home to Nauvoo and to their grieving loved ones. It was a mournful procession that bore the martyrs home — two rough wagons, a heartbroken sibling, and the bodies of two brothers who had lived, loved, and died together.

At the Mansion House, Samuel told his mother, "I have brought you the bodies of your sons, but I have a dire distress in my side,. . ." He collapsed in his mother's arms, and thirty-two days later he died from internal injuries sustained the previous day. Samuel had become the forgotten martyr of Carthage, because it took him longer to die. Three brothers whose devotion to each other was eternal were together at last.

"In life they were not divided, and in death they were not separated."

The news reached Emma sometime before midnight. Lorenzo Wasson rode into Nauvoo with the unenviable task of informing the families. Emma came rushing down the stairs when she heard the urgent tapping at the door. She flung it open, fear rising in her throat. A disheveled Lorenzo stood before her, his face wild and streaked with tears. And she knew.

"Joseph and Hyrum are both dead!"

"No-o-o!" came the wail. "No-o-o!" Emma threw back her head, giving vent to a cry of anguish. Dogs began to clamor, baying and moaning as if in grief.

"Aunt Emma! I fear for you. . . " Lorenzo began, but didn't finish, for she fainted into his arms. He carried her unconscious body into the house, where Julia came running out from her bedroom. "Get your grandmother," Lorenzo ordered. Julia stood there stock-still, her mouth agape.

Now, Lorenzo commanded the girl. "Go get your grandmother!"

Julia uttered a sob, and ran off. Lucy came down the stairs a few minutes later, her face ashen. Instinctively, she helped Lorenzo with Emma then demanded a full explanation. He broke the news as gently as he could. "Samuel and Willard are bringing the bodies home tomorrow."

Julia had returned and sat crying softly, holding her mother's hand. Tears rolled unheeded down Lucy's cheeks. But Emma remained unconscious. A blessed darkness enveloped her mind, giving her depleted body a chance to rest and her tortured mind some relief. Lorenzo left Joseph's household to go on to Hyrum's to repeat the grim task.

Who could say why Joseph and Hyrum were killed? Hundreds had clamored for their blood. Thousands had wished them dead. Most people in Illinois did not know Joseph, had never met him; their only information came from accusations made by Thomas Sharp, John C. Bennett, and William Law. Still, they had crowded the narrow streets of Carthage, calling for his blood. The murders were attributed to both the Carthage Greys and the Warsaw militia, but many other individuals were responsible for Joseph's murder, for they had set the stage. Then, as cowards will do, they fled the bloody scene even before the alarm was sounded, "The Mormons are coming!" But the saints were determined to honor Joseph's admonition to keep the peace. Far from being militant, Nauvoo was in deep mourning. Like specters, the virulent mobacrats who committed the deed slunk back into the shadows of the countryside.

Those specters, however, lived on in Emma's dreams. As if through a mist, she saw Joseph's battered body on the ground. *His visage was. . . marred more than any man.* She struggled toward him, but could not touch him. She wept and strained against invisible bonds, but he remained just beyond her reach. In her mind, she watched the senseless murder, again and again.

In the best of her dreams, Joseph rose from the courtyard, unmarred despite muskets going off all around him. He walked unscathed into her outstretched arms. The heinous sounds faded, and she and Joseph stood on the steps of the temple, looking out over the river. He kissed her brow, his words of love were as heavenly music that thrilled her ears, and then. . . and then, "she waked, he fled, and day brought back her night."

When the bodies of the martyrs were prepared and readied for viewing, they were dressed in shrouds and brought into the dining hall of the Mansion House. She wondered if she could ever enter this room again without this remembrance. William Huntington, the coroner, and his son, Dimick, along with Stake President William Marks, had washed and cleaned the bodies for burial. Some might have thought it a gruesome task, but for men who loved and revered their prophet and patriarch, it was an honor. Once the bodies were ready, the widows of Joseph and Hyrum were helped into the room.

Mary Fielding trembled with every step, nearly fell, but reached her husband's body, knelt down beside him and turned his face toward her. At the sight of the wound where the musket ball had entered, she began to lament, *"Oh, Hyrum, Hyrum! Have they shot you, my dear Hyrum — are you dead? Oh! speak to me, my dear husband. I cannot think you are dead, my dear Hyrum."*

Then her grief magnified until it choked off her words. Their children ran to her, gazing for the first time upon their father's lifeless form, and their spontaneous mourning echoed through the house.

Emma attempted to approach the body of her husband. She took a few steps, but her strength failed, as friends tried to support her. This was the culmination of her lifetime fear, and it was too much; she fainted, and they carried her from the room.

She rested in the parlor for a time, her friends soothing her forehead with cool cloths, fanning her, pressing her hand, and pleading for her to take heart. But Emma heard other voices from ministering angels, buoying her up.

Shortly, she revived. She thought she might have enough strength to look upon Hyrum first. Sorrow swept over her as she viewed those dear features, beloved as any brother's, a last time. Nearby, Hyrum's family embraced one other, and their strength gave Emma courage.

Then came Lucy Mack Smith, the seventy-year-old mother of the martyrs. She entered the room, trembling, and when the sobs of her children and grandchildren rushed upon her, she sank back into the arms of her friends. Finally she approached the bodies of her precious sons, her soul torn with grief, *"My God, my God, why hast thou forsaken this family?"*

Young Joseph ran to his father's body and embraced him. Kissing his cheek, he sobbed, "Oh father, my father!"

As Lucy watched her grandson, the answer came:

"I have taken them to myself that they might have rest."

She embraced Joseph III, and together they viewed their son and father. It was then she heard a familiar voice:

"Mother, weep not for us, we have overcome the world by love; we carried to them the gospel, that their souls might be saved; they slew us for our testimony, and thus placed us beyond their power; their ascendency is for a moment; ours is an eternal triumph."

Grandmother Lucy encouraged young Joseph to bring his mother forward. The eleven-year-old boy supported his mother at one arm, and Constable John P. Greene supported her at the other. When she finally reached the side of her husband, she went down on her knees, and clasped her hands upon his chest.

"Oh Joseph," she pleaded. "Just open your eyes one last time, and tell me that you forgive me!"

"Forgive you?" young Joseph asked. "Forgive you for what, Mother?"

Emma was stunned for a moment then replied, "I sent a letter to your father when he and your Uncle Hyrum had been told by God to flee from Nauvoo."

"What did the letter say?"

"I asked him to come home to us. The governor promised to protect him, but I never dreamed he would end up dead. Truly and to the end, I loved him."

"Truly and to the end, he loved you, Mother!" young Joseph cried.

Constable Greene tried to comfort her further, "Courage, Madam. Endure this thing and you will earn a crown."

Emma looked up at him through falling tears:

"Don't you understand? My husband was my crown; for my husband and my children I have suffered the loss of all things. . . Why, O God, am I now thus deserted? Why am I a widow, and why are my children widows, and why is my heart torn with this ten-fold anguish?"

O Joseph, my Joseph! Would to God that you could speak to me once more and tell me you still love me! Soon you will lie beneath the cold ground, and all I will have is your unknown grave. Once you wrote me that you were my only true friend on earth. Now, I vow that I will be your true friend, and I will never, never abandon you. All others may leave, but I will stay with you always, for I remember once — not long ago — you held me by the hand and sealed my soul to yours eternally. *Whither thou goest I will go; where thou diest I will die, and there will I be buried!* Now, neither mobs, nor heaven, nor hell can tear me from you — my dearest, my husband, my friend!

Joseph! My beloved!

Joseph's Lament

by Buddy Youngreen

Emma, from my Carthage twilight
I beheld our children, adrift
On the sea of your uncertainty,
And the light I saw in the mountain-west departed,
Leaving Julia, Joseph, Frederick,
Alexander, and David
Gazing darkly into the night of my departure.

Wife of my youth,
The seventh trouble is past
And I am here,
In the light that casts shadows of the temple
Across our Mansion House,
While Alvin, Thadeus, Louisa, little Joseph,
Don Carlos, and our silent babe,
Wait with me, for you,
Near the Bright and Morning Star.

Epilogue

The Master Weaver strings his loom with both dark and brilliant threads. He sets the shuttle moving, and time weaves a tapestry of the living into passionate designs, alternating love and hate, balancing the sublime, the debased, the tranquil, and the turbulent.

Capricious seasons of life play pranks with mankind's expectations. Prophets reveal events belonging to a later time but prophets, after all, must pass on, their worth judged by the fruits of their short season. No sooner does the body rest beneath the cool dark earth, than winds of change snatch up the brilliant threads.

Change dealt gently with the town at the bend of the great Mississippi River. Ambitious industry and growth departed with the Mormon exodus in 1846. Violence died away in a whisper of embarrassment once its object was removed, and a new breed of settlers brought a different way of life. Time's revolving seasons stamped the forsaken town with rotting fences, tumbled stones, and ghostly memories of beloved faces long departed. Thirty-five years brought the railroad to Illinois, but not to the City of Joseph, the sleepy hamlet at the river's edge. Horse and buggy, or a pair of stout boots, still prevailed as the chief means of transportation. Swamplands were thoroughly drained. New structures bedecked the bluffs where a magnificent temple once stood, while the flat was largely forsaken to melancholy memories. Along Water Street, the Mansion House still served as a hotel and, for some a historical curiosity.

Scattered puffs of white clouds strewed the sky over the wide, winding waterway. Migratory birds wheeled in whimsical patterns high above the sheltering oaks that shaded the quaint old town. Whence came the golden wealth of light gilding field and tree, spilling with reckless abandon over the elderly woman along the river road? Startled by the warm kiss of sunlight, she turned a searching gaze upon the sky. There, above the treetops — was it just a wisp of cloud or a familiar face that peeped at her? Self-conscious as a young girl, she smoothed her apron and patted her hair, while her fragile heart fluttered and a name formed upon her lips.

"Joseph?" she whispered. But no, the image thinned, then dissolved in cloudy wisps. Still, the warm fingers of late sunlight enfolded her like a caress, and she turned her reverie to the deep waters, stretching wide and running swiftly. Little islands braved the swirling currents — the island where she had visited him by night to steal a few precious hours. Now, a small boat bobbed across the water toward that bit of land which once afforded a beloved rendezvous.

Was it just a bit of breeze that brushed her cheek? His lips had felt like that — tender, warm, gentle on her skin. A trembling hand cupped a wilting rose. She bent her head and breathed the delicate scent. Emma-rose. *His* Emma-rose!

Time seemed to turn back. In her imagination, busy streets and dear friends took their phantom places on the desolate flat. Horses pranced as buggies whisked by, flowers bloomed, and she saw Nauvoo the Beautiful in its prime. Then, that vision passed, replaced by one of wagons heading down snow-encrusted Parley Street toward the river. From that procession, friends broke away to tell her good-bye, often begging her to join them, but Emma steadfastly refused their loving entreaties. They were heading west to find a place in the wilderness. She could have gone. . . but where would she live? In the western desert, she would pine for her beautiful river home and Joseph's secret grave. No, she could not forsake him. She could not give up her watchful care to vindictive mobs who vowed to find and desecrate his grave. So, she chose to stay, while she wept in remembrance of times past when she would have been counted among the pilgrims. Her love of Joseph had bound her to his unknown grave beside their old Homestead.

Now, the frail figure looked on her dearly beloved Homestead and Mansion House, and grievous memories were replaced by precious ones. Sweet children's faces flashed in rapid succession — their children — beautiful, innocent faces bearing the image of their father upon their features.

Alexander looked, perhaps, the most like Joseph, and that endeared him to her. He had stayed close by, gradually changing from protected child to protective son. Joseph III, so serious, was determined to properly represent his father. Weighing her cautious counsel, and urged by family friends, he had affiliated with the New Organization and presided as its head, these last nineteen years.

Julia's dark eyes and dark curls danced before her mother's dreamlike gaze, first as the adorable baby girl that filled the emptiness in Emma's aching heart, then the young woman – sometimes stormy, sometimes solemn — always helpful — and finally, the impetuous young bride leaving Nauvoo with high hopes. Those hopes had been dashed when her husband was killed in a steamboat explosion. The dark-haired beauty remarried and returned home to her mother becoming a daily comfort in Emma's life.

And other faces haunted the aging Emma. Freddy, with his dark laughing eyes, still made her smile. Stocky and dark-haired, with bold, brown eyes, he reminded her of her own father, and was determined that too much religion and too much gravity would taint his life. He could always make his mother smile with a kiss for her cheek and a story to lift her spirits. Now he too was lost to her, for this son had been cut down in the prime of life, leaving a wife and daughter.

Still more painful was the bewildered, sensitive face of her child of promise, David Hyrum. The memory of his birth was a firebrand on her heart. Still mourning, yet wanting to rejoice, still grieving, and too numb to respond to even friendship's compassionate hand, she had brought her precious son into the world amid silent tears, for his father was not there to rejoice in him. From the first, she doted on the boy, pampered him, and delighted to discover in him an artist's soul. But her David Hyrum, the poet, musician, painter, and dreamer, diagnosed with brain fever was eventually committed to an asylum. This had become Emma's "living trouble" and a sorrow that could not be assuaged.

Now, breaking her reverie, an unmistakable call rallied her attention. Clearly she heard Joseph's voice say, "Come with me, Emma."

In her excitement, she replied aloud. "Wait for me, Joseph. I'm coming!"

She turned round about to discover the source of the clarion voice sounding in her mind, but he wasn't to be seen. Only the breeze murmured through the boughs of the hickory trees. The joyful light faded from weary eyes, and she relapsed into a careworn figure who yearned for a lengthy rest.

In April, 1879, Emma fell ill. Alexander visited her at home, eager as a boy to see his mother. He prayed fervently for her recovery and wrote to his brother, "Joseph, if you expect to see mother alive, come quick."

Before Joseph III arrived, Emma related a vision she'd had. "Alexander, your father came to me last night. He said, 'Emma, come with me; it is time for you to come with me.' So, I put on my bonnet and my shawl and went with him. I did not think it was anything unusual. I went with him into a mansion of light — a beautiful mansion — and he showed me through the different apartments of that beautiful mansion."

The lines of her forehead seemed to smooth and fade. Her eyes brightened as she spoke. "And one room was a nursery. In that nursery was a babe in his cradle. I knew that babe, my Don Carlos that was taken away from me."

She gripped Alexander's arm with surprising strength. "I sprang forward, caught the child up in my arms, and wept with joy over him! When I recovered sufficiently, I turned to your father and said, 'Joseph, where are the rest of my children?'"

With a satisfied smile, she finished, "He said, 'Emma, be patient, and you shall have all of your children.'" Emma's face took on a tender glow. "it was then I saw, standing by his side, a personage of light, even our Lord and Savior, Jesus Christ."

Alexander held his mother's hand tightly in his own, knowing their time together would soon be gone. Julia and Joseph soon arrived at their mother's bedside to keep watch with Alex. Emma's bed stood beside a lace-curtained window, where cool breezes fanned her and she could look out upon the ever changing — yet, ever constant — winding river.

Through the night, they took turns watching and waiting and holding her hand. She coughed occasionally as she drifted further and further away from them. In the cool of the morning, before the first rays of dawn, while darkness still hung over the City of Joseph, a remarkable strength inspired her languid form.

Emma struggled to get up, but failing that, raised her left arm as high as she could raise it, extended her hand and joyfully cried out, "Joseph! Joseph!" Her countenance became momentarily youthful, joyful, and flooded with intense light as she called out, one last time, in a voice that rang with satisfaction, *"Joseph!"*

It was April 30, 1879, nearly thirty-five years after Joseph's passing.

Emma's spirit rose to meet the man whose soul had destined upon hers one fateful day in Harmony, Pennsylvania, and with whom she had been eternally bound in an upper room of their Nauvoo Mansion House. The Time and Seasons of their lives had woven a beautiful love story; a unique design in the great tapestry of history. Now the weaving was done; the shuttle was still, and the Master's purposes fulfilled.

Emma's spirit rose through a brilliant shaft of light, while Joseph came toward her with hand outstretched. Her spirit leaped form earth-bound shackles, flared with splendid fire, and rushed to join her Eternal Love near the Bright and Morning Star.

THE END

Authors' Notes

It has been said that the combination of theoretician, organizer, and leader in one person is the rarest thing that can be found on this earth; this combination makes the great man. While this explanation helps us to understand the uniqueness of the Prophet Joseph Smith, we must probe further to measure the significance and contribution of his helpmate, Emma Hale Smith.

In the past, the measure of our understanding has been determined more by what we did not know about Joseph's "Elect Lady," than by what we did. In response to the many questions we receive about her, we feel the need to explain a few circumstances of her life.

Emma married Lewis C. Bidamon on December 23, 1847, three years after Joseph's death. Keeping in mind that under civil law of the day a woman could not own property, Emma was subject to losing her home, which was the means of supporting her family. It was not surprising that she felt the need to marry again. It is interesting that she chose Joseph's birthday as the wedding day.

Lewis was apparently a good father to her children. However, he presented Emma with yet another challenge to her strict sense of propriety, fathering an illegitimate son. Emma took the child into her home, raised him as her own, and employed his mother in her hotel so she could be near him. Before her death, Emma obtained a promise from Lewis that he would marry the child's mother, thereby giving him a name and an inheritance. Following his pledge, Lewis married the young man's mother shortly after Emma's death. Such Christian charity speaks volumes about Emma's nature and stands as an interesting counterpoint to her difficulty with the celestial practice of plural marriage, being taught a profound lesson through the "telestial" application of the principle.

Emma did not go west with the body of the church for several reasons. We believe she felt her first obligation was to properly care for her children and protect the graves of Joseph and Hyrum. Additionally, the priesthood leadership of the church met with all five Smith widows and recommended against them leaving in February 1846. The intention was to send for them after the saints were settled. A trek west would have been terribly difficult for five widows with fifteen fatherless children between them and no adult man to help them on such a journey.

Finally, after all she had endured, Emma needed rest, and the prospect of starting over again in the wilderness, with no means of support and no husband to provide for her family, would have been daunting. She knew what her lot was in Nauvoo, but she did not know what it would be out West.

Joseph and Emma were married civilly January 18, 1827. Their sealing on May 28, 1843 was conditional, though they were assured if they continued, "true and faithful," the day would come when the eternal nature of their relationship would be confirmed upon them. On September 28, 1843, having received "the fullness of the priesthood," or "calling and election made sure," that sealing ordinance was confirmed by the Holy Spirit of Promise.

The supposition that Emma started the Reorganized Church of Jesus Christ of Latter Day Saints is false. After Joseph's death, she was anxious over the safety of her sons, his heirs, and attracted as little attention to herself and them as possible. She was always a religious woman, but rarely attended any church after the saints went west. She maintained that she did not leave the church; the church left her. Strictly speaking, that was true. The R.L.D.S. church movement, now the Community of Christ, was organized by others as early as 1852. When Joseph III felt a spiritual call to take his place at the head of that organization in 1860, Emma supported her son in his choice. Her subsequent involvement was negligible and, quite probably, out of a sense of duty.

It is our belief, after years of study, that Emma Hale Smith was, in every way, a righteous, dignified, supportive, and long suffering companion to the Prophet Joseph Smith. As with his memory, hers is deserving of the greatest reverence and honor.

Joseph and Emma have contributed a priceless legacy to the world by their unwavering dedication to the restored gospel of our Lord Jesus Christ.

Bibliography

Anderson, Karl Ricks. *Joseph Smith's Kirtland.* Salt Lake City: UT: Deseret Book Co., 1989.

Barrett, Ivan J. *Joseph Smith and the Restoration: A History of the LDS Church to 1846.* Provo, UT: Brigham Young University Press, 1973

Barron, Howard H. *Orson Hyde, Missionary, Apostle, Colonizer.* Bountiful, UT: Horizon Publishers, 1977.

Baugh, Alexander L. *A Call to Arms: the 1838 Mormon Defense of Northern Missouri.* Provo, UT: Joseph Fielding Smith Institute for Latter-day Saint History and BYU Studies, 2000

Brown, S. Kent, Donald Q. Cannon and Richard H. Jackson. *Historical Atlas of Mormonism.* New York, NY: Simon and Shuster, Inc., 1994

Bushman, Richard L. *Joseph Smith and the Beginnings of Mormonism.* Urbana and Chicago: IL, University of Illinois Press, 1984.

Cannon, George Q. *Life of Joseph Smith the Prophet.* Salt Lake City, UT: Deseret Book Co., 1964

Doctrine and Covenants of the Church of Jesus Christ of Latter-day Saints. Salt Lake City: UT, The Church of Jesus Christ of Latter-day Saints

Crowther, Duane S. *The Life of Joseph Smith.* Bountiful, UT: Horizon Publishers, 1989.

Evans, John Henry. *Joseph Smith An American Prophet.* New York, NY: The MacMillan Co., 1943.

Faulring, Scott H. *An American Prophet's Record, The Diaries and Journals of Joseph Smith.* Salt Lake City, UT: Signature Books, 1989.

Gentry, Leland H. *A History of the Latter-day Saints in Northern Missouri from 1836 to 1839.* Provo, UT: BYU Seminaries and Institutes of Religion, 1965.

Hill, Donna. *Joseph Smith: The First Mormon.* New York, NY: Doubleday & Co., 1977.

History of the Church of Jesus Christ of Latter-day Saints. Period I, History of Joseph Smith by Himself. 6 Volumes, Introduction and notes by B.H. Roberts, Salt Lake City, UT: Deseret Book Co., 1964

Jones, Gracia N. *Emma's Glory and Sacrifice, A Testimony.* Utah: Homestead Publishers and Dist., 1987.

Kirkham, Francis W. *A New Witness For Christ in America: The Book of Mormon.* Jackson County, MO: Press of Zion's Printing and Publishing Co, 1942

Leonard, Glen M. *Nauvoo: A Place of Peace, A People of Promise.* Salt Lake City, UT: Deseret Book Co., 2002

LeSueur, Stephen C. *The 1838 Mormon War in Missouri.* Columbia, MO: University of Missouri Press, 1987

Porter, Larry C. *A Study of the Origins of the Church of Jesus Christ of Latter-day Saints in the States of New York and Pennsylvania.* Provo, UT: Joseph Fielding Smith Institute for Latter-day Saint History and BYU Studies, 2000.

Proctor, Scot Facer. *The Revised and Enchanced History of Joseph Smith by His Mother, Lucy Mack Smith.* Salt Lake City, UT: Bookcraft, Inc., 1996.

Smith, Joseph Fielding. *Teachings of the Prophet Joseph Smith.* Salt Lake City, UT: Deseret Book Co., 1964.

Youngreen, Buddy. *Reflections of Emma.* Provo, UT: Maasai, Inc., 2001.